The U.S. Supreme Court's Modern Common Law Approach to Judicial Decision Making

This book studies the U.S. Supreme Court and its current common law approach to judicial decision making, from a national and transnational perspective. The modern Supreme Court's approach appears detached from and inconsistent with the underlying fundamental principles that ought to guide it, an approach that often leads to unfair and inefficient results.

This book suggests the adoption of a judicial decision-making model that proceeds from principles and rules treating them as premises to develop consistent unitary theories to meet current social conditions. This model requires judicial opinions to be informed by a wide range of considerations, beginning with established legal standards, but including the insights derived from deductive and inductive reasoning, the lessons learned from history and custom, and from an examination of the social and economic consequences of the decision. Under this model, the considerations made to reach a specific result should be articulated through a process that considers various hypothesis, arguments, confutations and confirmations, and it should be shared with the public.

Simona Grossi is a professor of law at Loyola Law School Los Angeles. She worked for the UN from 2000 to 2002. She then went into private practice, doing national and transnational litigation from 2002 to 2008 for Clifford Chance LLP and Bonelli Erede Pappalardo. She worked for Judge Charles Breyer at the United States District Court for the Northern District of California in 2010. Her scholarship focuses on civil procedure and transnational litigation. She is the author of the *Commentary to the Italian Code of Civil Procedure* (2010).

But one may criticize even what one reveres. Law is the business to which my life is devoted, and I should show less than devotion if I did not do what in me lies to improve it, and, when I perceive what seems to me the ideal of its future, if I hesitated to point it out and to press toward it with all my heart.

Oliver Wendell Holmes, Jr.
The Path of Law

The U.S. Supreme Court's Modern Common Law Approach to Judicial Decision Making

SIMONA GROSSI
Loyola Law School Los Angeles

CAMBRIDGE
UNIVERSITY PRESS

CAMBRIDGE
UNIVERSITY PRESS

32 Avenue of the Americas, New York NY 10013-2473, USA

Cambridge University Press is part of the University of Cambridge.

It furthers the University's mission by disseminating knowledge in the pursuit of education, learning and research at the highest international levels of excellence.

www.cambridge.org
Information on this title: www.cambridge.org/9781316612866

First published 2015
First paperback edition 2016

A catalogue record for this publication is available from the British Library

Library of Congress Cataloguing in Publication data
Grossi, Simona, author.
The U.S. Supreme Court's Modern Common Law Approach to Judicial Decision Making / Simona Grossi.
pages cm
ISBN 978-1-107-02805-0 (Hardback)
1. United States. Supreme Court–Decision making. 2. Judicial process–United States. 3. Forum non conveniens–United States. 4. Jurisdiction–United States. 5. Conflict of laws–Jurisdiction. I. Title. II. Title: US Supreme Court and the modern common law approach. III. Title: United States Supreme Court and the modern common law approach.
KF8748.G76 2015
347.73′262–dc23 2014021014

ISBN 978-1-107-02805-0 Hardback
ISBN 978-1-316-61286-6 Paperback

Contents

Introduction

Deciding cases is one of the most complex and fascinating tasks to which any legal professional may be called. The literature on judicial decision making is extensive; it explores a wide range of considerations from the pragmatic to the philosophic, and including studies of the various judicial bodies, their structure, and their procedures.[1] But these are the fundamental questions: What do judges do, how do they do it, and on what bases can their choices be justified?

The U.S. Supreme Court is perhaps the world's most influential judicial decision-making body. Its opinions have influenced not only the American legal system through the force of judicial review and binding precedent,[2] but also the legal systems of many other countries whose courts have often looked

[1] *See, e.g.*, ALEXANDER BICKEL, THE LEAST DANGEROUS BRANCH: THE SUPREME COURT AT THE BAR OF POLITICS (1962); BENJAMIN N. CARDOZO, THE NATURE OF THE JUDICIAL PROCESS (1975); JOHN HART ELY, DEMOCRACY AND DISTRUST (1980); JEROME FRANK, COURTS ON TRIAL: MYTH AND REALITY IN AMERICAN JUSTICE (1949). Ronald Dworkin, *The Model of Rules*, 35 U. Chi. L. Rev. 15 (1967–1968); Oliver Wendell Holmes, Jr., The Path of the Law, 10 Harv. L. Rev. 457 (1896–1897); McNollgast, *The Political Economy of Law: Decision-Making by Judicial, Legislative, Executive and Administrative Agencies*, available at http://papers.ssrn.com/sol3/papers.cfm?abstract_id=1153479; Roscoe Pound, *Mechanical Jurisprudence*, 8 Colum. L. Rev. 605 (1908); Roscoe Pound, *Juristic Science and Law*, 31 Harv. L. Rev. 1047 (1917–1918); Roscoe Pound, *Courts and Legislation*, 7 Am. Pol. Sci. Rev. 361 (1913); Roscoe Pound, *The Administrative Application of Legal Standards*, 42 Annu. Rep. A.B.A. 445 (1919); Roscoe Pound, *Common Law and Legislation*, 21 Harv. L. Rev. 383 (1907–1908); Martin Shapiro, *Supreme Court and Constitutional Adjudication: Of Politics and Neutral Principles*, 31 Geo. Wash. L. Rev. 587 (1963); Reinhold Zippelius, *"Trial and error" in Jurisprudence*, available at www.biblio.juridicas.unam.mx/libros/1/468/34.pdf.

[2] *Marbury v. Madison*, 5 U.S. (1 Cranch) 137, 177 (1803) ("It is emphatically the province and duty of the judicial department to say what the law is."); *Cooper v. Aaron*, 358 U.S. 1, 18 (1958) ("the federal judiciary is supreme in the exposition of the law of the Constitution").

to the U.S. Supreme Court for guidance.[3] As a lawyer and scholar educated and trained in both the civil law and common law systems, I have observed and studied the U.S. Supreme Court and its modern common law method in a series of procedural opinions and have come to the conclusion that this method is in serious need of reform.

The U.S. Supreme Court appears increasingly engaged in the development of doctrinal tests but insufficiently invested in the underlying principles and theories that should guide legal analysis and give uniformity to the relevant doctrines. The Court's analysis is often incomplete and fails to provide meaningful guidelines and directions for future developments in the areas of the law that are explored or revisited by the Court.

In the early twentieth century, Roscoe Pound described this type of jurisprudence as "mechanical," in that it elevates established formalities over common sense, "forgets the ends in the means," and uses conceptions as ultimate solutions rather than premises from which to reason.[4] This jurisprudence articulates narrow rules that confine judicial discretion and lead judges to try to fit the case to the rule rather than the rule to the case, as justice would instead demand.[5]

True, the common law method proceeds through case law, and judicial opinions are essential to give contour and content to principles and rules. This is, indeed, the beauty and strength of the common law system. However, in articulating and applying principles and rules, judicial opinions should not proceed mechanically and endorse mechanical tests and doctrines without exploring the facts before the court and the relationship between those facts and the underlying premises and ideas from which these tests and doctrines derive.[6]

Over a century ago, Pound sensed that the common law method was increasingly exposed to the risks of mechanical jurisprudence. Thus, he invited American scholars

> [t]o test the conceptions worked out in the common law by the requirements of the new juristic theory, to lay sure foundations for the ultimate legislative restatement of the law, from which judicial decision shall start afresh – this is as great an opportunity as has fallen to the jurists of any age.[7]

[3] Aaron B. Aft, *Respect My Authority: Analyzing Clims of Dimished U.S. Supreme Court Influence Abroad*, 18 Indiana Journal of Global Legal Studies, 421, 431–432 (2011) (challenging the thesis that the U.S. Supreme Court's influence over foreign jurisprudence is waning).

[4] Roscoe Pound, *Mechanical Jurisprudence*, 8 Colum. L. Rev. 605, 620–621 (1908).

[5] Roscoe Pound, *Courts and Legislation*, 7 Am. Pol. Sci. Rev. 361, 365 (1913).

[6] Roscoe Pound, *Mechanical Jurisprudence*, *supra* note 4, at 622–623.

[7] *Id.*

I take Pound's invitation, and I believe that in order to accomplish what Pound had in mind, any meaningful reform of legal analysis must necessarily involve both the judiciary and the legislature.

The judiciary and the legislature are organically bound together. They make the law jointly, one operating at a macro level and the other at a micro level. Thus, mechanistic legislation is likely to lead to mechanistic jurisprudence and, vice versa, mechanistic jurisprudence might implicitly "suggest" to the legislature that the adoption of mechanistic legislation is appropriate and required.

True, there are important differences between the judicial and the legislative processes. For instance, the judicial decision-making process is triggered by the need to resolve a specific case. Thus, differently from the legislature, which regulates issues from a less concrete factual perspective, the judge finds the law within a specific factual context and, because of that, his judgment might be improperly influenced by personal and subjective considerations that are triggered by the precise case in front of him.[8]

Since it is clear that both judges and lawyers make law, both the judicial and the legislative processes are law making in nature and both need the legislature's wisdom.[9] In fact, good legislation is premised on principles, a careful understanding of the relevant factual background to which the legislation might apply, and it is written in terms that permit application to a wide range of circumstances, some of which might be unforeseen. Likewise, good judicial decision making proceeds through a careful understanding of the facts, a consideration of the principles evoked by those facts, and the choice of a standard that is principled and durable in the sense that it can apply in a similar fashion to similarly situated cases.

Although this book contains suggestions for the legislative process, it is mainly focused on the judiciary and, more specifically, on the U.S. Supreme Court and that Court's modern common law method. It is also intended to promote a type of "legislative wisdom" that the U.S. Supreme Court seems to be currently lacking. Therefore, the studies in this book also include proposals for the restatement of judge-made procedural laws.

Chapter I introduces the reader to the common law method and suggests a perspective from which to assess and critique modern common-law judicial decision making. Chapters II and III analyze, respectively, personal jurisdiction and *forum non conveniens*, and the U.S. Supreme Court's common law approach to these topics. Both chapters offer a proposal for restatement of the

[8] *See* BENJAMIN N. CARDOZO, THE NATURE OF THE JUDICIAL PROCESS, 119–121 (1975).

[9] *Id.*, at 115.

developed common law principles and judge-made law in these areas. Chapter IV examines the law of personal jurisdiction, *forum non conveniens*, and conflict of laws rules in a transnational litigation context. It identifies important similarities between the civil law and common law approaches to these topics and suggests the possibility of harmonization. The purpose here is to open the modern common law method to principles and practices that may have been overlooked by the U.S. Supreme Court's mechanical jurisprudence. Chapter V studies the U.S. Supreme Court's common law method in the subject matter jurisdiction context as a paradigm example of the method gone awry. Chapter VI presents the reactions to the common law method by a selected group of judges, lawyers, and scholars from civil law systems. Finally, Chapter VII proposes the development of uniform guidelines for judicial decision making that would suit a democratic system of government and promote a global judicial dialogue.

1

The U.S. Supreme Court's Decision-Making Process: Deciding When and What to Decide

THE U.S. SUPREME COURT'S MODERN COMMON LAW METHOD AND ITS FLAWS: AN OVERVIEW

Roscoe Pound described three different judicial methods that reflect the arc of jurisprudential thinking over time: a jurisprudence of conceptions, a jurisprudence of premises, and an empirical jurisprudence. Under the jurisprudence of conceptions "[c]ertain fundamental conceptions are worked out from traditional legal principles, and the rules for the cause in hand are deduced from these conceptions by a purely logical process."[1] The jurisprudence of premises takes "the rules of a traditional system . . . as premises and . . . develop[s] these premises in accordance with some theory of the ends to be met or of the relation which they should bear, when applied, to the social condition of the time being."[2] Here, pure logic is thus tempered by consideration of the consequences, but still the analysis is cabined within the abstract legal standards and categories. Finally, an empirical jurisprudence begins with the facts and operates through a "process of inclusion and exclusion" and a method of "trial-hypothesis and confirmation" to discover the law.[3] Under this empirical approach, "[t]he tentative results of *a propriori* reasoning are corrected continually by experience. A cautious advance is made at some point. If just results follow, the advance goes forward, and in time a rule is developed. If the results are not just, a new line is taken, and so on until the best line is discovered."[4]

Pound thought that the first two categories of jurisprudence – conceptions and premises – were inadequate, as both were premised to some extent on the perceived immutability of established legal standards. If not based on natural

[1] Roscoe Pound, *Courts and Legislation*, *supra* note 5 (Introduction), at 371.
[2] *Id.*
[3] *Id.*
[4] *Id.*

law itself, they operated on the natural-law understanding that law can be perfectly established and, once so established, can serve as a sufficient tool for solving present claims and controversies, even those that were unanticipated by the law maker. Pound also found problems in the empirical jurisprudence, such as the slow pace at which the law must develop under a case-by-case approach, and he noted the "over-ambition of our courts to lay down universal rules," thus turning the empirical jurisprudence into a jurisprudence of conceptions.[5]

Despite its flaws, Pound considered empirical jurisprudence to be the best of the alternatives. He believed that the relationship between the legislative and the judicial law-making functions were essential to each other and to the full realization of the law. He saw the legislative role as laying the general standards from which the judiciary could discover what the law actually is in the context of pending cases. Thus, in his view, the legislature and the judiciary jointly make the law through the creation of standards, filtered through a judicial process of hypothesis, trial, corrections, and confirmations. At some point, the legislature should intervene to restate those confirmations and allow the judiciary to continue its process of discovery. Empirical jurisprudence is not experimenting for experimental sake: it is experimenting with the goal of testing old legal standards or discovering new ones and determining whether those standards are just and workable.

The current U.S. Supreme Court's modern jurisprudence seems not to fit any of the above categories. It is certainly not empirical, because its purported goal is to discover the true meaning of the law in original understandings and fundamental texts, often disregarding the facts before the Court. Thus, it thrives in fiction and not in fact. Moreover, the Court regularly denies that it is making the law; rather, it claims only to be revealing the established law. Yet, neither can the Court's modern common law method be viewed as a jurisprudence of conceptions or premises. While the Court often invokes established principles, it just as often ignores those principles or distorts them in service of unstated goals; for example, case management seems to be the subtext of many of the Court's procedural opinions. Of course, the Court will sometimes use conceptions, premises, and empiricism in deciding cases. But the occasional use of these tools does not reflect any particular judicial decision-making philosophy. Rather, cases and opinions sometimes seem mere opportunities for the Court to legislate, that is, to create rules designed

[5] *Id.*, at 372.

for future cases and contingencies.[6] To this end, the Court often endorses narrow rules and rigid multipart formulas that operate to closely constrain lower court discretion and judgment.[7] These narrow rules and formulas represent logic detached from principle and controlling facts. As such, they represent a return to the mechanical jurisprudence that Pound disparaged over a century ago.

When English case law was imported into the United States and the American legal system, American lawyers, judges, and scholars studied the relevant legal conceptions and considered the consequences to which their application would give rise. However, once the relevant legal theories were identified, the underlying conceptions were considered as established and were not reexamined. Principles lost their importance, and the law became an aggregate of increasingly narrow rules designed for easy, impersonal application that was seemingly infallible.[8] However, narrow rules are incapable of governing most aspects of human life, especially interests that are inherently

[6] As Kennth Culp Davis explained,

> [courts] always have the needed adjudicative facts, that is, the facts about the immediate parties – who did what, where, when, how, and with what motive or intent. But courts often have inadequate legislative facts, that is, the facts that bear on the court's choices about law and policy.

Kenneth Culp Davis, *Judicial, Legislative, and Administrative Lawmaking: A Proposed Research Service for the Supreme Court*, 71 Minn. L. Rev. 1, 7 (1986).

[7] *See, e.g.*, Frank Cross, Tonja Jabobi & Emerson Tiller, *A Positive Political Theory of Rules and Standards*, U. Ill. L. Rev. 1 (2012); Tom S. Clark, *A Principal-Agent Theory of En Banc Review*, 25 J.L. ECON. & ORG. 55, 76 (2008); Toby J. Heytens, *Doctrine Formulation and Distrust*, 83 Notre Dame L. Rev. 2045 (2008); Kirk A. Randazzo, *Strategic Anticipation and the Hierarchy of Justice in U.S. District Courts*, 36 AM. POL. RES. 669, 671–75 (2008); Tonja Jacobi & Emerson H. Tiller, *Legal Doctrine and Political Control*, 23 J.L. ECON. & ORG. 326, 329 (2007); Stefanie A. Lindquist, Susan B. Haire & Donald R. Songer, *Supreme Court Auditing of the U.S. Courts of Appeals: An Organizational Perspective*, 17 J. PUB. ADMIN. RES. & THEORY 607, 610 (2007); Tracey E. George & Albert H. Yoon, *The Federal Court System: A Principal-Agent Perspective*, 47 ST. LOUIS U. L.J. 819, 820–22 (2003); Susan B. Haire, Stefanie A. Lindquist & Donald R. Songer, *Appellate Court Supervision in the Federal Judiciary: A Hierarchical Perspective*, 37 LAW & SOC'Y REV. 143, 162–64 (2003); Sara C. Benesh & Malia Reddick, *Overruled: An Event History Analysis of Lower Court Reaction to Supreme Court Alteration of Precedent*, 64 J. POL. 534, 536 (2002); Tracey E. George & Michael E. Solimine, *Supreme Court Monitoring of the United States Courts of Appeals En Banc*, 9 SUP. CT. ECON. REV. 171, 175 (2001); Charles M. Cameron, Jeffrey A. Segal & Donald Songer, *Strategic Auditing in a Political Hierarchy: An Informational Model of the Supreme Court's Certiorari Decisions*, 94 AM. POL. SCI. REV. 101, 103 (2000); Matt Spitzer & Eric Talley, *Judicial Auditing*, 29 J. LEGAL STUD. 649, 670 (2000); Donald R. Songer, Jeffrey A. Segal & Charles M. Cameron, *The Hierarchy of Justice: Testing a Principal-Agent Model of Supreme Court–Circuit Court Interactions*, 38 AM. J. POL. SCI. 673 (1994).

[8] Roscoe Pound, *Mechanical Jurisprudence*, *supra* note 4, at 611–612.

complex.[9] And although narrow rules may seem easier to apply than general principles or standards, they cannot meet the needs of a developed legal system,[10] one that is not stable nor absolute, but fluid and changeable through a process of endless "becoming."[11] Pound thought that only a mature legal system could have the confidence to rely on reasoning rather than mechanical and rigid rules,[12] and that reasoning is an infallible and impersonal instrument but much superior in its results to mechanical forms.[13]

Indeed, principles and standards should be part of the analysis and guide it because, differently from narrow rules – more apt to govern property and business transactions – principles and standards are more apt to govern the conduct of enterprises and, in general, more complex situations that require the use of intuition more than rigid formulas.[14] Furthermore, general principles and conceptions allow courts to better identify and separate what is accidental and nonessential from what is instead essential and relevant to legal analysis.[15] They better unify and rationalize the particulars and may properly project and extend themselves to new cases,[16] thus inviting more efficient and fair results.

Now it remains to consider how we might assess and criticize what courts actually do.

LEGAL PROCESS: A MODEL TO CONSIDER

In an article written in 1994, Richard Fallon lamented a former teacher's observation that the study of federal courts had become an "intellectual backwater."[17] Fallon mounted a hearty defense to the charge, and in so doing

[9] Roscoe Pound, *The Administrative Application of Legal Standards*, *supra* note 1, at 454.
[10] *Id.*
[11] *See* BENJAMIN N. CARDOZO, THE NATURE OF THE JUDICIAL PROCESS, *supra* note 8.
[12] Roscoe Pound, *The Administrative Application of Legal Standards*, *supra* note 1, at 453.
[13] *Id.*
[14] *Id.*, at pp. 462–463.
[15] In this regard, Cardozo observed:

> The problem remains to fix the bounds and the tendencies of development and growth to set the directive force in motion along the right path at the parting of the ways. The directive force of a principle may be exerted along the line of logical progression this I will call the rule of analogy or the method of philosophy; along the line of historical development; this I will call the method of evolution; along the line of the customs of the community; this I will call the method of tradition; along the lines of justice, morals and social welfare, the *mores* of the day; this I will call the method of sociology.

See BENJAMIN N. CARDOZO, THE NATURE OF THE JUDICIAL PROCESS, 30 (1975).
[16] *Id.*, at 31.
[17] Richard H. Fallon, Jr., *Reflections on the Hart and Wechsler Paradigm*, 47 Vand. L. Rev. 953, at 955 (1994) (hereinafter Fallon, *Reflections*).

endorsed the continuing vitality of the legal process school, from which the scholarly discipline of "Federal Courts" emerged in the 1950s.[18] Despite this endorsement, Fallon noted that legal process theory was born of a different era – post-*Lochner* and pre-*Warren* Courts – and that modern circumstances and perceptions of the law and of the role of federal courts might require some modification of the animating principles and methodology.[19] He also called for future federal courts scholarship that would, among other things, use the legal process method to provide "critical analysis of cases and doctrines, proposals for law reform, [and] efforts to identify immanent values or purposes in light of which bodies of law might be rationalized."[20]

I agree with Fallon that legal process remains a worthy perspective from which to examine the law of federal courts and, more generally, the modern common law method and judicial decision making. I also agree with Fallon and others that legal process theory needs to be revitalized in light of current jurisprudential developments and insights.[21] I have some thoughts on the direction that the common law jurisprudence should take, an approach that both borrows and diverges from the legal process model.

As is well known, the legal process school is directly traceable to the work of Professors Henry Hart and Albert Sacks.[22] And while the influence of Hart and Sacks may have waned during the 1960s, their basic ideas have been woven into the common law jurisprudence and remain persistently influential. Professor Philip Frickey, a modern proponent of legal process, described the Hart and Sacks theory as follows:

> [Hart and Sacks] understood all law—including the legislature's role in statutory creation and the administrative and judicial roles of statutory implementation and application—as a purposive endeavor designed to promote social utility. They assumed the legislature to be made up of reasonable persons pursuing reasonable purposes reasonably, and the judges interpreting statutes to be engaged in the reasoned elaboration of those purposes as they could be made to fit within the broader legal fabric. Under this view, it was

[18] HENRY M. HART, JR. & HERBERT WECHSLER, THE FEDERAL COURTS AND THE FEDERAL SYSTEM (1953).

[19] Fallon, *Reflections*, *supra* note 17, at 959–960.

[20] *Id.*, at 977.

[21] Robert Post, *Theorizing Disagreement, Reconceiving the Relationship Between Law and Politics*, 98 Calif. L. Rev. 1319 (2010) (hereinafter Post, *Theorizing Disagreement*). Philip P. Frickey, *Getting from Joe to Gene (McCarthy): The Avoidance Canon, Legal Process Theory, and Narrowing Statutory Interpretation in the Early Warren Court*, 93 Calif. L. Rev. 397 (2005) (hereinafter Frickey, *The Avoidance Canon*).

[22] HENRY M. HART, JR., & ALBERT M. SACKS, THE LEGAL PROCESS: BASIC PROBLEMS IN THE MAKING AND APPLICATION OF LAW (Tentative edition, 1958).

> simply unacceptable to conclude that a statute lacked a sensible purpose. Moreover, unless it was impossible to conclude otherwise, courts were to avoid the perspective of cynical observers who might see only short-term political compromise rather than the embrace of reasonable public policy purposes.[23]

More specifically, legal process theory can be seen as premised on five interrelated elements: institutional settlement, antiformalism, rule of law, reasoned elaboration, and consistency with the broader legal fabric.[24]

The principle of institutional settlement posits that "decisions which are the duly arrived at result of duly established procedures … ought to be accepted as binding. …"[25] In this sense, institutional settlement determines what the law "is." That determination is legitimized by reference to institutional allocations and institutionally relevant procedures and practices through which the determination is made. The principle of institutional settlement elevates procedure above substantive law. In the words of Hart and Sacks, "these procedures and their accompanying doctrines and practices will come to be seen as the most significant and enduring part of the whole legal system, because they are the matrix of everything else."[26] In a sense, one could say, that from a legal process perspective, the way things are done will determine, to a large extent, what will and can be done.

The antiformalism principle rejects rigid interpretations of the law and posits that the law should instead be read in accord with evolving circumstances and a pluralistic range of norms and interests. As Hart put it, the law should be considered as "a continuous process of *becoming*. If morality [for example] has a place in the 'becoming,' it has a place in the 'is.'"[27] The antiformalism principle does not embrace legal realism, but attempts to stake out a middle ground between realism and positivism.[28] This approach to judicial decision making is sometimes described as "purposive."[29] It also strongly suggests that the judicial decision-making process consists of something more than merely finding and applying the law.

[23] Frickey, *The Avoidance Canon*, *supra* note 21, at 405.

[24] *See* Fallon, *Reflections*, *supra* note 12, at 963–970. Fallon identifies a sixth principle, structural interpretation. For reasons I will explain in the text, I treat that principle separately. *See infra*, text accompanying notes 46 to 52.

[25] HART & SACKS, THE LEGAL PROCESS, *supra* note 22, at 4.

[26] *Id.*, at 6.

[27] Henry M. Hart, Jr., *Holmes' Positivism – An Addendum*, 64 Harv. L. Rev. 929, 930 (1951).

[28] *See* Michael Wells, *Behind the Parity Debate: The Decline of the Legal Process Tradition in the Law of Federal Courts*, 71 B.U.L. Rev. 609, 619 (1991) (describing the distinction between Legal Realism and the Legal Process school in terms of the limits imposed on the adjudictory role by Legal Process) (hereinafter Wells, *The Parity Debate*).

[29] Post, *Theorizing Disagreement*, *supra* note 21, at 1332–1336.

The rule of law principle is not the "law of rules."[30] Nor is the rule of law principle meant to invite a return to formalism. Rather, as Fallon observes, the rule of law "implies courts"[31] and "requires the availability of judicial remedies sufficient to vindicate fundamental legal principles."[32] Thus, although legal process recognizes the authority of Congress to limit the jurisdiction of federal courts, the theory also recognizes that "the power to regulate jurisdiction is actually a power to regulate rights – rights to judicial process, whatever those are, and substantive rights."[33] As such, the power to regulate jurisdiction is subject to the rule of law principle that ensures the availability of courts to enforce substantive rights.[34]

The principle of reasoned elaboration means exactly what it suggests. For a judicial decision to be legitimate, it must be supported by a principled and logical explanation. It is this "role of reason" that distinguishes a legitimate judicial judgment from a nonjudicial political choice. That distinction is, in essence, one between the "exercise of reason" and an "an act of willfulness,"[35] with only the former being properly characterized as judicial in nature.[36]

Finally, the principle of consistency with the broader legal fabric, which is closely related to the principle of reasoned elaboration, requires that judicial decisions be premised on a legal principle that transcends the immediate facts of the case before the court. In his famous article, *Toward Neutral Principles of Constitutional Law*,[37] Herbert Wechsler explained that a "principled decision, in the sense I have in mind, is one that rests on reasons with respect to all the issues in the case, reasons that in their generality and their neutrality transcend any immediate result that is involved."[38] This has become known as the principle of "neutrality."

CRITICISM OF THE CLASSIC THEORY

I accept most of the above postulates of the classic legal process method, and particularly agree with the principles of reasoned elaboration and neutrality as further explained below. An opinion that is not consistent with these principles naturally leads to the suspicion that the decision is not legitimate.[39]

30 *Cf.* Antonin Scalia, *The Rule of Law as a Law of Rule*, 56 U. Chi. L. Rev. 1175 (1989).
31 Fallon, *Reflections*, *supra*, note 17, at 965.
32 *Id.*
33 *See* HART & WECHSLER, *supra* note 13, 317 ("Dialogue").
34 *Id.*, at 318.
35 Wechsler, *Neutral Principles*, *supra* note 6, at 11.
36 *See also id.*, at 31–35 (discussing the lack of reasoned analysis in the Equal Protection cases decided by *per curiam* opinions after *Brown v. Board of Education*).
37 *Id.*
38 *Id.*, at 19.
39 Fallon, *Reflections*, *supra* note 17, at 994, 999–1000.

Of course, I recognize that when deciding cases, judges will necessarily draw from their own personal experience and opinions,[40] since judges are not simply conduits through which the law flows. However, the principles of reasoned elaboration and neutrality, sensibly applied, provide a framework through which the legitimacy of a judicial decision can be measured from a shared perspective of legal principles and logic that should transcend the individual judge's policy preferences in a particular case. Moreover, these principles may help a judge check her personal instincts in a way that will bring greater consistency and fairness to the law.

Professor Robert Post has criticized the principle of reasoned elaboration to the extent that it is premised on the dichotomy between "reason" and "will." According to Post, this dichotomy is "far too crude to capture the difference between law and politics. Reason exists in politics and will exists in law."[41] At a descriptive and empirical level, I agree with Post. Reason and will play a role in both judicial and political decision making. Legal process does not deny that. It does, however, insist that a judicial decision be *justified* by reasoned elaboration, and recognizes that there is no such requirement that a political decision do so. In a sense, reasoned elaboration is an institutional requirement imposed on the judicial branch, while majority rule is the institutional requirement of the political process. In stating this disagreement with Post, I am not drawing a bright line between the judicial and the political processes, but I only recognize the requirement that a judicial decision be justified in terms other than will, even if that judicial opinion is the product of a five-to-four vote.

Post has also criticized the neutrality principle as being either trivial (i.e., the magistrate must be neutral as between the parties), incoherent (i.e., a "neutral principle" is an oxymoron), or an improper endorsement of non-consequentialism (i.e., the notion that a judge should ignore the consequences of her decisions).[42] I appreciate Post's critique, but I do not fully agree with it. The problem, as I see it, can be traced to Wechsler's unfortunate word choice – "neutral principles" – and to his somewhat incomplete and short-sighted defense of the principle.

As to "neutrality," the word itself is an easy target. If it is reduced to a call for a neutral magistrate, it states the obvious, and if it is meant to "neuter" values,

[40] *See* Wells, *The Parity Debate*, *supra* note 23, at 642–643; *but see* Fallon, *Reflections*, *supra* note 16, at 973 & n. 85 (responding to Wells).

[41] Post, *Theorizing Disagreement*, *supra* note 21, at 1328.

[42] *Id.*, at 1330–1331.

as Post suggests it might, it is pernicious. On the other hand, if it suggests no more than a nondiscriminatory application of a legal standard to a general pattern, then it might be entitled to more weight. I would read Wechsler's neutrality principle in this latter fashion. As such, I understand him to be saying that a "neutral principle" is one that must be durable and capable of application to a wide range of similarly situated cases. Neutrality here does not relate to magistrates or values, but to applications. Professor Kent Greenawalt captures this idea well when he observes that "A person gives a neutral reason, in Wechsler's sense, if he states a basis for a decision that he would be willing to follow in other situations to which it applies."[43]

Post's nonconsequentialist critique of neutrality is more troubling. Certainly, a judge must attend to both the long and short-term consequences of her decision, and the antiformalist principle fully supports this proposition. As Post amply demonstrates, a decision cannot be "purposive" and at the same time oblivious to consequences. As with neutrality, I would read Wechsler's admonition that judges should be aloof from the immediate consequences to mean that a judge should not alter a durable principle simply to avoid a result that is averse to her individual preferences. As Greenawalt puts it, "[t]he principles that support a decision must be … adequately general as well as neutral. They must reach out beyond the narrow circumstances of the case."[44]

That Wechsler can be interpreted more broadly, as Post suggests, may be a product of Wechsler's inability to discover a durable principle that would "reach out beyond the narrow circumstances" of *Brown v. Board of Education*[45] and justify the series of *per curiam* antiapartheid decisions that applied *Brown* in contexts other than public school education. Wechsler's failure to discover such a durable principle may have doomed "neutrality" as a persuasive ground from which to assess judicial decision making.

I strongly agree with Post that one should not adopt a vision of judicial decision making solely based on the judicial craft, i.e., on the ability to discover and apply the law. Rather, courts must recognize the long-term political and social consequences of their decisions and sometimes act as law-making statesmen, as the Court did in *Brown*. I also believe that Post and Frickey are correct when they assert that the classic legal process theory invites precisely this type of purposive statesmanship in appropriate and

43 Kent Greenawalt, *The Enduring Significance of Neutral Principles*, 78 Colum. L. Rev. 982, 985 (1978) (hereinafter Greenawalt, *Enduring Significance*).

44 *Id.*, at 987.

45 347 U.S. 483 (1954).

limited circumstances.[46] In short, I would interpret Wechsler's neutrality principle in a manner that avoids Post's nonconsequentialist criticism.

Some of the other legal process postulates also require closer examination and, as comprehensive as legal process may appear, it does not, in fact, present an exhaustive account of the purposes and foundations of the law of federal courts or of modern common law decision making. For example, the principle of institutional settlement exalts the primacy of procedure over substantive rights. It is true that without procedure there would be no enforceable substantive rights other than through the nonjudicial will of the sovereign. It is equally true, however, that without substantive rights there would be no point to having a system of procedure. Procedure is instrumental. It exists to ensure the fair and efficient delivery of justice, and the ends of justice necessarily include the vindication of substantive rights. Hence, a fully realized theory of legal process and judicial decision making ought to factor in the extent to which procedure accomplishes this ultimately substantive goal, namely, the protection of individual claims of right.

LEGAL PROCESS AND THE LAW OF FEDERAL COURTS

In their pathbreaking casebook, *The Federal Courts and the Federal System*, Hart and Wechsler added the principle of structural interpretation to the five principles of the classic legal process method, applicable specifically to the law of federal courts. The principle of structural interpretation focuses primarily on "our federalism" and also on the separation of powers. In fact, in the preface to their casebook, the very first sentence references the importance of "our federalism" to the study of federal courts,[47] and on the next page the authors offer a similar, albeit less insistent, respect to the principle of separation of powers.[48] The principle of structural interpretation is now often regarded as an essential component of the legal process method.[49] Thus, in determining the allocation of powers between federal courts and state courts, and between federal courts and the political branches of the federal government, federalism and separation of powers should, according to this expanded version of legal process theory, play a critical role.

In my view, the principle of structural interpretation is premised on a limited vision of constitutional values in that it emphasizes only two aspects

[46] *See* Post, *Theorizing Disagreement*, *supra* note 21, at 1323, 1332–1336; Frickey, *The Avoidance Canon*, *supra* note 16, at 454, 461.

[47] *See* HART & WECHSLER, *supra* note 13, xi.

[48] *Id.*, at xii.

[49] Fallon, *Reflections*, *supra* note 17, at 965.

of our constitutional system – federalism and separation of powers – at the expense of other equally weighty constitutional considerations, including the structural role of the federal judiciary in the vindication of individual claims of right. As the Court recognized in *Marbury v. Madison*:

> The very essence of civil liberty certainly consists in the right of every individual to claim the protection of the laws, whenever he receives an injury. One of the first duties of government is to afford that protection.... The government of the United States has been emphatically termed a government of laws, and not of men. It will certainly cease to deserve this high appellation, if the laws furnish no remedy for the violation of a vested legal right.[50]

The principle of structural interpretation thus needs to be more broadly conceived. Federalism means something more than "states' rights." It reflects a principle that defers to the states in matters constitutionally pertinent to the states, while recognizing the paramount interest of the national sovereign in matters pertinent to it. Similarly, separation of powers is not merely a limit on the scope of judicial authority; rather, it also imposes an affirmative responsibility on the judicial branch to act as a check on the political branches.

Finally, any complete theory of the law of federal courts and judicial decision making must incorporate the system of individual rights into the structural equation.[51] Of course, we can see this same balancing of principles in the individual rights component of constitutional structure as we do with federalism and separation of powers. Individual rights are always subject to countervailing constitutional interests. It is for this reason that no right is absolute. But individual rights are, emphatically, part of the constitutional structure. Hence, properly understood, the principle of structural interpretation ought to take into account the full dimension of constitutional considerations. Certainly, there is no case for making a one-sided vision of "our federalism" the primary focus of a jurisprudence of federal courts.[52]

[50] 5 U.S. 137, 163 (1803). Of course, famously, Mr. Marbury received no remedy from the U.S. Supreme Court. But this outcome was not because the law did not afford him a remedy, but because Mr. Marbury sought his remedy in a constitutional impermissible tribunal. The outcome, therefore, does not undermine the principle.

[51] Federalism and separation of powers can themselves indirectly protect individual rights by decentralizing the exercise of power. However, they do not necessarily operate in that fashion, and the founding generation in adopting the Bill of Rights eventually concluded that specific protections for individual rights were an essential additional component of the constitutional structure.

[52] We can see the "our federalism" principle dominance at work in the related contexts of the *Younger* doctrine (Younger v. Harris, 401 U.S. 37 (1971); Samuels v. Mackell, 401 U.S. 66 (1971);

In addition, the principle of structural interpretation potentially runs afoul of at least two other legal process principles, antiformalism and rule of law. As indicated above, the antiformalism principle provides that judicial interpretation should take into account a pluralistic array of interests in interpreting the law. Yet, the principle of structural interpretation appears to give singular and dominant weight to a narrow vision of structure over a vast array of other considerations, some of which have a constitutional dimension. In this sense, the principle of structural interpretation is itself a product of legal formalism, for it introduces a rigid hierarchy into the interpretive metrics. The clash with the rule of law principle is even more striking. That principle implies the availability of federal courts to vindicate federal rights. However, Hart and Wechsler's law of federal courts is premised more on power arrangements than it is on individual claims of right. Thus, the principle of structural interpretation illegitimately dominates the rule of law principle.

TOWARD A MODEL OF JUDICIAL DECISION MAKING

Drawing inspiration from Pound's studies and reflections, legal process theory, and the above-described critiques and responses, as well as from more than a century of the U.S. Supreme Court's jurisprudence and the jurisprudence and approaches adopted by the highest courts of other civil law and common law countries,[53] I believe that a successful jurisprudential method should begin with the framework of Pound's three jurisprudential categories – conceptions, premises, and empiricism.[54] My proposed model of judicial decision making should proceed from conceptions and rules treating them as premises to develop consistent with unitary theories in view of the ends to be met and the current relevant social conditions. This model should be flexible and subject to possible corrections suggested by experience.[55]

This judicial decision making should take into account the respective institutional roles of Congress and the judiciary; accept the purposive role of judicial decision making, including both the craft and the statesmen aspect of that role; examine the consistency of the decision with the rule of law and that principle's insistence on a judicial forum for the vindication of individual

Ohio Civil Rights Comm. v. Dayton Christian Schools, Inc., 477 U.S. 619 (1986); Pennzoil Co. v. Texaco, Inc., 481 U.S. 1, 11 (1987), and the Eleventh Amendment (Seminole Tribe of Florida v. Florida, 517 U.S. 44 (1996); Alden v. Maine, 527 U.S. 706 (1999)) – all cases in which access to the federal courts was denied, thus forcing litigants to take their federal claims to state court.

[53] *See* Chapter VI, *infra*.

[54] Roscoe Pound, *Courts and Legislation*, *supra* note 5 (Introduction), at 171.

[55] *Id.*, at 370–371.

claims of right; and measure the decision based on its fidelity to durable legal principles articulated through a reasoned elaboration. In addition, any such decision should reflect the full range of structural concerns that animate the Constitution, including a balanced approach to federalism, separation of powers, and individual rights. Legitimate judicial decision making should be informed by a wide range of considerations, beginning with established legal standards, but including the insights derived from deductive and inductive reasoning, the lessons learned from history and custom, and from an examination of the social and economic consequences of the decision. The considerations made to reach a specific result should be articulated through a process that considers various hypothesis, arguments, confutations and confirmations, and it should be shared with the public.

I have selected this approach as the proper judicial decision-making model because it is comprehensive, because it takes into account the full range of constitutional considerations, and because it places courts within the legitimate and recognized bounds of the judicial function. This model rejects "the mechanical and 'transcendental nonsense' of legal formalism"[56] and at the same time avoids an unrestricted endorsement of legal realism by inviting results that are premised on "predictable and nonsubjective conclusions."[57]

My proposal to reform legal analysis does not have anything to do with a "romantic," naïve view of law, nor with any idea of "natural law." My idea of law is quite pragmatic; my goal is to reform legal analysis by suggesting the adoption of a more mature judicial method that better meets the ends of a developed legal system like the American one.

THE SPECIAL CASE OF JUDICIAL REVIEW

The power of judicial review is the power to declare legislation (or action by the government) unconstitutional. Courts vested with this authority are properly denominated "constitutional courts," whether judicial review is their exclusive function, as is the case with the German Federal Constitutional Court or the Italian Constitutional Court, or whether judicial review is but one of their functions, as is the case with the Supreme Court of the United States. The basic point of judicial review is to insulate constitutional or fundamental law from the pressures of the transitory needs perceived by the immediate majority operating under the constitution.

[56] Post, *Theorizing Disagreement*, *supra* note 21, at 1320.

[57] Philip P. Frickey, *Faithful Interpretation*, 73 Wash. U. L. Q. 1085, 1090 (1995).

It is true that constitutional courts operate within the arena of politics, and it is also true that the decisions of constitutional courts, which are sometimes quite controversial, are subject to a type of political scrutiny. But, in my view, constitutional decision making cannot be divorced from politics. In fact, there is no separation between the constitutional and the political. The birth of judicial review in *Marbury v. Madison*[58] was a conspicuously political act designed to establish the U.S. Supreme Court's power to enforce the constitution against the legislative and executive branches. More generally, in the United States, the truly enduring decisions of the Supreme Court, such as *Brown v. Board of Education*,[59] have all been political in the very best sense of that word. They wrote from the present, but with an eye to the future.

To take this a step further, judicial review is, by its very nature, a form of law making. True, the principle of separation of powers purports to place the law making power in the legislature, leaving to the judiciary the power and responsibility to find and apply the legislatively created law. But this theoretical separation has never been complete. Thus, while the legislature has a type of primacy in the making of law, history shows that in both common law and civil law systems, courts make law when they interpret and apply the legislatively created standards and when they fill in any gaps left in the legislative program. This judicial law-making authority is even more evident in the context of judicial review where there is no legislative primacy. Here the constitution itself takes primacy, and the body of law designed to enforce that primacy is exclusively made by constitutional courts through the process of interpretation and application.

The important questions of constitutional law rarely involve a text that automatically resolves the question before the court. Rather, constitutional law flourishes in the interpretations and applications of open-textured phrases such as due process, equal protection, and federalism. Every such interpretation involves a choice among alternative views, and that choice is and ought to be informed by a wide range of considerations, beginning with established legal standards, but including the insights derived from deductive and inductive reasoning, the lessons learned from history and custom, and from an examination of the social and economic consequences of the decision. The choice made represents a political judgment and the resulting standard is enforceable as "law" in every sense of that word.

Certainly judicial decision making is law in the same sense as legislation. As the U.S. Supreme Court clearly and definitively established in *Cooper v.*

58 5 U.S. 137 (1803).
59 347 U.S. 483 (1954).

Aaron,[60] a case involving a state's resistance to the decision in *Brown*, the Supreme Court's interpretation of the Constitution in a specific case is the supreme law of the land, binding on anyone to whom it might apply now or in the future. That does not mean that constitutional courts exercise hegemony over constitutional interpretation. It does mean, however, that the constitution is precisely what the constitutional court says it is and that the court's statement of what constitutes the law of the constitution is the law.

There is, of course, a legitimate concern that judicial law making may stray into the realm of everyday politics. In addition, when constitutional courts are asked to decide high-profile, controversial issues, such as those pertaining to same-sex marriage or to a nation's participation in a larger political or economic community, it is inevitable that whatever the court decides will be deemed inappropriately political by some disappointed constituency. This is especially so when the court rules against the perceived majoritarian preference. The challenge is to find a way to justify the judicial choice on terms that transcend the particular case and promote a sense of legitimacy of the judicial decision-making process. The question is not whether the court has acted politically or has made law, but whether it has done so under circumstances and in a manner that will be perceived as legitimate and enduring. That the body of constitutional law is what a constitutional court declares it to be does not itself justify any specific exercise of that power. Hence, we do need a framework from which to assess the quality and legitimacy of judicial law making, and especially so in the context of constitutional law where the judicial determinations will impose deeply felt and enduring consequences. There must be a way to separate the good from the bad, the principled from the personal, and the enduring from the transient.

The judicial decision-making model I develop in this book may lessen some of the "political" discomfort that arises from the practice of judicial review. As anticipated above, my model suggests that constitutional decisions should be premised on "durable principles," by which I mean legal standards that can, by logic and analogy, be applied uniformly to a wide range of similarly situated cases. The articulation and application of those standards must be justified through a reasoned elaboration that takes into account the full sweep of constitutional text and tradition; considers the measure of evolving cultural norms, including new perspectives on established standards; and presents a fair and thorough consideration of real-world consequences. Taken together,

[60] 358 U.S. 1 (1958).

this decision-making process represents an act of creation, but does so within the breadth of the existing constitution.

Consistently with this approach, a constitutional court should not seek to justify its conclusions through a judicial monologue or argument that does no more than pave the path to a particular result. While a judge may be tempted to provide a sharp and confident description of what the law "is," pointing to any flaws and inconsistencies in the contrary point of view, an approach consistent with my model would identify the range of alternative interpretations to the constitutional principle at issue and, after careful examination of those alternatives, explain what the law "ought to be."

With this latter approach, which resembles a dialogue with the political community as opposed to a lecture to or imposition on that community, the decision-making process is more likely to reach conclusions that are understood and accepted by that community. In essence, judicial opinions that fairly consider and respond to counterarguments are more likely to be legitimate and accepted as such by the community. This may be because, so articulated, such opinions cohere with the broader perspective of the community and are therefore accepted as a moral imperative rather than as an imposition. Moreover, opinions that proceed through a carefully constructed framework of "trial and error" or "conjectures and refutations" appear more "scientific," rather than the product of personal preferences. Also, from a dissenter's perspective, opinions that truly consider the dissenter's views may be a product of having been taken seriously in the constitutional debate.

As with other powers vested in the state, the success of the judiciary depends on its relation with the community, not on its exalted status above the community. Durable principles and reasoned opinions would, therefore, bring constitutional courts the authority and public acceptance necessary to the success of the constitutional mission. Opinions perceived as usurpations will meet the resistance of the community and likely fail to endure.

Despite my acceptance of a constitutional court's law-making power, I do not see the practice of judicial review as somehow inconsistent with democracy. Rather, judicial review is part of the democratic process in the sense that the product of judicial review – constitutional law – must represent the full sweep of democratic history and progress, while legislation represents only the sentiments of a transient majority. In a constitutional system, there are, in essence, two democracies that must accommodate one another in creating an organic whole. Moreover, the tension between the politics of judicial review and the politics of the present majority is a natural consequence of the idea of constitutional law, of the notion that some principles, perhaps not fully realized in the text of a constitution, transcend the press of everyday politics.

Certainly the legislature should engage in its own analysis of constitutionality, since it has the authority and responsibility to interpret the constitution. That too is part of the organic law-making relationship between the court and the legislature. If the legislature defaults in this regard, then there is no constitutional dialogue. Under all circumstances, however, the Court, relatively insulated from the press of everyday politics, will have the final word.

Also, constitutional democracy and its constitutional court must recognize the "primacy of the political sphere" in the context of ordinary law. It is in this context that party politics and temporary majorities will usually prevail. Thus, constitutional courts must be attentive to the present-day will of the people, as reflected through established political processes. It is also my view that constitutional courts should not erect constitutional barriers to legislative action that undermine the legislature's ability to solve the practical problems confronting a democracy on a day-to-day basis. But in the context of constitutional law, where the transitory meets the fundamental, the "primacy of the political sphere" must give way to the primacy of constitutional law. Here the constitutional courts represent a broader democratic base – past, present, and future – and that base ought to determine the scope of enforceable constitutional principle.

A constitutional court should not operate in a fashion that replaces the legislative function in the everyday creation of ordinary law. But a constitutional court just as surely can require the government to comply with the constitution when such an order is appropriate to the enforcement of the underlying constitutional value. Thus, I would not characterize a court that requires a legislature to take action in "conformity to the constitution" as a "surrogate legislature." Nor would I so characterize a court that construed a statute to avoid a potential constitutional conflict. It seems to me that these are the normal tools of judicial decision making and quite consistent with the philosophy of judicial review. Indeed, both techniques invite the legislature to participate in the process of constitutional conformity as part of the organic law-making process.

It is certainly correct that a court vested with the power of judicial review should carefully consider the scope of any order that it enters. In some cases, perhaps in most, the remedy should be specific to the plaintiff. But in other cases, broader structural relief might be appropriate, including mandated legislative actions. The desegregation of schools in the United States, post-*Brown*, required judicial orders that one might call a form of "surrogate legislation"; however, the more precise question should be whether, under the circumstances presented, the judge or court properly ordered the structural relief. Was that relief necessary to the vindication of the constitutional right at stake? One solution here is for the court to invite the appropriate legislative body to submit a planned remedy for the constitutional violation. In this fashion, the organic law-making relationship is furthered, for the legislature can fully participate in the creation of the constitutional remedy. But if the legislature fails to submit an adequate remedy, the court, consistently with its judicial office, may order compliance with a judicially imposed plan. Indeed, a court's failure to provide a remedy for the constitutional violation would itself be unconstitutional. In this context, the "freedom" of the legislature is properly curtailed.

In sum, constitutional courts, by the very nature of their mission, engage in politics and, in the process, make law. The method should be cautious and premised on a respect for traditions, but always attentive to the potential consequences of the choices confronting the court. It is part craft, part art, and part science.

2

Personal Jurisdiction[1]

PREMISE

In the United States, as well as in most modern legal systems,[2] the law of personal jurisdiction is premised on two fundamental concepts: *connecting factors* and *reasonable expectations*. These two concepts, working in tandem, embrace fully the ideas of fairness, efficiency, and justice that are at the heart of due process. Thus, to properly establish personal jurisdiction, connecting factors must link the defendant to the forum under circumstances that invest her with a reasonable expectation of being sued there. That having been done, the exercise of personal jurisdiction over that defendant will be consistent with the idea of due process and, thus, proper.

Yet, despite the elegant simplicity of this formula, and its difference from most of the legal systems here considered,[3] the U.S. Supreme Court has failed to provide a coherent vision of the law of personal jurisdiction. In fact, the Court's fact-specific, case-by-case approach – what I call the "modern common law method" – has produced a widening doctrinal morass. As a consequence, the fundamental concepts and their attendant inquiry have been submerged beneath a series of mechanical tests that are both too broad and too narrow. Worse yet, these tests often invite an unnecessarily complex form of analysis wholly detached from any sensible understanding of due process. Here, the common law method has failed.

The dominant academic view of the Supreme Court's personal jurisdiction jurisprudence is that it represents a body of decisions that have progressively fined-tuned the relevant doctrine through a self-correcting process of trial and

[1] *See also* Simona Grossi, *Personal Jurisdiction: A Doctrinal Labyrinth with no Exit*, 47 Akron L. Rev. 617 (2014).

[2] *See* Chapter VI, *infra*.

[3] *Id.*

error.[4] Scholarship tends to work around the edges of the Court's mechanical jurisprudence. There is a body of literature that attempts to organize the developed doctrine into useful subcategories,[5] another that argues in favor or against various doctrinal developments,[6] and still another that focuses its attention on potential novel applications of established doctrine to emerging economic and social trends.[7] This scholarly endeavor is valuable indeed. It surely contributes to a better understanding of the judiciary's overall approach to the law of personal jurisdiction, thereby providing guidance to the legal profession and the scholarly community. My work does something different. It challenges the method itself, for it is the method that has led to the madness.

Through my civil law lens, but with due respect for the common law method properly applied,[8] I conclude that due process would be better served

[4] *See, e.g.*, CHARLES ALAN WRIGHT, et al., 4 Federal Practice and Procedure §1067.1 (3d. ed. 2013) (offering a positive narrative of the Court's personal jurisdiction jurisprudence); JACK H. FRIEDENTHAL, MARY KAY KANE & ARTHUR R. MILLER, CIVIL PROCEDURE 133–146 (4th ed. 1999) (describing the Court's refinement of the *International Shoe* standard) (hereinafter FRIEDENTHAL, CIVIL PROCEDURE). *But see* Douglas D. McFarland, *Drop the Shoe: A Law of Personal Jurisdiction*, 68 Mo. L. Rev. 753 (2003) (arguing for the abandonment of the *International Shoe* minimum contacts test).

[5] *See, e.g.*, Arthur T. von Mehren & Donald T. Trautman, *Jurisdiction to Adjudicate: A Suggested Analysis*, 79 Harv. L. Rev. 1121, 1136–1153 (1966) (drawing a distinction between general and specific jurisdiction); Mary Twitchell, *The Myth of General Jurisdiction*, 101 Harv. L. Rev. 610 (1988) (endorsing a more careful consideration of the distinction distinction between general and specific jurisdiction); Linda Sandstrom Simard, *Hybrid Personal Jurisdiction: It's Not General Jurisdiction, or Specific Jurisdiction, But Is It Constitutional?*, 48 Case W. Res. L. Rev. 559 (1998) (noting the emergence of a form of jurisdiction that is a "hybrid" of the general and specific categories). *See also* Carol Andrews, *Another Look at General Personal Jurisdiction*, 47 Wake Forest L. Rev. 999 (2012) (assessing the current status of general jurisdiction).

[6] *See, e.g.*, Stewart E. Sterk,*Personal Jurisdiction and Choice of Law*, 98 Iowa L. Rev. 1163 (2013) (critique on the current direction of doctrinal development); Allan Ides, *A Critical Appraisal of the Supreme Court's Decision in J. Mcintyre Machinery, Ltd. V. Nicastro*, 45 Loy. L.A. L. Rev. 341 (2012) (critique of the Court's stream of commerce decisions); Robin J. Effron, *Letting the Perfect Become the Enemy of the Good: The Relatedness Problem in Personal Jurisdiction*, 16 Lewis & Clark L. Rev. 867 (2012) (same); Todd David Peterson, *The Timing of Minimum Contacts*, 79 Geo. Wash. L. Rev. 101 (2010) (criticizing the Court for its lack of guidance as to the timeframe within which minimum contacts should be analyzed); Mona A. Lee, Burger King's *Bifurcated Test for Personal Jurisdiction: The Reasonableness Inquiry Impedes Judicial Economy and Threatens a Defendant's Due Process Rights*, 66 Temp. L. Rev. 945 (1993).

[7] *See, e.g.*, Sarah H. Ludington, *Aiming at the Wrong Target: The "Audience Targeting" Test for Personal Jurisdiction in Internet Defamation Cases*, 73 Ohio State Law J. 541 (2012); Megan M. La Belle, *Patent Litigation, Personal Jurisdiction, and the Public Good*, 18 George Mason Law Review 43 (2010); Veronica M. Sanchez, *Taking A Byte Out of Minimum Contacts: A Reasonable Exercise of Personal Jurisdiction in Cyberspace Trademark Disputes*, 46 UCLA L. Rev. 1671 (1999).

[8] *See* Chapter VI, *infra*.

by a statute that captures the essence of personal jurisdiction at a principled level, providing a durable standard capable of application across a wide range of cases. My proposed statute is designed to offer effective guidance to the courts that would apply it, but is not so narrow as to constrain the exercise of careful judgment on a case-by-case basis. Its goal is to help courts to see through the transitory particulars and reach what is permanent behind them.[9] True, proceeding along the basis of general principles, such as connecting factors and reasonable expectations rather than on highly specific mechanical tests requires, hard thinking and close reasoning.[10] However, what characterizes true judicial intelligence is the power to grasp the general.[11]

Of course, all statutes are subject to judicial interpretation as well as to the power of judicial review. That combination puts any statutory text at risk. Thus, my aim is not simply to replace the current jurisprudence with a statute, but to redirect the judicial method to its meaningful and legitimate function and return the jurisprudence of personal jurisdiction to the fundamental principles of due process that originally guided that law in the United States and that guide the law of jurisdiction in the developed world community. In short, this statutorily driven judicial method would invite results that are more consistent with the fundamental principles of due process and more likely to provide a coherent body of decisions.[12]

As noted, the statute would also make the law of personal jurisdiction in the United States more consistent with the law as currently practiced in the developed world community.[13] Of course, there is nothing inherently wrong with a multiplicity of solutions to a particular legal problem, and my goal is not simple conformity. But if the underlying concepts and principles are shared, which they are here, value might be gained from following those methods that seem to resolve the problem in a manner that is both consistent with the shared concepts and principles and that does so in a manner that is more coherent and transparent than other available options. The fact that the U.S. Supreme Court continues to revisit and readjust the law of personal jurisdiction, with no end in sight, suggests that there may be a better option.[14]

[9] *See* BENJAMIN N. CARDOZO, THE NATURE OF THE JUDICIAL PROCESS, 17 (1975).

[10] *See* Roscoe Pound, *The Administrative Application of Legal Standards*, 42 Annu. Rep. A.B.A. 445, 452–453 (1919).

[11] *Id.*, at 463.

[12] Philip P. Frickey, *Faithful Interpretation*, 73 Wash. U. L. Q. 1085, 1090 (1995).

[13] *See* Chapter VI, *infra*.

[14] After the several opinions rendered on personal jurisdiction and the last cases decided between 2011 and 2014 – Walden v. Fiore, 134 S.Ct. 1115 (2014); Daimler AG v. Bauman, 134 S.Ct. 746 (2014); J. McIntyre Mach., Ltd. v. Nicastro, 131 S. Ct. 2780 (2011); and Goodyear Dunlop Tires

CONNECTING FACTORS AND REASONABLE EXPECTATIONS

In the United States, the standards of personal jurisdiction have been shaped primarily by the U.S. Supreme Court's decisions.[15] Those decisions recognize two broad categories of circumstances under which jurisdiction may be exercised consistently with due process. The first category includes those exercises of jurisdiction that can be described as traditional, arguably tracing their origins to at least the late nineteenth century. The second category includes those exercises of jurisdiction that fall within the general contours of the "minimum contacts" test.

THE TRADITIONAL CATEGORY

The traditional bases of personal jurisdiction include domicile, voluntary appearance, consent to service of process, and physical presence. Each of these forms is consistent with the sovereignty principle announced in *Pennoyer v. Neff*,[16] the leading nineteenth-century decision on the topic. There, the Court saw due process as reflecting a principle of "territoriality" under which a state had complete jurisdictional dominion within its territory but virtually none beyond its borders (with some exceptions).[17] When jurisdiction is asserted on one of these traditional bases – that were generally recognized at the time the Fourteenth Amendment was ratified in 1868 – the exercise of jurisdiction categorically satisfies due process.

Territoriality aside, another way to describe the traditional bases is as a reflection of connecting factors and expectations that make the exercise of jurisdiction reasonable (and hence consistent with due process). The fit is not perfect, as we will see, but the parallels are significant. Thus, one's status as a domiciliary can be seen as a connecting factor that creates a reasonable expectation of being subject to suit within the state, given the tangible and intangible benefits that flow from citizenship. Essentially, a domiciliary has consented to the state's jurisdictional authority. Similarly, a person who has voluntarily appeared in court or contractually consented to jurisdiction within

Operations, S.A. v. Brown, 131 S. Ct. 2846 (2011) – the Court has recently granted certiorari in other two personal jurisdiction cases – DaimlerChrysler AG v. Bauman, No. 11-965 (cert. granted Apr. 22, 2013); and Walden v. Fiore, No. 12-574 (cert. granted Mar. 4, 2013).

15 *See generally* Christopher N. May and Allan Ides, Civil Procedure: Cases and Procedure 53-200 (4th ed. 2012); Friedrich K. Juenger, *American Jurisdiction: A Story of Comparative Neglect*, 65 U. Colo. L. Rev. 1, 2–17 (1993).

16 95 U.S. 714 (1877).

17 *Id.* at 722.

the forum has, by so acting, created a connecting factor that leads inexorably to a reasonable expectation of forum-based jurisdiction.

Connecting factors and reasonable expectations arising from them, however, cannot properly explain the exercise of jurisdiction over persons or property found within the forum. Although this form of jurisdiction is premised on a rather obvious geographic connection with the forum, it is not equally obvious that the connection universally creates (or ought to be seen as creating) a reasonable expectation of jurisdiction within the forum. One could argue that physical presence in the forum creates an expectation of jurisdiction based on *Pennoyer*'s territoriality principle. But that is a circular argument in which due process is dependent on a legal abstraction. Certainly, an expectation of jurisdiction is not an inherent characteristic of one's temporary presence within the territory (or from the fact that property is temporarily located within the jurisdiction). The "reasonableness" of any such expectation might well depend on the nature of the presence and the relationship between that presence and the claim asserted.

In sum, certain traditional forms of jurisdiction, although based on a sovereignty principle, can be seen as reflective of the due process principles of connecting factors and reasonable expectations. Domicile, voluntary appearance and consent would all fall into this category. On the other hand, the category of persons or property found within the jurisdiction, at least when applied rigidly, may be inconsistent with the reasonable expectation principle.

TRADITION EXTENDED – MINIMUM CONTACTS

Whenever the defendant is sued in a place other than his domicile, and whenever jurisdiction cannot be established on some other traditional bases, due process requires that there must be some indication that the defendant was otherwise on reasonable notice of the possibility of being sued there, either because he performed activities in that state or because his contacts with the state are such that the exercise of jurisdiction by a court of that state does not come as an unfair surprise to him. More specifically, in 1945, in *International Shoe Co. v. Washington*,[18] the Supreme Court held that "due process requires only that in order to subject a defendant to a judgment *in personam*, if he be not present within the territory of the forum, he *have certain minimum contacts* with it such that the maintenance of the suit does not offend 'traditional notions of fair play

[18] 326 U.S. 310 (1945).

and substantial justice.'"[19] The *International Shoe* formula clearly looked through the transitory particulars to reach what was permanent behind them.[20]

After *International Shoe* and on the premises of this opinion, the Court developed the minimum contacts test. Under the test, the nonresident defendant must have directed her conduct toward the forum state, for example, by engaging in activities there,[21] entering into contracts with residents of the forum state,[22] marketing or selling a dangerous or defective product there,[23] or causing an effect there.[24] In addition, the activities or contacts with the state must be related to the claim (specific jurisdiction)[25] or be so "continuous, substantial and systematic" that it is as if the nonresident defendant were "at home" there (general jurisdiction).[26] If these standards are satisfied, the exercise of jurisdiction is presumed to be reasonable, that is, consistent with due process. The nonresident defendant may, however, rebut that presumption by a strong showing to the contrary.[27]

We can see that both the traditional bases for asserting jurisdiction and the minimum contacts test share a salient characteristic; namely, they are both based on connecting factors that give rise to a reasonable expectation of being sued in the forum. The formula of connecting factors and reasonable expectations perfectly articulates the personal jurisdiction conception, and no particularized, narrow test can improve on it.

*****

[19] *Id.* at 316 (1945) (second emphasis added) (quoting *Milliken v. Meyer*, 311 U.S. 457, 463 (1940)).

[20] *See* BENJAMIN N. CARDOZO, THE NATURE OF THE JUDICIAL PROCESS, 17 (1975).

[21] *Id.*

[22] *See* Burger King Corp. v. Rudzewicz, 471 U.S. 462, 482 (1985).

[23] *See* J. McIntyre Mach., Ltd. v. Nicastro, 131 S. Ct. 2780 (2011); Asahi Metal Indus. Co. v. Super. Ct., 480 U.S. 102 (1987); World-Wide Volkswagen Corp. v. Woodson, 444 U.S. 286, 298 (1980).

[24] *See* Calder v. Jones, 465 U.S. 783, 789 (1984).

[25] *See* Nowak v. Tak How Inv. Ltd., 899 F. Supp. 25, 28 (D. Mass. 1995).

[26] Goodyear Dunlop Tires Operations, S.A. v. Brown, 131 S. Ct. 2846 (2011); Helicopteros Nacionales de Colombia, S.A. v. Hall. 466 U.S. 408, 415–16 (1984); Perkins v. Benguet Consol. Mining Co., 342 U.S. 437, 445–46 (1952). One can see general jurisdiction as an extension of the traditional basis of jurisdiction premised on domicile. In essence, the principle that jurisdiction is proper in the place of the defendant's domicile is expanded to say that, even when individuals or corporations are not formally "domiciled" in a state, if their activity there is continuous, substantial, and systematic, they may still be treated as if they were domiciled in that state, and the court may exercise general jurisdiction over them. Doing extensive activity in the forum state, however, is not considered a traditional basis of personal jurisdiction that, as such, does not require any fact-specific scrutiny to establish its consistency with due process and, therefore, its validity. A fact-specific analysis will always be required to find that, indeed, the activity done in the forum state is extensive and, by its very nature, a contact that should put the defendant on notice of the possibility of being haled into court there on any cause of action.

[27] *Asahi*, 480 U.S. at 115–16; *Nowak*, 899 F. Supp. at 33. In Daimler AG v. Bauman, 134 S.Ct. 746, 762 n.19 (2014), a majority of the Court ruled that the "second step" reasonableness inquiry is superfluous in once the standards for general jurisdiction have been satisfied.

Since the decision in *International Shoe*, which focused more on fundamental principles than on the niceties of doctrine, the Supreme Court has gradually but steadily moved from a jurisprudence of fundamental principles and conceptions, to a mechanical jurisprudence, that is, a technical and specialized approach to the law of personal jurisdiction. Instead of durable, transcendent principles, we can now think in terms of categories and subcategories of problems: activities in the forum, contracts with forum residents, tortious effects in the state, products liability cases, Internet cases, and so forth.

This process contradicts the very essence of the common law method. The common law method draws its generalizations from particulars, and the general formulas thus generated should yield results more in harmony with past particulars and more consistent with the social welfare.[28] This method of generalization from particulars is at the core of the common law system and represents one of its strengths.[29] A common law judge is not required to draw rules from a principle, but to provide "fresh illustration of the intelligent application of the principle to a concrete cause, producing a workable and a just result."[30]

The Supreme Court's personal jurisdiction jurisprudence, however, has not been faithful to this essential characteristic of the common law method and, rather than serving the fundamental principles of due process, the Court's jurisprudence has generated a fragmented, piecemeal discipline that often disserves the basic principles it seeks to further and renders legal analysis dry and meaningless. From a legal process perspective, the Court's jurisprudence falls short in a number of respects: the individual decisions often suffer from an absence of reasoned elaboration; the body of the Court's work is certainly not premised on a workable, durable principle; and, most importantly, overall approach runs afoul of the rule of law principle that demands the availability of courts to redress valid claims of right.

PROBLEMS WITH THE U.S. SUPREME COURT'S CURRENT APPROACH TO PERSONAL JURISDICTION

The ascendance of doctrine

What came in the wake of *International Shoe* was a process of redirecting the fundamental principles approach into narrower, more specific doctrinal

[28] *See* BENJAMIN N. CARDOZO, THE NATURE OF THE JUDICIAL PROCESS 25 (1975).

[29] Describing this common law method, Cardozo observed that "[t]his work of modification is gradual. It goes on inch by inch. Its effects must be measured by decades and even centuries. Thus measured, they are seen to have behind them the power and the pressure of the moving glacier." *Id.*

[30] Roscoe Pound, *Mechanical Jurisprudence*, 8 Colum. L. Rev. 605, 622 (1908).

categories. Some of that process has been informative as to the basic reach of the model and respectful of its fundamental principles. Other parts of the process, however, seem to have elevated doctrine over those principles, or at least have insinuated doctrine between the fundamental principles and the facts.

Most of the Supreme Court's jurisprudence following *International Shoe* exemplifies the ascendancy of mechanical jurisprudence, which Pound described and denounced.[31] This post–*International Shoe* jurisprudence does not reason from the particulars to the general nor engage in extensive analysis of the relevant premises. Rather, this jurisprudence reduces everything to multipronged formulas through which the guiding principles gradually lose their importance.[32] The Supreme Court has developed what Pound would call a "business-like procedure" that uses conceptions as empty words, not as premises from which to reason, a procedure motivated by the desire to get to pragmatic solutions quickly without engaging in extensive analysis of the relevant premises that would lead to those solutions.

FUNDAMENTAL PRINCIPLES ADRIFT

In its October 1957 term, the Supreme Court decided two personal jurisdiction cases. One might be characterized as informative but unnecessary; the other began the drift away from the fundamental principles approach endorsed in *International Shoe*.

The first, *McGee v. International Life Ins. Co.*,[33] involved a suit to enforce the provisions of a life insurance policy. The facts were simple. An insurance company from Texas solicited a reinsurance agreement with a resident of California via mail. The offer was accepted in California, and the insurance premiums were mailed from California to Texas, until the insured died. His mother, the beneficiary under the policy, filed a claim with the insurance company, but the company refused to pay. She then sued the company in a California state court, which upheld the exercise of personal jurisdiction over the insurance company and eventually entered a judgment in the plaintiff's favor. When the mother sought to enforce that judgment in Texas, however, Texas courts refused to give it full faith and credit on the theory that the California courts lacked jurisdiction over the Texas company.

The central issue before the Supreme Court was whether a single contact with the forum – the solicitation of one policy – could serve as a proper basis

[31] *Id.*, at 611–612.
[32] *Id.*, at 611–612.
[33] 355 U.S. 220 (1957).

on which to exercise personal jurisdiction. In fact, the Court in *International Shoe* had already given this question an affirmative response when it observed that a single act could be "deemed sufficient" to establish jurisdiction depending on the "nature and quality and the circumstances of [its] commission."[34] That principle having been established, there was little more that the Supreme Court needed to say about it. In upholding the California courts' exercise of personal jurisdiction, the Court explained, "[W]e think it apparent that the Due Process Clause did not preclude the California court from entering a judgment binding on respondent. It is sufficient for purposes of due process that the suit was based on a contract which had substantial connection with that State."[35]

The essence of this ruling was that the insurance company's solicitation of a contract in California established a connecting factor with that state and created a reasonable expectation in the insurance company that it might be sued there for breach of that contract. Thus, the Court's decision did not articulate any new doctrine. Rather, it policed the application of established principles and reiterated them for the guidance of lower courts. One might criticize the Court for being too engaged in correcting lower courts' case-specific errors; however, one could also say that its opinion served as a useful reminder of the fundamental principles and conceptions established twelve years earlier in *International Shoe*.

The *McGee* opinion represents a perfect example of a jurisprudence premised on fundamental principles, invited and made possible by the *International Shoe* due process formula. That formula was articulated through a general principle that provided courts with wide limits within which they could deal with and meet the demands of justice in each particular case. The *International Shoe* Court knew that the application of law involves not only logic, but also a measure of judicial discretion that, if eliminated, would reduce legal analysis to a purely mechanical exercise and eventually frustrate the ends of justice. Thus, the *McGee* Court did not create any specific rule or test out of the *International Shoe* due process formula, but it merely conformed its judgment to that formula and provided a fresh illustration of the formula's intelligent application to the concrete cause presented to the Court. The result was workable and just.

Six months after the decision in *McGee*, the Court returned to personal jurisdiction in *Hanson v. Denckla*.[36] The essential issue in *Hanson* was whether

[34] *Int'l Shoe*, 326 U.S. at 318 (citing Kane v. New Jersey, 242 U.S. 160 (1916); Hess v. Pawloski, 274 U.S. 352 (1927)).
[35] *McGee*, 355 U.S. at 223.
[36] 357 U.S. 235 (1958).

the courts of Florida could exercise jurisdiction over a Delaware trustee of a trust whose settlor had moved to Florida after the creation of the trust. The trustee continued to administer the trust on behalf of the Florida settlor for the following eight years, and the settlor exercised the power of appointment under the trust while in Florida. Still, the Court found that the trustee lacked minimum contacts with Florida sufficient to allow personal jurisdiction.

Relying on *International Shoe*, the *Hanson* Court described the due process standard as containing a "purposeful availment" requirement:

> [I]t is essential in each case that there be some act by which the defendant purposefully avails itself of the privilege of conducting activities within the forum State, thus invoking the benefits of protections of its laws.[37]

However, in *International Shoe*, the Court had merely noted:

> But to the extent that a corporation exercises the privilege of conducting activities within a state, it enjoys the benefits and protection of the laws of that state. The exercise of that privilege may give rise to obligations; and, so far as those obligations arise out of or are connected with the activities within the state, a procedure which requires the corporation to respond to a suit brought to enforce them can, in most instances, hardly be said to be undue.[38]

Here, the *International Shoe* Court was not imposing purposeful availment as a prerequisite to the exercise of personal jurisdiction. Rather, the Court was simply observing that it was reasonable for the state to exercise personal jurisdiction over someone who did purposefully benefit from the state's laws and protections. In other words, the condition of purposeful availment was *sufficient*, not necessary to validate the exercise of personal jurisdiction.[39] Instead, the *Hanson* Court transformed what *International Shoe* had considered a natural consequence of a defendant's activities in a state into a necessary precondition for the exercise of jurisdiction.

Hanson offers an example of the Supreme Court falling into a linguistic doctrinal trap[40] and endorsing a narrow, mechanical test inconsistent with the general principle that that test was supposed to apply – namely, the *International Shoe* formula.

In applying the new "purposeful-availment" test, the Court distinguished *McGee* by noting that, unlike the insurance company there, in *Hanson* the trustee had not performed any acts in the forum state that bore the same

[37] *Id.* at 253.
[38] 326 U.S. at 319.
[39] *See* Allan Ides & Simona Grossi, *The Purposeful Availment Trap*, 7 Fed. Cts. L. Rev. 118 (2013).
[40] *Id.*

relationship to the trust as did the solicitation of the insurance contract at issue in *McGee*. In fact, in the Court's view, the Florida proceeding could not be considered as one initiated to enforce an obligation arising from any privilege that the nonresident defendant trustee had exercised in Florida. Thus, according to the Court, the trustee had not "purposefully availed" itself of the benefits and protections of Florida law. Of course, as noted above, this purposeful availment requirement was a *Hanson* Court's own creation.

One wonders whether the *Hanson* Court's adoption of the purposeful availment requirement was intended to provide a neutral, narrow rule that would reduce lower court discretion as much as possible and eliminate any possible bias, or merely a rule that would be easier to apply. In either case, the rule is mechanical and inconsistent with the underlying principle. Pound described and critiqued this type of judicial decision making:

> Mechanical application of rule and rigid adherence to form admit of no personal bias and give no latitude for differences of individual opinion. Moreover, the process of decision, so conducted, is simple and easy, whereas to go beneath form to substance requires hard thinking and close reasoning . . . for a long time men distrusted reason as giving too much scope for the personality of the magistrate.[41]

Pound described a more advanced alternative as being premised on reasoning: "It is only in the maturity of law that men acquire confidence in reasoning as an infallible, impersonal instrument, quite as reliable as mechanical forms and much superior in its results."[42]

Furthermore, reliance on general principles allows a court to better identify and separate what is accidental and nonessential from what is instead essential and relevant to legal analysis. General principles better unify and rationalize the particulars and may properly project and extend themselves to new cases.[43] Thus, they invite more efficient and fair results.

It is possible that the *Hanson* Court's adoption of the purposeful availment requirement was intended to provide lower courts with a personal jurisdiction rule easier to apply than the general *International Shoe* formula. However, even if the Florida courts' judgment may have made it necessary for the *Hanson* Court to clarify the minimum contacts standard, in doing so the Court unfortunately did just the opposite by creating confusion over the nature of the contacts that would qualify as meaningful. It is certainly not true that the trust company

[41] Roscoe Pound, *The Administrative Application of Legal Standards*, 42 Annu. Rep. A.B.A. 445, 453 (1919).
[42] *Id.*
[43] *Id.*, at 31.

lacked meaningful connections with the state. Nor is it necessarily the case that the company could not have reasonably expected to be sued in Florida on a matter related to the trust. After all, the company was aware that the settlor had moved to Florida and continued to act as the trustee over the trust and to communicate with her in Florida with respect to trust business. Under *International Shoe*, Florida could be found to have jurisdiction over the trustee.

In his dissenting opinion, Justice Black argued that Florida had personal jurisdiction over the Delaware trustee. He observed that the object of the controversy was whether the settlor had properly exercised her power to appoint beneficiaries under the precise trust being administered by the trustee. In fact, the litigation arose when the legatees under the settlor's will brought an action in the Florida courts seeking a determination as to whether this appointment was valid. This disposition of her property had very close and substantial connections with Florida, since the settlor had appointed the beneficiaries in Florida, and all of the beneficiaries lived there. Thus, Florida had an interest in exercising jurisdiction and applying Florida law to determine whether the appointment was indeed valid. The connections between the appointment, the transaction, and the State of Florida were thus evident. And, of course, the trustee was necessarily implicated in this action. Therefore, in Justice Black's view, Florida courts should have the power to adjudicate a controversy arising out of transactions that were so connected to the state, unless litigation there would impose such a heavy and disproportionate burden on a nonresident defendant that it would offend "traditional notions of fair play and substantial justice." But, according to Justice Black, that was not the case, since the trustee "chose to maintain business relations with [the settlor] in that State for eight years, regularly communicating with her with respect to the business of the trust including the very appointment in question."[44] Moreover, the trustee's burden of participating as a formal (and collateral) party to this dispute over the appointment would have been minimal at best.

Justice Black's conclusion was more consistent with *International Shoe* and its premises. In fact, Justice Black was willing to attend to all of the connecting factors and expectations of the parties, while the majority, with its myopic focus on "purposeful availment," was not.

With the decision in *Hanson*, we see the beginning of a shift away from the fundamental principles that animated the decision in *International Shoe* toward a more technical and mechanical approach to the details of doctrine.[45] Thus, with *Hanson*, the minimum contacts test began to lose its inherent coherence and strength.

[44] *Id.* at 259.
[45] *Id.* at 253.

FUNDAMENTAL PRINCIPLES ALTERED

At issue in *Burger King v. Rudzewicz*[46] was whether a federal court sitting in Florida could exercise jurisdiction over a nonresident franchisee who had entered a long-term franchise agreement with the plaintiff, a corporate resident of the state. The bulk of the Court's opinion focused on the purposeful availment requirement, but the Court added a potential "exit" to the jurisdictional analysis under which a strong presumption of jurisdiction established by the connecting factors and the reasonable expectation arising of those factors could be rebutted under "compelling" circumstances.[47] In describing this standard, the Court suggested that it would apply only when the defendant established "the unconstitutionality of" the exercise of jurisdiction, as by showing a severe impairment of the defendant's ability to defend or assert a counterclaim.[48] The Court's application of this additional consideration essentially replicated *forum non conveniens* analysis,[49] strongly suggesting this element's redundancy.[50] The Court concluded, however, that the heavy presumption in favor of jurisdiction was not rebutted in the case before it.[51]

Two years later, in *Asahi Metal Industry Co. v. Superior Court*,[52] the Court applied the "unreasonableness" exit in a case that involved the enforcement of an indemnification agreement between two foreign entities. Here, the Court balanced the interests of the forum, the interest of the U.S. judicial system, potential foreign policy considerations, and the interests of the parties and concluded that the exercise of jurisdiction in that case would be unreasonable.[53] Again, the Court's analysis sounded more like a *forum non conveniens* than a personal jurisdiction analysis because it was not premised on connecting factors and reasonable expectations but on different considerations pertaining mostly to different interests.[54] Nor did the Court's analysis in *Asahi* suggest that there was any fundamental unfairness in the exercise of jurisdiction in the case before it.

The net result of *Burger King* and *Asahi* was that even when a plaintiff satisfied the connecting factors and the reasonable expectation requirements, a court might still decline to exercise jurisdiction under what was

[46] 471 U.S. 462 (1985).
[47] *Id.* at 477.
[48] *Id.* at 482–483.
[49] *See* Chapter III, *infra*.
[50] *Id.* at 482–486.
[51] *Id.*
[52] 480 U.S. 102 (1987).
[53] *Id.* at 113–116 (plurality opinion); *see also id.* at 116 (Brennan, J. concurring).
[54] *Id.*

essentially a balancing of interests, including the court's own interest in the exercise of jurisdiction.[55]

FUNDAMENTAL PRINCIPLES EXTENDED AND WITHDRAWN

In 1977, the Court revisited the theme of personal jurisdiction and, specifically, *quasi in rem* jurisdiction, in *Shaffer v. Heitner*.[56] There, Heitner filed a shareholder's derivative suit in Delaware against the Greyhound Corporation, its officers, members of its board of directors and one of its subsidiaries.[57] Heitner seized approximately 82,000 shares of Greyhound stock owned by twenty-one of the defendants in an attempt to establish *quasi in rem* jurisdiction over them in the Delaware court. However, the Supreme Court held that exercising jurisdiction would be inconsistent with due process because the property that was attached – that is, the shares – was not related to the plaintiff's claims, and thus the minimum contacts test had not been satisfied. Because these defendants had no apparent contacts with Delaware other than the shares that were attached, their contacts were insufficient to exercise personal jurisdiction consistent with due process. Since the defendants could not reasonably expect to be haled into court in Delaware on claims unrelated to their contacts there, said the Court, the Delaware court's exercise of jurisdiction over them was inconsistent with the connecting factors and reasonable expectations principles of due process.

Thus, in *Shaffer*, the Court took the fundamental principles of *International Shoe* and extended them to a traditional basis of jurisdiction, that is, the presence of the property within the forum state. In contrast to the Court's mechanical intervention in *Hanson*, which was not doctrinally necessary, the Court's taking of the *Shaffer* case was appropriate to endorse a new approach to *quasi in rem* jurisdiction and to make that form of jurisdiction consistent with the *International Shoe* due process formula. Here, again, no mechanical, narrow test was adopted. The *Shaffer* Court remained faithful to the *International Shoe* jurisprudence of general principles and conceptions by applying its due process formula to a case involving the presence of property within the forum.

The Court, however, abandoned this judicial method and engaged again in mechanical jurisprudence when, a few years later, it decided *Burnham v. Superior*

55 The *Burger King/Asahi* jurisdictional exit is remarkably similar to the subject matter jurisdiction exit used by the Court in the context of arising under jurisdiction. *See* Gunn v. Minton, 133 S.Ct. 1059 (2013). *See* Chapter III, *infra*.

56 433 U.S. 186 (1977).

57 *Id.*

Court.[58] There, with virtually no elaboration of the relevant premises and somehow inconsistent with them, the Court concluded that not all the traditional bases of personal jurisdiction need be consistent with the idea of connecting factors and reasonable expectations, that is, with due process. In *Burnham*, the nine justices concluded that a California state court could exercise personal jurisdiction over a nonresident defendant who was in the state for only three days attending to matters unrelated to the pending action, because he was personally served with process while voluntarily present within the state.[59] The Court believed that the exercise of this so-called tag jurisdiction did not violate the "'traditional notions of fair play and substantial justice'"[60] because "its validation is its pedigree."[61] Thus, the Court failed to conform this traditional method of jurisdiction to the fundamental principles of due process and instead relied on "pedigree" as a substitute for those principles. In this sense, tag jurisdiction – at least until Court revisits it – remains another fundamental-principles anomaly.[62]

FUNDAMENTAL PRINCIPLES SUPPRESSED

In *Kulko v. Superior Court*,[63] the Court considered whether a California court could exercise personal jurisdiction "over a nonresident, nondomiciliary

58 495 U.S. 604 (1990).

59 *Id.* Interestingly, however, Justice Brennan, commenting on Justice Scalia's reliance on historical precedents to justify transient jurisdiction in his concurring opinion, observed:

> [R]eliance solely on historical pedigree . . . is foreclosed by our decisions in *International Shoe Co. v. Washington* and *Shaffer v. Heitner*. . . The critical insight of *Shaffer* is that all rules of jurisdiction, even ancient ones, must satisfy contemporary notions of due process. . .

While our *holding* in *Shaffer* may have been limited to *quasi in rem* jurisdiction, our mode of analysis was not.

Id. at 629–30 (Brennan, J., concurring) (citations omitted). However, Justice Brennan's minimum contacts analysis, as applied to transient jurisdiction, was so broad as to be meaningless for the purpose of subjecting the transient jurisdiction analysis to the minimum contacts test. In fact, his test was such that persons transitorily present in the forum state would almost always have the necessary minimum contacts to make the exercise of transient jurisdiction valid. *See* Robert Taylor-Manning, *An Easy Case Makes Bad Law – Burnham v. Superior Court of California, 110 S. Ct. 2105 (1990)*, 66 WASH. L. REV. 623, 631–32 (1991).

60 *Int'l Shoe*, 326 U.S. at 316 (quoting Milliken v. Meyer, 311 U.S. 457, 463 (1940)).

61 *Burnham*, 495 U.S. at 621.

62 *See* FRIEDENTHAL, CIVIL PROCEDURE, *supra* note 4, at 171–172 (questioning whether the efficiencies of *Burnham*'s bright-line rule "outweigh the costs of the injustices it may allow"); Albert A. Ehrenzweig, *The Transient Rule of Personal Jurisdiction: The "Power" Myth and Forum Conveniens* 65 Yale L.J. 289, 303–304 (1956) (criticizing transient jurisdiction as a relic of *Pennoyer v. Neff*).

63 436 U.S. 84 (1978).

parent of minor children domiciled within the State."[64] The California Supreme Court had upheld the exercise of jurisdiction under the "effects test" – the father having sent his daughter into California to live permanently with her mother. In so ruling, the state high court explained why it thought that the father had purposefully availed himself of the benefits and protections of California law:

> [P]robably no parental act more fully invokes the benefits and protections of California law than that by which a parent permits his minor child to live in California. The parent thereby avails himself of the total panoply of the state's laws, institutions and resources—its police and fire protection, its school system, its hospital services, its recreational facilities, its libraries and museums, to mention only a few.[65]

The U.S. Supreme Court reversed, concluding that *Hanson*'s purposeful availment "requirement" had not been satisfied here. The Court disagreed with the California Supreme Court's purposeful availment analysis in a single sentence placed in a footnote: "[I]n the circumstances presented here, these services provided by the State were essentially benefits to the child, not the father, and in any event were not benefits that appellant purposefully sought for himself."[66]

Thus, instead of engaging in a realistic appraisal of the facts that would have lead it to identify the father's meaningful contacts with California and, thus, establish jurisdiction over him, the *Kulko* Court endorsed the mechanical, a-contextual purposeful availment requirement and concluded, without elaboration, that it was the child who was benefitting from California laws and protections, not the father. Thus, jurisdiction was not appropriate. Like the Court in *Hanson*, the Court in *Kulko* used the shortcut of a technical doctrine – a narrow, mechanical test that lead to results inconsistent with the personal jurisdiction conception and the *International Shoe* general principle that the Court was supposed to apply and articulate.[67]

The *Kulko* Court further confused the law of jurisdiction by observing, "In light of our conclusion that appellant did not purposefully derive benefit

[64] *Id.* at 86.

[65] Kulko v. Superior Court, 19 Cal.3d 514, 522 (1977), *rev'd*, 436 U.S. 84 (1978).

[66] 436 U.S. at 94 n.7.

[67] It is possible that the Court tortured the standard of personal jurisdiction in order to advance a policy of fairness in the context of child-support proceedings. But even that instinct was misplaced, since the father in *Kulko* had in fact waived any objection to personal jurisdiction in the child-custody proceeding (as opposed to the child-custody aspect of the proceeding). 436 U.S. at 88. Thus, any unfairness to the father in being required to defend the support proceeding would seem to have been misplaced.

from any activities relating to the State of California, it is apparent that the California Supreme Court's reliance on appellant's having caused an 'effect' in California was misplaced."[68] Here, the Court was referring to §37 of the Restatement (Second) of Conflict of Laws, the so-called "effects test."[69] Of course, that test contains no purposeful availment requirement and, in fact, it was specifically designed to embrace circumstances where purposeful availment could not logically be satisfied and yet where the exercise of jurisdiction would be consistent with due process.[70] By suggesting that purposeful availment was nonetheless a prerequisite to the effects test, the *Kulko* Court strayed further from the fundamentals of due process by allowing a court to deny the exercise of jurisdiction when due process would in fact be satisfied.

After *Kulko,* the Supreme Court's case-by-case, mechanical approach continued to erode the coherence and strength of the minimum contacts principles. In *Calder v. Jones,*[71] the Court applied the effects test in the context of an intentional tort. There, the Court held that California courts could exercise jurisdiction over nonresident defendant journalists who had written and edited a libellous story concerning the California activities of Jones, a California resident, knowing that Jones would feel the brunt of the harm there. The Court explained:

> The allegedly libelous story concerned the California activities of a California resident. It impugned the professionalism of an entertainer whose television career was centred in California. The article was drawn from California sources, and the brunt of the harm, in terms both of respondent's emotional distress and the injury to her professional reputation, was suffered in California. In sum, California is the focal point both of the story and of the harm suffered. Jurisdiction over petitioners is therefore proper in California based on the "effects" of their Florida conduct in California. . . .
>
> [Petitioners'] intentional, and allegedly tortious, actions were expressly aimed at California. Petitioner South wrote and petitioner Calder edited an article that they knew would have a potentially devastating impact upon respondent. And they knew that the brunt of that injury would be felt by respondent in the State in which she lives and works and in which the *National Enquirer* has its largest circulation. Under the circumstances,

[68] *Id.* at 96.

[69] Restatement (Second) of Conflict of Laws § 37 (1971). Section 37 provides, "A state has power to exercise judicial jurisdiction over an individual who causes effects in the state by an act done elsewhere with respect to any cause of action arising from these effects unless the nature of the effects and of the individual's relationship to the state make the exercise of such jurisdiction unreasonable."

[70] *Id.* at cmt. a.

[71] 465 U.S. 783 (1984).

> petitioners must "reasonably anticipate being haled into court there" to answer for the truth of the statements made in their article.[72]

If we were to take the above passage as merely descriptive of the Court's reasoning, it might be seen as an unremarkable application of the law of minimum contacts to the facts of the particular case. But as an endorsement of a particular doctrinal model, this passage proved troubling for two reasons.

First, it was completely unnecessary in light of the more general principles established in *International Shoe*. Clearly, both the writer and the editor who were sued in *Calder* had significant claim-related connections with California (as the above passage makes clear). These connecting factors should have led to an expectation of being subject to jurisdiction in a California court on a claim so closely tied to those connections. In other words, no special test was needed to establish jurisdiction under these facts.

Second, the doctrinal formula described by the Court was significantly narrower than the Restatement's version of the effects test. Under the Court's doctrinal formula, jurisdiction might be established under the effects test if: (1) the nonresident defendant committed an intentional tort, (2) that was aimed at the forum state, and (3) with the knowledge that the plaintiff would feel the "brunt" of the harm in the forum state.[73] The effects test under the Restatement (Second) of Conflict of Laws, however, can be satisfied "when the defendant did not intend to cause the particular effect in the state but could reasonably have foreseen that it would result from his act done outside the state."[74] This formula includes no requirement of "aim" or "brunt"; nor is this formula limited to intentional torts. Thus, differently from the *Calder* formula, by focusing merely on the meaningful contacts that the defendant has with the forum state, the Restatement version of the effects test embraces the full range of jurisdictional possibilities consistent with due process. The *Calder* formula, by contrast, is narrow, mechanical and, as such, inflexible and incapable of taking into account and measuring connections and expectations beyond the narrow contours of the doctrinal formula. Does *Calder* represent another example of mechanical jurisprudence that for apparently no reason erodes the jurisprudence of principles and conceptions originally intended to guide the law of personal jurisdiction?

One could view the *Calder* formula merely as a sufficient basis for asserting jurisdiction, not a necessary one. That would be a welcome reading. However,

[72] *See Id.* at 788–89.

[73] *Id.*

[74] Restatement (Second) of Conflict of Laws § 37.

this is not the reading that a majority of lower federal courts has adopted.[75] In fact, the Supreme Court recently revisited the effects test in *Walden v. Fiore*,[76] and adopted an approach to that test that seems even more mechanical and more restrictive than the formula applied in *Calder*.

It is as if the Court envisioned the evolution of the law of personal jurisdiction as something that could be achieved only through a series of narrow and specific tests, "shortcuts" that by deviating the lower courts' attention from the meaningful contacts in the case lead courts to achieve results inconsistent with the conceptions and principles that those tests purported to apply. Also, rather than offering better guidance to lower courts, these shortcuts ended up constraining judicial discretion, thus frustrating legal analysis.

Pound thought that constraining judges' discretion through narrow rules would frustrate the essence of law and the ends of justice,

> [f]or the application of law is not and ought not to be a purely mechanical process. Laws are not ends in themselves; they are means toward the administration of justice. Hence within somewhat wide limits courts must be free to deal with the individual case so as to meet the demands of justice between the parties. Any considerable narrowing of these limits, any confining of the judicial function by too many hard and fast rules soon defeats the purpose for which law exists. Application of law must involve not logic merely but a measure of discretion as well. All attempts to eradicate the latter element and to make the law purely mechanical in its operation have ended in failure. Justice demands that instead of fitting the cause to the rule, we fit the rule to the cause.[77]

The current Court's method, rather than improving legal analysis, in fact constrains it and prevents it from achieving the ends of justice and, thus, the ends of human beings. The narrow tests endorsed eliminate the lower courts' need to engage in meaningful legal analysis, to examine the relevant premises, the conditions of application as well as the conceptions and their logical consequences. Everything is reduced to simple deduction from the relevant premises. However, the deductions are not always reconcilable with the

[75] *See* Yahoo! Inc. v. La Ligue Contre Le Racisme Et L'Antisemitisme, 433 F.3d 1199, 1206 (9th Cir.) *cert. denied*, 547 U.S. 1163 (2006); Fielding v. Hubert Bunda Media, Inc., 415 F.3d 419, 429 (5th Cir. 2005); IMO Indus., Inc. v. Kiekert AG, 155 F.3d 254, 265–66 (3d Cir. 1998). *See also* IDES & MAY, note 15 *supra*, 137–138.

[76] 134 S.Ct. 1115 (2014) (denying personal jurisdiction over a nonresident defendant who had authored a knowingly false affidavit designed to prevent the return of unlawfully seized money to the plaintiff, who the defendant knew to be a resident of the forum State at the time the defendant executed the false affidavit).

[77] Roscoe Pound, *Courts and Legislation*, 7 Am. Pol. Sci. Rev. 361, 365 (1913)

premises from which they purport to flow. Legal analysis is reduced to a mechanical exercise[78] and judges to true interpreters rather than law-finders.[79] This Court's struggle to find a "more inclusive order,"[80] to prevent friction and eliminate the "waste, the arbitrary and illogical"[81] should be redirected to a "quest for the broad principle that will do the work of securing the most interests with the least sacrifice of other interests, and at the same time conserve judicial effort by flowing logically from or logically according with and fitting into the legal system as a whole."[82] The current Supreme Court's jurisprudence is, instead, myopic and in continuous need of corrections and adjustments not entirely justified by the changing needs and interests of society.

FUNDAMENTAL PRINCIPLES SUBMERGED

The "stream-of-commerce" doctrine provides yet another example of mechanical doctrine deflecting the jurisdictional inquiry from the fundamental principles and conceptions that ought to govern it. Moreover, this example of the phenomenon is particularly troubling since "stream of commerce" is a completely redundant doctrine, for the effects test (as contemplated in the Restatement) is itself fully capable of embracing all the situations to which stream of commerce potentially applies. In fact, there isn't a single stream-of-commerce decision that could not be fully and adequately resolved under the Restatement's effects test. In this sense, stream of commerce is a double-filtered deflection from the fundamental inquiry into due process.

The stream of commerce refers to the chain of distribution of a product that goes from the manufacturer to the ultimate consumer. A manufacturer producing a product in a state or foreign nation, and intentionally selling it through a chain of distribution that may employ exporters, importers, distributors, and retailers, is considered to have purposefully affiliated itself with the state where the ultimate consumer is located and the injury occurs.

This test traces its roots to *Gray v. American Radiator & Standard Sanitary Corp.*, a sensible 1961 decision by the Illinois Supreme Court that was premised largely on the fundamentals of due process and in which the phrase "stream of commerce" never appears.[83] In *Gray*, the plaintiff was injured

[78] *See, e.g.*, Roscoe Pound, *Mechanical Jurisprudence*, 8 Colum. L. Rev. 605, 611–612 (1908).
[79] *See* Roscoe Pound, *Courts and Legislation*, 7 Am. Pol. Sci. Rev. 361, 378 (1913).
[80] William James, The Will to Believe, 196 (196).
[81] Roscoe Pound, *Juristic Science and Law*, 31 Harv. L. Rev. 1047, 1063 (1917–1918).
[82] *Id.*
[83] 176 N.E.2d 761 (Ill. 1961).

when a water heater she purchased in Illinois exploded there, allegedly due to a defective safety valve. The valve was manufactured in Ohio and then shipped to Pennsylvania, where it was placed on the water heater. The water heater was then shipped into Illinois for retail purchase. The plaintiff sued both the manufacturer of the water heater, a Pennsylvania company, and manufacturer of the valve, an Ohio company, in an Illinois court. The valve manufacturer moved to quash service, arguing that it was not subject to personal jurisdiction in Illinois, as it did not do business there and had no registered agent for service there. The trial court quashed service, but the Illinois Supreme Court reversed. After holding that the Illinois long-arm statute was sufficiently broad to permit the exercise of jurisdiction over the valve manufacturer, the court turned to the question of whether the exercise of jurisdiction would comport with due process.

Interestingly enough, the Illinois Supreme Court did not use the phrase "stream of commerce." Nor did it purport to create a new jurisdictional doctrine. Rather, the court simply relied on fundamental principles derived from *International Shoe* and *McGee*, among other cases, to explain why the exercise of jurisdiction over the foreign manufacturer comported with due process:

> In the case at bar, defendant does not claim that the present use of its product in Illinois is an isolated instance. While the record does not disclose the volume of Titan's business or the territory in which appliances incorporating its valves are marketed, it is a reasonable inference that its commercial transactions, like those of other manufacturers, result in substantial use and consumption in this State. To the extent that its business may be directly affected by transactions occurring here, it enjoys benefits from the laws of this State, and it has undoubtedly benefited, to a degree, from the protection which our law has given to the marketing of hot water heaters containing its valves.[84]

Eventually, the Illinois Supreme Court's jurisprudence of general principles and conceptions that carefully considered and applied due process principles was reduced into a doctrine that acquired the "stream-of-commerce" label. Nearly twenty years after the decision in *Gray*, in *World-Wide Volkswagen Corp. v. Woodson*,[85] the U.S. Supreme Court endorsed the stream-of-commerce doctrine by way of dicta:

> The forum State does not exceed its powers under the Due Process Clause if it asserts personal jurisdiction over a corporation that delivers its products into

[84] *Id.* at 766.
[85] 444 U.S. 286 (1980).

> the stream of commerce with the expectation that they will be purchased by consumers in the forum State. *Cf. Gray v. American Radiator & Standard Sanitary Corp.*, 22 Ill.2d 432, 176 N.E.2d 761 (1961).[86]

Given the fundamentals of the due process standard as embodied in the minimum contacts test, this endorsement would seem to have been completely superfluous. After all, the Illinois state court had properly understood *International Shoe* and applied it in a "stream-of-commerce" context through a jurisprudence of conception that reached the same result that *World Wide Volkswagen* official "stream-of-commerce" doctrine would have reached. The problem with the *World Wide Volkswagen* opinion is, in fact, not the result it reached, but its endorsement of another doctrinal layer with the potential of becoming a mechanical test. The stream-of-commerce test further fragmented the analysis and general conception that that analysis was supposed to articulate and apply, and it further reduced the range of jurisdictional possibilities that *International Shoe* and due process would have allowed.

Of course, the specific "act or conduct" sufficient to meet the due process requirement must be identified and described by a court applying the minimum contacts test, but this description need not, in itself, create new doctrine. If each such description creates a new jurisdictional doctrine or an offshoot of settled doctrine, the law of due process becomes nothing more than a complex web of fact-specific outcomes, further and further removed from the core principles of the due process standard. And, under such an evolving-standards model, each fact-specific decision by the Supreme Court will inevitably offer new possibilities of gaps in the existing web, generating yet another neatly labeled jurisdictional doctrine.

Gradually, the law of personal jurisdiction became an aggregate of very specific and narrow rules, incapable of governing the complexity of human life and interests[87] and of a developed legal system.[88]

A few years after *World Wide Volkswagen* incanted the magic phrase "stream of commerce," the Court granted certiorari in *Asahi Metal Industry Co. v. Superior Court*[89] to resolve a conflict that had arisen in lower courts over the scope of what had become the stream-of-commerce test. Indeed, the danger of this type of mechanical jurisprudence is that the tentative results of a *priori* reasoning often generate confusion thus requiring continuous interventions by

[86] *Id.* at 298–99.
[87] Roscoe Pound, *The Administrative Application of Legal Standards*, 42 Annu. Rep. A.B.A. 445, 454 (1919).
[88] *See* Roscoe Pound, *The Administrative Application of Legal Standards*, *supra* note 155.
[89] 480 U.S. 102 (1987).

the Supreme Court. This leads to an inefficient use of the very limited judicial resources available and, as illustrated above, to a fragmented legal analysis that ends up frustrating the ends of justice.

At the time the Court granted certiorari in *Asahi*, some lower courts required that a manufacturer whose goods reached the forum state through the stream of commerce have also taken some affirmative action to promote the sales of its products within that state, that is, a so-called "plus factor." Other courts did not require the plus factor. The Supreme Court intervened to solve the conflict. However, the Court did not succeed in the endeavor, and instead split four-to-four, with one justice declining to address the question.[90]

While the *Asahi* Court did not provide any direction to the lower courts as to the scope of the stream-of-commerce test, it made it clear that the unresolved question – plus or no plus? – was quintessentially technical and doctrinal, and not premised on the fundamental due process questions pertaining to connecting factors, expectations or, more generally, fairness and reasonableness. Basically, *Asahi* made it clear that the controversy was over the details of a mechanical test and, by endorsing such mechanical approach, it pressed *International Shoe* and its jurisprudence of general principles and conceptions further into the background.

The Court's most recent foray into the stream-of-commerce test came in 2011 with the decision in *J. McIntyre Machinery Ltd. v. Nicastro*.[91] In *McIntyre*, the Court admitted that "This Court's *Asahi* decision may be responsible in part for [the state] court's error regarding the stream of commerce, and this case presents an opportunity to provide greater clarity."[92] In short, it was time to eliminate the confusion.[93] However, despite the Court's good intentions, no greater clarity was provided and, worse, as Justice Ginsburg convincingly explained in her dissent, *International Shoe* and the minimum contacts test would have easily resolved the case and demanded a different outcome. In many ways, the decision in *McIntyre* provides a perfect exemplar of the potential deficiencies of the modern, mechanical case-by-case doctrinal approach to due process.

In *McIntyre*, the plaintiff, Nicastro, severely injured his hand while using a metal-shearing machine manufactured by J. McIntyre Machinery, Ltd. (McIntyre UK). Nicastro filed a products-liability action against McIntyre UK and others in a New Jersey state court. The accident occurred in

90 *Id.*
91 131 S.Ct. 2780 (2011).
92 *Id.* at 2787.
93 As Professor Arthur Miller has observed, "Trying to determine what the diverging opinions [in *McIntyre*] mean to counsel in the coming years presents a bit of a mystery." 4 Federal Practice and Procedure §1067.4 (3d. ed. 2013).

New Jersey, but the machine was manufactured in England, where McIntyre UK was incorporated and operated. McIntyre UK did not directly market its products in New Jersey nor did it ship any of them there. However, McIntyre UK had a relationship with an independent distributor, McIntyre Machinery America, Ltd. (McIntyre America), that promoted and sold McIntyre's machines in the U.S. market. In addition, McIntyre UK's representatives attended trade shows in Chicago, Las Vegas, New Orleans, Orlando, San Diego, and San Francisco, all to promote sales of its products throughout the United States. At one of those conventions in Las Vegas, where McIntyre UK was an exhibitor, Nicastro's employer learned of McIntyre UK's machine and decided to buy one. McIntyre America then shipped the machine to New Jersey, where it eventually injured Nicastro. The New Jersey Supreme Court upheld the exercise of jurisdiction in New Jersey over McIntyre UK.

On appeal, the U.S. Supreme Court reversed. There was no majority opinion for the Court. The four-person plurality opinion authored by Justice Kennedy correctly observed that the stream-of-commerce test – which it called a "metaphor" – was not a substitute for due process analysis, but then went on to define stream of commerce in a manner that created a shield to any consideration of the due process fundamentals. The plurality's definition of stream of commerce was concise, but virtually empty of content. In the words of the *McIntyre* plurality, "The defendant's transmission of goods permits the exercise of jurisdiction only where the defendant can be said to have targeted the forum."[94] The "target" metaphor is left unexplained, though it seems akin to the "aim" element of the effects test. The plurality narrow, doctrinal "metaphor" thus created a further gatekeeping standard preventing consideration of the fundamental fairness principles established in *International Shoe*. By a similar mechanical approach, Justice Breyer's concurring opinion adopted his own "single-sale" limitation on the use of the stream-of-commerce approach, thereby obviating any need to look into the fundamental due process concerns triggered by the facts in such cases.[95]

As Justice Ginsburg noted in her dissent:

> McIntyre UK's regular attendance and exhibitions . . . was surely a purposeful step to reach customers for its products "anywhere in the United States." At least as purposeful was McIntyre UK's engagement of McIntyre America as the conduit for sales of McIntyre UK's machines to buyers "throughout the United States." Given McIntyre UK's endeavors to reach and profit from the

[94] *McIntyre*, 131 S.Ct. at 2789.
[95] *Id.* at 2792 (Breyer, J., concurring).

> United States market as a whole, Nicastro's suit, I would hold, has been brought in a forum entirely appropriate for the adjudication of his claim. He alleges that McIntyre UK's shear machine was defectively designed or manufactured and, as a result, caused injury to him at his workplace. The machine arrived in Nicastro's New Jersey workplace not randomly or fortuitously, but as a result of the U.S. connections and distribution system that McIntyre UK deliberately arranged.[96]

Justice Ginsburg was right. The *International Shoe* Court would have recognized these connecting factors as creating a reasonable expectation of a lawsuit in those forums where the marketing strategy succeeded and where a product-based injury occurred.[97] However, although her instinct was correct, Justice Ginsburg also took a misstep. Rather than focusing on the fundamental principles established in *International Shoe*, she then tried to fit the case into her own re-formulation of the stream-of-commerce test, one with a "national contacts" overlay. More specifically, she noted:

> In sum, McIntyre UK, by engaging McIntyre America to promote and sell its machines in the United States, "purposefully availed itself" of the United States market nationwide, not a market in a single State or a discrete collection of States. McIntyre UK thereby availed itself of the market of all States in which its products were sold by its exclusive distributor.[98]

[96] *Id.* at 2797.

[97] She observed:

> A foreign industrialist seeks to develop a market in the United States for machines it manufactures. It hopes to derive substantial revenue from sales it makes to United States purchasers. Where in the United States buyers reside does not matter to this manufacturer. Its goal is simply to sell as much as it can, wherever it can. It excludes no region or state from the market it wishes to reach. But, all things considered, it prefers to avoid products liability litigation in the United States. To that end, it engages a U.S. distributor to ship its machines stateside. Has it succeeded in escaping personal jurisdiction in a state where one of its products is sold and causes injury or even death to a local user? Under this Court's pathmarking precedent in International Shoe Co. v. Washington, 326 U. S. 310 (1945), and subsequent decisions, one would expect the answer to be unequivocally, "No." But instead, six justices of this Court, in divergent opinions, tell us that the manufacturer has avoided the jurisdiction of our state courts, except perhaps in states where its products are sold in sizeable quantities. Inconceivable as it may have seemed yesterday, the splintered majority today "turn[s] the clock back to the days before modern long-arm statutes when a manufacturer, to avoid being haled into court where a user is injured, need only Pilate-like wash its hands of a product by having independent distributors market it." Weintraub, A Map Out of the Personal Jurisdiction Labyrinth, 28 U. C. Davis L. Rev. 531, 555 (1995)."

Id. at 2794.

[98] *McIntyre*, 131 S. Ct. at 2801.

Justice would have demanded the use of judicial discretion to find jurisdiction over McIntyre. However, the current mechanical personal jurisdiction tests constrained judicial discretion to the point that the only thing left for the justices to do was to try to fit the case to the available mechanistic jurisdictional tests,[99] and, not so surprisingly, the case did not fit them.

One of the ironies of *McIntyre* is that the New Jersey state courts understood the fundamental principles and ran the analysis on the basis of them. Also, the state courts displayed a stronger intuitive sense of the scope and operation of those principles[100] than did the Supreme Court. Unfortunately, the justices of the Supreme Court appeared to be trapped in and confused by their own personalized tests and by the interpretations of their own interpretations. As a consequence, what was in fact a relatively simple case of a nonresident defendant whose commercial activities manifested its intent to submit to the state's jurisdiction set the stage for yet further confusion and new doctrinal twists.[101] In short, the New Jersey Supreme Court recognized what was obvious and fundamental and got it right, but the U.S. Supreme Court's mechanical jurisprudence did not.

As noted above, stream of commerce is, in essence, a specialized version of the effects test. By manufacturing a product outside of the state and then placing it into the stream of commerce with the expectation and indeed the hope that it will reach the forum state, if the product in fact reaches that state and injures a consumer there, the manufacturer has caused a totally foreseeable effect in the forum state through activities undertaken elsewhere. Not surprisingly, the Restatement therefore considers "stream of commerce" to be an expression of the effects test:

> The causing of effects in a state by means of an act done outside the state is today a jurisdictional basis of immense importance. Many of the current court decisions involve this basis. It plays a particularly significant role in the area of product liability. A common situation is where a product is taken from one state to another and there causes injury or is the subject of some other claim as, for example, one for breach of warranty. The question then arises whether the state to which the product has been taken has judicial jurisdiction over, as the case may be, the out-of-state manufacturer, assembler, importer, distributor or ultimate seller. Frequently, the answer will be in the affirmative.[102]

[99] Pound, *Courts and Legislation*, 7 Am. Pol. Sci. Rev. 361, 365 (1913).

[100] Nicastro v. McIntyre Mach. Am., Ltd., 945 A.2d 92, 96 (N.J. Super. Ct. App. Div. 2008), *aff'd*, 987 A.2d 575 (N.J. 2010).

[101] *See* Allan Ides, *A Critical Appraisal of the Supreme Court's Decision in J. McIntyre*, *supra* note 6.

[102] *See* Restatement (Second) of Conflict of Laws, Commentary to § 37.

Thus, for the same reasons that the effects test (as contemplated by the Restatement) is a product of the fundamentals of due process – connecting factors and reasonable expectations – so too is the stream-of-commerce test. But to the extent that either the effects test or the stream-of-commerce test operates as a mechanical gatekeeper to the fundamental questions of due process, the test undermines the principles it should in fact serve.

From this review of the Supreme Court's post–*International Shoe* cases, it should be clear that the lack of uniform rules, and the development of redundant, misguided, and increasingly fact-specific and mechanical tests, have fragmented the law of personal jurisdiction and confused the Supreme Court as to the real scope of the minimum contacts test. As a consequence, the results have been often contradictory and inconsistent and increasingly distant from the fundamental principles of due process. This is evident in the jurisprudence of state courts as well as lower federal courts.

*DOCTRINAL CONFUSION IN STATE AND LOWER FEDERAL COURTS – THE POST-*HANSON *MEANING OF "PURPOSEFUL AVAILMENT"*

Two predictable results of mechanical jurisprudence are inefficiency and unfairness. The multitude of narrow tests requires continuous corrections and adjustments. Also, the applications of such tests are often contradictory and, as such, unfair to the litigants. The mechanical jurisprudence of the Supreme Court in the area of personal jurisdiction has yielded precisely these types of results.

The "purposeful availment" requirement established in *Hanson* has led not only to confusion but also to the denial of jurisdiction in cases where its exercise would comport with the due process analysis as articulated in *International Shoe*. The decision of the California Supreme Court in *Sibley v. Superior Court*[103] provides an illustrative example.

In that case, the question was whether an out-of-state guarantor on a contractual performance to be undertaken in California could be subjected to jurisdiction in a California court based simply on having caused an effect in the state. The California Supreme Court held that despite the obvious effect caused by the guarantor – the guaranty led to a contract that was to be performed in California – jurisdiction could not be exercised over the non-resident guarantor, consistently with *Hanson*, since the guarantor had not sought any California benefit from the transaction, or, stated differently, he

[103] 16 Cal.3d 442 (1976), *cert. denied*, 429 U.S. 826 (1976).

had not "purposefully availed himself of the privilege of conducting business in California or of the benefits and protections of California laws."[104] In essence, *Sibley* applied "purposeful availment" literally,[105] thus creating a doctrinal limitation on jurisdiction wholly inconsistent with due process principles of connecting factors and reasonable expectations.

The decision in *Sibley* should not be seen as aberrational or a maverick. As recently as 2012, the Supreme Court of Kansas declared that the

> "effects" test in *Calder* does not, however, replace the need to demonstrate minimum contacts that constitute purposeful availment, that is conduct by the nonresident defendant that invoked the benefits and protections of the state or was otherwise purposefully directed toward a state resident.[106]

Under this approach, the effects test is rendered superfluous: whether or not it is satisfied, the jurisdictional decision must ultimately rest on the principle of "purposeful availment." While the Kansas court to its credit rejected a mechanical reliance on the "effects test," it then fell back on another mechanical test, namely, "purposeful availment."

Hanson and its absolute "purposeful availment" requirement has even infected the realm of statutory interpretation. In fact, by way of interpretation, courts seek to inject the purposeful availment requirement into their jurisdictional statutes so as to preserve the statutes' constitutionality. Thus, in *Ehrenfeld v. Bin Mahfouz*,[107] the New York Court of Appeals, interpreting the state's long-arm statute, imposed a type of purposeful availment requirement on the exercise of jurisdiction that excluded use of the effects test in situations where its application would in fact have been totally consistent with due process. Hence, the doctrinal error of *Hanson* was imported into the statutory law of New York.

At the same time, other courts construed "purposeful availment" to embrace jurisdiction premised on a nonresident defendant's merely having caused an effect in the forum state.[108] Eventually, some courts came to recognize that the purposeful availment standard was at best incomplete since it did not encompass anything like the full range of jurisdictional possibilities

[104] *Id.* at 447.

[105] *Sibley* was overruled by Kulko v. Superior Court, 19 Cal.3d 514 (1977).

[106] *See* Aeroflex Wichita, Inc. v. Filardo, 275 P.3d 869, 885 (Kan. 2012).

[107] 881 N.E.2d 830 (N.Y. 2007).

[108] *See, e.g.*, Rosenblatt v. Am. Cyanamid Co., 86 S.Ct. 1 (1965) (in chambers opinion of Justice Goldberg) (holding that the purposeful availment standard generally requires "requirement that the defendant must have taken voluntary action calculated to have an effect in the forum state." (quoting David P. Currie, *The Growth of the Long Arm*, U. Ill. L. F. 533, 544 (1963))); Walker v. Newgent, 583 F.2d 163, 168 (5th Cir. 1978) (purposeful availment satisfied if defendant's out of state actions have "foreseeable effects" in the forum). Leasco Data Processing Equip. Corp. v. Maxwell, 468 F.2d 1326, 1340 (2d Cir. 1972) (caused consequences in the forum).

permitted under the due process clause. As the Ninth Circuit explained in *Yahoo! Inc. v. La Ligue Contre Le Racisme et L'Antisemitisme*,[109] the phrase "purposeful availment" is inappropriate in situations where a nonresident has committed an intentional tort outside the state with foreseeable effects in the state. In that context, even though the defendant cannot be said to have availed himself of the forum's benefits, the exercise of jurisdiction would nevertheless be consistent with due process. It is enough, said the Ninth Circuit, that the defendant's relationship with the state was a product of "purposeful direction."[110] Thus, by asking the right question – what factors connect the defendant's activity to the forum state? – the Ninth Circuit wisely moved the doctrine back toward the fundamentals of due process by its willingness to jettison a requirement of "purposeful availment" in favor of a realistic appraisal of connecting factors.[111]

THE EFFECTS TEST

As noted above, the measure of jurisdiction for activities taking place outside a state that cause an effect within the state should require no more than a straightforward application of the due process standards described by the Court in *International Shoe*. If that activity causes a foreseeable effect in the state, the party who engaged in that activity will likely have a reasonable expectation of being sued in the forum on a claim arising out of that effect. The Restatement version of the effects test was written to capture the wide range of possibilities that might arise in this context. The doctrinal version of the effects test that has emerged from the decision in *Calder v. Jones*,[112] however, appears to be more circumscribed and less likely to embrace the full range of due process possibilities. As a consequence, under the *Calder* formula, plaintiffs are often denied access to a forum to which they are otherwise entitled.

Lower federal courts opinions applying the effects test can be correctly described as including a "mixture of broad and narrow interpretations."[113] As one court phrased it, in an obvious understatement, federal courts "have struggled somewhat with *Calder*'s import."[114] The range of interpretations does, however, appear to share a common premise: the elements that the

[109] 433 F.3d 1199 (9th Cir. 2006).
[110] *Id.* at 1205.
[111] *Id.* at 1205–06.
[112] 465 U.S. 783 (1984).
[113] IMO Indus., Inc. v. Kiekert AG, 155 F.3d 254, 261 (3d Cir. 1998).
[114] Bancroft & Masters, Inc. v. Augusta Nat. Inc., 223 F.3d 1082, 1087 (9th Cir. 2000). *See generally* Allan Ides, *A Critical Appraisal of the Supreme Court's Decision in J. McIntyre*, note 6, *supra*, at 137–138.

Calder Court identified as being sufficient to satisfy due process – that is, an intentional tort, aimed at the forum, with the brunt of the harm felt there – have been transformed from the sufficient into the necessary. Hence, a set of circumstances under which due process was deemed to have been satisfied is now treated as defining the limits of due process. Thus, the doctrine has come to trump the constitutional due process standard and has rendered it almost impossible to engage in the type of legal analysis that Pound was advocating, that is, an analysis that would fit the rule to the cause, rather that the cause to the rule.

Consistent with the foregoing, the Third Circuit has limited the effects test to the following circumstances:

> (1) The defendant committed an intentional tort; (2) The plaintiff felt the brunt of the harm in the forum such that the forum can be said to be the focal point of the harm suffered by the plaintiff as a result of that tort; (3) The defendant expressly aimed his tortious conduct at the forum such that the forum can be said to be the focal point of the tortious activity. . . .[115]

As to the first element, the First Circuit has taken even a narrower view and suggested that the effects test should be limited to defamation cases only.[116] And as to the third element, "aim," the Fifth Circuit requires that (1) the subject matter of and (2) the sources relied upon for the article to have been from the forum state.[117] On the other hand, the Ninth Circuit has somewhat softened the edges of the second element, the "brunt" requirement, by demanding only a "foreseeable harm" in the forum.[118] At the same time, however, it has refused to apply the effects test to a contracts claim,[119] which is somewhat peculiar since the effects test was specifically designed to reflect personal jurisdiction decisions involving contracts.[120] And the one circuit court decision that appeared to adopt a more open-ended approach to the effects test has been limited by a subsequent decision of that same circuit.[121]

Ironically, in some cases where the elements of the three-part effects test would be in fact satisfied, a federal court will nonetheless conclude that the assertion of jurisdiction would violate due process, without reference to the

[115] *See* IMO Indus., Inc., 155 F.3d at 265–66.

[116] *See* United States v. Swiss Am. Bank, Ltd., 274 F.3d 610, 624 (1st Cir. 2001).

[117] Fielding v. Hubert Bunda Media, Inc., 415 F.3d 419, 426 (5th Cir. 2005).

[118] Fiore v. Walden, 657 F.3d 838, 848–53 (9th Cir. 2011).

[119] McGlinchy v. Shell Chemical Co., 845 F.2d 802, 817 (9th Cir. 1988).

[120] Restatement (Second) of Conflict of Laws, § 37 cmt. a.

[121] *See* Janmark, Inc. v. Reidy, 132 F.3d 1200 (7th Cir. 1997) ("effects" jurisdiction sustained in the absence of aim); *but see* Tamburo v. Dworkin, 601 F.3d 693, 705–06 (7th Cir.), *cert. denied*, 131 S. Ct. 567 (2010) (interpreting *Janmark* as requiring "something more" directed at the forum).

effects test. For example, in *Fox v. Boucher*,[122] a landlord in New York brought diversity action for a *prima facie* tort against the father of a tenant. The defendant was a resident of Massachusetts. The plaintiff landlord alleged that the defendant made a single telephone call from Massachusetts to the plaintiff in New York, and that the comments of the defendant during that phone call caused the plaintiff extreme mental and physical suffering. Finding that the defendant's contacts with New York were not sufficient to satisfy due process, a New York court held that:

> One single telephone call made to New York State is insufficient contact to support a suit initiated in that forum against an out-of-state resident under either the contract or tort provisions [of New York's long-arm statute] of CPLR 302. The mere possibility of foreseeable consequences in New York does not give New York *in personam* jurisdiction. As the Supreme Court states, there must be "some act by which the defendant purposefully avails itself of the privilege of conducting activities within the forum State, thus invoking the benefits and protections of its laws." It would offend "minimum contacts" due process principles to force [the defendant], a Massachusetts resident, to litigate in a New York forum on the basis of one telephone call.[123]

Here, although the tort consisted in a single contact, that is, a single phone call to the state, the three-part effects test seems to have been satisfied: (1) the defendant committed an intentional tort (i.e., an act constituting intentional infliction of emotional distress); (2) the phone call was aimed at the plaintiff in the forum state (in fact, the defendant dialed the New York area code when making the phone call); and (3) the defendant knew that the plaintiff lived in New York and, thus, that he would have felt the brunt of the harm there. The doctrinal "tripping" point for the *Fox* court seems to have been the abstraction of purposeful availment, an appendage to the principles of due process imposed by the Court in *Hanson*. But the Court in *International Shoe* made it clear that even a single contact could be a sufficient basis on which to assert jurisdiction,[124] and reaffirmed that principle in *McGee*. Perhaps the exercise of jurisdiction in *Fox* would have been unreasonable under the circumstances, but that question differs markedly from issues pertaining to the sufficiency of the connecting factors.[125]

[122] 794 F.2d 34 (2d Cir.1986).

[123] *Id.* at 37 (citations omitted).

[124] *Int'l Shoe*, 326 U.S. at 318 (citing Kane v. New Jersey, 242 U.S. 160 (1916); Hess v. Pawloski, 274 U.S. 352 (1927)).

[125] To be precise, it is not proper to talk about "purposeful availment" in a tort situation. As the Ninth Circuit has correctly indicated, in torts contexts it is more appropriate to say that, by

State courts, often relying on federal precedents, have adopted similarly narrow versions of the effects test. *Pavlovich v. Superior Court*,[126] a decision by the California Supreme Court, provides a good example. In that case, the licensor of an encryption technology used to prevent the copying of DVDs containing motion pictures sued a resident of Texas for misappropriation of trade secrets for having posted on the Internet the source code that would allow the decryption and copying of those DVDs. The suit was filed in a California state court. The assertion of jurisdiction was premised on the theory that the defendant should have known that his actions would have an adverse impact on the motion picture industry located in that state. In ruling that jurisdiction could not be asserted consistently with due process, the California Supreme Court relied largely on federal precedents interpreting the scope of the effects test, and in so doing, endorsed the Third Circuit's three-part formula.[127] The specific issue before the California Supreme Court was whether the "aim" prong of the test could be satisfied by the mere knowledge that the posting would have an adverse effect in California. The court concluded that mere knowledge was insufficient to satisfy that prong. Thus, the California Supreme Court participated in the refinement of a doctrine – knowledge does not satisfy aim – that is ever more precise and yet ever more removed from the fundamental due process inquiry.[128]

As one might infer from *Pavlovich*, the mechanical, case-by-case method can be expected to give rise to yet further doctrinal complications in cases involving the Internet. While beyond the scope of this discussion, it is fair to note that jurisdictional law relating to the Internet, like the effects test itself, tends to deflect the jurisdictional consideration away from the fundamentals of due process and into the technicalities of the "*Zippo*" doctrine[129] and other like "refinements" on the law of jurisdiction.

committing the tort, the nonresident defendant "purposefully directs" his activity towards the forum State, rather than saying that he "purposefully avails" himself of the benefit and protection of the laws of the state. Yahoo! Inc. v. La Ligue Contre Le Racisme et L'Antisemitisme, 433 F.3d 1199, 1205–1206 (9th Cir. 2006).

[126] 58 P.3d 2 (Cal. 2002).

[127] *Id.* at 8.

[128] State courts have taken an array of approaches to the effects test. *See, e.g.*, Aeroflex Wichita, Inc. v. Filardo, 275 P.3d 869 (Kan. 2012) (effects test requires a separate showing of purposeful availment); Davis v. Simon, 963 N.E.2d 46, 54 (Ind. Ct. App. 2012) (noting that some federal courts treat the three-part test as mandatory, but declining to take a position on that question); Baldwin v. Fischer-Smith, 315 S.W.3d 389, 393 (Mo. Ct. App. 2010) (three-part test, but "knowledge that the effects would be felt" in the forum substituted for "brunt"); Pitts v. Fink, 698 S.E.2d 626, 632 (S.C. Ct. App. 2010) (strict three-part test).

[129] Zippo Mfg. Co. v. Zippo Dot Com, Inc., 952 F. Supp. 1119 (W.D. Pa. 1997).

THE STREAM-OF-COMMERCE TEST

The stream-of-commerce test has provided a considerable source of confusion and inconsistencies in lower federal courts. As one commentator has observed:

> Personal jurisdiction analysis now varies depending on which circuit a litigant files in. If a plaintiff is savvy enough to pick a circuit embracing Brennan's foreseeability view, minimum contacts will likely be found. This is particularly true where that same jurisdiction, after finding "purposeful conduct" then transfers the burden to the defendant to demonstrate "unfairness." Conversely, if a plaintiff files in the First, Fourth, Sixth, or Eleventh Circuits, a finding of personal jurisdiction may be less likely, given the same facts, because those circuits employ the O'Connor test requiring a much more specialized showing to reach "purposeful conduct."[130]

Prior to the 2011 decision in *McIntyre*, the First,[131] Fourth,[132] and Sixth[133] Circuits had adopted the O'Connor stream-of-commerce plus test, while the Fifth,[134] Seventh,[135] and Eighth[136] Circuits opted for Brennan's pure stream-of-commerce formula.[137] Other federal circuit courts declined to decide the issue and instead used both tests as well as Justice Stevens's alternate approach.[138] Panels in the Eleventh Circuit have both adopted the plus test

[130] Angela M. Laughlin, *This Ain't the Texas Two-Step Folks: Disharmony, Confusion, and the Unfair Nature of Personal Jurisdiction Analysis in the Fifth Circuit*, 37 CAP. U.L. REV. 681, 682–83 (2009). Note that the Eleventh Circuit has taken contrary positions on this issue. *Compare* Madara v. Hall, 916 F.2d 1510, 1519 (11th Cir. 1990) (O'Connor plus) *with* Vermeulen v. Renault, U.S.A., Inc., 985 F.2d 1534.,1548 (11th Cir.), *cert. denied*, 508 U.S. 907 (1993) (opting not to make a choice).

[131] Boit v. Gar-Tec Prods., Inc., 967 F.2d 671, 683 (1st Cir. 1992) (same).

[132] Lesnick v. Hollingsworth & Vose Co., 35 F.3d 939, 945–46 (4th Cir. 1994), *cert. denied*, 513 U.S. 1151 (1995) (same).

[133] Fortis Corporate Ins. v. Viken Ship Mgmt., 450 F.3d 214, 220 (6th Cir. 2006).

[134] Luv N' Care v. Insta-Mix, Inc., 438 F.3d 465, 470 (5th Cir.), *cert. denied*, 548 U.S. 904 (2006).

[135] Dehmlow v. Austin Fireworks, 963 F.2d 941, 947 (7th Cir. 1992).

[136] Clune v. Alimak AB, 233 F.3d 538, 542 (8th Cir. 2000), *cert. denied*, 533 U.S. 929 (2001).

[137] *See, e.g.*, Barone v. Rich Bros. Interstate Display Fireworks Co., 25 F.3d 610, 613–15 (8th Cir.), *cert. denied*, 513 U.S. 948 (1994) (following Justice Brennan's stream-of-commerce test); Ruston Gas Turbines, Inc. v. Donaldson Co., 9 F.3d 415, 420 (5th Cir. 1993) (same); Dehmlow v. Austin Fireworks, 963 F.2d 941, 947 (7th Cir. 1992) (same).

[138] *See, e.g.*, Kernan v. Kurz-Hastings, Inc., 175 F.3d 236, 244 (2d Cir. 1999); Pennzoil Products Co. v. Colelli & Assoc's, Inc., 149 F.3d 197 (3d Cir. 1998); Akro Corp. v. Luker, 45 F.3d 1541, 1545 (Fed. Cir.), *cert. denied*, 515 U.S. 1122 (1995) (following *Int'l Shoe* purposeful availment test for patent infringement cases); Vermeulen v. Renault, U.S.A., Inc., 985 F.2d 1534, 1548 (11th Cir.), *cert. denied*, 508 U.S. 907 (1993).

and declined to adopt it.[139] And at least one circuit has noted the substantial confusion over the content of the doctrine.[140] Federal district courts are in an equal state of disarray.[141] And as noted above, the decision in *McIntyre* did nothing to allay that confusion.

Not surprisingly, state courts have also struggled with the stream- of-commerce concept. Some have adopted the stream-of-commerce-plus test,[142] sometimes leading to results that fly in the face of fundamental due process principles.[143] Others have adopted the Brennan model.[144] And still others have declined to resolve the question.[145] In addition, various state courts have come up with their own unique formulations of the doctrine. Here are a few examples of those variations with rising and falling levels of specificity and generality:

> It is sufficient that, as here, the defendant purposefully sets his product or his designs into the stream of commerce, knowing or having reason to know that they will reach the forum state and *that they create a potential risk of injury*.[146]
> (Alaska Supreme Court)

> This court has decided that purposeful minimum contacts are established when an out-of-state manufacturer places its products in the stream of interstate commerce, *because under those circumstances it is fair to charge*

[139] *Compare* Madara v. Hall, 916 F.2d 1510, 1519 (11th Cir. 1993), (O'Connor plus) *with* Vermeulen v. Renault, U.S.A., Inc., 985 F.2d 1534, 1548 (11th Cir.), *cert. denied*, 508 U.S. 907 (1993) (opting not to make a choice).

[140] *See* Commissariat A L'Energie Atomique v. Chi Mei Optoelectronics Corp., 395 F.3d 1315, 1322 (Fed. Cir. 2005).

[141] *See, e.g.*, Askue v. Aurora Corp. of Am., No. 1:10-cv-0984-JEC, 2012 WL 843939, at *5 (N.D. Ga. 2012); Newman v. European Aero. Def. & Space Co., No. 09-10138-DJC, 2011 WL 2413792, at *5 (D. Mass. 2011); Belden Tech., Inc. v. LS Corp., 829 F. Supp. 2d 260, 269 (D. Del. 2010); Step2 Co., LLC. v. Parallax Group Intern., LLC., No. 5:08CV2580, 2010 WL 3783151, at *6 (N.D. Ohio 2010).

[142] *See, e.g.*, Spir Star AG v. Kimich, 310 S.W.3d 868, 873 (Tex. 2010); State v. N. Atl. Ref. Ltd., 999 A.2d 396, 406 (N.H. 2010); CSR, Ltd. v. Taylor, 983 A.2d 492, 483 (Md. 2009).

[143] *See, e.g.*, 983 A.2d 492, at 508 (For example, a Maryland court of appeals applied the O'Connor stream-of-commerce test and held that cargo "introduced into the stream of commerce with the expectation that it w[ill] arrive in th[e] forum," was sufficient to constitute purposeful availment to Maryland. Hence, after granting foreign distributor's petition for writ of certiorari, the court held that the foreign distributor's act of shipping raw asbestos through port at which stevedores worked did not constitute the requisite purposeful availment for the Maryland court to be able to exercise jurisdiction over the distributor).

[144] *See, e.g.*, Ex parte DBI, Inc., 23 So.3d 635, 647 (Ala. 2009); Kopke v. A. Hartrodt S.R.L., 629 N.W.2d 662, 674-65 (Wis. 2001), *cert. denied*, 534 U.S. 1079 (2002).

[145] *See, e.g.*, State ex rel. Edmondson v. Native Wholesale Supply, 237 P.3d 199, 207 (Okla. 2010), *cert. denied*, 131 S.Ct. 2150 (2011); Etchieson v. Cent. Purchasing, LLC, 232 P.3d 301, 307 (CA Colo. 2010); State v. Grand River Enter., Inc., 757 N.W.2d 305, 313-15 (S.D. 2008); Ruckstuhl v. Owens Corning Fiberglas Corp., 731 So.2d 881, 889 (La.), *cert. denied*, 528 U.S. 1019 (1999).

[146] Modern Trailer Sales, Inc. v. Traweek, 561 P.2d 1192, 1196 (Alaska 1977) (emphasis added).

> *the manufacturer with knowledge that its conduct might have consequences in another state.*[147]
>
> (Washington Supreme Court)

> [I]njuries were caused by products introduced into the stream of commerce by defendants *whose primary interest was to benefit economically from their use in other states.* Correspondingly, the forum states had an overriding interest in the protection of their citizens from injuries resulting from the use of these products.[148]
>
> (Hawai'i Supreme Court)

> In placing their goods in the flow of interstate commerce, the respondents must have had the reasonable expectation that such items *would be shipped indiscriminately throughout the United States.* If dangerously defective goods are placed in the interstate flow of commerce, those whose negligence created the defect should be prepared to defend themselves *wherever injury should occur.*[149]
>
> (Idaho Supreme Court)

The critical point here is that the stream-of-commerce test has no set meaning in federal or state courts and it has no apparent utility that could not be achieved more effectively by reference to the *International Shoe* jurisprudence of conception (or even by application of the effects test). Moreover, given the stream-of-commerce test elasticity, it necessarily invites an arbitrary pattern of results that violate fundamental principles of due process.

At this point, one might legitimately ask whether a statute governing personal jurisdiction might be the solution, and whether the legislature might be better than judges in dealing with the law of personal jurisdiction. It might, if framed in a way that allowed courts the necessary discretion to run meaningful legal analysis on the basis of the relevant general premises and deal with individual cases so as to meet the demands of justice between the parties.

Before trying to draft an effective personal jurisdiction statute, however, an important lesson may be learnt from the states' long-arm statutes.

A LESSON FROM TAILORED LONG-ARM STATUTES

Tailored long-arm statutes provide relatively detailed specifications of the circumstances under which a court may exercise personal jurisdiction. As a consequence, one might think that the relatively precise guidance provided by

147 Grange Ins. Ass'n v. State, 757 P.2d 933, 938 (Wash. 1988) (emphasis added).
148 Kailieha v. Hayes, 536 P.2d 568, 572 (Haw. 1975) (emphasis added).
149 Doggett v. Elecs. Corp. of Am., 454 P.2d 63, 68–69 (Id. 1969) (emphasis added).

such statutes would eliminate the never-ending layering of doctrine upon doctrine caused by the case-by-case minimum contacts approach. Yet this has not been so for three reasons. First, if jurisdiction is to be exercised, the application of a tailored long-arm statute is merely a prelude to the application of due process, not a substitute. Thus, any application of a long-arm statute's must still be tested against the Due Process Clause. Second, as noted above, in an effort to capture the fact-specific rulings of due process doctrine, states find themselves in a never-ending process of amending and interpreting their long-arm statutes. Thus, case-by-case due process doctrine constantly invades the territory of the tailored long-arm statute and often end up distorting their wording and original rationales. This is especially true in those states that do not interpret their tailored long-arm statutes as embracing the full extent of due process.[150] Finally, the highly specified nature of a tailored long-arm statute operates much like fact-specific doctrine in that it deflects courts from a direct consideration of the fundamental due process principles at stake in the personal jurisdiction analysis and instead focuses a court's attention on the technicalities of the statutory specifications.

The struggle to conform Georgia tailored long-arm statute to modern reality is instructive.[151] Section 9-10-91(2) of the Georgia long-arm statute provides Georgia courts the authority to exercise jurisdiction over a nonresident

150 These states are Georgia, Mississippi, New York, Ohio, Puerto Rico, Vermont, West Virginia, Wisconsin.

151 The current Georgia long-arm statute provides:

> A court of this state may exercise personal jurisdiction over any nonresident or his or her executor or administrator, as to a cause of action arising from any of the acts, omissions, ownership, use, or possession enumerated in this Code section, in the same manner as if he or she were a resident of this state, if in person or through an agent, he or she:
>
> (1) Transacts any business within this state;
> (2) Commits a tortious act or omission within this state, except as to a cause of action for defamation of character arising from the act;
> (3) Commits a tortious injury in this state caused by an act or omission outside this state if the tortfeasor regularly does or solicits business, or engages in any other persistent course of conduct, or derives substantial revenue from goods used or consumed or services rendered in this state;
> (4) Owns, uses, or possesses any real property situated within this state; or
> (5) With respect to proceedings for divorce, separate maintenance, annulment, or other domestic relations action or with respect to an independent action for support of dependents, maintains a matrimonial domicile in this state at the time of the commencement of this action or, if the defendant resided in this state preceding the commencement of the action, whether cohabiting during that time or not, notwithstanding the subsequent departure of one of the original parties from this state and as to all obligations arising from alimony, child support, apportionment of debt, or real or personal property orders or agreements, if one party to the marital

defendant who "[c]ommits a tortious act or omission within this State…." Georgia courts initially interpreted this statutory language as not covering tortious acts committed outside the state.[152] In response, the legislature added subsection (3) to §9-10-91, expressly vesting Georgia courts with the power to exercise jurisdiction over a nonresident defendant who caused an effect in the state by a tortious act or omission committed outside the state "if the tortfeasor regularly does or solicits business, or engages in any other persistent course of conduct, or derives substantial revenue from goods used or consumed or services rendered in this state."[153] In a case interpreting both sections, and despite the text of subsection (2), the Georgia Supreme Court, somewhat oddly, held that both subsections (2) and (3) permitted the exercise of jurisdiction over defendants who had committed tortious acts or omissions outside the state.[154] The state high court later revisited that decision and returned to a "literal construction" of §9-10-91, ruling that only subsection (3) permitted the exercise of jurisdiction when the tortious act occurred outside the state.[155]

While interpreting subsections (2) and (3) of §9-10-91, Georgia courts were also busy interpreting subdivision (1) of the same statute and held that that provision, which was triggered when a nonresident defendant transacted "any business within the state," applied only in contract cases or where the nonresident defendant was physically present within the state. The Georgia courts reached this conclusion even though the text of the statute did not literally impose either requirement.[156]

This was the state of the law when the Georgia Supreme Court granted certiorari in *Innovative Clinical & Consulting Services, LLC v. First Nat. Bank of Ames*,[157] a case involving a combination of tort and contract claims premised

relationship continues to reside in this state. This paragraph shall not change the residency requirement for filing an action for divorce.

(6) Has been subject to the exercise of jurisdiction of a court of this state which has resulted in an order of alimony, child custody, child support, equitable apportionment of debt, or equitable division of property, notwithstanding the subsequent departure of one of the original parties from this state, if the action involves modification of such order and the moving party resides in this state, or if the action involves enforcement of such order notwithstanding the domicile of the moving party.

GA CODE ANN. § 9-10-91 (West 2012).

152 Castleberry v. Gold Agency, 185 S.E.2d 557 (1971); O'Neal Steel v. Smith, 169 S.E.2d 827 (1969).

153 *See* note 151, *supra*.

154 Coe & Payne Co. v. Wood-Mosaic Corp., 195 S.E.2d 399, 400-01 (1973).

155 Gust v. Flint, 356 S.E.2d 513 (1987).

156 *See* Innovative Clinical & Consulting Serv., LLC. v. First Nat. Bank of Ames, 620 S.E.2d 353, 355 (Ga. S.Ct. 2005) (discussing this state of affairs).

157 620 S.E.2d 353 (Ga. S.Ct. 2005).

largely on activities arising outside of the state, but having an adverse effect in the state. The state court of appeals had held that jurisdiction could not be asserted over the tort claims under subsections (1), (2), or (3) of the state's long-arm statute.[158] The Georgia Supreme Court agreed that neither subsection (2) nor (3) was satisfied under the facts presented, but concluded that subsection (1) – the transacting business section – could be used in tort cases since it vested Georgia courts with jurisdiction to the full extent permitted by due process of law.[159]

The serpentine interpretation of the Georgia long-arm statute is instructive.[160] A tailored long-arm statute operates in much the same fashion as mechanical jurisprudence. The focus of the jurisdictional inquiry is deflected from the fundamentals of due process – connecting factors and reasonable expectations – and centers instead on the details of the text and on judicial interpretations and reinterpretations of that text. Instead of attending to fundamental principles, courts and litigants fight over the words, the gaps between words, and the inconsistencies that form within any body of interpretation. Hence, while a tailored long-arm statute may seem like a path to clarity, the opposite has often been true. This would be, to borrow from Pound's terminology, an example of mechanical legislation that, as much as mechanical jurisprudence, is not capable of effectively guiding legal analysis.

We can observe these same patterns and interpretive stretches in other states that have not construed their long-arm statutes as going to the full extent of due process. For example, in West Virginia, a commentary on the West Virginia's long-arm statute expands the scope of the term "business" to include noncommercial activities:

> To assume that the legislature intended W.Va.Code §56-3-33 to apply only to commercial activities of unincorporated businesses would be to apply an unduly limited meaning to that phrase. The term "business" need not necessarily imply an activity tinged with commercial aspects; it is enough if the activity undertaken by the nonresident defendant is such that the nonresident can or should expect to derive a benefit therefrom. The nonresident defendant's activity must be purposeful, but it need not be intimately intertwined with the defendant's livelihood.[161]

[158] *Id.* at 355.

[159] *Id.*

[160] In fact, we've described only the tip of iceberg of the interpretive complexities generated by Georgia's long-arm statute. *See* Jeffrey A. Van Detta & Shiv K. Kapoor, *Extraterritorial Personal Jurisdiction for the Twenty-First Century: A Case Study Reconceptualizing the Typical Long-Arm Statute to Codify and Refine International Shoe After Its First Sixty Years*, 3 SETON HALL CIRCUIT. REV. 339 (2007).

[161] Harman v. Pauley, 522 F. Supp. 1130, 1135 (D.W.V. 1981); *see also* 11B M.J. *Jurisdiction* § 15 (2011).

It is, however, hard to describe as "business" an activity from which the nonresident defendant might gain only a moral or personal benefit.[162] Still, such noncommercial activity would seem to be covered by the West Virginia long-arm statute, as explained by the relevant commentary.[163] But in a way, all of this is beside the point, for whether a particular form of activity can be properly characterized as "business" has no bearing on whether that activity represents a due-process-sufficient connecting factor with the forum.

Similar interpretative questions arose in *Kopke v. A. Hartrodt S.R.L.*,[164] where the Wisconsin Supreme Court confronted the text of its long-arm statute in the context of a products liability suit. Kopke, a truck driver, was injured when he opened a cargo container in Neenah, Wisconsin. The injury occurred when a pallet loaded with paper fell out of the container and landed on him. The pallet had been loaded into the cargo container in Italy by L'Arciere, an employee-owned Italian cooperative. Kopke brought a personal injury claim against L'Arciere and others in a Wisconsin state court. L'Arciere moved to dismiss for lack of personal jurisdiction. The County Circuit Court denied this motion and ruled that L'Arciere's acts of stabilizing the products being shipped by surrounding the product with air bags, and installing bracing beams and boards into the cargo container, brought the defendant within the scope of section 4(b) of the state's long-arm statute and that the exercise of jurisdiction was consistent with due process. L'Arciere's appeal was eventually certified to the state Supreme Court.

The Wisconsin long-arm statute, §801.05(4), authorized the exercise of personal jurisdiction over nonresidents whose act or omission committed outside of Wisconsin gives rise to an injury within the state under specified circumstances:

> A court of this state having jurisdiction of the subject matter has jurisdiction over a person served in an action pursuant to §801.11 under any of the following circumstances:
>
> . . .
>
> (4) Local injury; foreign act. In any action claiming injury to person or property within this state arising out of an act or omission outside this state by the defendant, provided in addition that at the time of the injury, either:

[162] *But see* CHARLES DICKENS, A CHRISTMAS CAROL ("Business!" cried the Ghost, wringing its hands again. "Mankind was my business. The common welfare was my business; charity, mercy, forbearance, and benevolence, were all my business. The dealings of my trade were but a drop of water in the comprehensive ocean of my business!")

[163] The courts of New York have also construed the "transacting business" component of the state's long-arm statute as not being restricted to commercial activities. Best Van Lines, Inc. v. Walker, 490 F.3d 239, 247 n.10 (2d Cir. 2007).

[164] 629 N.W.2d 662 (2001), *cert. denied*, 534 U.S. 1079 (2002).

> ...
>
> (b) Products, materials or things *processed*, serviced or manufactured by the defendant were used or consumed within this state in the ordinary course of trade.[165]

The critical issue was whether L'Arciere had "processed" products, materials, or things that were used or consumed within Wisconsin. As the State Supreme Court phrased it, "The question presented is, therefore, whether the word 'process' means to bring about a physical transformation upon the products, materials, or things themselves, as urged by L'Arciere ... or whether process is a broader term," i.e., one that would include the preparation of goods for transit.[166] In concluding that the latter, more inclusive definition was more consistent with the goals of the long-arm statute, the state high court relied on an earlier decision by the Seventh Circuit, *Nelson by Carson v. Park Industries, Inc.*,[167] construing §801.05(4)(b):

> The verb "to process" certainly may refer to the narrower concept of preparing something in the sense of manufacturing it. However, it also has the broader definitions of subjecting something to a particular system of handling to effect a particular result and preparing something for market or other commercial use by subjecting it to a process. *See* Webster's Third New International Dictionary of the English Language (1963).[168]

With that broad interpretation as its guide, the Wisconsin Supreme Court concluded that the loading activities engaged in by L'Arciere fell within the scope of §801.05(4)(b) as a form of processing. In so ruling, the court rejected the reasoning of the Fifth Circuit, construing a virtually identical Florida statute as pertaining only to the process of manufacturing and thus excluding activities pertaining to the shipment of the goods.[169] The Wisconsin court explained the differing conclusions as being the product of different interpretive principles. The court also found that the exercise of jurisdiction over L'Arciere was consistent with due process, applying Justice Brennan's pure stream-of-commerce model.[170]

Given the broad interpretation employed by the Wisconsin Supreme Court, the Wisconsin long-arm statute did not prevent the court from examining the

165 WIS. STAT. ANN. § 801.05(4) (West 2012) (emphasis added). It is worth noting that also the Wisconsin long-arm statute treats the stream-of-commerce as an expression of the effect test.
166 *Kopke*, 629 N.W.2d at 669.
167 *See generally* Nelson by Carson v. Park Indus. Inc., 717 F.2d 1120 (7th Cir. 1983).
168 *Id.* at 1124 n.5.
169 *See generally* Mallard v. Aluminum Co. of Canada, 634 F.2d 236 (5th Cir. 1981).
170 *Kopke*, 629 N.W.2d at 674-75.

fundamentals of due process (albeit through the misdirected lens of the stream-of-commerce test). The result in the Florida case was, however, quite different. The Fifth Circuit's interpretation of the statute blocked any consideration of fundamental due process principles. On the one hand, the interpretation adopted by the Wisconsin Supreme Court seems to be a bit of a stretch. On the other hand, it seems unlikely that the Florida legislature intended to draw the manufacturer–shipper distinction that the language of the statute suggests. The simple point is this: Whether the "product, material, or things" were "processed" has virtually nothing to do with connecting factors, expectations, or fundamental principles and conceptions of fairness and justice at the heart of the law of personal jurisdiction. These general principles should have instead engaged the court and guided the analysis.

PROPOSAL: A FUNDAMENTAL–PRINCIPLES DUE PROCESS STATUTE

From the above analysis of long-arm statutes and jurisprudence interpreting the same, we can learn an important lesson. Because these statutes were too narrow and mechanical, the courts could not run any meaningful legal analysis intended to fit the rule to the cases. Rather, they tried to fit the cases to the rule, thus giving conflicting interpretations of the rule itself – as in the case of personal or moral gain that was interpreted as falling within the scope of a rule that applies to "business" contacts with the state.

To be successful, a rule governing personal jurisdiction should be broad enough to allow courts a margin of discretion. It should resemble a jurisprudence of fundamental principles rather than a mechanical one. In fact, the legislature and the judiciary are organically bound together. They make the law jointly, one operating at a macro level and the other at a micro level. Thus, mechanistic legislation is likely to lead to mechanistic jurisprudence and, vice versa, mechanistic jurisprudence might implicitly "suggest" to the legislator that the adoption of mechanistic legislation is appropriate and required. Because the law does not exist in nature but is rather the product of a fiction, of human needs, human ends, and human minds, we can say that law is not found, but made. Thus, both the judicial process and the legislature's process are legislative in nature, and they both demand a legislator's wisdom.[171]

True, there are important differences between the judicial and the legislative processes. The judicial decision-making process is triggered by a specific case.

[171] *See* BENJAMIN N. CARDOZO, THE NATURE OF THE JUDICIAL PROCESS, 115 (1975).

Thus, differently from the legislator who regulates issues somehow in the abstract, the judge finds the law within specific contexts; because of that, his judgment might be improperly influenced by personal and subjective considerations that are triggered by the specific case in front of him.[172]

A proper legislative intervention – at both the state and federal levels – should effectively address the topic and significantly reduce current inconsistencies and confusion resulting from the increasingly fragmented and mechanical case-by-case approach.

Indeed, immediately after *International Shoe*, state and federal legislative bodies might have stepped in and adopted statutes that articulated the basic ideas contained in that opinion, thus offering a stable, principled approach to answering many of the issues that the Court has had to later confront on a case-by-case basis – and not always successfully, as the Court itself recently admitted.[173]

As noted in the introduction, all statutes are subject to judicial interpretation and judicial review. Hence, the Supreme Court will have the final say as to the constitutionally permissible scope of any proposed statute. It is possible that the Court will insist on enforcing its mechanical approach to personal jurisdiction. But it is also possible that the guidance offered by a conception, general principles statute might allow the Court to redirect its analysis back to the fundamental principles of due process.

In any event, as Cardozo noted,

> [j]udges have, of course, the power, though not the right, to ignore the mandate of a statute and render judgment in despite of it. They have the power, though not the right, to travel beyond the walls of the interstices, the bounds set to judicial innovation by precedent and custom. None the less, by that abuse of power, they violate the law.[174]

The proposed statute takes a middle course between an open-ended due process statute and the typical tailored long-arm statute. It rejects the due process statute because it provides too little guidance and would generate the same problems that the Supreme Court has created in interpreting the due process clause. It also rejects the tailored long-arm statute for the reasons offered above. This is because tailored long-arm statutes mirror the misguided mechanical jurisprudence of due process and are therefore not premised on

[172] *Id.*, at 119–21.

[173] In **J. McJutyre v. Nrcastro**, 131 S. Ct. 2780, 2786 (2011), the Court observed, "This Court's *Asahi* decision may be responsible in part for that court's error regarding the stream of commerce, and this case presents an opportunity to provide greater clarity."

[174] *See* BENJAMIN N. CARDOZO, THE NATURE OF THE JUDICIAL PROCESS, 129 (1975).

a durable standard capable of application to a wide range of cases. The proposed statute is intended to articulate precisely such a durable standard without the baggage of the Court's mechanical formulas or the state courts' acrobatics to interpret their long-arm statutes.

PROPOSED STATUTE

The proposed statute, which is addressed to Congress and state legislatures,[175] reads as follows:

> Section 1. The district courts may exercise personal jurisdiction over an individual or entity not a resident of the state in which the court is located when the individual or entity has engaged in activities in that state or outside that state that have caused effects therein, when those in-state activities or in-state effects are such as to give that individual or entity a reasonable expectation of being sued in that state. A "reasonable expectation of being sued in the forum" shall take account of both the quality and quantity of the contacts, including the relationship or lack thereof between those contacts and the plaintiff's claims.
>
> Section 2. The district courts may not decline the exercise of jurisdiction provided under Section 1 of this Title unless authorized to do so by Congress.

A. Commentary to the Proposed Statute

SECTION 1

This Section is premised on the due process principles of connecting factors and reasonable expectations arising from those connections. This standard does not draw any distinction between the traditional and minimum contacts bases of jurisdiction, nor between general and specific jurisdiction, nor among the various subcategories of doctrine developed over the past several decades, e.g., purposeful availment, effect test, stream of commerce, etc. Rather, this Section asks a simple and direct question and, at the same time, encompasses a wide range of jurisdictional possibilities, all traceable to the fundamental principles of due process.

Within some limits, courts are left free to run meaningful legal analysis through which to adapt the standard to the various cases; they are free to deal

[175] The text of the statute is directed toward its application in the federal judicial system. The text, however, could be easily revised to make it applicable in state courts.

with individual cases to meet the demands of justice between the parties. This Section returns the law of personal jurisdiction from its modern mechanical nature to its original dimension of conceptions and general principles.

As articulated above, most of the Supreme Court's major decisions on personal jurisdiction could be resolved and explained by reference to this elegant standard. For example, the activities of the International Shoe Company in the State of Washington were of such a nature to give that company reasonable expectation of a suit in the forum based on those contacts. Similarly, the contractual relationships in *McGee* and *Burger King* were sufficiently connected to the forum state to give the parties to the contracts a reasonable expectation of suit in the forum on claims arising from those contacts. Even the decision in *Calder* can be explained as premised on the nonresident defendants' connections with the forum state; such connections gave rise to a reasonable expectation of suit in the forum. The Section 1 standard also explains the denial of jurisdiction in *World Wide Volkswagen* and *Shaffer*, where the absence of meaningful factors connecting the nonresident defendants with the forum indicated the absence of a reasonable expectation of suit against them in that forum.[176]

Section 1 would overrule *Burnham* since that case is inconsistent with the standard at the heart of this provision, namely, connecting factors and reasonable expectations arising therefrom.[177]

Undoubtedly, there is some tension between this standard and some of the Court's decisions, at least if those decisions are examined under the Fourteenth Amendment perspective. This might occur in a federal forum under the standards of Federal Rule of Civil Procedure 4(k)(1)(A), or in a state forum that has adopted the proposed statute. Certainly the results in *Hanson*, *Kulko*, and *McIntyre* can be seen as inconsistent with the standard described in Section 1. This is because in those cases, the Court insinuated an artificial test between the fundamental principle and the facts. Thus, in these cases, the personal jurisdiction analysis was driven by irrelevant questions. Of course, it is possible that the current Court would insist on a continuation of this practice, thus rendering Section 1 ineffective and potentially unconstitutional. But it is also possible that the Court would accept an invitation from Congress to reconsider its personal jurisdiction jurisprudence from the more principled perspective provided in Section 1.

With respect to the exercise of personal jurisdiction by federal courts, the Fourteenth Amendment constitutional issue should disappear, since the

[176] *See infra* text accompanying notes 55.

[177] *See infra* text accompanying notes 85–86.

exercise of jurisdiction by federal courts is constrained by the due process clause of the Fifth Amendment. In other words, the exercise of personal jurisdiction here would not present a question of jurisdiction under Federal Rule of Civil Procedure 4(k)(1)(A), which incorporates the Fourteenth Amendment, but under Federal Rule of Civil Procedure 4(k)(1)(C), which vests federal courts with personal jurisdiction pursuant to a congressionally enacted statute. Under these circumstances, the constitutionality of any application of Section 1 would look at the connecting factors between the non-resident defendant and the United States as a whole.

Given the foregoing, it is quite likely that under the proposed statute, a federal court would be able to exercise personal jurisdiction in cases presenting fact patterns similar to those in *Hanson*, *Kulko*, and *McIntyre*. In *McIntyre*, for example, the foreign manufacturer clearly had contacts with the United States as a whole, since it targeted the entire North American market, and those contacts were certainly sufficient to establish a reasonable expectation of suit in the United States premised on effects of that marketing felt there. Under Section 1, Justice Ginsburg's analysis in *McIntyre* would be unassailable, since the standard would be, in fact, national contacts as a matter of the Fifth Amendment due process clause.

Although Section 1 does not expressly reference the traditional grounds of jurisdiction, as explained above, most of them are encompassed by its standard.[178] For example, an individual who is domiciled in the state in which the court is located will be subject to the jurisdiction in that state since domicile in a state creates a reasonable expectation of suit there, given both the quality and quantity of the defendant's contacts with the forum. In other words, domicile is a meaningful contact that gives the defendant a reasonable expectation of suit in the forum.[179] Similarly, consent to jurisdiction in a forum inherently creates a connection with the forum that leads to reasonable expectation of suit there.

SECTION 2

The purpose of Section 2 is to replace the "unreasonableness" exit of the personal jurisdiction analysis with a legislatively defined and carefully circumscribed *forum non conveniens* doctrine.[180] I have proposed the adoption of

[178] *See infra* text accompanying notes 2–17. *See also* Restatement (Second) of Conflict of Laws §29 & cmt. a (2012) (domicile); *id.* §41 & cmts. a & b (place of incorporation); *id.* §32 (consent); *id.* §33 (waiver or appearance).

[179] See Chapter IV, *infra*.

[180] *See infra* text accompanying notes 2–17.

precisely such a *forum non conveniens* statute.[181] That statute is essentially a companion to the proposed personal jurisdiction statute. The combined goal of these proposed statutes is to redirect courts' personal jurisdiction analysis to a method that is more legitimate and efficient. The two statutes define the scope of personal jurisdiction, providing guidance as to the limited circumstances under which a court may decline the exercise of an otherwise legitimate exercise of jurisdiction.

*****

The above proposed personal jurisdiction statute fully incorporates the fundamental principles of due process recognized by the Court in *International Shoe*. It also embraces the traditional grounds of jurisdiction, but only to the extent that those traditional grounds are consistent with *International Shoe*'s individual rights conception of the due process of law. Moreover, its application requires no mechanical formulas, nor any doctrinal tests other than those

[181] See Chapter III, *infra*. The proposed forum non conveniens statute reads as follows:

1. In any civil action of which a district court has original jurisdiction, the district court may stay or dismiss the action under the doctrine of *forum non conveniens* only if:
   a. The defendant files a timely motion to dismiss on grounds of *forum non conveniens*, such timeliness to be measured under the standards applicable to a motion under Federal Rule of Civil Procedure 12(b)(2); and
   b. The moving party demonstrates and the district court finds that there is an available alternate forum with jurisdiction over the action and the defendants, that, as a practical matter, the plaintiff will have access to that forum, that such forum provides a suitable substantive remedy for the claim or claims asserted by the plaintiff, and that such forum adheres to the fundamental standards of due process; and
   c. The district court finds that the available alternate forum provides a substantially more suitable forum for the adjudication of the claim or action, and that the maintenance of the claim or action in the district court would impose substantial injustice on the moving party.
2. For good cause shown, the court may extend the period set forth in Section 1a for the filing a *forum non conveniens* motion.
3. If the district court finds that the standards in Section 1 have been satisfied, it may stay or dismiss the claim or action on any condition it deems just. Such conditions may include the defendant's waiver of any statute of limitation or lack of jurisdiction defense he might otherwise have in the alternate forum.
4. When granting a motion to dismiss an action on *forum non conveniens* grounds, the district court shall retain jurisdiction to enforce its dismissal order and any related stipulations or conditions attached thereto.
5. A court that grants or denies a motion to stay or dismiss an action pursuant to this statute shall set forth specific findings of fact and conclusions of law supporting the court's order.
6. An order granting or denying a motion to dismiss on *forum non conveniens* grounds is immediately appealable. The findings of fact shall be reviewed under a clearly erroneous standard. The conclusions of law shall be reviewed under *de novo* standard.

that focus on the forum-relating connecting factors and the reasonable expectations that make the exercise of jurisdiction reasonable.

While courts will be required to apply this statute in specific factual contexts, those applications should not operate as an invitation to create new doctrine or rewrite the statute, as has occurred with so many state long-arm statutes. Rather, those applications should provide no more than exemplars of what a particular court did under a particular set of facts, consistent with the specific language of the statute. To be sure, the perceived wisdom of those particular applications may well influence the direction of statutory interpretation, but the critical question must always be whether the application respects the fundamental principles of due process.

CONCLUSION

In 1966, von Mehren and Trautman identified problems with the then emerging personal jurisdiction formula; these problems became even more evident in the years that followed. At that time, they predicted that significant changes were going to occur and that, among those changes, a less mechanical and more effective methodology would emerge.[182] Instead, under the guidance of the Supreme Court, quite the opposite has occurred.

The importance of personal jurisdiction cannot be overstated. As noted earlier, personal jurisdiction is deeply intertwined with the litigants' due process rights. Also, the outcome of cases is significantly influenced, if not entirely determined, by decisions on jurisdiction and choice of law, with the latter often deeply influenced by the former.

Those skeptical of rules might raise the question as to whether a statute would really solve the issues that the Court's standards have thus far not been able to solve. Indeed, even after a statute is passed, judges will still be the ones to interpret and apply it. However, as illustrated above, the proposed statute and its underlying ideas and principles would not generate the same problems that the current personal jurisdiction judge-made formula were generating because the statute would clearly invite a jurisprudence of fundamental principles rather than a mechanical one, a jurisprudence that would carefully guide lower courts through a meaningful analysis intended to fit the rule to the cause and not vice versa.[183]

[182] *See* Arthur T. von Mehren and Donald T. Trautman, *Jurisdiction to Adjudicate: A Suggested Analysis*, 79 HARV. L. REV. 1121 (1966).

[183] *See* Pound, *Courts and Legislation*, 7 Am. Pol. Sci. Rev. 361, 365 (1913).

Indeed, by endorsing the clear and straightforward formula of connecting factors and the reasonable expectations to which those factors can give rise, the proposed statute reminds courts that the jurisdictional inquiry is a fact-specific analysis and that no more specific doctrinal test is needed to decide when meaningful connections with the forum state give rise to a reasonable expectation of being sued there. True, judges might view facts differently. However, the basic idea is that for the exercise of personal jurisdiction to be consistent with due process, that exercise should be reasonably expected by the defendant based on his or her meaningful contacts with the forum. At least that's the right question to ask.

The proposed personal jurisdiction statute would not be the first jurisdictional statute to provide clear and effective guidance to federal courts. Indeed, 28 U.S.C. §1367 governing supplemental jurisdiction can be considered illustrative in this respect. When §1367 was adopted, in 1990, courts were confused as to when they could properly exercise supplemental jurisdiction, for the Court's earlier opinions[184] had left some questions unanswered.[185] Congress decided to intervene by passing §1367. Subsections (a) and (c) of that statute adopt a fundamental principles approach to supplemental jurisdiction that, through a general formula – "claims that are so related . . .that they form part of the same case or controversy under Article III" – and general criteria that a court might consider to "decline to exercise supplemental jurisdiction" – gives courts sufficient guidance as to the scope of the standards, avoiding the need for further doctrinal developments and inviting a jurisprudence of general principles and conceptions that fit the rule to the cause. The guidance that the statute offered under subsections (a) and (c) was indeed effective, for the Court has not had to revisit the related issues again. On the other hand, the Court's intervention was necessary to clarify the scope of subsection (b) of the same statute,[186] which, unlike the other two provisions, takes a mechanical approach. Learning from that experience, the proposed personal jurisdiction statute mirrors the general principles and conceptions format of subsections (a) and (c) of the supplemental jurisdiction statute.

184 *See* United Mine Workers v. Gibbs, 383 U.S. 715 (1966); Owen Equipment & Erection Co. v. Kroger, 437 U.S. 365 (1978).

185 Aldinger v. Howard, 427 U.S. 1, 17–18 (1976).

186 *See* Exxon Mobil Corp. v. Allapattah Services, Inc., 545 U.S. 546 (2005).

3

Forum Non Conveniens[1]

INTRODUCTION

In *American Dredging Co. v. Miller*,[2] Justice Scalia, writing for the Court, observed (with characteristic confidence):

> At bottom, the doctrine of *forum non conveniens* is nothing more or less than a supervening venue provision, permitting displacement of the ordinary rules of venue when, in light of certain conditions, the trial court thinks that *jurisdiction* ought to be declined.[3]

Justice Scalia was wrong. While *forum non conveniens* incorporates certain venue-transfer techniques, the doctrine itself does more than displace the ordinary rules of venue. In fact, it displaces the ordinary rules of jurisdiction because the case is not transferred to another proper venue, but is instead dismissed and filed in a different judicial system. Moreover, as a consequence of the dismissal, the case will be subject to a different set of procedures and different standards of substantive law. None of these effects occur on a §1404(a) motion to transfer venue. There, if the motion is granted, the case is transferred from one proper venue to another within the same judicial system, and the applicable procedural and substantive rules remain the same. Thus, the effects of a dismissal on *forum non conveniens* grounds are different and much more dramatic than the effects of a §1404(a) motion to transfer venue.

Beginning with the earliest examples of *forum non conveniens*, and working through more recent applications of the doctrine within the federal judicial

[1] *See also* Simona Grossi, *Forum Non Conveniens as a Jurisdictional Doctrine*, 75 U. Pitt. L. Rev. __ (2014).

[2] 510 U.S. 443 (1993).

[3] *Id.* at 453 (emphasis added).

system,[4] I offer an alternative to the venue-premised and relatively untethered approach to *forum non conveniens* now in vogue. I argue that some of the problems in the contemporary approach to *forum non conveniens* are a consequence of the improper classification of the doctrine as primarily pertaining to venue. The result of this classification is the importation of an open-textured, venue-based test that calls for nothing more than a balancing of conveniences. That invitation to balance vests district courts with a wide range of discretion to decline the exercise of jurisdiction otherwise properly invoked. The consequence of this somewhat boundless approach to *forum non conveniens* is that often, as a practical matter, the district court's decision to dismiss represents the death knell of the litigation. By repositioning *forum non conveniens* as a jurisdictional doctrine, I attempt to cabin district court discretion within the legitimate confines of jurisdictionally relevant considerations to eventually make the *forum non conveniens* analysis more consistent with due process.

THE DUE PROCESS MODEL OF JURISDICTION AND VENUE

To more clearly understand the proper scope and operation of *forum non conveniens*, it will be useful to review briefly some of the fundamentals of due process, jurisdiction and venue. The purpose here is not to provide a detailed account of those topics, but to offer a context from which to view and critique the modern usages of *forum non conveniens* and on which to build a more carefully and jurisdictionally circumscribed doctrine.

DEFINING DUE PROCESS

Defining procedural due process is necessary to a proper understanding of the doctrines of jurisdiction and venue, since each of these doctrines represent particular articulations of due process, namely, the power of the court over the person of the defendant and the convenient geographical location of the lawsuit. Each of these concepts and its related formula is intended to identify the forum that will better meet litigants' expectations and the ends of justice, which are, in essence, the precise goals due process is intended to achieve.

Due process requires a rule-based system through which adverse parties may resolve their disputes efficiently and fairly. Its chief characteristics may be described as follows: fair and predictable access to a neutral forum created by law and operated under rules and standards that are uniformly interpreted and

[4] *See* Allan Stein et al., *Coming to American to File Suit: Foreign Plaintiffs and the Forum Non Conveniens Barrier in Transnational Litigation*, 65 OHIO ST. L.J. 659 (2004).

applied by a neutral magistrate. In *Logan v. Zimmerman Brush Co.*,[5] the Supreme Court explained,

> The Court traditionally has held that the Due Process Clauses protect civil litigants who seek recourse in the courts, either as defendants hoping to protect their property or as plaintiffs attempting to redress grievances.... [T]he Fourteenth Amendment's Due Process Clause has been interpreted as preventing the States from denying potential litigants use of established adjudicatory procedures, when such an action would be "the equivalent of denying them an opportunity to be heard upon their claimed right[s]." *Boddie v. Connecticut*, 401 U.S. 371 (1971)[6]

Due process thus entails a correlative right of each party to be heard, i.e., to assert a claim and/or to defend against one, under the established rules of the forum. A plaintiff's right to assert a claim is the converse of the defendant's right to resist that claim. In this sense, due process protects both sides in a lawsuit. Hence, due process entails the right of access to courts by plaintiffs and defendants,[7] and its overarching principle is one of predictable fairness. That predictable fairness is a product of the neutrality of the established rules under which the system operates, including those pertaining to access to the forum, the consistency with which those rules are applied, and the effectiveness of the system in efficiently approximating the truth and in delivering justice. Conversely a system that is not predictable, that is less rule-based than it is fact-based, i.e., one that operates on an *ad hoc* basis, and is characterized by open-ended balancing or the investiture of broad discretion in the magistrate, is not fair in the predictable sense and cannot be described as fully comporting with the due process of law.

In this sense, the principle of due process is a-contextual and hardly lends itself to mechanical jurisprudence. It transcends the particular facts or contexts in which the principle may come into play. Rather, due process begins with the specific articulated principles described above, which must then be applied to particular facts and contexts. The contexts reflect the various applications of the principles of due process, but they are not substitutes for the principles themselves. It is true that a particular context may reveal something about the principle's application that requires alteration, but that perception is merely a manner of shedding new light on the fundamental principle at stake, which should itself be unchanging.[8]

[5] 455 U.S. 422 (1982).
[6] *Id.* at 429.
[7] *Id.* at 430 n.5.
[8] *See* Chapter I, *supra*.

PERSONAL JURISDICTION

The standards of personal jurisdiction measure the scope of a court's power to issue a judgment binding on a party to a lawsuit. The law of personal jurisdiction has both a statutory and a constitutional dimension. As to the statutory component, Federal Rule of Civil Procedure 4(k)(1)(A) allows a federal district court to borrow the long-arm statute of the state in which it sits. This borrowing provision applies in the vast majority of cases filed in federal courts. From a constitutional perspective, the scope of a district court's authority to issue a binding judgment is limited (in most cases) by the due process guarantees of the Fourteenth Amendment. This combination of Rule 4(k)(1)(A) and the limits imposed by the Fourteenth Amendment places a district court on the same footing as the courts of the state in which that district court sits. In other words, district courts have been instructed to comply with the jurisdictional standards of state law and the Fourteenth Amendment.

A federal court's exercise of personal jurisdiction over a party is consistent with due process if it complies with either "traditional" jurisdictional standards or with the "minimum contacts" test as formulated in *International Shoe Co. v. Washington*.[9] As explained and more deeply explored in Chapter II, the traditional grounds for asserting jurisdiction include transient or tag jurisdiction, voluntary appearance or waiver, and consent and domicile. In addition, even if no traditional ground of jurisdiction is satisfied, a federal court may exercise personal jurisdiction over a party whose purposeful contacts with the state are either so related to the claim or so extensive, both quantitatively and qualitatively, as to make the exercise of jurisdiction over that party presumptively reasonable.[10] A party objecting to the exercise of jurisdiction under the minimum contacts test may rebut this presumption of reasonableness, but he must present a "compelling case" to do so.[11]

The traditional bases of personal jurisdiction and the minimum contacts test can be sensibly reduced to two essential concepts: "connecting factors" and "reasonable expectations" arising from those connecting factors. These concepts fully embody the complex bundle of due process rights. A forum in which these standards are satisfied can be considered the "natural forum" for the case. One of those expectations is the plaintiff's expectation that a court of competent jurisdiction will exercise power in accord with statutory and due process standards. There are no apparent exceptions to this rule, at least not

[9] 326 U.S. 310, 316 (1945).
[10] *See generally* Nowak v. Tak How Inv. Ltd., 899 F. Supp. 25 (D. Mass. 1995).
[11] Burger King Corp. v. Rudzewicz, 471 U.S. 462, 477 (1985).

within the discipline of personal jurisdiction. In other words, while a defendant has a right to resist the exercise of personal jurisdiction when either statutory or constitutional standards have not been satisfied, a plaintiff has a correlative right to insist that jurisdiction be exercised over the defendant when those standards have been met.

Notice that there is no aspect of personal jurisdiction doctrine that allows a court to decline the exercise of jurisdiction based on something other than the standard formula. True, a nonresident defendant may seek to rebut the presumption of reasonableness under the minimum contacts test, but that rebuttal, if successful, identifies a violation of due process, not an invitation to decline an otherwise properly invoked jurisdiction. Either the standards are satisfied and jurisdiction is compelled or they are not, and the case must be dismissed. Declining to exercise personal jurisdiction when it would otherwise be proper is, therefore, potentially arbitrary and in violation of due process because it takes from the plaintiff the court to which he or she is entitled.

VENUE

Venue is a statutorily based, nonjurisdictional doctrine that identifies the proper geographic location or locations for a lawsuit within an identified jurisdictional system.[12] While the overall concept of venue may be premised on the balance of conveniences among the parties and the judicial system, that convenience determination is not typically *ad hoc*. Rather the "convenient" forum is defined by way of statutes (e.g., 28 U.S.C. §§1391, 1394, 1395, 1396, 1400, 1402) that, on the basis of meaningful connecting factors, identify the proper venue for each and every case.

If the venue selection is statutorily proper and subject matter and personal jurisdiction standards have been satisfied, the plaintiff's choice of venue will be given significant weight. A transfer to another proper venue will be allowed under 28 U.S.C. §1404(a) only if the alternative federal forum is substantially more convenient than the chosen forum.[13] This is the only instance where Congress has authorized district courts to make an *ad hoc* determination as to the relative convenience of alternative venues. Moreover, a transfer of venue under §1404(a) does not involve a loss of federal jurisdiction. Rather, jurisdiction is retained within the federal system, and only the geographic location of the lawsuit – the venue – is changed. Hence, the balance of conveniences

[12] *See* 28 U.S.C. §1390(a) ("the term 'venue' refers to the geographic specification of the proper court or courts").

[13] 28 U.S.C. §1404(a) (West 2012).

analysis mandated by §1404(a) pertains only to location within the federal system, and the related fact that the system retains jurisdiction over the case makes it clear that such transfers present classic venue-premised questions and not power-based jurisdictional questions. In addition, in a diversity case, if a transfer motion is granted, the substantive law that would have been applied by the transferring court must travel with the case. In other words, such a change of venue will not alter the substantive law to be applied to the case.[14]

Finally, if the venue is proper in the plaintiff's chosen forum, there is no statute or formal federal rule that allows a federal court to dismiss the lawsuit based on the inconvenience of the forum. Like personal jurisdiction, a statutorily proper venue vests the plaintiff with a rule-of-law-based expectation that the case will proceed in that venue or some other statutorily proper venue to which the case may be transferred. Thus, once a plaintiff's choice of venue is determined to have been proper, the only statutory option is to retain or transfer within the federal system.

The doctrines of personal jurisdiction and venue are intimately related. In fact, starting from the same due process premise, they both use meaningful connecting factors linking the controversy and the defendant to the forum, thus identifying the forum or forums that would be suitable for the parties and the judicial system as a whole. Still, the two concepts of personal jurisdiction and venue are distinct and demand different analyses. While the doctrine of venue is rule-based, the jurisdiction doctrine is not so,[15] thus requiring a careful case-by-case approach to find whether its exercise is consistent with due process.

ORIGINS OF THE DOCTRINE OF *FORUM NON CONVENIENS*

Forum non conveniens, in its modern form, operates as a trump on the due process system of personal jurisdiction and venue. It is a judge-made doctrine that may upset the legitimate constitutional and statutory expectations of the parties and operates under a standard that vests district courts with a relatively broad discretion to dismiss a case under principles pertaining more to case management than to any constitutional principle or policy. The origins of *forum non conveniens* reveal that the doctrine was not always so broadly conceived.

[14] *See generally* Van Dusen v. Barrack, 376 U.S. 612 (1964); Ferens v. John Deere Co., 494 U.S. 516 (1990).

[15] *See* Chapter II, *supra* (suggesting the adoption of a statute governing personal jurisdiction).

SCOTLAND AND ENGLAND

It is generally accepted that the modern doctrine of *forum non conveniens* traces its roots to the Scottish doctrine of *forum non competens*, which was developed by Scottish courts as early as the seventeenth century to decline the exercise of otherwise proper jurisdiction.[16] This doctrine was initially used to ameliorate potential abuses of process in the context of *arrestment ad fundandam jurisdictionem*, a form of jurisdiction that allowed Scottish courts to assert jurisdiction over foreigners by attaching and seizing their moveable assets.[17] Hence, at least in this earliest form, the doctrine was plainly jurisdictional in that it was used to limit the exercise of seemingly proper, but potentially exorbitant, exercises of jurisdiction.[18]

By the late nineteenth century, the Scottish doctrine had evolved from an "abuse of process" concept toward one that permitted a stay of proceedings in deference to the "more suitable" forum. Consistently with that evolution, the nomenclature of "*forum non conveniens*" replaced the earlier usage of "*forum non competens*."[19] However, the re-named doctrine remained narrow in scope. It required a showing by the defendant that there was an alternate forum most suitable to promote the ends of justice and a demonstration by the defendant that the plaintiff would gain an "unfair advantage" were the case to remain in the Scottish forum.[20] In addition, the doctrine was not applied in cases involving domestic defendants until 1978.[21] In other words, until very recently, defendant's home forum was deemed per se to be a convenient forum.

[16] RONALD A. BRAND & SCOTT R. JABLONSKI, FORUM NON CONVENIENS: HISTORY, GLOBAL PRACTICE, AND FUTURE UNDER THE HAGUE CONVENTION ON CHOICE OF COURT AGREEMENTS 7, n.2 (2007); ALAN DASHWOOD ET AL., A GUIDE TO THE CIVIL JURISDICTION AND JUDGMENTS CONVENTION 425 n.76 (1987). *But see* Allan Stein, *Forum Non Conveniens and the Redundancy of Court-Access Doctrine*, 133 U. PA. L. REV. 781, 796–797 (1985) (casting doubts on the Scottish origins of the doctrine).

[17] VERONICA RUIZ ABOU-NIGM, THE ARREST OF SHIPS IN PRIVATE INTERNATIONAL LAW 40–42 (2001).

[18] *See* Alexander Reus, *Judicial Discretion: A Comparative View of the Doctrine of Forum Non Conveniens in the United States, the United Kingdom, and Germany*, 16 LOY. L.A. INT'L & COMP. L.J. 455, 459 (1994); *see also* ANDREW D. GIBB, THE INTERNATIONAL LAW OF JURISDICTION IN ENGLAND AND SCOTLAND 213 (1926).

[19] Paxton Blair, *The Doctrine of Forum Non Conveniens in Anglo-American Law*, 29 COLUM. L. REV. 1, 8–9, n.7 (1929); Reus, *supra* note 18, at 459–60.

[20] Sim v. Robinow, 19 R. 665, 667–68 (Scot); Longworth v. Hope, 3 M. 1049, 1052-59 (Scot.).

[21] *See* MacShannon v. Rockware Glass Ltd., [1978] A.C. 795 (H.L.) (appeal taken from Eng.); *see also* Reus, *supra* note 18, at 460.

Forum non conveniens was embraced by English courts in 1906 with the decision in *Logan v. Bank of Scotland*.[22] There, a Scottish plaintiff sued a Scottish bank in an English court for false representations in the prospectus of a Scottish company. Jurisdiction was established in England on the basis of the defendant's London branch bank. The court granted the defendant's motion to stay the proceedings in deference to a Scottish forum, citing what the court deemed as a "serious injustice" to the defendant in trying the suit in London.[23]

The English version of *forum non conveniens* was applied only under exceptional circumstances, typically where allowing the lawsuit to proceed in England would be extremely vexatious or oppressive for the litigants and the court itself. Moreover, the doctrine was used mainly to correct a gross unfairness that a rigid application of the jurisdictional doctrines or rules might otherwise produce. That happened, most often, when the litigants were both from foreign countries, or when only the defendant was. In *Société du Gaz de Paris v. Société Anonyme de Navigation "Les Armateurs Français,"* decided by the House of Lords on appeal from the Scottish Court of Session, a French shipper sued a French ship owner in a Scottish court, obtaining jurisdiction by attaching the defendant's property. The plaintiff claimed damages for the loss of its cargo due to the unseaworthiness of one of the defendant's vessels, which had foundered on a voyage from Scotland to France. The defendant filed a *forum non conveniens* motion, which was initially denied by the trial court but then granted by the Court of Session and, eventually, by the House of Lords. The judges based their decision on a Scottish opinion, *Clements v. Macaulay*,[24] in which the Scottish court offered the following principle:

> If in the whole circumstances of the case it be discovered that there is a real unfairness to one of the suitors in permitting the choice of a forum which is not the natural or proper forum, either on the ground of convenience of trial or the residence or domicile of parties, or of its being either the *locus contractus*, or the *locus solutionis*, then the doctrine of *forum non conveniens* is properly applied.[25]

Each of the elements cited by the court in the above quotation has a counterpart in the modern doctrines of personal jurisdiction: defendant's domicile as a "natural" forum; place of contract or contract performance as a connecting factor with the forum; and "real unfairness," suggestive of the unreasonableness prong of the minimum contacts test. Thus, even as it evolved, *forum non conveniens* remained closely tied to jurisdictional principles and concerns.

[22] *See* Logan v. Bank of Scotland. [1906] 1 K.B. 141 (Eng).

[23] *Id.* at 151–52.

[24] 4 Macpherson (Sess. Cas., 3d Ser.) 583 (1866).

[25] *Id.* at 20.

Another leading and instructive English precedent is *Egbert v. Short*.[26] There, the plaintiff was an alien domiciled in India and the defendant was an Indian solicitor. The suit was one for breach of a trust agreement made in India and governed by Indian law. The suit was filed in England. The court applied the *forum non conveniens* doctrine, finding that the casual presence of the defendant in England and the service upon him there were not enough to justify the exercise of jurisdiction, given that the litigation in England would have been extremely vexatious for the defendant since all the relevant evidence was located in India. In other words, the *forum non conveniens* doctrine operated to correct the unfairness that arose from an exorbitant application of transient or tag jurisdiction, much like the earlier *forum non competens* cases.[27]

Similarly, in *Williamson v. Northeastern Ry. Co.*,[28] the court sustained a plea of *forum non conveniens* to correct the unfairness to which an exercise of *quasi in rem* jurisdiction would have led. There, the widow of a man domiciled in Scotland sued an English company in Scotland for having negligently caused her spouse's death at a private grade crossing in England. She established *quasi-in-rem* jurisdiction over the defendant in Scotland by attaching its property there. Despite the fact that the plaintiff was from Scotland and despite the attachment of defendant's property there, the court sustained the plea of *forum non conveniens*:

> The event occurred in England; the witnesses to prove it are in England; the law which apparently rules it is English; and there is said to be involved in it a question of right of way which English law must decide. It is true that the pursuer is in Scotland, but the general rule is *actor sequitur forum rei*, and the appropriate and suitable forum in this case seems to me to be English, not necessarily because it is the *forum delicti*, but because it is also the most convenient for the trial of this case.[29]

One might think of *Williamson* as a precursor to the decision in *Shaffer v. Heitner*,[30] in which the Supreme Court imposed a modern due process standard on the exercise of the *quasi in rem* jurisdiction, thus undercutting the need to rely on *forum non conveniens* in such cases.

The leading Scottish and English cases discussed above demonstrate that *forum non conveniens* was used primarily to correct extreme excesses to which

[26] Egbert v. Short [1907] 2 Ch. 205.

[27] *See* Albert A. Ehrenzweig, *The Transient Rule of Personal Jurisdiction: The "Power" Myth and Forum Conveniens* 65 Yale L.J. 289, 292 (1956) (describing *forum non conveniens* as the antidote for the inconvenience case by transient jurisdiction).

[28] 11 Rettie (Sess. Cas., 4th Ser.) 596 (1884).

[29] *Id.* at 598.

[30] 433 U.S. 186 (1977).

the application of jurisdictional rules would give rise, thus avoiding potentially unfair proceedings. In each of these cases, jurisdictional considerations and, more specifically, due process considerations, played a significant role. Where there were no factors connecting the case to the forum, that is where the forum was technically proper but not the natural forum, the court would examine the potential unfairness of the proceeding in that forum and eventually dismiss the case. The considerations that the courts made in each case closely resemble those that American courts currently make under the unreasonableness prong of the minimum contacts test – i.e., when deciding that the exercise of jurisdiction would be unreasonable despite the satisfaction of the minimum contacts test.[31]

FORUM NON CONVENIENS ARRIVES IN THE UNITED STATES

In the United States, the term *forum non conveniens* made one of its earliest appearances in 1929, in an influential article by Professor Paxton Blair.[32] While Blair's endorsement of *forum non conveniens* was conceptually broad, his specific aim seems to have been to solve a problem of calendar congestion then facing the New York state court system. In this regard, Blair viewed *forum non conveniens* as an effective case-management tool that was "incontestably necessary to the effective performance of judicial functions."[33] In Blair's view, courts had "inherent powers" to dismiss or stay on grounds of *forum non conveniens*,[34] and even to raise the issue *sua sponte*.[35] Hence, all that was needed to provide proper relief to court congestion in New York (and elsewhere) was a greater judicial willingness to use this handy doctrine.[36]

In his article, Blair noted that it was "apparent that the courts of this country have been for years applying the doctrine."[37] This was because American courts were using the doctrine without always identifying it by

[31] *See generally* Asahi Metal Indus. Co., Ltd. v. Super. Ct., 480 U.S. 102 (1987); *see also* Metal Indus. Co. v. Super. Ct. of Cal., 480 U.S. 102 (1987); Nowak v. Tak How Invs. Ltd., 94 F.3d 708 (1st Cir. 1996).

[32] *See* Blair, *supra* note 19.

[33] *Id.*, at 1.

[34] *Id.*

[35] *See* Collard v. Beach, 81 N.Y.S. 619, 622 (1903), s.c., 87 N.Y.S. 884 (1904). *See also* Great W. Ry. Co. v. Miller, 19 Mich. 305, 315-13616 (1869).

[36] *See* John R. Wilson, Note, *Coming to America to File Suit: Foreign Plaintiffs and the Forum Non Conveniens Barrier in Transnational Litigation*, 65 OHIO ST. L.J. 659, 673 (2004).

[37] *See* Blair, *supra* note 19, at 21. According to John Wilson:

> Blair's thesis was that forum non conveniens should be more widely used to "reliev[e] calendar congestion by partially diverting at its source the flood of litigation by which our

name.[38] Blair explained that American courts applying the doctrine looked to factors such as the availability of witnesses, the burden on the state's citizens, the possible differences among tribunals in terms of rights and remedies, the ability to enforce a judgment when foreign law governs the dispute and, most of all, the complexity of the governing foreign law.[39]

To appreciate fully the precise nature of Blair's vision and the doctrine he endorsed, it is important to note that in his view, the classic case inviting an application of *forum non conveniens* was one in which neither party was a resident of the forum state and in which there were no factors connecting the forum with the activities out of which the suit arose. Under such circumstances, the state's interest in providing a forum was, at the very least, substantially diminished. Hence, while the factors described in the preceding paragraph outline a type of *forum non conveniens* methodology, it is clear that the focal point of Blair's article was the congestion caused by lawsuits that had no natural connection with the forum.

While Blair did not equate *forum non conveniens* with jurisdiction, he did at least recognize a critical relationship between the two. Essentially, he viewed a *forum non conveniens* motion as an invitation to decline the otherwise proper exercise of jurisdiction:

> [S]ince the basis of the [*forum non conveniens*] objection is the impropriety of the court's exercising *jurisdiction* over the subject matter rather than an absolute lack of such *jurisdiction*, the usual rule that want of *jurisdiction* of the subject matter cannot be waived by a failure to raise the objection *in limine*, or at any particular stage of the proceedings, is not strictly applicable.[40]

Blair was not the only one who saw that *forum non conveniens* doctrine was rooted in jurisdictional considerations. In 1947, shortly after Blair's piece, Robert Braucher noted:

> Early Scottish cases dealing with a plea of "*forum non competens*" suggest that the question litigated was one of power or jurisdiction rather than discretion; but as early as 1845 it was recognized that the question was one "on the

courts are being overwhelmed." The cause of the flood, Blair said, was forum shopping, which "merits the unequivocal condemnation of bench and bar.

John R. Wilson, quoting Blair in Wilson, *supra* note 36, at 673.

38 Blair observed that "while the doctrine has but rarely been referred to by name in American cases, yet decisions showing applications of it are numerous." *See* Blair, *supra* note 19, at 2.

39 *See Id.*, at 23.

40 *Id.* at 3 (emphasis added).

> merits" rather than one of jurisdiction, and the English words 'inconvenient forum' were used to point out the inaccuracy of the traditional Latin form.[41]

In brief, *forum non conveniens* was seen by Blair and others as a method for achieving what are essentially jurisdictional ends, specifically, responding to the abusive invocation of jurisdiction at a time when there was no other doctrinal method for doing so. The filing of a case in a forum other than a natural forum triggered the application of the doctrine because of the potential for jurisdictional abuse. According to Blair, under such circumstances, it might then be appropriate for a court to decline the exercise of jurisdiction after considering such matters as witness availability, the burden on forum citizens, the complexity of the governing foreign law, and, most significantly, the potential impact on rights, remedies, and enforceability. Differently from the Scottish and English courts, Blair considered the doctrine of *forum non conveniens* as a valid and legitimate case-management tool, but to be used only under the above described circumstances.

DEVELOPMENTS OF THE DOCTRINE OF FORUM NON CONVENIENS

In examining Supreme Court *forum non conveniens* precedent and lower court applications of that precedent, we must keep in mind the critical elements of that doctrine as it took root in the United States, namely, the absence of meaningful connecting factors establishing a natural forum, the presence of considerations suggestive of the unfairness of the forum choice, and countervailing concerns regarding potential unfairness to the plaintiff should the case be dismissed.

SUPREME COURT PRECEDENT

The Supreme Court first addressed the doctrine of *forum non conveniens* in *Gulf Oil Corp. v. Gilbert*.[42] There, the plaintiff, a resident of Virginia, sued a Pennsylvania corporation in a New York federal court on a nonfederal cause of action that had arisen entirely in Virginia. Jurisdiction over the defendant was apparently proper in New York since the defendant was qualified to do business there. Aside from that qualification to do business, the lawsuit had no other

[41] Robert Braucher, *The Inconvenient Federal Forum*, 60 HARV. L. REV. 908, 909. (1947).

[42] 330 U.S. 501 (1947), *superseded by statute*, 28 U.S.C. §1404 (2006), *as recognized in* Am. Dredging Co. v. Miller, 510 U.S. 443 (1994).

connections with the forum state. In other words, although the forum choice was technically proper, that forum was not a natural forum for the action. The defendant filed a motion to dismiss on *forum non conveniens* grounds, the more convenient forum being in Virginia where the plaintiff resided, where most of the witnesses were to be found, where the claim arose, and where jurisdiction over the defendant could readily be established. The district court granted the motion. The court of appeals reversed. The Supreme Court upheld the decision of the district court. In the Court's view, given the lack of connections with New York and the obvious connections with Virginia, this was one of those "rather rare" cases where the doctrine of *forum non conveniens* could be applied despite the technical propriety of jurisdiction and venue in New York.[43] In so ruling, the Court emphasized the absence of natural connecting factors with New York and the absence of any plausible explanation for the plaintiff's choice of a New York forum.[44] In short, the forum was not a natural forum.

The Court in *Gilbert* also described the public and private interest factors that should be considered in determining whether to apply *forum non conveniens*. These interests include but are not limited to: the relative ease of access to sources of proof; the availability of compulsory process for the attendance of the unwilling and the cost of obtaining attendance of willing witnesses (private factors); the administrative difficulties that follow for courts when litigation is piled up in congested centers instead of being handled at its origin; jury duty – which should not be imposed upon the people of a community with no relation to the litigation; and a local interest in having localized controversies decided at home (public factors).[45] In addition, implicit in the Court's description and application of these factors was the unquestioned availability of a suitable alternate forum.

The application of *forum non conveniens* in *Gilbert* did not operate as a denial of jurisdiction within the federal system since the case could be re-filed in a federal court sitting in Virginia. In this sense, *Gilbert* was, in essence, a venue-transfer case, and the standards there developed with those appropriate to a change of venue motion. Indeed, today *Gilbert* would be treated as a transfer case under §1404(a).[46]

The *Gilbert* "transfer" analysis cannot be considered sufficient for *forum non conveniens* purposes, because there the alternate forum is outside of the federal

[43] *Gilbert*, 330 U.S. at 509.
[44] *Id.* at 509–10.
[45] *Id.* at 508–09.
[46] Section 1404(a) was adopted in 1948 as a response to and partial affirmation of *Gilbert*. 62 Stat. 937 (1948).

system. In the *forum non conveniens* context, an otherwise legitimate invocation of jurisdiction is not deflected to another more convenient court within the system but is denied altogether. In other words, *forum non conveniens* doctrine does not represent a change of venue, but a change of sovereign jurisdictions.

Koster v. Lumbermens Mutual Casualty Co.,[47] which was decided on the same day as *Gilbert*, also involved an intra-system determination as to whether one federal forum was substantially more convenient than another. The plaintiff in *Koster* also failed to explain why he chose a forum where no events giving rise to the claim occurred and where the defendant did not reside. Hence, *Koster* qualified as another of those rare cases where the plaintiff's chosen forum would not be honored. Moreover, both *Gilbert* and *Koster* can be seen as representing circumstances where the plaintiff, taking advantage of overly generous jurisdictional and venue provisions, used its choice of forum as a form of harassment to seek a vexatious advantage over the defendant. In this sense, *forum non conveniens* operated as an antidote to the exorbitance to which the jurisdictional and venue rules had given rise. This use of *forum non conveniens* was consistent with the doctrine's original idea and rationale, as Paxton Blair had endorsed.

The *Koster* Court also added a new wrinkle to the doctrine by describing the scope of *forum non conveniens* as involving a disjunctive test. Thus, the doctrine could be applied on

> a clear showing of facts which *either* (1) establish such oppressiveness and vexation to a defendant as to be out of all proportion to plaintiff's convenience, which may be shown to be slight or nonexistent, *or* (2) make trial in the chosen forum inappropriate because of considerations affecting the court's own administrative and legal problems.[48]

The Court cited no authority for splitting the doctrine into a disjunctive form, but by doing so the Court elevated the case-management aspect of the doctrine thus inviting applications of *forum non conveniens* premised solely on a standard pertaining to the convenience of the court. The Court continues to cite this disjunctive form of the doctrine authoritatively.[49]

Justice Black dissented in both *Gilbert* and *Koster*. His objection to the decision in *Gilbert* rested on the obligation of a district court to exercise the jurisdiction conferred by Congress:

> Neither the venue statute nor the statute which has governed jurisdiction since 1789 contains any indication or implication that a federal district court, once

[47] 330 U.S. 518 (1947).

[48] *Id.* at 524 (emphasis added).

[49] *See, e.g.*, Am. Dredging Co., 510 U.S. at 448; Piper Aircraft Co. v. Reyno, 454 U.S. 235, 241 (1981).

> satisfied that jurisdiction and venue requirements have been met, may decline to exercise its jurisdiction. Except in relation to the exercise of the extraordinary admiralty and equity powers of district courts, this Court has never before held contrary to the general principle that "the courts of the United States are bound to proceed to judgment and to afford redress to suitors before them in every case to which their jurisdiction extends. They cannot abdicate their authority or duty in any case in favor of another jurisdiction."... Never until today has this Court held, in actions for money damages for violations of common law or statutory rights, that a district court can abdicate its statutory duty to exercise its jurisdiction for the alleged convenience of the defendant to a lawsuit.[50]

Justice Black thus rejected the notion that a judicially created balance of conveniences could trump the statutory scheme of jurisdictional power and identified conveniences created by Congress. He argued convincingly that when Congress confers jurisdiction and venue in a case at law, courts have no discretion to decline to exercise this power:

> It may be that a statute should be passed authorizing the federal district courts to decline to try so-called common law cases according to the convenience of the parties. But whether there should be such a statute, and determination of its scope and the safeguards which should surround it, are, in my judgment, questions of policy which Congress should decide.[51]

Thus, for Black, the difference between the obligatory exercise of jurisdiction in a case at law and the discretionary exercise of jurisdiction of an equitable abstention doctrine was critical. In the majority opinion, Justice Jackson never explained why a federal court may decline the exercise of granted jurisdiction, and instead treated that point as noncontroversial without fully confronting the dissent's critique.

The *forum non conveniens* doctrine was expanded significantly in *Piper Aircraft Co. v. Reyno*,[52] a case that arose out of an airplane crash in Scotland. A representative of the estate of the deceased Scottish passengers brought a suit in a California state court against the manufacturer of the plane (Piper) and the manufacturer of the propeller (Hartzell). The defendants successfully removed the case to the appropriate California federal district court, which, on defendants' motion, ordered the case transferred to a district court in Pennsylvania, Piper's state of incorporation[53] and the location of the airplane's

[50] *Gilbert*, 330 U.S. at 512–13 (Black, J., dissenting) (quoting Hyde v. Stone, 61 U.S. 170, 175 (1857)).
[51] *Id.* at 515.
[52] 454 U.S. 235 (1981).
[53] Brief for Respondent, Piper Aircraft Co. v. Reyno, 454 U.S. 235 (1981) (Nos. 80-883, 80-848) 1981 WL 390479 (Piper Aircraft Co. was incorporated in Pennsylvania).

manufacture. The defendants then filed *forum non conveniens* motions to dismiss, the more convenient forum allegedly being one in Scotland. The district court granted the motion and the Supreme Court ultimately affirmed that decision.

As noted above, *Gilbert* and *Koster* were essentially transfer of venue cases and would be so treated under today's standards. *Piper* was initially a transfer case as well – the transfer from California to Pennsylvania – and the absence of connecting factors with California bears a striking similarity to the facts in *Gilbert* and *Koster*. But once Piper, in the Pennsylvania district court, sought to dismiss on *forum non conveniens* grounds, the case became markedly different from *Gilbert* and *Koster* since the question was no longer one of transfer but one of dismissal from the federal system altogether. The *Piper* Court, however, failed to recognize this critical distinction and simply assumed that the standards of *Gilbert* should apply. Thus, without any due consideration, venue standards became a means to defeat jurisdiction.

There are several other noteworthy aspects of the *Piper* decision. First, the Court held that a foreign plaintiff's choice of forum, when merely dictated by the desire to benefit from a more favorable law or outcome, is not entitled to the same level of deference as a domestic plaintiff's choice of forum. Essentially, the nonresident foreigner's choice of a United States forum was given no presumptive weight whatsoever.

Second, the Court ruled that a change of law unfavorable to the plaintiff should rarely justify a denial of a *forum non conveniens* motion.[54] As to this point, the Court explained that an extensive choice of law analysis as to the relative favorableness of the alternate forum's law would be inconsistent with the policy behind *forum non conveniens* since such an analysis would unnecessarily complicate the *forum non conveniens* inquiry.[55] Hence, unlike the motions to transfer under §1404(a), which effect no change in the law, a *forum non conveniens* dismissal can be accompanied by a very unfavorable change in the law. Indeed, it is not unreasonable to assume that the motion is often filed to advance that goal. The Court did make it clear that there must be an alternate available forum, but the Court provided little guidance as to what might constitute such a forum other than to observe that "if the remedy

[54] 454 U.S. at 239.

[55] *Id.* at 253–54. In fact, as previously noted, transferring a case from one forum to another under §1404(a) does not produce any change in the applicable substantive law; however, there is such a change when a case is dismissed on *forum non conveniens* grounds and then filed in another forum.

provided by the alternative forum is so clearly inadequate or unsatisfactory that it is no remedy at all," the forum would not be adequate.[56]

Next, and significantly, the Court granted substantial deference to the district court's application of the *Gilbert* factors and chastised the appellate court for giving too little deference in this regard. It is also important to note that the district court identified no particular unfairness to the defendants should the case proceed in Pennsylvania – certainly nothing amounting to a due process violation; rather, the district court focused solely on the relative convenience of the forums (which the Supreme Court recognized as presenting a close question) and on the difficulties the district court would face in managing a case involving foreign law. The fact that *Piper* was being sued in its state of domicile – typically considered a significant connecting factor – appeared to play no role in the district court's calculus.[57]

Oddly enough, the Supreme Court's majority opinion actually references the ease of obtaining jurisdiction and venue as a reason for needing a flexible *forum non conveniens* doctrine.[58] In other words, the *Piper* Court saw *forum non conveniens* as a potential check on and antidote for the untoward consequences of liberal jurisdiction and venue standards. Yet, the antidote appears to have been totally unnecessary in the pending case when one considers that the lawsuit was pending in Piper's home state and in the location where the airplane was manufactured, hence, in a natural forum. Surely, this was not a case of vexatious or exorbitant jurisdiction.

Piper is thus responsible for a dramatic expansion of the classic range of *forum non conveniens* cases, where the absence of connecting factors was a critical threshold consideration. Essentially, *Piper* endorsed and invited a much more robust application of the doctrine of *forum non conveniens*, placing primary responsibility for the doctrine's application in the district courts and leaving very little room for appellate review.[59]

After *Piper*, the Court has continued to add wrinkles to the *forum non conveniens* doctrine. In *American Dredging Co. v. Miller*,[60] for example, the Court held that a state court exercising concurrent jurisdiction over an admiralty claim

[56] *Id.* at 254.

[57] The *Piper* Court's vesting of broad discretion in the district court has led to a doctrine that is open-textured, subject to unpredictable outcomes, and seemingly beyond the law. For an illuminating discussion of this phenomenon, see Cassandra Burke Robertson, *Forum non Conveniens on Appeal: The Case for Interlocutory Review*, 18 Southwestern J. Int'l L. 445 (2012).

[58] 454 U.S. at 250.

[59] *See* American Dredging Co. v. Miller, 510 U.S. 443, 445 (1993) ("The forum non conveniens determination. . .is committed to the sound discretion of the district court.")

[60] 510 U.S. 443 (1993).

was not required to adhere to the federal doctrine of *forum non conveniens* when state law would have banned application of the doctrine in that case. And in *Sinochem International Co. v. Malaysia International Shipping Corp.*,[61] the Court ruled that a federal court could dismiss a case under the *forum non conveniens* doctrine before definitively ascertaining its own jurisdiction "when considerations of convenience, fairness, and judicial economy so warrant."[62] Finally, in *Quackenbush v. Allstate Insurance Co.*,[63] the Court compared *forum non conveniens* to various abstention doctrines and suggested, somewhat ironically, that the constitutionally driven abstention doctrines were more circumscribed in application than the relatively unconstrained *forum non conveniens* doctrine.[64]

In sum, the doctrine of *forum non conveniens* as elaborated by the Supreme Court is significantly more open-textured than the original doctrine as envisioned and applied in Scotland and England and equally so with respect to the doctrine described and endorsed by Paxton Blair in his article. In these early forms of the doctrine, the threshold consideration involved a lack of connecting factors with the chosen forum, i.e., the absence of a natural forum, sometimes described as constituting an abuse of process, and what certainly could be described as an exorbitant and unfair invocation of jurisdiction. These factors kept the doctrine within reasonable bounds even when the doctrine's primary purpose might be perceived as pertaining to housekeeping matters such as docket reduction or case management.

The decision in *Piper* and the Supreme Court cases decided in its wake to treat *forum non conveniens* as a venue doctrine that vests broad discretion in district courts to decline the exercise of jurisdiction based on an *ad hoc* balancing formula that is appropriate to change of venue situations (as in *Gilbert* and *Koster*), but inadequate to justify the denial of constitutionally valid and statutorily vested jurisdiction, where jurisdiction may be defeated only under compelling circumstances.[65] These decisions ignore the doctrine's jurisdictional roots in service to an open-textured balancing of conveniences. Moreover, the doctrine today may even be applied in cases, such as *Piper*, where there are significant connecting factors with the forum and where jurisdiction over the defendant is both fair and premised on traditional grounds.

[61] 549 U.S. 422 (2007). The approach endorsed in *Sinochem* is troubling since it permits a court, that may not have jurisdiction, to enter an order that may end up altering the plaintiff's substantive rights, sometimes resulting in the death knell of the plaintiff's claim. *See* Robertson, *supra* note 57, at 449.

[62] *Id.* at 432.

[63] 517 U.S. 706 (1996).

[64] *Id.* at 722–723.

[65] Burger King Corp. v. Rudzewicz, 471 U.S. 462, 477 (1985).

CURRENT PRACTICES WITHIN THE FEDERAL JUDICIAL SYSTEM

With *Piper* as their guide, lower federal courts have taken widely disparate approaches to *forum non conveniens*.[66] There is confusion over the types of cases to which the doctrine applies, over how the various elements of the doctrine are to be applied, over which party bears the ultimate burden of persuasion, and over the scope of appellate review. Indeed, there is no agreement as to whether the doctrine is meant to protect defendants from a truly inconvenient forum or whether the doctrine is simply meant to identify the most suitable forum.[67] As one commentator has observed:

> As typically happens when trial courts of varying predilections are directed to "exercise discretion" in weighing a large number of incommensurate factors, the result has been a welter of decisions that are difficult if not impossible to harmonize. More disturbing, many *forum non conveniens* dismissals have plainly been granted on the basis of factors not endorsed in *Gilbert*, not fairly disclosed by the deciding court, and not, on closer examination, rationally supportive of dismissal.[68]

Of course, much of this confusion and uncertainty is a product of the fact that *forum non conveniens* is a judge-made doctrine, unbounded by constitutional constraint and unguided by statute or rule.

VARIABILITY AS TO TYPES OF CASES TO WHICH THE DOCTRINE APPLIES

The indeterminacy of *forum non conveniens* allows courts to favor certain types of claims over others, even though all such claims are statutorily vested within a federal court's jurisdiction. For instance, the Alien Tort Claims Act (ATCA) vests federal courts with jurisdiction over tort claims by aliens for a narrow range of violations of international law.[69] As such, ATCA represents

[66] *See* Robertson, *supra* note 57, at 455–464 (describing and critiquing variable standards); Elizabeth T. Lear, *Congress, the Federal Courts, and Forum Non Conveniens: Friction on the Frontier of the Inherent Power*, 91 Iowa L. Rev. 1147, 1156–1159 (2006) (documenting a wide range of conflicting approaches); Martin Davies, *Time to Change the Federal Forum Non Conveniens Analysis*, 77 Tul. L. Rev. 309 (2002) (same).

[67] Robertson, *supra* note 57, at 460 (citing conflicting authorities).

[68] Peter G. McAllen, *Deference to the Plaintiffs in Forum Non Conveniens*, 13 S. ILL. U. L.J. 191, 194 (1989).

[69] 28 U.S.C. §1350 provides, ""The district courts shall have original jurisdiction of any civil action by an alien for a tort only, committed in violation of the law of nations or a treaty of the

a congressional exercise of its power to enforce the "law of nations" and to recognize the juridical obligations of the United States in this regard.[70] Yet, despite this specific congressional investiture of jurisdiction, ATCA claims often fall victim to *forum non conveniens* dismissals. Thus, in *Mastafa v. Australian Wheat Bd. Ltd.*[71] the plaintiffs, Kurdish women whose husbands were allegedly imprisoned, tortured, and killed by the Saddam Hussein regime in Iraq, brought a class action on behalf of themselves and others similarly situated against defendants Australian Wheat Board Limited aka AWB Limited ("AWB"), AWB (U.S.A.) Limited, and Banque Nationale De Paris Paribas. They alleged violations of the law of nations and the Torture Victims Protection Act ("TVPA") and asserted jurisdiction pursuant to ATCA. The defendants moved to dismiss on *forum non conveniens* grounds, the more convenient forum being the defendants' home forum of Australia. The court granted a conditional dismissal and noted:

> ATCA and the TVPA permit adjudication of foreigners' claims for certain violations of international law. However, they have not "nullified, or even significantly diminished, the doctrine of *forum non conveniens*." Adjudication of foreign claims under ATCA is certainly appropriate where an adequate foreign forum is unavailable or there is reason to think that the foreign forum lacks an interest in pursuing such an adjudication or that litigation in the United States would be more convenient for the parties. But where, as here, there is an adequate foreign forum with a profound interest in adjudicating the dispute and litigation here would be significantly less convenient, the abstract interest of the United States in enforcing international law does not compel an assertion of jurisdiction. Accordingly, the interests of the parties, of judicial economy, and of Australia and the United States are better served by adjudication of this dispute in Australia.[72]

The presumed congressional judgment that the courts of the United States should be open to such claims apparently played no role in the district court's *forum non conveniens* analysis. Such ATCA dismissals are frequently entered despite the specific jurisdictional mandate from Congress, often sending

United States." *See* Kiobel v. Royal Dutch Petroleum, 133 S.Ct. 1659 (2013) (narrowing the scope of ATCA based on a presumption against the extraterritorial application of U.S. law); *but see Id.* at 1669 (Kennedy, J., concurring) (supplying the critical fifth vote and suggesting that extraterritorial activity in violation of the Torture Victims Protection Act might fall within the scope of the ATCA).

70 U.S. CONST., art. I, §8, cl. 10 (granting Congress power "To define and punish . . . Offences against the Law of Nations.").

71 No. 07 CIV. 7955 (GEL), 2008 WL 4378443 (S.D.N.Y. Sept. 25, 2008).

72 *Id.* at 9.

litigants back to the forum where the violations of international law are alleged to have occurred[73] or ringing the death knell of the litigation.[74] Yet not all federal courts are equally inhospitable to ATCA claims.[75] Thus, *forum non conveniens* permits a district court broad discretion to dismiss ATCA claims despite a clear congressional mandate that federal courts be available to vindicate international law claims arising under that statute.

On the other hand, the Supreme Court has suggested that federal courts generally may not dismiss federal antitrust suits on the basis of *forum non conveniens*,[76] though, as can be expected with such an open-ended doctrine, there are a few cases to the contrary.[77] This decidedly less aggressive use of *forum non conveniens* remains the case even when the lawsuit involves activities that take place on foreign soil. The reason for this reluctance is sound. Congress has specifically vested federal courts adjudicating such cases with the broadest possible scope of personal jurisdiction (minimum contacts with the United States) and with the most generous venue options for the plaintiffs.[78] In essence, the express will of Congress to vest broad jurisdictional and venue authority in district courts has been deemed to trump or (at the very least) substantially diminish the judge-made doctrine of *forum non conveniens*.

The jurisprudential distinction between ATCA suits, where *forum non conveniens* is often considered part of the defendant's rights, and antitrust suits, where it is generally not, is not clear. Certainly, there is nothing inherent in *forum non conveniens* that requires this differential treatment. Nor is there anything about ATCA that supports this approach. Both types of cases (ATCA and federal antitrust) may involve activities taking place on foreign soil and

[73] *See* Aldana v. Del Monte Fresh Produce N.A., Inc., 578 F.3d 1283 (11th Cir. 2009); *but see* Bigio v. Coca-Cola Co., 448 F.3d 176 (2d Cir. 2006).

[74] Robertson, *supra* note 57, at 449.

[75] *See* Wiwa v. Royal Dutch Petroleum Co., 226 F.3d 88, 99–108 (2d Cir. 2000) (reversing a *forum non conveniens* dismissal in favor of a British forum and stating that "[i]f in cases of torture in violation of international law our courts exercise their jurisdiction conferred by the 1789 Act only for as long as it takes to dismiss the case for forum non conveniens, we will have done little to enforce the standards of the law of nations").

[76] *See* U.S. v. Nat'l City Lines, 334 U.S. 573, 596–597 (1948) (holding that *forum non conveniens* could not be used to transfer an antitrust suit to a more convenient forum within the United States); Indus. Inv. Dev. Corp. v. Mitsui & Co., Ltd., 671 F.2d 876, 890 (5th Cir. 1982) (common law doctrine of *forum non conveniens* not applicable to suits brought under the United States antitrust laws).

[77] *See, e.g.*, Capital Currency Exchange, N.V. v. National Westminister Bank, PLC, 155 F.3d 603 (2d Cir. 1998)(Sherman Act claim dismissed on *forum non conveniens* grounds).

[78] 15 U.S.C. § 22 ("Any suit, action, or proceeding under the antitrust laws against a corporation may be brought not only in the judicial district whereof it is an inhabitant, but also in any district wherein it may be found or transacts business; and all process in such cases may be served in the district of which it is an inhabitant, or wherever it may be found.").

both come with an express and specific grant of jurisdiction over the "foreign" activities at issue. The reasons for the differential treatment could be political, that is, it might be because the State Department often asks courts to dismiss ATCA cases. Or it could simply depend on the fact that human rights cases are fraught with jurisprudential and political challenges beyond those confronted in international antitrust cases. Or, it could be based on a judgment about the economic importance of antitrust litigation. Or, it could be based on the courts' greater sympathy for one class of plaintiffs over another. In any event, in both types of cases, Congress was very clear about granting federal jurisdiction to federal courts over the respective claims arising outside the United States. The fact that *forum non conveniens* is flexible enough to allow variances from one subject matter to another is itself a sign of the arbitrariness of the underlying doctrine.

DOCTRINAL INDETERMINACY

To prevail on a *forum non conveniens* motion, the defendant must establish the availability of an adequate alternate forum and demonstrate that the balance of the private and public factors (the *Gilbert* factors) weigh strongly in favor of dismissal.[79] This simple description opens the door to a complex web of results, for the factors that inform a district court's decision to grant or deny a *forum non conveniens* motion are more or less unconstrained and thus vary widely from court to court and case to case.[80] As Justice Scalia observed for the Court in *American Dredging Co. v. Miller*, "The discretionary nature of

[79] CHARLES ALAN WRIGHT, ET AL., 14D FEDERAL PRACTICE AND PROCEDURE §3828 (3d 2013).

[80] In 2010, Joel Samuels published a study drawing on a review of every published federal court decision since 1982 that had considered the doctrine of *forum non conveniens*. The study considered 1,500 decisions and was intended to see how federal courts were applying the doctrine. The data collected revealed that:

> far too often, courts conflate the two prongs [alternate forum and convenience] – treating both as discretionary, bypassing the first prong altogether, or considering AAF [available alternate forum] without meaningful review and analysis. Lower courts struggle to apply the two-part *Piper* inquiry. However, by its very nature, that second prong is ad hoc and not susceptible to closer scrutiny. This capricious process is unfair to plaintiffs and defendants alike and undermines the authority of the judiciary – at least when ruling on *forum non conveniens* motions.

Joel H. Samuels, *When Is an Alternative Forum Available? Rethinking the Forum Non Conveniens Analysis*, 85 Indiana Law Journal 1059, 1061 (2010). *See also* Robertson, *supra* note 57, at 448–456. For a contrary view, *see* Christopher Whytock, *The Evolving Forum Shopping* System, 96 Cornell L. Rev. 481 (2011).

the doctrine, combined with the multifariousness of the factors relevant to its application ... make uniformity and predictability of outcome almost impossible."[81]

As to the burden of establishing *forum non conveniens*, courts generally hold that the defendant bears the burden of proving both prongs of the *Piper* test, i.e., that there is an adequate alternate forum and that the balance of private and public interests weigh strongly in favor of dismissal,[82] in practice, the actual allocation of the burden is more elusive. For example, if the defendant shows that it is amenable to suit in the alternate forum, some courts hold that the burden shifts to the plaintiff to demonstrate the inadequacy of the presumptively adequate forum.[83] While it remains the case that the defendant bears the ultimate burden of persuasion, somehow the plaintiff's failure to provide affirmative evidence of inadequacy legitimates a finding of adequacy, suggesting that, in fact, the plaintiff bears the burden of proof on the question of adequacy once the defendant satisfies a relatively low threshold.[84]

Concerning the courts' overall approach to the existence of an available alternative forum, Professor Joel Samuel's empirical study of post-1982 federal cases deciding *forum non conveniens* motions found that courts conducted an

[81] 510 U.S. at 455 (citation omitted).

[82] *See, e.g.*, Abdullahi v. Pfizer, Inc., 562 F.3d 163, 189 (2d Cir. 2009); *see also* CHARLES ALAN WRIGHT, ET AL., 14D FEDERAL PRACTICE AND PROCEDURE §3828.2 (3d 2013) ("Federal courts are unanimous in concluding that the defendant bears the burden of persuasion on all elements of the forum non conveniens analysis.")

[83] *See, e.g.*, Jackson v. Am. Univ., 52 F. App'x 518, 519 (D.C. Cir. 2002) (rejecting plaintiffs' argument that Egypt was not an appropriate forum because the plaintiffs offered no evidence in the district court "to rebut the [defendant's] affidavit from an Egyptian attorney regarding the adequacy of the forum"); Presbyterian Church of Sudan v. Talisman Energy Inc., 244 F. Supp. 2d 289, 337–38 (S.D.N.Y. 2003) (assuming the adequacy of the alternate forum based on plaintiff's failure to show otherwise). State St. Bank & Trust Co. v. Inversiones Errazuriz, Limitada, 230 F. Supp. 2d 313, 319–20 (S.D.N.Y. 2002) (treating plaintiff's failure to challenge the adequacy of the proposed alternative forum as somehow dispositive of the question of adequacy).

[84] In Abdullahi v. Pfizer, Inc., the court the elusive burden as follows:

> The defendant bears the burden of establishing that a presently available and adequate alternative forum exists, and that the balance of private and public interest factors tilts heavily in favor of the alternative forum. Absent a showing of inadequacy by a plaintiff, "considerations of comity preclude a court from adversely judging the quality of a foreign justice system." Accordingly, while the plaintiff bears the initial burden of producing evidence of corruption, delay or lack of due process in the foreign forum, the defendant bears the ultimate burden of persuasion as to the adequacy of the forum.

562 F.3d at 189 (internal citations omitted). *See* CHARLES ALAN WRIGHT, ET AL., 14D FEDERAL PRACTICE AND PROCEDURE §3828.3 (3d 2013) (describing trial court opinion in *Abdullahi* as implicitly shifting the burden of proof to the plaintiff).

available-alternative-forum analysis only 69 percent of the time.[85] But much more shocking is Samuel's finding that in 24 percent of the *forum non conveniens* dismissals, the court's opinion included no alternative forum analysis.[86] In addition, according to Samuels, the *Piper* Court contributed to the lower courts' confused approach to the available alternative forum by inviting those courts to blur the line between available alternative forum analysis and the balancing of public and private conveniences:

> Instead of articulating a doctrine that should be invoked to dismiss cases in federal courts only in "rare cases," the *Piper* AAF [Available Alternative Forum] inquiry creates an opposite presumption (amenability to service of process is sufficient): an alternative forum is presumed to be available, except in rare circumstances. Second, the exception to the presumption of availability involves a single inquiry into whether "the remedy offered by the other forum is clearly unsatisfactory." Courts have been left wide ambit to interpret that condition narrowly or broadly as they see fit. Moreover, factors that actually involve the availability of [an alternative forum] but that do not fit into the exception to AAF carved out in *Piper* are simply thrown into the mix of public factors considered under the second prong of the *forum non conveniens* analysis.[87]

For those courts that do conduct an alternative forum analysis, the inquiry is often "cursory" and "limited," vesting the defendants with a tool that effectively puts the plaintiff out of court.[88] One leading commentator has even expressed doubts as to whether district courts are capable of appraising "the competence or character of a foreign tribunal."[89] Not surprisingly, the extent of the inquiry into the "availability" and "adequacy" of the alternate forum is ill defined, though it generally appears to impose a very low threshold, requiring only that the defendant be subject to service of process and that the courts of the forum provide some remedy.[90] Beyond that, it is unclear whether courts should take into account the substantive law that the foreign court would apply to the case[91]; and equally unclear is the extent to which the

85 Samuels, *supra* note 80, at 1077. Samuels offers examples of federal courts' opinions that do not give adequate consideration, or do not consider at all, the adequate alternative forum. *See, e.g.*, *In re* Union Carbide Corp. Gas Plant Disaster at Bhopal, India in Dec., 1984, 634 F. Supp. 842, 844 (S.D.N.Y. 1986), *aff'd as modified*, 809, F. 8422d 195 (2d Cir. 1987).

86 Samuels, *supra* note 80, at 1077.

87 *Id.*, at 1070.

88 CHARLES ALAN WRIGHT, ET AL., 14D FEDERAL PRACTICE AND PROCEDURE §3828.3 (3d 2013).

89 *Id.*

90 *Id.*

91 *See e.g.*, Presbyterian Church of Sudan, 244 F.Supp.2d at 335–337 (closely examining both the substantive and procedural rights available in the alternate forum).

alternate forum must offer procedural guarantees that comport with due process.[92] In other words, there is no accepted definition as to what constitutes an adequate alternate forum.

There is a similar dispersal of doctrine with respect to how one values the plaintiff's choice of forum. A large number of decisions defer to the plaintiff's choice, where he has chosen his own district or state of residence as the forum. However, where the plaintiff is not a resident of the forum – in many ATCA cases, for example, the plaintiff will be an alien nonresident – this deference, under *Piper*, will not come into play. Some courts will give added weight to the plaintiff's choice of forum if that is the forum where the defendant resides or does substantial business. Yet it is now often the case that corporate defendants object to their corporate residence as a proper forum, seeking instead to place the litigation in a foreign nation, where there is the likelihood of a more favorable result.[93]

Next, while the *Gilbert* factors outline the public and private considerations to be weighed in the balance of conveniences, nothing in the *Gilbert* opinion or in any subsequent Supreme Court opinion explains how to weigh and apply those factors. Not surprisingly, there is no consistency of approach in the lower federal courts.[94] Nor has the Supreme Court provided any guidance as to how modern litigation practices, enhanced by technology and the global legal marketplace, might alter *Gilbert*'s antique matrix.[95]

[92] *See generally In re* Union Carbide Corp. Gas Plant Disaster at Bhopal, India in Dec., 1984, 634 F. Supp. 842, 844 (S.D.N.Y. 1986) (district court reviewed the complaint and dismissed on *forum non conveniens* grounds condition on defendants compliance with the federal discovery rules), *affirmed and modified*, 809 F.2d 195 (2d Cir. 1987). *But see* Mercier v. Sheraton Int'l, Inc., 981 F.2d 1345, 1352-53 (1st Cir. 1992); Zermeno v. McDonnell Douglas Corp., 246 F. Supp. 2d 646, 659 (S.D. Tex. 2003); Carney v. Sing. Airlines, 232. 940 F. Supp. 1496, 1505 n.6 (D. Ariz. 1996) (showing that case law is clear that an alternative forum ordinarily is not considered "inadequate" merely because its courts afford different or less generous discovery procedures or different procedures than those that would available under American rules.).

[93] See Whytock, *supra* note 80, at 527-528 (citing a potential bias against foreign plaintiffs).

[94] For a description of the inter- and intra-circuit splits on the *Gilbert* balancing formula, see Davies, *supra* note 66, at 352–353 (citing authorities).

[95] Considering that well over 90 percent of all cases are disposed of prior to trial, one wonders what weight should be given to the "trial-based" *forum non conveniens* private interest factors, such as the location of physical evidence, existence of a compulsory process, ability to viewing the scene, etc. After all, if the case is unlikely to go to trial, why care about this? Also, given modern technology, how real are these concerns? Shouldn't things like Skype or video conferencing, videos of an accident scene, computer recreations, etc., eliminate most of these concerns even for those few cases that do go to trial? The obvious answers to these questions seem to suggest that *forum non conveniens* is simply another procedural tool in the hands of courts used to avoid adjudicating cases on their merits. *See also* Ronald A. Brand, *Comparative*

Ultimately, it is hard to fully capture the reasoning behind each *forum non conveniens* decision at any detailed level, since most such decisions are quite brief and do little more than recite the legal standards, followed by a holding that the balance tips in favor of dismissal or not. If appealed, most are affirmed under an "abuse of discretion" standard,[96] though even that standard varies from circuit to circuit in the intensity of its application.[97]

*****

We are left with a doctrine unbounded by rules or standards and ungrounded in any clearly stated policy.[98] Most observers find that the results are unpredictable and unfair in both practice and perception.[99]

This confusion regarding the proper scope and limits of the *forum non conveniens* doctrine, coupled with its growing complexity and apparent attractiveness, add significant costs to litigation. The determination of jurisdiction (and proper venue), however, should not be so costly. Rather, a lawyer should be able to predict with a high degree of accuracy whether the proper standards of jurisdiction and venue are satisfied in a particular forum. This is where the absence of a statute or rule is particularly telling.

Forum Non Conveniens and the Hague Convention on Jurisdiction and Judgments, 37 Texas TEX. INT'L LJ. 467, 485 (2002).

96 *Gilbert*, 330 U.S. at 502.

97 *See* Iragorri v. Unitd Tech. Corp., 274 F.3d 65, 72 (2d Cir. 2001) (district court decision on *forum non conveniens* may be reverse only if discretion "clearly abused"); Bank of Credit and Commerce Int'l (Overseas) Ltd. v. State Bank of Pakistan, 273 F.3d 241, 246 (2d Cir. 2001) (appellate review of *forum non conveniens* decision "severely cabined"). However, some appellate courts do recognize the "abuse" and do reverse trial courts' opinions when they clearly depart from the essential requirements of the doctrine. *See, e.g.*, Cariajano v. Occidental Petroleum Corp., 626 F.3d 1137 (9th Cir. 2010) *opinion withdrawn and superseded on reh'g sub nom.* Carijano v. Occidental Petroleum Corp., 643 F.3d 1216 (9th Cir. 2011) (reversing trial court's order granting a motion to dismiss on *forum non conveniens* grounds due to district court's failure to consider full range of factors); *see also* Robertson, *supra* note 57, at 462–463 (citing variable applications of the standard, from strict to highly deferential).

98 *See* Stein, *supra* note 16, at 832 (noting that, "[t]here have been ninety-three reported *forum non conveniens* decisions by federal courts of appeals since the *Gulf Oil* decision, only twenty-seven of which were reversals. Only fifteen cases in which the district court retained jurisdiction under forum *non conveniens* reached the courts of appeals, and, of these, all but two were affirmed"); *see also* Robertson, *supra* note 57, at 455–464.

99 See David W. Robertson & Paula K. Speck, *Access to State Courts in Transnational Personal Injury Cases: Forum Non Conveniens and Antisuit Injunctions*, 68 TEX. L. REV. 937, 971, 75 (1990) (describing forum non conveniens as "vague and amorphous, yielding little predictability and virtually guaranteeing against clear explanation of the outcomes"); Stein, *supra* note 16, at 785 (describing a "crazy quilt of ad hoc, capricious, and inconsistent [*forum non conveniens*] decisions"); Robertson, *supra* note 57, at 454–455 (noting the perception and reality of injustice).

A common law, judge-made rule, when not reduced to a statue or rule, tends to evolve and grow ever more complicated and with conflicting doctrinal tentacles. In any event, as matters now stand, litigants will not know in advance or, at least, will not be certain as to which factors the court will consider in deciding whether the case should proceed or be dismissed in deference to an alternate forum. This relatively boundless approach to jurisdiction and venue creates the opposite of due process. It creates a system of discretionary jurisdiction that is unbounded by the rule of law and, hence, often arbitrary in application.

The general confusion on the doctrine confirms that *forum non conveniens* has, indeed, become an arbitrary doctrine, often used as a case-management tool, intended to dismiss cases presenting complex conflict of laws issues, or, more generally, complex issues of law in which the chosen forum is not interested in investing its resources. The *forum non conveniens* doctrine, as it exists today, hardly resembles the original quasi-jurisdictional doctrine developed by Scottish and English courts between the seventeenth and the twentieth centuries and later introduced to the United States. The contemporary federal doctrine is neither one of jurisdiction nor one of venue. It is not venue, because it does not pertain to a geographic location within a judicial system, but to a change from one judicial system to another. Yet, it is not truly jurisdictional since it employs a form of *ad hoc* balancing of convenience factors that can defeat jurisdiction on much less than a compelling case. What then, is it? It is simply a judge-made doctrine that gives a district court arbitrary power to dismiss a case if the court concludes that the case can proceed elsewhere for any one of a number of reasons or for no reason at all other than that the judge deems the alternate forum superior.

REPOSITIONING *FORUM NON CONVENIENS* AS A JURISDICTIONAL DOCTRINE

Stated at its most general level, the doctrine of *forum non conveniens*, as enforced by federal courts, vests district courts with broad and virtually unfettered discretion to decline the exercise of otherwise properly asserted jurisdiction and venue if, in the judgment of the district court, there is an available alternate forum where the case can be more conveniently litigated. The district court's judgment in this regard will not be reversed unless that judgment reflects an abuse of discretion (and in some circuits that abuse must be "clear" to warrant reversal). Given that 28 U.S.C. §1404(a) permits a district court to transfer a case to another district under a similar balance-of-conveniences analysis, the doctrine of *forum non conveniens* will only come into play when the alternative forum is in a foreign nation. Hence, *forum non conveniens* in federal courts is a dismissal doctrine.

As I have shown, *forum non conveniens* cannot be properly characterized as a supervening venue provision. It neither provides for a transfer of venue within the federal judicial system, as does §1404(a), nor does it establish the propriety of venue in the alternate foreign forum, a virtual impossibility. The only "venue" characteristic of *forum non conveniens* is that it uses the same type of ad hoc balancing that applies (with congressional sanction) in the context of venue transfers under §1404(a). However, this commonality of technique (without congressional sanction) does not transform *forum non conveniens* into a venue provision. Rather, this jot-for-jot borrowing raises a suspicion that something is amiss with *forum non conveniens*. For unlike a venue transfer, which is both intra-system and congressionally sanctioned, *forum non conveniens* involves a denial of congressionally conferred and constitutionally sanctioned jurisdiction and removes the case completely from the federal judicial system. In addition, given the Supreme Court's decision in *Piper*, a *forum non conveniens* dismissal can, unlike a §1404(a) transfer, lead to a significant change in the law and remedies available to the plaintiff, including the distinct possibility that the case will not be re-filed in the alternative forum.

If we instead view *forum non conveniens* realistically for what it is and what it does, we must conclude that it is or ought to be part of the jurisdictional calculus. *Forum non conveniens* was born and nurtured in the context of exorbitant exercises of jurisdiction and used as an antidote for that exorbitance. That foundation can serve as a significant limiting factor on the application of the doctrine while at the same time preserving its utility for those cases where the plaintiff's choice of forum represents an abuse of process or places the defendant at a distinct litigation disadvantage.

We might find an appropriate constitutional standard in the law of personal jurisdiction. The basic minimum contacts test is premised on meaningful connections that link the forum, the defendant, and the asserted claim. These connecting factors create a reasonable expectation of amenability to being sued in the forum and thereby create a strong presumption of reasonableness. The defendant can rebut that presumption only by presenting a compelling case. This means that the defendant must show that the exercise of jurisdiction would be objectively unfair under the circumstances presented. This same standard would give constitutional weight to *forum non conveniens* and thus provide a narrowly circumscribed basis for the occasional refusal to exercise jurisdiction that was otherwise properly invoked. Thus, instead of continuing to employ the "soft focus" balancing formula taken from the law of venue, which undermines the obligation to exercise conferred jurisdiction, *forum non conveniens* would borrow the sharply focused due process reasonableness inquiry to validate a court's refusal to exercise jurisdiction. In fact, in the interests of clarity, *forum non conveniens*, as so circumscribed, could replace the unreasonableness prong of the minimum contacts test and permit that test to focus exclusively on minimum contacts analysis.[100]

Since its origin, *forum non conveniens* has been used in response to exorbitant exercises of jurisdiction. It was designed to remedy situations where the exercise of jurisdiction would have brought a serious disadvantage to the defendant by imposing a real unfairness on her ability to defend a lawsuit. By contrast, the contemporary *forum non conveniens* doctrine – at least its federal version – has the effect of denying an otherwise proper assertion of jurisdiction and of significantly altering the rights and remedies at stake in the proceedings, without a defendant's having to demonstrate any real unfairness. The contemporary doctrine's balancing of conveniences, often unarticulated, thus serves as the talisman of a broad discretion to dismiss, providing yet more evidence that federal judges are less and less judges than they are managers of their docket.

Professor Judith Resnik long ago noted with alarm the growth of managerial judges, prompted by "changes initiated by judges themselves in response to work load pressures."[101] As she has correctly noted, such alterations in the judicial function toward a more managerial role are made "privately, informally, off the record, and beyond the reach of appellate review"[102] and hence provide a threat to the core judicial function, which is the delivery of justice.

A PROPOSED CODIFICATION OF *FORUM NON CONVENIENS*

Several States have codified the doctrine of *forum non conveniens*.[103] After reviewing a number of these provisions and considering the factors that ought to inform the scope of the federal doctrine, I propose the following

[100] *See* Chapter II, *supra*.

[101] Judith Resnik, *For Owen M. Fiss: Some Reflections on the Triumph and the Death of Adjudication Managerial Judges*, 96 HARVARD L. REV. 374, 391 (1982).

[102] *Id.* at 426.

[103] *See, e.g.*, Alabama Code §6-5-430; California Cal Code Civ. Proc. §410.30; Colorado C.R.S. 13-20-1004; Fla. R. Civ. P. 1.061; Mass. Gen. Laws Ann. Ch 223A, §5; N.Y.C.P.L.R. §327(a)

codification. This codification seeks to transform the current amorphous common-law doctrine into a much narrower tool that judges would employ only rarely, and whose invocation would be subject to a more meaningful review on appeal.

PROPOSED CODIFICATION

1. In any civil action of which a district court has original jurisdiction, the district court may stay or dismiss the action under the doctrine of *forum non conveniens* only if:
   a. The defendant files a timely motion to dismiss on grounds of *forum non conveniens*, such timeliness to be measured under the standards applicable to a motion under Federal Rule of Civil Procedure 12(b)(2), but for good cause shown, the court may extend the period set forth in this Section for the filing a *forum non conveniens* motion; and
   b. The moving party demonstrates and the district court finds that there is an available alternate forum with jurisdiction over the action and the defendants, that, as a practical matter, the plaintiff will have access to that forum, that such forum provides a suitable substantive remedy for the claim or claims asserted by the plaintiff, and that such forum adheres to the fundamental standards of due process; and
   c. The district court finds that the available alternate forum provides a substantially more suitable forum for the adjudication of the claim or action, and that the maintenance of the claim or action in the district court would impose substantial injustice on the moving party.
2. If the district court finds that the standards in Section 1 have been satisfied, it may stay or dismiss the claim or action on any condition it may deem just. Such conditions may include the defendant's waiver of any statute of limitation or lack of jurisdiction defense that defendant might otherwise have in the alternate forum.
3. When granting a motion to dismiss an action on *forum non conveniens* grounds, the district court shall retain jurisdiction to enforce its dismissal order and any related stipulations or conditions attached thereto.

(McKinney); 12 Okl. St. §140; 42 Pa. C.S. §532; Tenn. Code Ann. §20-15-104; Tex. Civ. Prac. & Rem. Code Ann. §71.051; W.Va. Code §56-1-1a; Wisconsin Wis. Stat. Ann. §801.52 (West).

4. A court that grants or denies a motion to stay or dismiss an action pursuant to this statute shall set forth specific findings of fact and conclusions of law supporting the court's order.
5. An order granting or denying a motion to dismiss on *forum non conveniens* grounds is immediately appealable. The findings of fact shall be reviewed under the clearly erroneous standard. The conclusions of law shall be reviewed under the *de novo* standard.

COMMENTARY AND CONCLUDING REMARKS

Section 1 requires a district court to determine whether it has jurisdiction over the case prior to any consideration of a *forum non conveniens* motion. The purpose of this decision-making sequence is to position the *forum non conveniens* inquiry within the contours of the district court' obligation to exercise jurisdiction. In addition, this sequencing requirement prevents a court without power over the controversy from resolving, in effect, substantive rights of the parties. This provision would overrule *Sinochem* to the extent that *Sinochem* permits a district court to decide a *forum non conveniens* motion without first resolving the question of jurisdiction.

Subsection 1a imposes a timeliness requirement that is keyed to the federal rules. Hence, in most cases, the defendant would be required to file a motion to dismiss on *forum non conveniens* grounds within 21 days of having been served with the complaint.[104] This Section also vests the district court with discretion to extend the time within which to file the motion for good cause shown. For example, good cause might permit a tardy *forum non conveniens* motion to be filed when materials gathered during discovery establish firm grounds on which to file such a motion and where no such grounds were apparent at the outset of the litigation.

Subsection 1b makes it clear that it is the moving party's burden to establish the existence and practical availability of an alternative forum. This subsection also defines what constitutes an available alternative forum. It includes a requirement that the court consider the practical consequences of the dismissal on the plaintiff and that those consequences be central to the determination of whether there is an alternative adequate forum.

[104] Federal Rule of Civil Procedure 12(a)(1)(A)(i).

Subsection 1c narrows the scope of the district court's discretion to dismiss on *forum non conveniens* grounds. While the "substantially more suitable alternative forum" language does permit the district court to take into account the practical interests of the judicial system, the "substantial injustice" requirement precludes the court from dismissing a case on mere case-management considerations. In addition, this subsection requires that the district court find that the alternative forum is "substantially" more suitable and that retention of jurisdiction would impose "substantial injustice" on the moving party. The first requirement makes it clear that the doctrine may not be enforced based simply on a finding that an alternative forum is "more" convenient, but only on a finding that such a forum is "substantially" more suitable. The "substantial injustice" requirement is meant to meld *forum non conveniens* with the unreasonableness prong of the minimum contacts test, thus limiting the application of *forum non conveniens* to circumstances where the moving party will suffer an injustice commensurate to a violation of due process.[105]

Section 2 permits the district court to impose conditions on a *forum non conveniens* stay or dismissal and specifies two non-exclusive examples of such conditions.

Section 3 requires that the district court retain jurisdiction to enforce any of the conditions or stipulations in any order of dismissal. This conditional dismissals gives the dismissing court an opportunity to monitor the proceeding in the foreign court to make sure the remedy provided is not clearly inadequate.[106] Of course, federal courts are free to do this, but there is no rule that requires them to do so.

Section 4 requires a district court to make specific findings of fact and conclusions of law when ruling on a *forum non conveniens* motion. The purpose here is threefold: 1) avoid the open-textured approach to *forum non conveniens* that has come to characterize district court practice; 2) provide appellate courts with a clear statement of the district

[105] *See* Chapter II, *supra* (endorsing such an intersection between the law of personal jurisdiction and the law of forum non conveniens).

[106] *See, e.g.*, Mastafa v. Australian Wheat Bd. Ltd., No. 07.CIV. 7955 (GEL), 2008 WL 4378443, at 9 (S.D.N.Y. Sept. 25, 2008) (providing for a renewal of jurisdiction if the alternate forum turns out to be unavailable). This option is also provided by some state code provisions. *See e.g.*, CAL. CIV. PROC. CODE § 410.30 (West 2012) (providing that "[w]hen a court upon motion of a party or its own motion finds that in the interest of substantial justice an action should be heard in a forum outside this state, the court shall *stay* or dismiss the action in whole or in part on any conditions that may be just" (emphasis added).

court's decision, thereby making appellate review more meaningful and less speculative; and 3) provide a foundation from which appellate courts can create a coherent doctrine that lends itself to predictability of application.

Section 5 works together with Section 4 to ensure robust appellate review of district court decisions.

*****

The federal doctrine of *forum non conveniens* has drifted far from his jurisdictional beginnings. It has now morphed into a device that allows district courts to decline jurisdiction on policy choices that range well beyond the legitimate sphere of the judicial function. In part, this state of affairs is a product of the facile treatment of *forum non conveniens* as a "superseding" venue doctrine, freighted with an *ad hoc* balancing of conveniences appropriate to venue transfer motions, but quite out of place in a motion that calls for a jurisdictional dismissal and the attendant substantive consequences of such a dismissal. By repositioning *forum non conveniens* as a jurisdictional doctrine, my goal is to return *forum non conveniens* to its legitimate scope and usage.

4

Personal Jurisdiction and *Forum Non Conveniens* in a Transnational Context[1]

INTRODUCTION

The adoption of an international convention on conflict of laws could be achieved through a "harmonization" process. To harmonize means "to make or form a pleasing or consistent whole."[2] Harmonization is often used to mean "the process by which we make everything the same, a sort of rush to the bottom to further facilitate the globalization of advanced capitalism."[3]

However, as observed by Professor Laura Spitz: "'Harmony' is by definition diverse. 'Harmonization' is by definition layered. Like 'globalization,' harmonization is not necessarily a normative claim, but rather a tool. . . As with music, the difficult question is which aspects should be similar, and which different, in order to create a pleasing or appropriate relationship."[4] Spitz further observed:

> Globalization has been described as the process of increasing interconnectedness between societies such that events on [sic] one part of the world more and more have effect on people and societies far away. It is a consequence of increased human mobility, enhanced communications, greatly increased trade and capital flows and technological developments.[5]

This leads to an increase in transnational litigation on business transactions and to the consequent need for uniform rules governing the same.

[1] *See also* Simona Grossi, *Rethinking the Harmonization of Jurisdictional Law*, 86 Tul. L. Rev. 623 (2012).

[2] THE CONCISE OXFORD DICTIONARY OF CURRENT ENGLISH 538 (8th ed. 1990).

[3] Laura Spitz, *The Gift of Enron: An Opportunity to Talk About Capitalism, Equality, Globalization, and the Promise of a North-American Charter of Fundamental Rights*, 66 OHIO ST. L.J. 315, 337 (2005).

[4] *Id.* at 338.

[5] *Id.* at 338–39 (footnote omitted) (internal quotation marks omitted).

This work suggests the adoption of an international convention on conflict of laws – that is, a uniform convention on choice of law, jurisdictional law, and recognition and enforcement of judgments – applicable to civil and commercial matters.[6] However, this work will focus only on the harmonization of choice of law and jurisdictional rules, considering the harmonization of the rules on recognition and enforcement of judgments a natural corollary of the harmonization of the first two sets of rules. In contrast to the comparative analyses carried out by the authoritative common law[7] and civil law[8] scholars, which focus on the differences between civil and common law jurisdictional rules, I follow and expand the approach taken by the very scarce literature, which instead focuses on the similarities between civil and common law jurisdictional rules.[9]

DEFENDING HARMONIZATION

We should consider harmonization as a phenomenon that follows as a natural consequence of, and is instrumental to, "globalization." However, even if increased interconnectedness between societies and transnational litigation is undeniable, no consensus has been reached as to the necessity and feasibility of harmonization of rules that would facilitate transnational litigation.

[6] This expression resembles the one used in the various regulations of the European Communities as well as in the Hague Conventions governing procedural issues, for example, the Hague Convention on the Taking of Evidence Abroad and the Hague Convention on the Service of Process Abroad. If the convention applies to "civil and commercial matters," it means that it does not apply to tax, customs and administrative issues, family law, competition, arbitration, social security, bankruptcy, or wills and successions. *See, e.g.*, Council Regulation 44/2001, on Jurisdiction and the Recognition and Enforcement of Judgments in Civil and Commercial Matters 2001 O.J. (L 12) (EC) [hereinafter Council Regulation 44/2001]; Convention on the Taking of Evidence Abroad in Civil or Commercial Matters, Mar. 18, 1970, 847 U.N.T.S. 231 [hereinafter Hague Evidence Convention]; Convention on the Service Abroad of Judicial and Extrajudicial Documents in Civil or Commercial Matters, Nov. 15, 1965, 658 U.N.T.S. 163 [hereinafter Hague Service Convention].

[7] *See* Kevin M. Clermont, *Jurisdictional Salvation and the Hague Treaty*, 85 CORNELL L. REV. 89 (1999); Linda Silberman, *Comparative Jurisdiction in the International Context: Will the Proposed Hague Judgments Convention Be Stalled?*, 52 DEPAUL L. REV. 319 (2002); Arthur T. von Mehren, *Drafting a Convention on International Jurisdiction and the Effects of Foreign Judgments Acceptable World-Wide: Can the Hague Conference Project Succeed?*, 49 AM. J. COMP. L. 191 (2001).

[8] *See* Peter F. Schlosser, *Lectures on Civil-Law Litigation Systems and American Cooperation with Those Systems*, 45 U. KAN. L. REV. 9, 17 (1996).

[9] *See* Ronald A. Brand, *Jurisdictional Common Ground: In Search of a Global Convention*, *in* LAW AND JUSTICE IN A MULTISTATE WORLD: ESSAYS IN HONOR OF ARTHUR T. VON MEHREN 11 (James A.R. Nafziger & Symeon C. Symeonides eds., 2002).

The drafters of the ALI/UNIDROIT Principles of Transnational Civil Procedure,[10] when explaining the reasons and rationales behind those principles, pointed out that "the costs and distress resulting from legal conflict can be mitigated by *reducing* differences in legal systems, so that the same or similar 'rules of the game' apply no matter where the participants may find themselves."[11] Furthermore, harmonization reduces uncertainty and the costs related to it, as well as forum shopping,[12] and leads to significant social benefits by "break[ing] down local bar monopolies by opening up legal practice to persons from outside the jurisdiction."[13]

Through a harmonization process, the procedural legal systems are brought into line with one another by eliminating their "exorbitant" rules.[14] This might eventually lead to internal reforms intended to improve efficiency because, all things being equal, exorbitant rules and devices are most likely to be less efficient than other more widely accepted rules and devices.[15] In fact, harmonization processes usually go beyond the mere achievement

[10] *See* ALI/UNIDROIT, PRINCIPLES OF TRANSNATIONAL CIVIL PROCEDURE (2004), *available at* http://www.unidroit.org/english/principles/civilprocedure/main.htm.

[11] Geoffrey C. Hazard, Jr. et al., *Introduction to the Principles and Rules of Transnational Civil Procedure*, 33 N.Y.U. J. INT'L L. & POL. 769, 769 (2001) (emphasis added).

[12] *See* Harold J. Berman, *Is Conflict of Laws Becoming Passé? An Historical Response* 43–44 (Emory Univ. Sch. of Law Pub. Law & Legal Theory Research Paper Series, Research Paper No. 05-42, 2005), *available at* http://ssrn.com/abstract=870455.

[13] Geoffrey P. Miller, *The Legal-Economic Analysis of Comparative Civil Procedure*, 45 AM. J. COMP. L. 905, 917 (1997).

[14] "Exorbitant" rules are rules that are valid within the legal systems where they have been adopted, but they appear unreasonable to nonnationals because of the grounds used to justify them. *See, e.g.*, Kathryn A. Russell, *Exorbitant Jurisdiction and Enforcement of Judgments: The Brussels System as an Impetus for United States Action*, 19 SYRACUSE J. INT'L L. & COM. 57, 59 (1993). When the Hague Convention on the Service of Process Abroad was adopted, notification *au parquet* was used by five countries: Belgium, France, Greece, Italy, and the Netherlands. 3 1964 Conférence de la Haye de Droit International Privé, Actes et Documents de la Dixième Session (Notification) 75 (1964).

To outsiders, these rules of jurisdiction appear unreasonable when they believe that the court seised does not possess a sufficient connection with the parties to the case, the circumstances of the case, the cause or subject of the action, etc. Examples of exorbitant rules of jurisdiction include: article 14 of the French Civil Code, which bases jurisdiction on nationality (that is, a French national living in the United States could sue an American citizen in France to seek damages suffered as a consequence of an accident that occurred in China), article 23 of the German Code of Civil Procedure, which provides that German courts have jurisdiction over nonresident defendants who own property in Germany, irrespective of the cause of action and the value of the property, and the American "tag" or "transient" jurisdiction. *See* CODE CIVIL [C. CIV.] art. 14 (Fr.); ZIVILPROZESSORDNUNG [ZPO] [CODE OF CIVIL PROCEDURE], Sept. 21, 1994 BUNDESGESETZBLATT [BGBL.] 2494, as amended, § 23 (Ger.); discussion *infra*.

[15] *See* Russell, *supra* note 14, at 61–62.

of uniformity and end up crafting the best solutions to given legal problems, thus also accomplishing a developmental function.[16]

The arguments offered against harmonization are not strong enough to outweigh the benefits that harmonization would bring to transnational litigation on civil and commercial matters. Against harmonization, some authors argue that the adoption of uniform rules may reduce legal risk[17]; but this comes with costs, and in any event, an optimal level of legal risk is greater than zero.[18] Furthermore, these authors observe that in order for these rules to be clear, they should provide more detailed instructions and cover a greater number of eventualities. However,

[16] *See* Sandeep Gopalan, *From Cape Town to the Hague: Harmonization Has Taken Wing*, 5 U. PA. J. INT'L L. & POL'Y (2006–07), www.law.upenn.edu/journals/jil/jilp/articles/1-1_Gopalan_Sandeep.pdf.

[17] There are different definitions of "legal risk." For a comprehensive illustration of these theories and a proposal of a new definition of legal risk, see Tobias Mahler, *Defining Legal Risk* (Turku Univ. of Applied Scis. Conf. on Com. Contracting for Strategic Advantage – Potentials and Prospects, 2007), *available at* http://papers.ssrn.com/sol3/papers.cfm?abstract_id=1014364. According to the author:

> There are many different definitions of legal risk, but most seem to fall into one of the following two groups. The first set of definitions links legal risk to *legal uncertainty*. Most other definitions define legal risk by giving a number of examples, which include, in addition to legal uncertainty, *uncertainty about factual elements*.

Id. at 3–4.

[18] *See* Paul B. Stephan, *The Futility of Unification and Harmonization in International Commercial Law* 4 (Univ. of Va. Sch. of Law Legal Studies Working Paper Series, Working Paper No. 99-10, 1999), *available at* http://papers.ssrn.com/paper.taf?abstract_id=169209. In line with this reasoning, Professor Helmut Wagner notes:

> [F]ull harmonization may (at first sight) seem to be an adequate instrument for reducing the costs of cross-border legal uncertainty; however, full harmonization itself tends to imply high economic costs, so that it is not generally recommendable. Nevertheless, a gradual (partial) harmonization process could, in some circumstances, be beneficial.
>
> . . .
>
> Legal uncertainty can be regarded as a non-tariff trade barrier. But from this it does not follow that full harmonization is necessary, because harmonization itself generates substantial costs. These include not only direct costs for developing new bureaucracies or demolishing old structures, but also costs arising from a loss of the advantages of system competition, the advantages being an adaptation to the variety of preferences, efficiency advantages of regulative competition, and the minimization of "rent-seeking" costs caused by bureaucrats/politicians. Nevertheless, from the point of view of the economy as a whole, welfare gains could possibly be realized through more harmonization.

Helmut Wagner, *Costs of Legal Uncertainty: Is Harmonization of Law a Good Solution?*, *in* MODERN LAW FOR GLOBAL COMMERCE: PROCEEDINGS OF THE CONGRESS OF THE UNITED NATIONS COMMISSION ON INTERNATIONAL TRADE LAW HELD ON THE OCCASION OF THE FORTIETH SESSION OF THE COMMISSION 53, 53, 59 (2011), *available at* www.uncitral.org/pdf/english/congress/09-83930_Ebook.pdf.

rather than predictability and certainty, the parties to transnational commercial transactions, and, more generally, parties to transnational litigation on civil and commercial matters might prefer alternatives and flexibility.[19]

Yet a feasible and successful harmonization process is one that leads to the adoption of principles, standards, and models that can be adapted (by legislatures and courts) to the various legal systems.[20] The rules of an international convention would necessarily be framed using terminology and concepts that could be assimilated in all legal traditions, which would necessarily leave legislators little room for variation and flexibility. Thus, there would always be a level of legal risk greater than zero. The goal of a proper harmonization project is not to eliminate legal risk – which is neither possible nor desirable – but rather to reduce it to the benefit of the parties and the legal systems.

Another author has observed that harmonization carries economic costs. One of the most important of these economic costs is the elimination of human capital that has been built up among the local bar on the operation of a given procedural system. In this context, according to this author, lawyers should be retrained.[21]

However, not all lawyers would have to be retrained. A harmonization process cannot be pursued for all the rules applicable in a legal system. Usually, harmonization is suggested only for cases that may involve commercial transactions, transnational litigation, or both. A harmonization process is usually intended for this restricted category of cases only, and certainly not for purely domestic matters, which may also be deeply intertwined with fundamental public policy considerations (such as family, estate, tax, and administrative law issues). Therefore, if any lawyers must be retrained, they will be those lawyers who deal with transnational commercial transactions or transnational litigation on civil and commercial matters – the same lawyers who most likely must "train" or "retrain" every time they approach a new foreign legal system or transnational litigation issue.

Furthermore, whether harmonization "removes diversity from the procedural system, and thus reduces the available menu of options that can be looked to as models for procedural reform," depends on how the uniform rules are conceived.[22] A good harmonization process would not eliminate diversity, but would instead build on it. Such a process would combine the best elements of

[19] *See* Stephan, *supra* note 18, at 4.

[20] For an excellent example of the harmonization process of procedural rules, see ALI/UNIDROIT, *supra* note 10.

[21] *See* Miller, *supra* note 13, at 917.

[22] *Id.*

various systems and leave national legislatures and courts some room to adapt the uniform rules to the peculiarities of their own legal systems, without destroying the overall objectives of the project.

Professor Louis Visscher believes that "it remains to be seen if harmonized law indeed would result in more legal certainty (problems of different interpretation and application of the legal rules may still result in non-uniform law)," and that

> there is no empirical evidence that differences between legal systems indeed significantly impede international trade, nor that harmonization of law would result in more international transactions... According to several responses, problems in the functioning of the internal market are more caused by language barriers, cultural differences, distance, habits, and divergence in other areas of law, such as tax law and, noteworthy, procedural law.[23]

However, these are exactly the obstacles that a harmonization process considers, trying to reduce the negative effects that such obstacles have on the efficiency and fairness of transnational litigation without pretending to eliminate them. The legal risk will necessarily always be greater than zero.

It is also said that a harmonization process "will not necessarily generate efficient rules, because it is likely to be carried out by elites selected in a political process, who may not necessarily give a high value to the efficiency of the rules they adopt."[24] However, assuming that we appreciate the benefits of having uniform rules governing certain aspects of transnational litigation, we cannot renounce such benefits merely because we believe that the procedure for adopting these rules is not structured as it should be. Rather, we should consider any problem in the procedure and eliminate it through careful consideration.

[23] Louis Visscher, *A Law and Economics View on Harmonization of Procedural Law* 9–10 (Rotterdam Inst. of Law & Econ. Working Paper Series, Paper No. 2010/09), *available at* http://ssrn.com/abstract=1669944. Although Visscher takes a position which is strongly opposed to harmonization, he recognizes:

> [C]lear rules regarding choice of law and regarding recognition and execution of foreign titles seems like a much better approach. In as far as "best practices" exist which would also be used in other jurisdictions, regulatory competition enables bottom-up harmonization because other jurisdictions may incorporate similar solutions.
>
> ...
>
> ... [T]he scope for harmonization of procedural law from a Law and Economics point of view hence is at best limited and it should have an optional character.

Id. at 20–21.

[24] *See* Miller, *supra* note 13, at 917–18.

It is true, though, that thus far, the harmonization of procedural law has made much less progress than the harmonization of substantive law.[25] This is due to the perceived existence of some irreconcilable differences in the various civil procedure systems. However, there were many instances when differences originally viewed as irreconcilable did not stop countries from adopting uniform procedural rules, some of which turned out to be extremely successful.

International conventions on service of process,[26] on the abolition of legalization,[27] and on the taking of evidence abroad[28] are perfect examples of instances when existing differences among countries did not prevent harmonization.[29] They all demonstrate that exorbitant rules adopted by some

[25] According to some authors, harmonization of procedural law "has been impeded by the assumption that national procedural systems are too different from each other and too deeply embedded in local political history and cultural tradition to permit reduction or reconciliation of differences among legal systems." *See* Hazard et al., *supra* note 11, at 770. There, the authors also note:

> [T]he pioneering work of Professor Marcel Storme has demonstrated that harmonization is possible in such procedural matters as the formulation of claims, the development of evidence, and the decision procedure. This project to develop transnational rules for civil procedure has drawn extensively on the work of Professor Storme.
>
> . . .
>
> This project endeavors to draft procedural rules that a country could adopt for adjudication of disputes arising from international transactions. The project is inspired by the desire to unite many diverse jurisdictions under one system of procedural rules as was accomplished in the United States a half-century ago with the enactment of the Federal Rules of Civil Procedure.

Id. at 771 (footnotes omitted). See generally Stephen B. Burbank, *The Rules Enabling Act of 1934*, 130 U. PA. L. REV. 1015 (1982), for a discussion on the adoption of the Federal Rules of Civil Procedure.

[26] See Hague Service Convention, supra note 6.

[27] See Convention Abolishing the Requirement of Legalisation for Foreign Public Documents, Oct. 5, 1961, 527 U.N.T.S. 189 [hereinafter Convention Abolishing the Requirement of Legalisation for Foreign Public Documents].

[28] *See* Hague Evidence Convention, *supra* note 6.

[29] As it has been observed:

> Until the Convention [on the service abroad] was implemented, the contracting nations followed widely divergent practices for serving judicial documents across international borders, some of which did not ensure any notice, much less timely notice, and therefore often produced unfair default judgments. Particularly controversial was a procedure, common among civil-law countries, called notification au parquet, which permitted delivery of process to a local official who was then ordinarily supposed to transmit the document abroad through diplomatic or other channels. Typically, service was deemed complete upon delivery of the document to the official whether or not the official

countries could be set aside in favor of harmonization and that the international community as a whole could greatly benefit from uniform rules.

Through the adoption of standardized rules, these conventions introduced cheaper and faster mechanisms to handle transnational commercial litigation, thus eventually enhancing international judicial cooperation and improving international dispute resolution.[30] Harmonization is possible and worth pursuing, especially in the area of conflict of laws. Considering the benefits – namely, uniformity, efficiency, and fairness – that this convention could achieve, as well as the fact that such a convention does not exist, leads one to believe that there must be irreconcilable differences preventing such an achievement. Yet the existing differences among conflict of laws rules are not irreconcilable and are merely the product of recent developments. Moreover, when conflict of laws rules were originally introduced, the mechanisms that such rules adopted were very simple and hardly lent themselves to different interpretations and applications. Furthermore, the original purpose of conflict of laws rules was to harmonize the differences and bring unity while preserving such differences. This purpose should still be preserved.

> succeeded in transmitting it to the defendant and whether or not the defendant otherwise received notice of the pending lawsuit.
> The United States delegation to the Convention objected to notification au parquet as inconsistent with the requirements of due process of law under the Federal Constitution. The head of the delegation has derided its [i]njustice, extravagance [and] absurdity...
> In response to this and other concerns, the Convention prescribes the exclusive means for service of process emanating from one contracting nation and culminating in another.

GARY B. BORN, INTERNATIONAL CIVIL LITIGATION IN UNITED STATES COURTS 829 (3d ed. 1996) (internal quotation marks omitted). In other words, despite the original differences and the presence of exorbitant rules in the participating member states, a consensus was reached.

30 Professor Hélène van Lith observed:

> The desirability for unification of jurisdiction rules at a world-wide level should be understood as a need for an international legal framework regulating cross-border commercial activities and its disputes in a 'globalizing world', rather than a process that forms part of an economic and a political integration... As a general rule, unification of law is still considered to be desirable if it meets the 'specific needs of international legal business'. In that respect it is undeniable that the desirability of unification of jurisdiction lies in the fact that the international community would benefit from jurisdictional certainty and predictability in cross-border activities and transnational commercial contracts.

HÉLÈNE VAN LITH, INTERNATIONAL JURISDICTION AND COMMERCIAL LITIGATION: UNIFORM RULES FOR CONTRACT DISPUTES 18–19 (2009).

CONFLICT OF LAWS RULES

Terminology

Strangely, though the term "private international law" was introduced by an American, Joseph Story, it prevails in Europe,[31] while the term "conflict of laws," first used by a European, Ulrich Huber, prevails in the United States.[32] In European private international law, the word "international" is used to identify cases having a transnational dimension, and the word "private" indicates controversies not involving states. Most of the time, European conflict of laws rules are codified. American conflict of laws, on the other hand, focuses on the "conflict" between different applicable laws or jurisdictions that is not resolved ex ante by an applicable rule, but rather is resolved by courts at the time the issue arises through the analysis and the approach that they consider more valuable.[33] In both cases, conflict of laws or private international law involves three areas of law: choice of law, jurisdictional law, and recognition and enforcement of judgments.

Until recently, the differences reflected in the different terminology were not so evident, especially because American conflict of laws subscribed to the same premises and aspirations as Savigny's classical theory.[34] In fact, while most American law derives from English common law, American conflict of

[31] Symeon C. Symeonides, *The American Revolution and the European Evolution in Choice of Law: Reciprocal Lessons*, 82 TUL. L. REV. 1741, 1784 (2008).

[32] *See id.*

[33] *See id.*

[34] Friedrich Carl von Savigny was a German scholar who lived between the end of the eighteenth century and the first half of the nineteenth century. In the words of Professor Friedrich Juenger:

> According to Savigny, the conflict of laws serves the purpose of allocating each legal relationship to a particular legal system to avoid disparate treatment of the same transaction at the hands of judges in different states. Because he focused on the need for a uniform treatment of legal transactions irrespective of the forum, he rejected the statutists' unilateralist doctrine as well as the primacy of forum law Wächter had advocated. In Savigny's words,
>
> 'in many conflicts cases there is concurring jurisdiction in different places, so that in a particular case the plaintiff is free to choose the forum. Accordingly, if ... [Wächter's] principle should control, the local law applicable in each case depends not only on fortuitous circumstances, but on a litigant's unilateral choice.'

Friedrich K. Juenger, *Jurisdiction, Choice of Law and the Elusive Goal of Decisional Harmony*, *in* LAW AND REALITY: ESSAYS ON NATIONAL AND INTERNATIONAL PROCEDURAL LAW 137, 138 (1992).

laws rules derive from continental European law, mainly Roman and German law. Therefore, American and European conflict of laws rules share deep historic roots.[35]

Originally, both American conflict of laws and European private international law aimed to achieve international or interstate uniformity of choice of law decisions, regardless of where litigation occurred. In this context, there was no room for interest analysis, forum-law favoritism, or protectionism of forum litigants. Until the middle of the twentieth century, most countries' conflict of laws rules had to be neutral in the sense that foreign and forum laws had to be applied equally.[36]

THE ROMANIST ORIGINS OF CONFLICT OF LAWS PRINCIPLES: USING "CONNECTING FACTORS" TO DETERMINE CHOICE OF LAW AND JURISDICTION

According to Professor Friedrich Juenger, the origins of conflict of laws can be traced back to Roman law of the twelfth century, when Western scholars began to study and teach the Justinian Code in Northern Italy.[37] Usually, a conflict of laws problem arose when a citizen of one city sued a citizen of another city, and the judge had to identify the law applicable to the controversy. The same occurred elsewhere in Western Europe, including France, England, and Germany, where not only issues concerning conflicts of urban laws, but also conflicts of feudal, mercantile, royal, and ecclesiastical laws arose.[38]

[35] *See* EUGENE F. SCOLES ET AL., CONFLICT OF LAWS 18–19 (4th ed. 2004). The principle that the courts of the place where the defendant resides have personal jurisdiction over the defendant, which was spelled out in *Milliken v. Meyer*, comes from the Justinian Code. *See* CODE JUST. 3.13.2 (Diocletian & Maximian); Milliken v. Meyer, 311 U.S. 457, 463–64 (1940). Roman law also provided the concept of limited jurisdiction, according to which the plaintiff could sue in tort at the place of wrongful conduct, could bring contract claims at the place of contract execution or performance, and could bring property right claims at the situs. Under Roman law, courts usually applied the same connecting factors to identify the law applicable to the controversy: the law of the place where the contract was entered into (*lex loci contractus*), the law of the place where the tort or the crime was committed (*lex loci delicti*), and the law of the place where the property in dispute was situated (*lex rei sitae*). American courts adopted these connecting factors and conflict of laws rules too. *See* discussion *infra*.

[36] *See* SCOLES ET AL., *supra* note 35, at 40.

[37] *See* Berman, *supra* note 12, at 45. However, private international law had somehow already emerged in Greece with the growth of Greek city-states around the fourth century B.C. *See* FRIEDRICH K. JUENGER, CHOICE OF LAW AND MULTISTATE JUSTICE 6 (2005).

[38] Berman, *supra* note 12, at 45.

The Romanist scholars who commented on the Justinian Code derived fundamental conflict of laws concepts and doctrines from the canon law applied in the ecclesiastical courts. According to one such doctrine, when a choice of law had to be made, courts should apply the law of the place where the contract was entered into (*lex loci contractus*), the law of the place where the tort or the crime was committed (*lex loci delicti*), the law of the place where the property in dispute was situated (*lex rei sitae*), or the law of the place where the marriage was celebrated (*lex loci celebrationis*).[39] These were all connecting factors,[40] which linked the controversy to a particular jurisdiction. In any event, justice should prevail over formal choice of law rules when the application of a formal rule would be unjust.[41] These principles were very simple, fair, and relatively predictable.

The same connecting factors would, in most instances, identify the judge with jurisdiction over the case and the parties. Thus, in some legal settings, the determination of jurisdiction was the choice of law.[42] That was true in

[39] *Id.* at 46–47.

[40] Connecting factors are the factors that link an event, a transaction, or a person to a country. *See* ABLA J MAYSS, PRINCIPLES OF CONFLICT OF LAWS 3 (3d ed. 1999).

[41] *See* Berman, *supra* note 12, at 46. According to Professor Hessel Yntema:

> The analysis indicates that by the fourteenth century a considerable structure for the solution of statutory conflicts according to the nature and subject matter of the statutory provisions had been developed. In this scheme, a number of principles, which have since become common property, were set forth, e.g. – That questions of form are governed by the *lex loci actus*. That *litis ordinatio*, the conduct of litigation or, as we should say today, questions of procedure, are governed by the law of the place of suit, the *lex fori*. That *litis decisio*, viz. of matters affecting the performance of a contract, if arising conformably to the contract at the time of its conclusion, is governed by the law of the place of contract; if arising *ex post facto* as a result of negligence or delay in performance, by the law of the place of performance. That liability for delicts is governed by the *lex loci delicti* except when a foreigner may justifiably plead ignorance of an unusual local law. That questions of rights arising out of things are governed by the *lex rei sitae*. That questions affecting the quality or status of persons are governed by the personal law, which applies only to subjects.
>
> With variants in detail, the technique of statutory interpretation dominated conflicts law for five centuries. The reasons why it was ultimately superseded are implicit in Bartolus' commentary. The spheres of application of conflicting statutes cannot be resolved by their pretensions; therefore, the method necessarily involved recourse to fluctuating formalistic and equitable considerations on which the doctors disagreed in concrete cases. By the sixteenth century, d'Argentré observed that the subject had become so complicated with divergent scholastic distinctions, opinions, and precedents that confused masters left their readers more confused.

Hessel E. Yntema, *The Historic Bases of Private International Law*, 2 AM. J. COMP. L. 297, 304 (1953).

[42] The idea that by choosing the law applicable to a controversy, the parties would choose the judge with jurisdiction over the parties and the case, is very old. Around the fourth century B.C.,

England, but also true in any conflict between civil and ecclesiastical courts. In fact, no civil court would have taken jurisdiction of a case against a cleric or a case involving marriage and then apply canon law, nor would an ecclesiastical court have heard a case of novel disseisin. Less obviously, a manorial court would not have applied the common law, which in England was tied to the system of royal writs.[43] Therefore, the origins of choice of law rules tell us much about the origins of choice of jurisdiction.

After all, jurisdictional law and choice of law are branches of conflict of laws, and although authors often forget this and treat jurisdictional law as a separate and independent doctrine, the opposite is true.[44] When conflict of laws rules were first adopted and used, these rules used the same connecting factors to identify both the law applicable to a controversy and the judge with jurisdiction over the controversy and the parties. This approach to conflict of laws rules proved successful and efficient. A joint study and analysis of choice of law and jurisdictional law and their origins and evolutions helps us better identify the flaws that have developed over the years, think about the reasons why they have developed, and formulate hypotheses for reform.

ROMAN AND AMERICAN CONFLICT OF LAWS RULES SHARE RELEVANT ROOTS

Roman conflict of laws – from which civil law derives – and American conflict of laws share some relevant roots. For example, the Justinian Code provided the maxim *actor sequitur forum rei*,[45] thus anticipating the decision in *Milliken v. Meyer*, according to which the courts of the place where the defendant

contracts between Egyptians and Greeks contained "implicit choice-of-law rule[s]" and "[s]pecifying language as the pertinent connecting factor for jurisdictional purposes, it recognized the principle of party autonomy: by choosing the idiom, the parties could select the court and thus, indirectly, the applicable law." JUENGER, *supra note 37, at 8. Likewise, when the Germanic tribes invaded Rome, they blended the Roman law with their own customary laws, and inhabitants of Rome continued to be ruled under Roman law while the "barbarians" were ruled by their own law. When conflicts arose over which law to apply, the parties would make a* professio iuris: *"[A] declaration originally meant to evidence the parties' ethnicity ... by professing to belong to a particular ethnic group, a party could in effect stipulate the law it wished to govern."* Id. *at 10.*

43 In England, after 1066, the church had exclusive authority over ecclesiastical matters and "manorial courts ... dealt with the peasants who worked monastic and other ecclesiastical lands." *See* HUNT JANIN, MEDIEVAL JUSTICE: CASES AND LAWS IN FRANCE, ENGLAND AND GERMANY, 500–1500, at 69 (2004).

44 The other branch being recognition and enforcement of foreign judgments.

45 *See* CODE JUST. 3.19.3 (Valentinian, Theodosius & Arcadius 385), 3.13.2 (Diocletian & Maximian).

resides have personal jurisdiction over him.[46] Roman law also provided the concept of "limited jurisdiction," according to which the plaintiff could sue in tort at the place of wrongful conduct, bring contract claims at the place of contract execution or performance, and bring property right claims at the situs.[47] The same connecting factors were used to identify the law applicable to the controversy: courts usually applied the law of the place where the contract was entered into (*lex loci contractus*), the law of the place where the tort or the crime was committed (*lex loci delicti*), or the law of the place where the property in dispute was situated (*lex rei sitae*).[48]

As Professor Juenger observed, "[F]ourteen hundred years before *International Shoe*, the civil law, unhampered by constitutional doctrine and territorialist dogma, already premised jurisdiction on 'minimum contacts,' and this idea continues to inform current European jurisdictional law."[49] This is because, while most of American law derives from English common law, American conflict of laws rules derive from continental European law.[50] Additionally, as Professor Symeon Symeonides observed:

> It is therefore natural that, even after its formative period, American conflicts law continued to share some basic characteristics with its European counterpart. Indeed, until the middle of the twentieth century, the two systems shared the same general goals and followed similar methods. They aspired for international/interstate uniformity and "conflicts justice" and employed the same general methodology—multilateral selectivism—and the same basic choice-of-law syllogism consisting of characterization, localization, and application of the predesignated law, with *ordre public*[51] and *renvoi*[52] functioning as occasional exceptions.[53]

[46] 311 U.S. 457, 463–64 (1940).

[47] *See* Friedrich Juenger, *Judicial Jurisdiction in the United States and in the European Communities: A Comparison*, 82 MICH. L. REV. 1195, 1203–04 (1984).

[48] *See id.*

[49] *Id.* at 1204. In other words, despite what many authors and commentators still believe, European jurisdictional law is not based on a territorialist dogma; rather, it is premised on "minimum contacts" as much as American jurisdictional law is. *See* discussion *infra*.

[50] *See* SCOLES ET AL., *supra* note 35, at 18–19.

[51] *Ordre public* means "public order."

[52] *Renvoi*, a conflict of laws device, means "sending back." When *renvoi* is accepted as a valid conflict of laws device, it means that when the forum court's conflict of laws rules point to a law of another state as the one applicable to the controversy, they make reference to the entirety of that state's law, including that state's conflict of laws rules. If these rules point back to the forum court's law as the one applicable to the controversy, then this is the law that should apply, assuming the forum court recognizes *renvoi*.

[53] Symeonides, *supra* note 31, at 1744–45 (second emphasis added) (footnotes omitted).

At some point, however, the American and the continental European systems began diverging, or at least this is the idea that we must have had if we accepted the assumption that adopting a uniform convention on conflict of laws rules was utopian. The proposed Hague Convention on Jurisdiction and Recognition and Enforcement of Judgments – that is, an international convention that was supposed to harmonize two branches of conflict of laws – failed, allegedly due to irreconcilable differences existing between civil law and common law systems.[54] Perhaps a brief overview of a few civil law and common law countries considered to be fairly representative of the respective systems could help us understand whether this belief is well grounded and whether reasons exist to stop pursuing the original goal of harmonizing conflict of laws rules while preserving differences.

CHOICE OF LAW RULES

General Features of the Systems Under Consideration

The phrases "choice of law" and "conflict of laws" are often used interchangeably.[55] However, as clarified above, choice of law is only an area of conflict of laws, and choice of law rules identify, in cases of conflict between potentially applicable laws, the substantive law that should apply and govern a specific controversy.[56]

The following analysis focuses on the choice of law systems adopted by Italy, Germany, France, England (as well as some uniform choice of law rules adopted in Europe), and the United States, considering these systems as fairly representative of the civil law (Italian, German, and French) and common law (English and American) systems. Civil law systems come from Roman law, which first strongly influenced and shaped most of the European systems, and later influenced Latin America and some Asian countries (such as China and Japan). Common law began developing in England and was then adopted in the United States. Due to colonization and various dominations by common law countries such as England and the United States, the Philippines, the

[54] *See Convention on Choice of Court Agreements, Concluded 30 June 2005*, HAGUE CONF. ON PRIVATE INT'L L., www.hcch.net/upload/conventions/txt37en.pdf (last visited Jan. 18, 2012) [hereinafter *Convention on Choice of Court Agreements*]; *see also* THE HAGUE CONVENTION ON JURISDICTION AND JUDGMENTS (Andreas F. Lowenfeld & Linda J. Silberman eds., 2001) [hereinafter RECORDS].

[55] *See, e.g.*, Jeffrey M. Shaman, *The Vicissitudes of Choice of Law: The* Restatement *(First, Second) and Interest Analysis*, 45 BUFF. L. REV. 329 (1997).

[56] *See* discussion *supra*.

African and Asian parts of the British Commonwealth, South Africa, Liberia, Scotland, Sri Lanka, and Guyana were strongly affected by the common law system, but they were also influenced by the civil law system.[57]

ITALY

In Italy, the international private law is Law No. 218 of 31 May 1995 for the Reform of the Italian System of Private International Law (Italian PIL).[58] Choice of law rules are therefore codified, and case law does not create new rules, but merely interprets the existing rules. The Italian PIL contains more than forty articles dealing with choice of law. Chapter I contains the general provisions on applicable law, while the other chapters deal with capacity and rights of natural persons, companies, family relations, succession, property rights, and contractual and noncontractual obligations. The latter two are now regulated by Rome I and Rome II, respectively.[59] *Renvoi* is accepted (article 13 Italian PIL).[60] Therefore, if Italian courts find that the applicable law is that of a foreign state, they must determine whether the choice of law rules of the foreign law refer to the law of a different country. If this is the case, they have to apply the Italian law if the foreign law refers back to Italian law (*rinvio all'indietro*) or, when the choice of law rules designate the law of a third state (*rinvio altrove*), they have to apply the law of that third state if the law of that state accepts *renvoi*, that is, considers itself applicable in the particular case. After determining the applicable law, the Italian court can still refuse to apply it to the particular case if the result would be contrary to the *ordre public*, that is, a fundamental principle of Italian law (article 16 Italian PIL). The statute also recognizes the existence of mandatory rules of the *lex fori* that must be applied in all cases, even when the choice of law rules would designate a foreign law as the applicable law (article 17 Italian PIL).

As observed by Professors Tito Ballarino and Andrea Bonomi: "These rules require a different approach to conflicts issues. Here the judge does not have to determine the law applicable to a certain legal relationship, but to ask

[57] *See* UGO A. MATTEI ET AL., SCHLESINGER'S COMPARATIVE LAW 190–97 (7th ed. 2009). This analysis does not take into account the so-called "religious systems" (like the Islamic one) because, in those cases, there are too many variables to consider, and that analysis would exceed the scope of this work. However, with the premises made above, those systems could consider this analysis too.

[58] For more information on Italian private international law and transnational litigation, see SIMONA GROSSI, Italy, in Transnational Litigation: A Practitioner's Guide (Richard H. Kreindler et al., 2010).

[59] *See infra.*

[60] *See* Legge 31 Maggio 1995, n. 218 (It.).

whether the object and purpose (in other words, the policy) of the domestic rule imposes its application in the particular case."[61] This method is similar to the functional policy-oriented approach adopted in the United States under the influence of Professor David Currie's interest analysis[62]; however, it is limited to cases where an important interest of the forum is at stake.[63] Therefore, *ordre public* and rules of mandatory application function as occasional exceptions.

Some choice of law rules aim to achieve a particular substantive result that is the expression of a certain policy of the law of the forum. In this case, policy considerations influence the choice of the applicable law in order to ensure that a certain result is achieved. This is done through alternative connecting factors and optional rules. Alternative connecting factors are used to uphold the formal validity of certain activities like marriage, recognition of an illegitimate child, and testamentary wills, while optional rules are sometimes used to protect the party who is considered weaker in the legal relationship.[64] In all areas where the statute contains policy-oriented choice of law rules, it also makes exceptions to the general rule on *renvoi*, which could otherwise nullify the intent of the legislature in these circumstances.[65]

Most Italian choice of law rules can be regarded as "jurisdiction-selecting" rather than "result-selecting." This means that the court determines the applicable law without taking into account the contents of the law designated by the choice of law rules. However, the Italian choice of law rules become result-selecting when *ordre public* or a rule of mandatory application should apply. As observed by Ballarino and Bonomi:

> Codification of the rule of mandatory application, on the one hand, and the introduction of some result-oriented choice-of-law rules, on the other hand, are expressions of the "methodological pluralism" that constitutes one of the distinguishing characteristics of private international law in Europe in the

[61] Tito Ballarino & Andrea Bonomi, *The Italian Statute on Private International Law of* 1995, 2 Y.B. PRIVATE INT'L L. 99, 111 (2000).

[62] *See* discussion *infra*.

[63] *See* Ballarino & Bonomi, *supra* note 61, at 112.

[64] For instance, legitimacy and legitimation of children is governed, alternatively, by the national law of the child and its parents, whereby the law more favorable to the creation of a relation of kinship prevails.

[65] For instance, as far as legitimacy and legitimation are concerned, *renvoi* must be applied only if it promotes the policy underlying the choice of law rule, that is, if it leads to the application of a law that favors the establishment of the parental link. *See* Paolo Venturi, *Sul c.d. rinvio in favorem nel sistema italiano di diritto internazionale privato*, 35 RIVISTA DI DIRITTO INTERNAZIONALE PRIVATO E PROCESSUALE 525 (1999) (It).

> modern or rather post-modern era, as professors Jayme and Brilmayer would put it. This syncretism is generally considered a sign of maturity.[66]

Furthermore, the adoption of this method moves European private international law closer to American choice of law.[67] Foreign law is not considered as a "fact" that must be proved by the parties; rather, the judge is required to ascertain the content of foreign law ex officio. When doing so, the judge can use experts in the field.

GERMANY

In Germany, the statutory bases for the application of foreign substantive law are set forth in the Introductory Act to the Civil Code (German PIL).[68] Articles 3 to 38 of the German PIL form the foundation of German private international law. German choice of law rules are governed by black-letter rules and not by open-ended provisions indicating the considerations to be taken into account when deciding which law should govern the case. Like Italian courts, German courts may interpret rules governing private international law, but they are not free to change statutory provisions. *Renvoi* is accepted (article 4(I) German PIL), and when German conflict of laws rules identify a foreign law as the one applicable to a controversy, but this law manifestly violates German public policy, the foreign law is not applied, applied differently, or substituted by German domestic law (article 6 German PIL).[69]

German courts tend to refrain from using public policy as an "escape clause" to avoid the application of an otherwise applicable foreign law that would lead to a different result. This enhances predictability and reduces the chance of arbitrary decisions. As Professor P.B. Carter observed, public policy is an escape route from the application of the relevant choice of law rule, which denotes the shortcoming of choice of law rules.[70] In Italy and Germany, codification helped limit the use of public policy as an escape device.

[66] *See* Ballarino & Bonomi, *supra* note 61, at 112 (footnote omitted).

[67] *See* discussion *infra*.

[68] EINFÜHRUNGSGESETZES ZUM BÜRGERLICHEN GESETZBUCHE [EGBGB] [Introductory Act to the Civil Code], Sept. 21, 1994, BGBL. §§ 3-38 (Ger.).

[69] *Id.* $$ 4, 6.

[70] P.B. Carter, *The Rôle of Public Policy in English Private International Law*, 42 INT'L & COMP. L.Q. 1, 1 (1993). Carter also observes:

> Public policy historically has been, and continues to be today, only one of several fairly well-trodden escape routes. Others include contrived characterisation of an issue, (occasionally) misuse of the doctrine of *renvoi*, doctrinaire inhibitions about penal and revenue laws, the so-called "public law" mystique, and, of course, in modern times the

FRANCE

In contrast to Italy and Germany, France has no choice of law statute. The main source of choice of law rules is case law. Some of the case law solutions were adopted during the prerevolutionary time in order to solve conflicts among local customary laws in fields like succession and matrimonial property. Subsequent and more recent attempts to codify private international law were unsuccessful. First, the legislature introduced specific choice of law rules while reforming certain areas of domestic family law, and then the European Union adopted some EC Regulations that provided France with codified choice of law rules.[71] There is also, however, a general codified choice of law rule in France. The rule states, "Statutes relating to public policy and safety are binding on all those living in the territory. [Real estate located within the French territory is] governed by French law even when owned by aliens."[72]

As it happens, under the Italian and German PIL, *renvoi* is excluded by French private international law where its application would be inconsistent with the purposes underlying the conflicts rule. The French *Cour de Cassation* has held that the "escape device" of public policy should be invoked when the foreign law is found to offend "principles of universal justice deemed of absolute international value by common French opinion."[73] Following an approach that resembles Currie's "governmental interest analysis," a foreign law may also be set aside by French law because it is incompatible with the French legislative policy on the matter, at least when the case has specific contacts with the forum.[74] When refusing to apply a foreign law due to a public policy issue, a French court must consider the intensity of the policy underlying the competing French rule, or the significance of the controversy's connecting factors with France, or both, thus combining considerations of policy and contacts with considerations pertaining to the content of the foreign law (a result-selecting approach).[75]

> elaborate pseudo-methodological pantomime of governmental interest analysis. As contrasted with some of these other routes public policy may be seen as having the disadvantageous merit of being blatantly frank and obvious.

Id. at 2–3.

[71] EC Regulations are immediately applicable in each Member State, while European directives are implemented by all Member States through enactment of national legislation, which must reflect the directive but may be interpreted by each Member State. *See* discussion *infra*.

[72] CODE CIVIL [C. CIV.] art. 3 (Fr.).

[73] INTRODUCTION TO FRENCH LAW 455 (George A. Bermann & Etienne Picard eds., 2008).

[74] *See* discussion *infra*.

[75] This happens, for instance, in maintenance obligations.

Although the application of domestic laws to transnational situations should be the exception and not the rule, the opposite is happening in France, because French courts are increasingly applying domestic rules rather than foreign rules that might otherwise be applicable, based on the legislature's assumed intent and without any reference to the normally applicable bilateral choice of law rule.[76] Such "mandatory rules" are referred to in French law as laws of "immediate application" or *lois de police*, under article 3, paragraph 1 of the French Civil Code.[77] The scope of these rules as well as the circumstances under which they should apply are very uncertain and unpredictable.

ENGLAND

Before the beginning of the seventeenth century, English common law courts exclusively applied English law to controversies, ignoring any foreign element that these controversies involved. English choice of law rules were introduced in the early years of the seventeenth century, when English courts had to face conflict issues, specifically those involving the courts of common law and the courts of equity, conflicts between custom and statute, statute and precedent, and general and local custom.[78] At that time, a body of uniform choice of law rules finally developed in England.[79]

The most significant sources of the English choice of law rules are statutes, decisions of the courts, and opinions of jurists. However, statutes are the most important source. Various connecting factors have been adopted to identify the applicable laws, which more or less resemble those adopted by the other European systems.[80]

English use of public policy as an escape device is rare when compared to the French use of public policy.[81] This approach has been considered a

[76] INTRODUCTION TO FRENCH LAW, *supra* note 73, at 456.

[77] Article 3, paragraph 1 of the French Civil Code provides that statutes relating to public policy and safety are binding on all those living in the territory. CODE CIVIL [C. CIV.] art. 3 (Fr.).

[78] For the origins of conflict of laws in the United Kingdom, see generally KIRSTY J HOOD, CONFLICT OF LAWS WITHIN THE UK (2007).

[79] Common law and equity were brought to America by the colonists. This body of law did not vary among the colonies to which the colonists took such laws. Thus, there were originally no differences between the laws of Virginia and Massachusetts, New York and Connecticut, or Pennsylvania and Maryland, and, on the face of it, there were no conflict of laws issues. The only significant conflict of laws issue that existed at that time was the conflict among different jurisdictions. *See* HOOD, *supra* note __.

[80] *See* discussion *infra*.

[81] However, public policy has played a substantial role in the area of recognition of foreign judgments. *See* Carter, *supra* note 70, at 1.

consequence of the "*forum*-orientated bias which is built into many English choice of law rules" rather than of any "inter-nationalist" attitude on the part of English courts.[82] In other words, because English internal law should apply on several occasions – for example, in family matters like divorce, voidability of marriage, judicial separation, adoption, and maintenance – there is no need to refer to public policy to avoid the application of a foreign law.[83] Similarly, public policy rarely comes into play in tort actions. English law provides that there is no action in tort unless the tort is actionable under English domestic law.[84] On the other hand, in the area of commercial contracts, where English choice of law rules are more "internationalist," public policy is often invoked with regard to choice of law.[85]

UNITED STATES

In the United States, choice of law rules are judge-made law to which various approaches have been suggested and adopted throughout the years.[86] The first approach to choice of law issues was the traditional "vested rights" approach proposed by the Restatement (First) of Conflict of Laws (First Restatement).[87] Under this approach, the law of the state in which the parties' rights "vested," that is, were created, had to apply to any given case.[88] This approach was abandoned and substituted by the "most significant relationship" approach introduced by the Restatement (Second) of Conflict of Laws (Second Restatement), according to which the law of the state having the most significant relationship to the parties and the transaction in light of the particular issues applies.[89] This approach ends up being not so different from the vested rights approach or from the approach originally adopted and still present in Europe.

The European and the American approaches to conflict of laws seemed to diverge when American courts started following Currie's approach, the so-called "governmental interest analysis."[90] Under this approach, when determining which law to apply to the controversy, the court should consider the

82 *Id.* at 3.

83 In these cases, choice of law rules in other countries would call for the application of the foreign *lex causae*.

84 *See* Carter, *supra* note 70, at 3.

85 *See Id.*

86 For a comprehensive description of American conflict of laws, on which this work is also based, see DAVID P. CURRIE ET AL., CONFLICT OF LAWS: CASES-COMMENTS-QUESTIONS (8th ed., 2010).

87 *See* RESTATEMENT (FIRST) OF CONFLICT OF LAWS (1934).

88 *See generally* CURRIE ET AL., *supra* note 86 (examining American conflict of law rules).

89 RESTATEMENT (SECOND) OF CONFLICT OF LAWS § 145 (1971).

90 *See* CURRIE ET AL., *supra* note 86.

underlying policies of the states involved and the interest of the states in furthering those policies. This is because Currie believed that the forum courts were instruments of state policy; thus, they had to apply forum laws whenever legitimate interests were present. Once the policies are defined, the court should determine which state has the strongest interest in applying its own law to the specific issue. If the court finds that only one of two or more states with allegedly conflicting laws has a legitimate interest in applying its law, then a "false conflict" exists, and the court should apply the law of the interested state.[91] Conversely, where more than one state has a legitimate interest in having its law applied to the issue and the laws of the interested states conflict, then there is a "true conflict," and various methods can apply to identify the applicable law.[92]

American courts, most of which have adopted the most significant relationship approach, have abandoned the traditional vested rights approach.[93] The most significant relationship approach is more flexible and takes into account the fact that controversies may give rise to different issues, each of which relates to a different state and a different substantive law – considerations which a "single contact" approach would not be able to consider. This approach is also referred to as the "center of gravity" approach, which was developed in *Babcock v. Jackson*.[94] In that case, plaintiffs and defendants were from New York. They took a trip to Ontario, where an accident occurred. Instead of applying Ontario

[91] *Id.*

[92] Professor David Currie suggests that, in this case, the court should recognize the interests of the forum by applying its own law, even though this would defeat the interests of the other states involved. Applying the forum non conveniens doctrine, the forum should dismiss the case. Otherwise, the forum should apply the law of one of the interested states, choosing the applicable law by: (1) considering which law is better or sounder or (2) considering which law most resembles its own. There may also be a case where neither the forum nor the other states involved have an interest in applying their respective law, the so-called "unprovided case." In this case, Professor Currie suggests four possible solutions: (1) apply the law of that state providing the better solution to the underlying social and economic problems; (2) protect the local defendant against the claims of foreign plaintiffs; (3) reach the same result as in (2) by applying a more sophisticated rule that would treat foreign plaintiffs as they would be treated in their home states; or (4) apply the law of the forum, because application of another state's law is not justified. Professor Currie prefers the fourth alternative. Professor Lawrence Baxter suggests another approach, which is to run a "comparative impairment" analysis, through which a federal court would assume jurisdiction in cases of true conflict and would apply the law of the state whose underlying policies would be most impaired if its laws were not applied to resolve the case. Baxter believes that if neither of the two conflicting states could resolve the conflict, but if an impartial federal court could do so, Currie's solution of having each state apply its own law could be avoided. Professor Robert Leflar proposes the "better law" approach, which rejects rules and formulas, and selects the better law on the basis of particular considerations.

[93] This approach is the one adopted by the Second Restatement. *See* RESTATEMENT (SECOND) OF CONFLICT OF LAWS § 145 (1971); discussion *infra*.

[94] 191 N.E.2d 279 (N.Y. 1963).

law – which denied recovery – as the vested-rights approach suggested, the New York court applied New York law, considering that the parties were from New York and that the trip began and would end in New York. Thus New York was the place where the parties' relationship was centered. In other words, the most significant contacts had to be traced to New York.[95]

On the other hand, in *Dym v. Gordon*, the court adopted the governmental interest analysis approach.[96] In that case, two students from New York, while attending the University of Colorado, went on a trip together and were involved in an accident. One was driving; the other was a passenger. The passenger claimed that the driver's negligence caused the accident, and she sued the driver before a New York court. Colorado law permitted recovery only for "willful and wanton" behavior by the driver.[97] The New York court held that because the most significant contacts were with Colorado, Colorado law applied.[98] Another reason the New York court applied Colorado law was because New York's public policy gave high priority to claims of innocent third-party victims.[99]

Usually, courts adopting the Second Restatement approach identify the state with the most significant relationship with reference to a "governmental interest," thus combining the two approaches. Therefore, despite the original intent of the Second Restatement, uniformity and predictability of outcomes seem hard to achieve because different courts may reach different conclusions regarding what is significant or not in light of underlying public policies.

In recent years, legal scholars have suggested other approaches to choice of law rules, but these approaches lend themselves to the same critiques applicable to the governmental interest analysis approach.[100] American choice of

[95] *Id.* at 284–85.

[96] 209 N.E.2d 792 (N.Y. 1965), *overruled in part by* Tooker v. Lopez, 249 N.E.2d 394 (N.Y. 1969).

[97] *Id.* at 793.

[98] *Id.* at 797.

[99] *Id.* at 796.

[100] Professors Arthur von Mehren and Donald Trautman, as well as Professor Russell Weintraub, proposed the adoption of a "functional analysis" approach, which substitutes the term "concerned jurisdiction" for "interested state" under the governmental interest approach. *See, e.g.*, Arthur T. von Mehren & Donald T. Trautman, *Jurisdiction to Adjudicate: A Suggested Analysis*, 79 HARV. L. REV. 1121 (1966). The forum should locate concerned jurisdictions, identify the "predominantly concerned jurisdiction," and apply the law of that state to the particular issue in question. In the absence of a predominantly concerned jurisdiction, this approach requires the forum to "weigh" the status of the conflicting laws, considering the policies behind the laws in terms of both their effectiveness and current trends in the law. Professor Weintraub's approach follows governmental analysis up to the point of a "true conflict," when he then proposes a rational solution based on the underlying policies of the interested states and general trends in the law. *See, e.g.*, Russell J. Weintraub, *Interest Analysis*

law rules today are somewhat chaotic. As illustrated above, there are different approaches to choice of law rules, such that the same case tried in two different states might have different choice of law rules applied and therefore have quite different substantive rules applied.[101] Furthermore, the Second Restatement principles are, in practical application, extremely manipulable and therefore nonuniform in application. Also, the states have very little control over choice of law rules through constitutional due process.[102]

COMMONALITIES BETWEEN EUROPEAN AND AMERICAN CHOICE OF LAW SYSTEMS

The preceding analysis of the general features of the systems under consideration shows that these systems share many similarities. As far as codification is concerned, the Italian, German, and English systems have codified choice of law provisions.[103] Although France is a civil law system – code-based by definition – in the past, French choice of law rules were mainly found in case law. However, with the adoption of EC Regulations governing choice of law, today France also has codified choice of law rules. The American legal system does not have binding codified choice of law provisions; however, by following the Second Restatement, American courts and the American legal system in general show an interest in "systematization," suggesting that codification would not be unacceptable to the United States. Furthermore, by applying various methods to identify the applicable substantive law, both the European and the American choice of law rules adopt a "methodological pluralism," which ensures flexibility and fairness.

The most significant relationship approach adopted by the American courts is very similar to the European courts' approach if one only considers that what renders a relationship among the controversy, the parties, and a specific place "most significant" is the presence of connecting factors tying that controversy and the parties to a specific place.[104] After all, these connecting

in the Conflict of Laws as an Application of Sound Legal Reasoning, 35 MERCER L. REV. 629 (1984).

[101] *See* Herma Hill Kay, *Theory into Practice: Choice of Law in the Courts*, 34 MERCER L. REV. 521, 591–92 (1983) (listing the states that apply different systems of choice of law rules).

[102] But see *Phillips Petroleum Co. v. Shutts*, 472 U.S. 797 (1985), for one of the very few cases where the United States Supreme Court has applied the due process clause to limit the ability of a state to apply its own law to a dispute.

[103] It is worth noting that, as observed above, the English legal system is a common law system, which traditionally considers case law as the main source of law. However, in England, the main sources of choice of law rules are statutes.

[104] As observed by Friedrich K. Juenger:

factors do not – and cannot – vary substantially from system to system, because the underlying goal is to make the applicable law predictable to the parties. Most of the time, whenever a choice of law needs to be made, courts apply the law of the place where the contract is made, the law of the place where the tort is committed, or the law of the place where the property in dispute is situated.[105] This is the law of the place that is "most significantly" or substantially connected to the case.

All the civil law and common law systems consider "public policy" as an exception to the application of foreign law – that is, as an "escape device."[106] The American governmental interest analysis, despite its name, is quite similar to the European public policy analysis. The only difference between the two approaches lies in the extent to which the government's interest, forum's interest, or public policy is used to prevent the application of an otherwise applicable foreign law that would lead to a different result. France and the United States, however, appear to rely on the escape device more so than other systems.

> The European panelists have given us an ambivalent answer to the question whether American conflicts learning can be exported to their shores. On the one hand, they tell us that there has been no "Americanization" of European conflicts law. But in the same breath they give us many examples of European conflicts developments that look distinctly American. For example, analogues to the Second Restatement's "most significant relationship" formula are found in the conflicts statute of Austria, the Swiss draft, and in a European draft convention. Also, Common Market nations have emulated American practice by combining what we would call full faith and credit with a long-arm statute to produce the Brussels Convention on Jurisdiction and Enforcement of Civil and Commercial Judgments.
>
> Family law, too, affords good illustrations of European conflicts ideas that parallel our own...
>
> Despite such striking parallels, the European panelists deny the Americanization of their conflicts law.

Friedrich K. Juenger, *American and European Conflicts Law*, 30 AM. J. COMP. L. 117, 117–18 (1982) (footnotes omitted).

105 *See* discussion *supra*, **Romanist Origins**, 113 f.

106 CODE CIVIL [C. CIV.] art. 3 (Fr.); EGBGB § 6 (Ger.); Legge 31 Maggio 1995, n. 218, arts. 16–17. See also discussion *supra* Part IV.A.4-5 for the English and American approaches, respectively. Choice of law analyses always considered public policies. Since the origins of conflict of laws in the twelfth century, codified connecting factors were applied unless *justice* demanded otherwise. However, in all these contexts, public policy considerations made in the interest of justice were only the exception, not the rule. Professor Currie's idea that courts are instruments of state policy and, thus, they should apply forum laws whenever there are legitimate interests, necessarily leads to different results and disuniformity and runs against the idea of harmonization and with Savigny's theory, according to which the main goal of private international law is international (or interstate) uniformity of choice of law decisions, regardless of where litigation occurs.

In any event, the existing similarities among these systems' choice of law rules and approaches outweigh their differences. By focusing on the predominating similarities, this analysis intends to prove that harmonization of choice of law and, more broadly, conflict of laws rules is possible. Despite the apparently different approaches adopted by the various systems, the outcomes are similar. Perhaps it is because, notwithstanding the different paths or labels adopted by the legislatures, scholars, and judges, choice of law rules cannot totally depart from their original goals of uniformity and adherence to due process.[107]

Given the limited scope of this work, this analysis will not consider each and every single choice of law problem in the systems considered. Instead, it will focus on a few areas and issues that might arise in the context of transnational litigation on civil and commercial matters. The preceding overview of the main features of the five countries here considered should provide some preliminary ideas of the approaches used by these systems, as well as the bases to better understand the following analysis, which intends to further support the thesis that harmonization of conflict of laws rules is possible.

A FEW CHOICE OF LAW RULES THAT MIGHT BE HARMONIZED

As indicated above, while American choice of law rules have not been codified, the vast majority of American courts tend to follow, interpret, and apply the Second Restatement uniformly. Most of the European Union Member States's choice of law rules have been codified but not harmonized; however, European choice of law rules dealing with contractual and noncontractual obligations have been harmonized through the adoption of European Regulations.[108] This means that whenever a controversy concerning contract or torts issues involves parties from different European countries, the harmonized rules will apply rather than the Member States's domestic choice of law rules.[109] The analysis that follows focuses on European and American choice of law rules governing contracts and torts.

CONTRACTUAL OBLIGATIONS

Controversies on contractual obligations pending between citizens of different European Union Member States are governed by Council Regulation 593/2008

[107] *See* discussion *supra*.

[108] *See* discussion *infra*.

[109] It is interesting to see how, despite language barriers and the differences existing in the European conflict of laws systems, EU Member States were still able to reach a consensus on a set of uniform conflict of laws rules.

of the European Parliament and of the Council of 17 June 2008 on the Law Applicable to Contractual Obligations (Rome I), which replaced the original 1980 Rome Convention.[110] The Regulation applies only to "civil and commercial matters"; that is, it does not apply to revenue, customs, and administrative matters, or matrimonial and family relationships.[111]

The central feature of the system established by the Regulation is the principle of freedom of choice, according to which the parties to a contract are free to choose the law applicable to it. Where the parties have not determined the applicable law, the law of the country with which the contract has the closest connection governs.[112] The contract is presumed to be connected with the country where the party who will perform the characteristic performance habitually resides.[113]

[110] Council Regulation 593/2008, on the Law Applicable to Contractual Obligations (Rome I), 2008 O.J. (L 177) (EC) [hereinafter Rome I], available at http://eur-lex.europa.eu/LexUriServ/LexUriServ.do?uri=OJ:L:2008:177:0006:01:EN:HTML. The 1980 Convention was not applicable to the ten Member States who joined the Union in 2004, and it was necessary to have a proper Community instrument – that is, an EC Regulation automatically applicable in all Member States – rather than an international agreement applicable to only some Member States.

[111] *Id.* art. 1; *see also supra.*

[112] This formula resembles the Second Restatement's most significant relationship formula.

[113] Generally, the decision on who renders the characteristic performance must be taken in regard to the center of gravity of the various parts of the contract. According to the Council Report on the Convention on the Law Applicable to Contractual Obligations:

> [T]he characteristic performance defines the connecting factor of the contract from the inside, and not from the outside by elements unrelated to the essence of the obligation such as the nationality of the contracting parties or the place where the contract was concluded.
>
> In addition it is possible to relate the concept of characteristic performance to an even more general idea, namely the idea that [t]his performance refers to the function which the legal relationship involved fulfils in the economic and social life of any country. The concept of characteristic performance essentially links the contract to the social and economic environment of which it will form a part.

Council Report on the Convention on the Law Applicable to Contractual Obligations, 1980 O.J. (C 282) 1, 20 (by Mario Giuliano & Paul Lagarde). However, as observed by Mireille M.M. van Eechoud:

> The latter part of the above quote seems to imply that policies of substantive law play a role in determining the characteristic performance and therefore in determining the law applicable to a contract. However, the doctrine of characteristic performance entails the categorisation of different types of contracts and the determination of a (standard) connecting factor for each, with little or no consideration for the actual social or economic function of the various contracts.
>
> As in modern societies the counter-performance in many contracts is the payment of a sum of money, such payment is not regarded as the characteristic performance…

In the absence of the parties' choice as to the applicable law, article 4(1) of Rome I dictates that the law governing the contract is for contracts for the sale of goods, the law of the country where the seller has his habitual residence; for contracts for the provision of services, the law of the country where the service provider habitually resides; for contracts relating to a right in rem in immovable property or to a tenancy of immovable property, the law of the country where the property is situated; for franchise contracts, the law of the country where the franchisee habitually resides; for distribution contracts, the law of the country where the distributor habitually resides, etc.[114] However, when it is clear from all the circumstances of the case that the contract is manifestly more closely connected with a country other than the one indicated above, the law of that other country shall apply.[115] Additionally, when the law applicable to the contract cannot be determined by the rules stated above, the law of the country to which the contract is most closely connected shall govern.[116] Other special provisions identify the law applicable to other specific types of contracts (for example, employment contracts, consumer contracts, and insurance contracts). This approach closely resembles the American approach in the Second Restatement.[117]

> Identification of the characteristic performance then also becomes easy: this lies with the party that sells property, or takes on the obligation to do work, or transport goods, etc.

MIREILLE M.M. VAN EECHOUD, CHOICE OF LAW IN COPYRIGHT AND RELATED RIGHTS: ALTERNATIVES TO THE LEX PROTECTIONIS 198 (2003) (footnote omitted).

114 Rome I, *supra* note 110, art. 4.

115 *Id.*

116 *Id.*

117 Interestingly, recital 19 to the Regulation provides:

> Where there has been no choice of law, the applicable law should be determined in accordance with the rule specified for the particular type of contract. Where the contract cannot be categorised as being one of the specified types or where its elements fall within more than one of the specified types, it should be governed by the law of the country where the party required to effect the characteristic performance of the contract has his habitual residence. In the case of a contract consisting of a bundle of rights and obligations capable of being categorised as falling within more than one of the specified types of contract, the characteristic performance of the contract should be determined having regard to its *centre of gravity*.

Id. recital 19 (emphasis added). Recital 21 also provides:

> In the absence of choice, where the applicable law cannot be determined either on the basis of the fact that the contract can be categorised as one of the specified types or as being the law of the country of habitual residence of the party required to effect the characteristic performance of the contract, the contract should be governed by the law of the country with which it is *most closely connected*. In order to determine that country, account should be taken, *inter alia*, of whether the contract in question has a very close relationship with another contract or contracts.

Id. recital 21 (first emphasis added).

In the United States, section 186 of the Second Restatement provides, "Issues in contract are determined by the law chosen by the parties in accordance with the rule of §187 and otherwise by the law selected in accordance with the rule of §188."[118] Similar to Rome I, the Second Restatement provides the parties with the power to select the law applicable to their contract. Only when the parties have not exercised this power does §188 apply. Section 188 identifies a series of connecting factors that can be used to identify such law.

In particular, the first paragraph of section 188 of the Second Restatement provides that "[t]he rights and duties of the parties with respect to an issue in contract are determined by the local law of the state which, with respect to that issue, has the *most significant relationship* to the transaction and the parties under the principles stated in §6."[119] Then, the second paragraph lists the relevant connecting factors in the absence of the parties' choice. The list includes "(a) the place of contracting, (b) the place of negotiation of the contract, (c) the place of performance, (d) the location of the subject matter of the contract, and (e) the domicil[e], residence, nationality, place of incorporation and place of business of the parties."[120]

American courts usually apply these principles, following the "center of gravity" and "most significant relationship" approaches.[121] Under the center of gravity approach, the various contacts in the case are considered so that the law of the place where there is a preponderance of contacts will be applied.[122] Under the most significant relationship approach, the above connecting factors should identify the place that is most significantly related to the controversy.[123] This is exactly what happens in Rome I, which looks at the country with which the contract has the closest connection in order to identify the law applicable to the contract, absent the parties' choice.[124]

However, American courts following the Second Restatement generally identify the state with the most significant relationships not only by looking at the "specific contacts" but also by considering the interests of the states involved. In other words, starting from the assumption that choice of law problems should be considered in light of underlying policies – that is, purposes or functions of the laws of the involved states and the respective interests of those states in furthering such policies – courts identify the law applicable to the controversy by considering these policies. The forum court

118 RESTATEMENT (SECOND) OF CONFLICT OF LAWS § 186 (1971).
119 *Id.* § 188 (emphasis added).
120 *Id.*
121 *See* discussion *supra.*
122 *Id.*
123 *Id.*
124 Rome I, *supra* note 110.

will then consider the contacts and interests of each state involved and apply the law of the state having the most significant relationship with the parties and the transaction in light of the particular issue before the court. Other modern decisions have adopted the governmental interest approach to choice of law, in which the forum applies its own law if it has an interest in doing so.

This seems to set the American approach apart from the European one. However, as explained above, this is not true for several reasons. First, the states most likely to be interested in the outcome of a given case dealing with contract issues are those presenting one of the above listed contacts with the parties' transaction. These are the states having the closest connection with the contract, or the states having a fundamental (exceptional) public policy that might be affected by certain outcomes of the case. Second, European conflict of laws rules also consider public policy issues.[125] When the law identified as applicable to the contract dispute conflicts with a fundamental public policy, the latter is enforced and the conflicting law does not apply. In any event, good conflict of laws rules should be drafted in such a way that there is no need to make public policy considerations to avoid unwanted results, unless rare and exceptional circumstances occur.[126]

The general idea behind both the European and the American choice of law rules governing contract disputes is the same: the choice of the parties should prevail, and where the parties have not exercised their power to choose, the contract will be subject to the law of the place that is most significantly "related" or "connected" to the contract. In addition, public policy issues are – or should be – taken into account only when they really pertain to a fundamental public policy that needs to be preserved.

One would then begin to wonder whether it would be useful to engage in the process of harmonizing rules that, after all, are quite similar. The problem with the lack of uniform rules is the unpredictability of outcomes. Even if most of the time the outcome of the controversy should be the same, it may not be. Thus, uniform rules would reduce unpredictability and favor efficiency.

[125] *See, e.g.*, CODE CIVIL [C. CIV.] art. 3 (Fr.); EGBGB § 6 (Ger.); Legge 31 Maggio 1995, n. 218, arts. 16–17. Recital 37 of Rome I also provides:

> Considerations of public interest justify giving the courts of the Member States the possibility, in exceptional circumstances, of applying exceptions based on public policy and overriding mandatory provisions. The concept of "overriding mandatory provisions" should be distinguished from the expression "provisions which cannot be derogated from by agreement" and should be construed more restrictively.

Rome I, *supra* note 110, recital 37. Also, article 21 provides, "The application of a provision of the law of any country specified by this Regulation may be refused only if such application is manifestly incompatible with the public policy (*ordre public*) of the forum." *Id.* art. 21.

[126] *See* discussion *infra*.

An example might better clarify this. A seller from California enters into a contract with a French buyer; the contract is to be performed in New York. The parties do not choose the law applicable to this contract. The seller performs the contract but the buyer fails to pay; the seller then files a suit before a California state court for breach of contract. The California judge, applying California choice of law rules and following section 188 of the Second Restatement, might decide that California law applies, because California is the state where the seller is domiciled and California has an interest in protecting its sellers. This result would be consistent with the applicable European rules.[127] But what if the California seller sues the French buyer before a New York judge? This judge, following section 188 of the Second Restatement, might decide that New York law should apply because New York was the place of performance and because New York has an interest in the dispute and in applying its own law because it must ensure investments and business relationships that occur within the state are honored.

In this case, despite the original similarities between the American and the European choice of law rules, the differences prevail and the outcome of the litigation might be different. Uniform rules would avoid nonuniformity of outcomes and enhance predictability, fairness, and efficiency by identifying a limited number of connecting factors, allowing the judge to disregard them and apply a different law only when the identified law conflicts with a fundamental public policy of the forum or when the contract is manifestly more substantially connected with another country whose law should apply. Uniform rules would indicate the law to apply in transnational litigation on civil and commercial matters, leaving little room for a governmental interest analysis. That analysis would potentially come into play under exceptional circumstances only.

NONCONTRACTUAL OBLIGATIONS

In Europe, Council Regulation 864/2007 of the European Parliament and of the Council of 11 July 2007 on the Law Applicable to Non-Contractual Obligations (Rome II) contains the choice of law rules applicable to noncontractual obligations in civil and commercial matters, including product

[127] Article 4(1) of Rome I provides:

> To the extent that the law applicable to the contract has not been chosen in accordance with Article 3 and without prejudice to Articles 5 to 8, the law governing the contract shall be determined as follows . . . a contract for the sale of goods shall be governed by the law of the country where the seller has his habitual residence.

Rome I, *supra* note 110, art. 4(1).

liability, *negotiorum gestio* (activities carried on by someone relating to the affairs of somebody else, in the interest of the latter), and *culpa in contrahendo* (noncontractual obligations arising out of dealings that precede the conclusion of a contract).[128]

As Rome I harmonizes the Member States's choice of law rules dealing with contractual obligations, Rome II harmonizes the Member States's choice of law rules governing noncontractual obligations so that, no matter where in the European Union a noncontractual action is brought, the rules determining the applicable law will always be the same. Rome II is of universal application, that is, the law specified is applied whether or not it is the law of a Member State.[129]

As a general rule, and in order of priority, the law applicable to noncontractual obligations is (1) the law of the country where the damage occurs (principle of territoriality), (2) the law of the country where both parties habitually resided when the damage occurred, and (3) the law of the country with which the case is manifestly more closely connected than the other countries.[130] However, article 4 of Rome II also authorizes the parties to choose, by mutual agreement, the law applicable to their obligation. The agreement may also be entered into after the event giving rise to the damage takes place, or, when all the parties to the agreement are pursuing commercial activity, may be freely negotiated before the event giving rise to the damage takes place.[131] The choice must be explicit or evident from the circumstances and must not prejudice the rights of any third party. In any event, when all the elements relevant to the situation relate to a country other than the one chosen, the agreement by which the parties chose to apply a different law becomes invalid. Similarly, European Community law overrides the law of a non-EU country chosen by the parties when all the elements of the situation are located in one or more EU Member States.

[128] *See* Council Regulation 864/2007, on the Law Applicable to Non-Contractual Obligations (Rome II), 2007 O.J. (L 199) (EC) [hereinafter Rome II], *available at* http://eur-lex.europa.eu/LexUriServ/LexUriServ.do?uri=OJ:L:2007:199:0040:0040:EN:PDF. The Regulation does not apply to revenue, customs and administrative matters, the liability of the state, or matrimonial and family relationships. *See supra* text accompanying note 6.

[129] *See* Berthiaume v. Dastous (1929), [1930] 1 D.L.R. 849 (Can. Que.).

[130] According to Symeon Symeonides, Europeans do not accept Professor Currie's interest analysis. However, the drafters of choice of law rules should identify and resolve false conflicts, and this is what the drafters of Rome II have tried to do by adopting the common domicile rule. They recognized that in certain cases, the state of the tort has no claim to apply its law to a dispute that involves only codomiciliaries of another state. *See* Symeonides, *supra* note 31, at 1760–62.

[131] *See* Rome II, *supra* note 128, art. 14.

Rome II gives very limited recognition to the role of state interests, and its explanatory report explains most of its rules in terms of the parties' expectations. However, recital 32 in the preamble to the Regulation provides:

> Considerations of public interest justify giving the courts of the Member States the possibility, *in exceptional circumstances*, of applying exceptions based on public policy and overriding mandatory provisions. In particular, the application of a provision of the law designated by this Regulation which would have the effect of causing noncompensatory exemplary or punitive damages of an excessive nature to be awarded may, depending on the circumstances of the case and the legal order of the Member State of the court seised, be regarded as being contrary to the public policy (*ordre public*) of the forum.[132]

Furthermore, article 26 of the Regulation provides, "The application of a provision of the law of any country specified by this Regulation may be refused only if such application is *manifestly incompatible with the public policy* (*ordre public*) of the forum."[133] In other words, recourse to public policy to prevent the application of an otherwise applicable law must be made only under exceptional circumstances. This approach is not so different from the modern approach most American courts adopt.

In the United States, the original approach to torts was the traditional vested rights approach, which determined the existence of tort liability according to the law of the place of the wrong (*lex loci*).[134] The Second Restatement abandoned this approach and adopted the most significant relationship approach.[135] More specifically, the first paragraph of section 145 of the Second Restatement provides, "The rights and liabilities of the parties with respect to an issue in tort are determined by the local law of the state which, with respect to that issue, has the most significant relationship to the occurrence and the parties under the principles stated in §6."[136] The second paragraph of section 145 lists the contacts that can be taken into account to determine the applicable law. Such contacts include: "(a) the place where the injury occurred[;] (b) the place where the conduct causing the injury occurred[;] (c) the domicil[e], residence, nationality, place of incorporation and place of business of the parties[;] and (d) the place where the relationship, if any, between the parties is centered."[137] This is exactly what Rome II provides.[138] These

[132] *Id.* recital 32 (emphasis added).

[133] *Id.* art. 26 (emphasis added).

[134] *See* discussion *supra*.

[135] *See* discussion *supra*.

[136] RESTATEMENT (SECOND) OF CONFLICT OF LAWS § 145 (1971).

[137] *Id.*

[138] *See* discussion *supra*.

contacts should be evaluated according to their relative importance with respect to the particular issue, while also taking into account the interests of the states involved.[139]

Although in theory, the Second Restatement should have shifted from the old vested rights approach to a modern approach, which takes governmental interest into account and applies the law of the forum sometimes even when there is a true conflict, the reality is that the modern approach is not so different from the old vested rights approach of the First Restatement. Furthermore, American courts continue to apply the law of the state where the tort occurred in several patterns of tort conflicts, thus reaching the same result they would reach were they to follow the First Restatement.[140]

Therefore, the American and the European approaches also share important similarities concerning the law governing noncontractual obligations.[141] A recent study by Symeonides explained:

> [D]espite using different approaches and invoking varied rationales, [American] courts that have joined the revolution have reached fairly uniform results in resolving cross-border tort conflicts: they have applied the law of the state of either the injurious conduct or the resulting injury, but, in the vast majority of cases (86 percent), they have applied whichever of the two laws favored the tort victim. Another finding is that the vast majority of recent conflicts codifications around the world (a total of twenty) have adopted the same solution: they apply whichever law favors the victim, by authorizing either the court or the victim directly to make the choice.[142]

JURISDICTIONAL LAW

Brief overview of European jurisdictional law

Council Regulation 44/2001 of 22 December 2000 on Jurisdiction and the Recognition and Enforcement of Judgments in Civil and Commercial

[139] *See* RESTATEMENT (SECOND) OF CONFLICT OF LAWS § 145.

[140] In some other cases, American courts apply the law of the state of the conduct rather than the law of the state of the injury. *See* Symeonides, *supra* note 31, at 1746–47.

[141] Rome II was only recently adopted; therefore, it is too early to get significant empirical data concerning its application and the connecting factors that courts are applying. However, it would not be surprising to see that, in fact, European courts are mainly applying the law of the place where the wrong occurred when this is the law more favorable to the victim. This is consistent with Symeonides's study. *See id.* at 1764-68.

[142] Symeon C. Symeonides, Choice of Law in Cross-Border Torts 1 (Willamette Univ. Coll. of Law Working Paper Series, 2009), available at http://ssrn.com/abstract=1328191. According to Symeonides, the choice-of-law revolution that has taken place in the United States "succeeded in demolishing the old regime in forty-two U.S. jurisdictions, but failed to replace it with anything resembling a unified system." *Id.*

Matters (EC Regulation 44/2001) governs jurisdiction in Europe when parties are from different EU Member States.[143] EC Regulation 44/2001 contains various provisions identifying the judge with jurisdiction over specific cases, and it applies when the defendant is domiciled in a Member State of the European Union.[144] The Regulation aims to establish certain rules and to identify, with some level of certainty, the judge with jurisdiction over every case. This is why the Regulation does not adopt the doctrine of forum non conveniens,[145] which would require the courts to exercise their discretion to establish the convenience (or inconvenience) of the exercise of jurisdiction, thus making the identification of the "competent" judge uncertain, in contrast with the fundamental aim of the Regulation.[146] This Regulation, as well as Rome I and Rome II,[147] applies to civil and commercial matters.[148]

As a general rule of jurisdiction, persons domiciled in a Member State may be sued in the courts of that Member State, regardless of their nationality, subject to the rules of jurisdiction applicable to the nationals of that State (article 2).[149] The defendant's domicile is considered the preferred forum for legal disputes, and, as the European Court of Justice explained, this is because the defendant may defend himself more easily there. Accordingly, the criteria for special jurisdiction or the cases where the plaintiff may file the action before the court of the Member State where he is domiciled are exceptions and should be interpreted and applied narrowly.[150] Regardless of the defendant's domicile, the courts of the Member States where the property is located have exclusive jurisdiction over actions concerning rights in rem in real estate

[143] Council Regulation 44/2001 substituted the Brussels Convention on jurisdiction and the recognition and enforcement of judgment in civil and commercial matters of 1968. *See* Council Regulation 44/2001, *supra* note 6.

[144] *See id.* Therefore, it will not apply when the defendant is domiciled in the United States, but it will apply if a French national sues an Italian, or vice versa. In controversies involving non-Europeans, the EU Member States apply their national laws, that is, their conflict of laws rules, which are, most of the time, codified.

[145] This doctrine is not known to civil law systems. But see the discussion *infra* for further discussion on this point.

[146] *See* Case C-288/92, Custom Made Commercial Ltd. v. Stawa Metallbau GmbH, 1994 E.C.R. I-2913, 2956.

[147] *See* Rome I, *supra* note 110; Rome II, *supra* note 128; Council Regulation 44/2001, *supra* note 143.

[148] *See* Council Regulation 44/2001, *supra* note ___, art. 1; discussion *supra* __.

[149] Domicile is determined in accordance with the domestic law of the Member State where the matter is brought before a court. Legal persons or firms are considered domiciled in the state in which they have their statutory seat, central administration or principal place of business. *See* Council Regulation 44/2001, *supra* note 143; art. 60.

[150] Case C-26/91, Jakob Handte & Co. GmbH v. Traitements Mécano-chimiques des Surfaces SA, 1992 E.C.R. I-3967, 3995.

or tenancies of real estate.[151] Also, in matters relating to a contract, if the action may be combined with an action against the same defendant in matters relating to rights in rem in real estate, a person domiciled in a Member State may be sued in the court of the Member State in which the property is situated.[152]

The Regulation provides different rules of special jurisdiction, according to the type of controversy considered. In these cases, the person can also be sued at a place different from their domicile. However, as indicated above, these special jurisdiction criteria are exceptions to the general principle of domicile as the place where the defendant should be sued and should be interpreted and applied narrowly.[153]

In controversies "in matters relating to a contract," a person domiciled in a Member State may be sued in another Member State where the contract was performed or had to be performed.[154] The place of performance must be determined for each obligation separately, and the court must refer to the specific obligation object of the controversy.[155] If a claim is based on different obligations or causes of action, the main obligation determines the place of performance.[156] The place of performance should be determined according to the private law referred to by the choice of law rules of the forum, unless article 5(1)(b) of the Regulation applies.[157]

In order to identify the judge with jurisdiction over a case concerning contracts, EC Regulation 44/2001 uses very predictable connecting factors.[158] It is reasonable, and thus predictable, that a party to a contract can be sued before the court of the place where the contract was performed or was to be performed. This is the place to which the controversy arising out of the

[151] *See* Council Regulation 44/2001, *supra* note 6, art. 22. This idea resembles the idea of proper and exclusive venue for *local actions* in the United States, according to which actions concerning title or possession of real estate must be brought before the court of the place where that property is located.

[152] *See id.* art. 6. The location of the *res* also identifies the law applicable to the controversy dealing with real estates (*lex rei sitae*). *See* Rome I, *supra* note 110, art. 4.

[153] Case C-26/91, *Jakob Handte & Co.*, 1992 E.C.R. at I-3995.

[154] Council Regulation 44/2001, *supra* note 143, art. 5. In contracts for the sale of goods, unless where otherwise agreed, this is the place where the goods were delivered or should have been delivered; in the case of the provision of services, this is the place where the services were provided or should have been provided. *Id.*

[155] Case 14/76, Ets. A. de Bloos, S.P.R.L. v. Société en commandite par actions Bouyer, 1976 E.C.R. 1497.

[156] Case 266/85, Shenavai v. Kreischer, 1987 E.C.R. 239, 256.

[157] This is the so-called "Tessili Rule." *See* Case 12/76, Industrie Tessili Italiana Como v. Dunlop AG, 1976 E.C.R. 1473, 1485.

[158] *See* Council Regulation 44/2001, *supra* note 143, art. 5.

contract is more closely connected – that is, the place with which the controversy has "minimum" or better "substantial contacts." The plaintiff, therefore, is free to decide whether to sue the defendant in the place of the latter's domicile (general jurisdiction, general forum), or in the place where the contract was performed or was to be performed (alternative and specific forum).[159]

Likewise, in matters relating to torts, the person who is domiciled in a Member State can be sued in the courts of the place where the harmful event occurred or may occur under article 5 of the EC Regulation 44/2001.[160] This provision applies to all claims seeking to establish the liability of a defendant that does not arise out of a "matter relating to contract" within the meaning of article 5(1) of the Regulation.[161] This is because, under the principle of ubiquity, the claimant can choose between the courts of the place where the damage occurred and the courts of the place of the event giving rise to the damage. Damage under article 5(3) refers to the place where the tortious activity directly harmed the immediate victim of that event, as opposed to mere indirect consequences.[162]

159 This approach is consistent with the approach adopted by Rome I, which provides that in the absence of the parties' choice as to the law applicable to the contract, the contract is governed by the law of the country with which it has the closest connection. While Council Regulation 44/2001, in order to identify the judge with jurisdiction over the case, adopts a general formula – the judge of the place where the contract was performed or had to be performed – and Rome I adopts a more complex and detailed formula to identify the law applicable to contracts absent the parties' choice, the connecting factors that they respectively adopt to identify the judge with jurisdiction over the case or the law applicable to the contract are factors that tie the controversy to a specific place. *See* Rome I, *supra* note 110, art. 4; Council Regulation 44/2001, *supra* note 6, art. 5. The place where the contract was or had to be performed is often the place where the party who has to perform the contract resides and the place where the controversy occurs. Therefore, rather than having two different provisions – one to identify the judge with jurisdiction over the case, and another one to identify the applicable law – a single provision using the same reasonable criterion could be adopted for both tasks. "Substantial" contacts – the same contacts – between the controversy, the defendant, and the place should point at the competent judge and the applicable law.

160 *See* Council Regulation 44/2001, *supra* note 143, art. 5.

161 Case 189/87, Kalfelis v. Bankhaus Schröder, Münchmeyer, Hengst & Co., 1988 E.C.R. 5565, 5585, 5587.

162 Article 4 of Rome II provides that the law applicable to torts is: (1) the *law of the country where the damage occurs* (principle of territoriality), (2) the law of the country where both parties were habitually resident when the damage occurred, or (3) the law of the country with which the case is manifestly more closely connected than the other countries. The connecting factor used by Council Regulation 44/2001 to identify the competent judge – "place where the harmful event occurred or may occur" – is not different from the connecting factor used by Rome II to identify the law applicable to the contract – "the law of the country in which the damage occurs" – given that, under the principle of ubiquity, article 5 of Council Regulation 44/2001 gives the claimant the power to choose whether to sue the defendant before the court

These are only a few examples of the rules contained in EC Regulation 44/2001. All of them identify the judge with jurisdiction over cases on the basis of very clearly defined connecting factors; thus, very little room is left for judges to create "new" rules while purporting to interpret the existent ones. The defendant is therefore put on notice that the judge of the place where these connecting factors are located will be the one with jurisdiction over the case,[163] and most of the time, the place where the same connecting factors exist would also identify the applicable law.[164]

When the defendant is domiciled in a Member State of the European Union and proceedings involving the same cause of action[165] and the same parties (lis pendens) are brought before the courts of different Member States, any court other than the one where the action was first brought[166] *should*, sua sponte, stay the proceeding until the court where the action was brought first has declared its jurisdiction or lack of jurisdiction over the case. Once the court first seised declares that it has jurisdiction over the case, the other courts where the same case between the same parties was brought should decline jurisdiction in favor of the first court.[167]

of the place where the damage occurred or the court of the place of the event giving rise to the damage. Rome II, *supra* note 128, art. 4; Council Regulation 44/2001, *supra* note __, art. 5. Here, again, the adoption of two separate conventions is not the best solution. A single criterion connecting the controversy to a specific place should simultaneously identify the judge with jurisdiction over the case and the law applicable to it. This would render the handling of the controversy by the judge easier because the judge will, most of the time, be applying his own law. Alternative connecting factors would be adopted to make sure that justice prevails over formalistic results.

[163] See Council Regulation 44/2001, *supra* note 6, arts. 8–17, for jurisdiction in matters relating to insurance (articles 8–14) and for jurisdiction over consumer contracts (articles 15–17).

[164] The connecting factors used by the Council Regulation 44/2001 to identify the judge with jurisdiction over specific cases are often similar to the connecting factors used by Rome I and Rome II that identify, respectively, the law applicable to contractual obligations and the law applicable to noncontractual obligations. *See* discussion *supra*.

[165] The European Court of Justice has clarified that two proceedings involve the same cause of action when the same subject matter lies "at the heart of the two actions." Case 144/86, Gubisch Maschinenfabrik KG v. Palumbo, 1987 E.C.R. 4871, 4876.

[166] A court is considered as "first seised" at the time when the complaint (or an equivalent document) is filed with the court, or when the document should be first served and then filed with the court, at the time when it is received by the authority responsible for the service. *See* Council Regulation 44/2001, *supra* note 143, art. 30.

[167] *See id.* art. 27. In order to determine whether there is lis pendens, the court first seised should consider the facts and the rule of law relied on as the basis of the action, the aims of the action, and the object of the action. *See* Case C-406/92, Tatry v. Maciej Rataj, 1994 E.C.R. I-5439, 5475. On the other hand, the procedural positions of the parties as well as the grounds of defense raised by the defendant are not relevant. *See* Case C-111/01, Gantner Elec. GmbH v. Basch Exploitatie Maatschappij BV, 2003 E.C.R. I-4207, 4236. With reference to the requirement concerning parties' identity, in *Drouot Assurances SA v. Consolidated*

Also, the judge before whom an action related to another action is brought *may* stay the action. Actions are considered "related" when they are so closely connected that it is expedient to hear and determine them together in order to avoid the risk of irreconcilable judgments resulting from separate proceedings.[168] In making this discretionary determination, courts consider the degree of relatedness and risk of irreconcilability, the progress of the proceedings already reached, and the connection of the courts to the issue.[169]

Articles 27 and 28 implement the objectives of recital 15 of EC Regulation 44/2001, according to which:

> *In the interests of the harmonious administration of justice* it is necessary to minimise the possibility of concurrent proceedings and to ensure that irreconcilable judgments will not be given in two Member States. There must be a clear and effective mechanism for resolving cases of *lis pendens* and related actions and for obviating problems flowing from national differences as to the determination of the time when a case is regarded as pending.[170]

When determining that the court that was first seised in cases of lis pendens or related actions is the "most convenient" forum in the best interest of justice, the European legislature adopted a doctrine which makes considerations similar to the considerations underlying the American doctrine of forum non conveniens. However, it is clear that Europeans give courts much less discretion to determine whether one forum is "more convenient" than another.[171]

Parties may also consent to jurisdiction or waive any objection they may have for lack of jurisdiction. A court of a Member State before which a defendant enters an appearance may have jurisdiction by virtue of such a filing.[172] However, the filing of an appearance merely to contest the jurisdiction will not provide the court with jurisdiction over the case. Similarly, if another court has exclusive jurisdiction over the case under the Regulation,

Metallurgical Industries, the European Court of Justice held that two parties formally not identical are nevertheless deemed to be "the same person" if there is such a degree of identity between their interests that a judgment delivered against one of them would have the force of res judicata against the other. *See* Case C-351/96, Drouot Assurances SA v. Consol. Metallurgical Indus., 1998 E.C.R. I-3075, 3088. In the United States, a similar procedural device is provided for proceedings pending before federal courts, except that the first court *may* enjoin the second action, or the second court *may* dismiss, stay, or transfer the action to the first court. *See* ALLAN IDES & CHRISTOPHER N. MAY, CIVIL PROCEDURE: CASES AND PROBLEMS 695 (3d ed. 2009).

[168] *See* Council Regulation 44/2001, *supra* note 143, art. 28.

[169] *See id.*; Case C-129/92, Owens Bank Ltd. v. Bracco, 1994 E.C.R. I-117, 154.

[170] *See* Council Regulation 44/2001, *supra* note 143, recital 15 (first emphasis added).

[171] For further discussion on the point, see *infra*.

[172] *See* Council Regulation 44/2001, *supra* note 143, art. 24.

then the filing of the appearance will not give the "nonexclusive" court jurisdiction over the case.[173] Furthermore, lack of jurisdiction must be raised no later than in the first statement of the defendant, which most of the time, according to the applicable national laws (*lex fori*), constitutes a defense against the claim.[174] In addition to the defendant doing so, the court may also declare lack of jurisdiction sua sponte. When a defendant domiciled in one Member State is sued in a court of another Member State and does not enter an appearance, the court shall declare sua sponte that it has no jurisdiction unless it derives its jurisdiction from the provisions of the Regulation.[175]

Europe does not apply the common law doctrine of forum non conveniens,[176] which allows a court with jurisdiction over a case to decline to exercise jurisdiction if an adequate alternative forum that is more convenient for the case exists.[177] Therefore, the defendant in a proceeding will not be able to challenge the jurisdiction of a EU Member State on the basis of that doctrine, but he will still be able to argue that there is a situation of lis pendens or related actions that might make the forum less convenient than another one for the action.[178]

BRIEF OVERVIEW OF AMERICAN JURISDICTIONAL LAW

In the United States, rules of jurisdiction[179] have been shaped primarily by U.S. Supreme Court decisions.[180] Consistent with the traditional Justinian maxim *actor sequitur forum rei* and the European approach,[181] the United States recognizes the jurisdiction of the court of the place where the defendant is domiciled.[182] This principle is expanded to say that, even when

[173] *See id.* art. 22.

[174] *See* Case 150/80, Elefanten Schuh GmbH v. Jacqmain, 1981 E.C.R. 1671, 1686.

[175] *See* Council Regulation 44/2001, *supra* note 143, art. 26.

[176] *See* discussion *infra*.

[177] *See* Piper Aircraft Co. v. Reyno, 454 U.S. 235 (1981).

[178] *See* discussion *infra*.

[179] In contrast to European jurisdictional law, American jurisdictional law distinguishes between personal jurisdiction – jurisdiction over the person or property by reason of the person's location within the territory of the state, or by virtue of the person's contacts with the territory – and subject matter jurisdiction – which, by looking at the subject matter of the litigation, indicates whether a case falls within the jurisdiction of a federal or state court. Having in mind the scope of this project, which deals with transnational commercial transaction litigation, this analysis focuses on personal jurisdiction only.

[180] *See generally* IDES & MAY, *supra* note 167, at 53-200; Friedrich K. Juenger, *American Jurisdiction: A Story of Comparative Neglect*, 65 U. COLO. L. REV. 1, 2–17 (1993).

[181] *See* Council Regulation 44/2001, *supra* note 143, art. 2.

[182] Pennoyer v. Neff, 95 U.S. 714, 723 (1877), *overruled in part by* Shaffer v. Heitner, 433 U.S. 186 (1977). On the concept of domicile, see Major Wendy P. Daknis, *Home Sweet Home:*

individuals or corporations are not formally "domiciled" in a state but their activity there is continuous, substantial, and systematic, they may still be treated as if they were domiciled in that state, and the court may exercise "general jurisdiction" over them.[183]

In *Perkins v. Benguet Consolidated Mining Co.*, the president of Benguet, a corporation from the Philippines, moved to Ohio and carried out all of the corporation's activities there during World War II.[184] The Supreme Court held that due process did not prevent the Ohio court from exercising jurisdiction over Benguet, because the activities that Benguet carried out in Ohio were continuous, substantial, and systematic, and Benguet could have reasonably expected to be haled into court there on any cause of action, even if it were unrelated to the corporation's contacts with the forum state. Therefore, Ohio courts could exercise jurisdiction over Benguet consistently with due process.

In the United States, jurisdiction may also be based on consent or agreement. Additionally, an objection for lack of personal jurisdiction is waived if not raised by the defendant's first defense.[185]

Furthermore, whenever the defendant is sued in a place different from his domicile, there must be some indication that he was on notice of the possibility to be sued there, either because he performed activities in that state or because his contacts with that state are such that the exercise of jurisdiction by the court of that state does not come as an "unfair surprise" to him. More specifically, in *International Shoe Co. v. Washington*, the U.S. Supreme Court held that "due process requires only that in order to subject a defendant to a judgment *in personam*, if he be not present within the territory of the forum, he *have certain minimum contacts* with it such that the maintenance of the suit does not offend 'traditional notions of fair play and substantial justice.'"[186] On the basis of *International Shoe* and its progeny, a court may

A Practical Approach to Domicile, 177 MIL. L. REV. 49 (2003), and Gadi Zohar, Comment, *Habitual Residence: An Alternative to the Common Law Concept of Domicile?*, 9 WHITTIER J. OF CHILD & FAM. ADVOC. 169 (2009).

183 *See* Goodyear Dunlop Tires Operations, S.A. v. Brown, 131 S. Ct. 2846 (2011); Helicopteros Nacionales de Colombia, S.A. v. Hall, 466 U.S. 408 (1984); Perkins v. Benguet Consol. Mining Co., 342 U.S. 437 (1952).

184 342 U.S. at 447.

185 In federal courts, by motion to dismiss for lack of personal jurisdiction under Federal Rules of Civil Procedure 12(b)(2) or by answer, whichever comes first. *See* FED. R. CIV. P. 12(b)(2), (h)(1).

186 326 U.S. 310, 316 (1945) (second emphasis added) (quoting Milliken v. Meyer, 311 U.S. 457, 463 (1940)).

exercise jurisdiction over a nonresident defendant consistent with due process if the "minimum contacts test" is satisfied.

Under the minimum contacts test, there should be an applicable long-arm statute that gives the courts of the state the power to exercise jurisdiction over the nonresident defendant, and the nonresident defendant must have availed himself of the benefits and protection of the laws of the state (purposeful availment) – for example, by engaging in activities there,[187] entering into contracts with residents of the forum state,[188] sending products there through the "stream of commerce,"[189] or by satisfying the effects test.[190] In addition, the activities or contacts with the state must be related to the claim (specific jurisdiction)[191] or be so "continuous, substantial, and systematic" that it is as if the nonresident defendant was domiciled there (general jurisdiction).[192] Finally, the exercise of jurisdiction must be reasonable.[193]

Furthermore, jurisdiction may be properly established by attaching the property that the nonresident defendant owns in the forum state. This is called quasi in rem jurisdiction or in rem jurisdiction.[194] However, even when a

[187] *Id.*

[188] Burger King Corp. v. Rudzewicz, 471 U.S. 462, 482 (1985).

[189] J. McIntyre Mach., Ltd. v. Nicastro, 131 S. Ct. 2780 (2011); Asahi Metal Indus. Co. v. Superior Court, 480 U.S. 102 (1987); World-Wide Volkswagen Corp. v. Woodson, 444 U.S. 286, 298 (1980).

[190] *See* Calder v. Jones, 465 U.S. 783, 789 (1984).

[191] Nowak v. Tak How Inv. Ltd., 899 F. Supp. 25, 28 (D. Mass. 1995).

[192] Goodyear Dunlop Tires Operations, S.A. v. Brown, 131 S. Ct. 2846 (2011); Helicopteros Nacionales de Colombia, S.A. v. Hall. 466 U.S. 408, 415–16 (1984); Perkins v. Benguet Consol. Mining Co., 342 U.S. 437, 445–46 (1952).

[193] *Asahi*, 480 U.S. at 115–16; *Nowak*, 899 F. Supp. at 33.

[194] The court has quasi in rem jurisdiction over some property, tangible or intangible, that is located within its territory. By attaching the property at the commencement of the action and serving the defendant owner of that property with process, the court has jurisdiction over him, but jurisdiction is limited to the property and its value. In other words, quasi in rem actions only affect the interests of particular persons in the attached property, namely, those who have been made parties to the suit. In *Shaffer v. Heitner*, the Supreme Court significantly limited the scope of quasi in rem jurisdiction to those cases where the exercise of such jurisdiction would be consistent with the minimum contacts test. 433 U.S. 186 (1977). Examples of quasi in rem actions include: suits to foreclose on a mortgage or lien; suits to repossess goods; and suits for money damages instituted by attaching a defendant's house, farm, car, bank account, or other real or personal property. An in rem action is one that establishes rights or interests in property as "against all the world." It binds everyone, wherever they reside, whether or not they are parties to the suit, even if their identity or interest in the property is unknown to the court. Only a few types of suits qualify as truly in rem, for example, actions to register or quiet title, actions to condemn or confiscate property, libels in admiralty, probate actions, and bankruptcy proceedings. *See* IDES & MAY, *supra* note 167, at 66.

court exercises quasi in rem jurisdiction over the nonresident defendant, the contacts that the defendant has with the forum state must be such that the defendant may reasonably expect to be haled into court there.

In *Shaffer v. Heitner*, Heitner filed a shareholder's derivative suit in Delaware against the Greyhound Corporation, one of its subsidiaries, and some members of Greyhound's board of directors and officers.[195] Heitner seized approximately 82,000 shares of Greyhound stock owned by twenty-one of the defendants in an attempt to establish quasi in rem jurisdiction over the defendants in the Delaware court. However, the Supreme Court held that exercising jurisdiction would be inconsistent with due process because the property that was attached – that is, the shares – was not related to the plaintiff's claims, and thus, the minimum contacts test had not been satisfied. In other words, because the defendants did not have any contacts with Delaware other than the shares that were attached at the commencement of the Delaware proceeding, the contacts were insufficient to exercise personal jurisdiction consistent with due process. The shares were not related to the plaintiff's cause of action, therefore, the defendants could not expect to be haled into court in Delaware, and the Delaware court's exercise of jurisdiction was thus inconsistent with due process.

Likewise, a contract case falls within the jurisdiction of a court if the nonresident defendant who is a party to the contract has sufficient contacts with the forum state such that he could reasonably expect this exercise of jurisdiction. In *Burger King Corp. v. Rudzewicz*, John Rudzewicz and Brian MacShara, both residents of Michigan, entered into a franchise agreement with Burger King, a corporation with its headquarters located in Miami, Florida.[196] Rudzewicz and MacShara failed to make the monthly payments due to Burger King under the franchise agreement, and Burger King sued them in Florida for breach of contract. After examining the franchise agreement, the Supreme Court held that the contract had substantial connections with Florida because it had been negotiated in Florida, it was entered into with a Florida corporation, and it was subject to Florida substantive law. Moreover, payments due under the contract had to be sent to Florida, training took place in Florida, etc. It was evident that, by entering into a contract with Burger King, the Michigan defendants availed themselves of the benefits and protection of the laws of Florida. Therefore, they could reasonably expect to be haled into court there for breach of that contract, and Florida courts could exercise jurisdiction over them consistent with due process.

[195] 433 U.S. at 186.
[196] 471 U.S. 462 (1985).

A defendant to a tort action must have the same due process guarantees, and here again, the exercise of jurisdiction over him will only be proper if he can reasonably expect to be haled into the forum state court based on his contacts with the state. In *Calder v. Jones*, the plaintiff, actress Shirley Jones, sued the defendants, the *National Enquirer*, its distributor, a writer, and Calder, the editor in chief of the magazine, over an article in which Jones alleged she had been libeled.[197] Jones lived in California and, although the article was written and edited in Florida, Jones sued the defendants in a California state court. The Supreme Court held that the California court had jurisdiction over the defendants because the defendants intentionally defamed Jones, they knew that she lived and worked in California, that she was going to suffer the "brunt of the harm" there, and that their publication was sold there in large numbers. Therefore, they could have reasonably expected to be haled into court in California, and the exercise of jurisdiction by a California court over them was consistent with due process.

Similar considerations apply to product liability and stream of commerce cases.[198] In *World-Wide Volkswagen Corp. v. Woodson*, Harry and Kay Robinson purchased an Audi from Seaway Volkswagen, Inc., in New York.[199] While they were traveling through Oklahoma with their two children, their car collided with another vehicle, and members of the family were severely injured. The Robinsons filed an action in Oklahoma against the automobile's manufacturer (Audi), its importer (Volkswagen of America), its regional distributor (World-Wide Volkswagen Corp.), and its retailer dealer (Seaway Volkswagen). The Supreme Court held that Oklahoma did not have jurisdiction over the regional distributor or the retailer because they had no contacts with the state of Oklahoma, and the car had left the stream of commerce once it was sold in New York. The regional distributor and the retailer had carried out no activity in Oklahoma, had no office there, and had not advertised the car there. In other words, the regional distributor and the retailer had no "minimum contacts" with Oklahoma such that they could reasonably expect to be haled into court there. Therefore, the exercise of jurisdiction by Oklahoma courts over these two defendants was inconsistent with due process.

American jurisdictional law also recognizes "tag" or "transient" jurisdiction and the doctrine of forum non conveniens. Tag or transient jurisdiction is

[197] 465 U.S. 783 (1984).

[198] The "stream of commerce" is the chain that goes from the manufacturer to the consumer. Under the "stream of commerce" theory discussed in *World-Wide Volkswagen Corp. v. Woodson*, when the manufacturer places a product within the stream of commerce with the expectation that the product will be sold in a state, he has availed himself of the benefits and protection of the law of the state, and can reasonably expect to be haled into court there. *See* 444 U.S. 286, 298 (1980).

[199] *Id.*

personal jurisdiction based on service properly made upon the defendant while he is voluntarily present within the territory of that state, even when his presence is only transitory and unrelated to the object of the litigation.[200]

Under the forum non conveniens doctrine, even when an American court has jurisdiction (personal and subject matter) over a specific case, in its sound discretion and by balancing private and public considerations, it could grant a motion to dismiss on forum non conveniens grounds when it believes that there is another adequate forum that is substantially more convenient for the case. The doctrine of forum non conveniens was developed mainly by three U.S. Supreme Court decisions: *Gulf Oil Corp. v. Gilbert*,[201] *Koster v. Lumbermens Mutual Casualty Co.*,[202] and *Piper Aircraft Co. v. Reyno*.[203]

In *Gulf Oil*, the Court held:

> In all cases in which the doctrine of *forum non conveniens* comes into play, it presupposes at least two forums in which the defendant is amenable to process . . .
>
> The principle of *forum non conveniens* is simply that a court may resist imposition upon its jurisdiction even when jurisdiction is authorized by the letter of a general venue statute. . .
>
> . . .
>
> Wisely, it has not been attempted to catalogue the circumstances which will justify or require either grant or denial of remedy. The doctrine leaves much to the discretion of the court to which plaintiff resorts, and experience has not shown a judicial tendency to renounce one's own jurisdiction so strong as to result in many abuses.[204]

The Court also noted that, when exercising discretion in the application of the forum non conveniens doctrine, a court should give strong deference to the plaintiff's choice of forum.[205] The Court identified two groups of factors, private and public, that should guide courts when deciding to stay or dismiss a

[200] *See* Burnham v. Superior Court, 495 U.S. 604 (1990).

[201] 330 U.S. 501 (1947), *superseded by statute*, 28 U.S.C. § 1404 (2006), *as recognized in* Am. Dredging Co. v. Miller, 510 U.S. 443 (1994).

[202] 330 U.S. 518 (1947).

[203] 454 U.S. 235 (1981).

[204] 330 U.S. at 506–08.

[205] The Court noted:

> [While] the plaintiff may not, by choice of an inconvenient forum, "vex," "harass," or "oppress" the defendant by inflicting upon him expense or trouble not necessary to his own right to pursue his remedy . . . unless the balance is strongly in favor of the defendant, the plaintiff's choice of forum should rarely be disturbed.

Id. at 508 (footnote omitted).

case in favor of another forum. The private factors include the relative ease of access to sources of proof, the availability of compulsory process for attendance of unwilling, and the cost of obtaining attendance of willing witnesses. The public factors include: the administrative difficulties that follow for courts when litigation is piled up in congested centers instead of being handled at its origin; jury duty – which should not be imposed upon the people of a community with no relation to the litigation; and a local interest in having localized controversies decided at home.[206]

It has been observed:

> Among the greatest beneficiaries of forum non conveniens are American corporate defendants sued for products liability and other tort claims in the United States by foreign plaintiffs. When American courts use forum non conveniens to stop these lawsuits from reaching the merits, foreign plaintiffs experience delay and uncertainty in achieving a remedy in a forum outside the United States.[207]

However, American courts need the forum non conveniens doctrine because of the reach of state long-arm statutes and tag or transient jurisdiction.[208] Because plaintiffs have such a wide range of forum choices, given the extremely long arms of the state statutes and the generous scope of jurisdiction allowed by minimum contacts under the due process clause, some mechanisms must be available to save the defendants (and to some degree the courts) from the consequences of an aggressive plaintiff's forum choice.[209] Because European courts generally do not allow such a wide choice of courts to plaintiffs, they might not need the doctrine of forum non conveniens as much as American courts do.[210]

COMPARING EUROPEAN AND AMERICAN JURISDICTION LAW: ARE THE DIFFERENCES TRULY IRRECONCILABLE?

When negotiations for the adoption of international conventions occur, delegates often take to the negotiating table the views that are prevalent in their respective countries. In the case of the proposed Hague Convention on

206 *Id.* at 508–09.

207 John R. Wilson, Note, *Coming to America to File Suit: Foreign Plaintiffs and the Forum Non Conveniens Barrier in Transnational Litigation*, 65 OHIO ST. L.J. 659, 659 (2004).

208 *See* discussion *infra*.

209 This was Paxton Blair's idea too. In fact, as noted by John Wilson, "Blair's thesis was that forum non conveniens should be more widely used to *reliev[e] calendar congestion* by partially diverting at its source the flood of litigation by which our courts are being overwhelmed." Wilson, *supra* note 207, at 673 (emphasis added) (internal quotation marks omitted). The cause of the flood, Blair said, was forum shopping, which "merits the unequivocal condemnation of bench and bar." *Id.* (internal quotation marks omitted).

210 *See* discussion *infra*.

jurisdictional rules, Europeans had prejudices, false assumptions, and misconceptions of the functioning of juries, punitive damages, discovery, class actions, etc. On the other hand, Americans shared the same criticism and skepticism on European civil procedure being codified, inflexible, and thus, unable to find the truth.[211]

However, from the preceding overview, European and American jurisdictional law appear quite similar, with the exceptions of tag jurisdiction and the doctrine of forum non conveniens. In any event, both tag jurisdiction and forum non conveniens are merely permitted but not required by American due process. The two do not constitute a serious impasse to the harmonization of jurisdictional rules because, as will be further explained *infra*, Europeans could agree on a specific provision allowing the use of the forum non conveniens doctrine and Americans could give up tag jurisdiction for the limited purposes of the international convention.[212]

[211] See HENRY M. HART, JR. & ALBERT M. SACKS, THE LEGAL PROCESS: BASIC PROBLEMS IN THE MAKING AND APPLICATION OF LAW 723–73 (1994), in which the authors note their concern with the adverse effects of legal codification on the ability of the law to grow with society. Hence, the American preoccupation with codified rules of jurisdiction would constrain American courts' ability to adapt jurisdictional bases to meet the needs of a changing world. *See* SAMUEL P. BAUMGARTNER, THE PROPOSED HAGUE CONVENTION ON JURISDICTION AND FOREIGN JUDGMENTS: TRANS-ATLANTIC LAWMAKING FOR TRANSNATIONAL LITIGATION 14, 29 (2003). In favor of codifying jurisdictional rules, however, Professor Linda Silberman observed:

> My predilections for rule-oriented jurisdictional standards lead me not only to a defense of "tag" jurisdiction but to a critique of modern jurisdictional jurisprudence more generally.
>
> . . .
>
> A model that establishes a set of clear and presumptive jurisdiction rules and takes into account the compelling interests of plaintiffs and defendants in formulating those rules satisfies the need for identifying a litigationally appropriate forum. "Reasonableness" as an additional overlay should be eliminated as a constitutional standard for jurisdiction and should be incorporated only as part of discretionary *forum non conveniens*. This type of jurisdictional interpretation would leave substantial discretion to the trial judge to determine whether or not jurisdiction should be exercised and the decision would rarely be overturned.

Linda Silberman, *Reflections on* Burnham v. Superior Court: *Toward Presumptive Rules of Jurisdiction and Implications for Choice of Law*, 22 RUTGERS L.J. 569, 578, 590 (1991) (footnotes omitted). An example of "codification" of jurisdictional rules in the United States, however, is offered by states' long-arm statutes. *See* IDES & MAY, *supra* note 167, at 87.

[212] *See* discussion *infra*.

STRONG SIMILARITIES BETWEEN EUROPEAN AND AMERICAN JURISDICTIONAL LAW

In the United States, as in Europe, the defendant's domicile is considered a "traditional" basis of jurisdiction that poses no due process concern. By being domiciled in a forum, the defendant has certainly availed himself of the benefits and protections of the laws of that forum, and thus, he can expect to be haled into court there.[213]

American "general jurisdiction" seems to have expanded the concept of "domicile" to include situations where, even if not formally domiciled in a state, a defendant is acting as if he were domiciled there. This happens when the defendant engages in continuous, substantial, and systematic activity in that state. If this happens, the defendant may be sued in that state on any cause of action, and the court of that state will have general jurisdiction over him. This exercise of jurisdiction is considered consistent with due process.

"Doing-business jurisdiction" is a category of general jurisdiction premised on due process: the state has jurisdiction over the nonresident defendant because his activity is so continuous, substantial, and systematic within that forum state that he could reasonably expect to be haled into court there.[214] Thus, by virtue of his activity within the forum state, the defendant is acting as

[213] See *Int'l Shoe Co. v. Washington*, 326 U.S. 310 (1945), for the idea that the exercise of jurisdiction must be consistent with due process and meet defendant's expectations as to the forum where he can be sued.

[214] In *Moulin v. Trenton Mutual Life & Fire Insurance Co.*, the Supreme Court of New Jersey observed:

> The corporation, it is true, were [sic] drawn into the forum of a foreign sovereignty to litigate; but having voluntarily entered that jurisdiction, and transacting business there; having invoked the comity and the protection of the laws of that sovereignty for their own benefit, can they complain that the contracts there made are enforced within that sovereignty and in accordance with its laws? Does it involve the violation of any principle of *natural justice* or that protection which is due to the citizens of our own state? If the corporation were carrying on its business within the state of New York at the time of the service of the process, the court has already intimated its opinion that the service would be valid. "I think," says Justice Elmer, "under such circumstances natural justice requires that corporations should be subject to the laws of the state whose comity they thus invoke. For the purpose of being sued, they ought to be regarded as voluntarily placing themselves in the situation of citizens of that state."

25 N.J.L. 57, 62–63 (1855) (quoting Moulin v. Trenton Mut. Life & Fire Ins. Co., 24 N.J.L. 222, 234 (1853) (emphasis added)). The reference to "natural justice" here seems to refer to the European idea of a "natural judge." Put in these terms, American general jurisdiction does not seem so different from European general jurisdiction and the European "natural judge." Here, the American court even expressly mentions the idea of "natural justice" and a defendant's expectations concerning the judge with jurisdiction over him.

if he were domiciled there. The contemporary general jurisdiction doctrine emanates from the pre-*International Shoe* fictional premise of a corporation's constructive presence through doing business in the forum.[215]

General jurisdiction, so conceived, does not seem so distant from the European concept of general jurisdiction, that is, jurisdiction of the state where the defendant is domiciled. In fact, as observed by Professor Ronald Brand:

> U.S. law takes the defendant's presence much further in creating general jurisdiction than does the traditional civil law concept of *actor sequitur forum rei*.
>
> This does not mean, however, that common ground ends with a rule providing for general jurisdiction at the place of the defendant's domicile. It has been stated that "[f]ourteen hundred years before *International Shoe*, the civil law, unhampered by constitutional doctrine and territorialist dogma, already premised jurisdiction on 'minimum contacts,' and this idea 'continues to inform current European jurisdictional law.'" This reference was explicitly directed at paragraphs (1) and (3) of Article 5 of the Brussels Convention, dealing with tort and contract jurisdiction, but applies equally to paragraph (5) of that Article, authorizing jurisdiction over disputes arising out of the operation of a branch, agency or establishment in the forum state.[216]

However, it has been argued that Europeans reject, among other things, American doing-business jurisdiction.[217] This is perhaps due to the fact that, in contrast to the guidelines provided by the U.S. Supreme Court in its two foundational cases,[218] which set a very high threshold for the exercise of doing business jurisdiction, American state courts began to uphold doing-business jurisdiction even when this high threshold had not been met.[219] Under a due process point of view, this exercise of jurisdiction was unacceptable to Europeans.

In a recent decision, the Supreme Court clarified that, if need be, doing-business jurisdiction may be exercised only when, by virtue of the activity carried out in the forum state, the defendant behaves as if domiciled there.[220]

215 *See* 326 U.S. at 318; Charles W. "Rocky" Rhodes, *Clarifying General Jurisdiction*, 34 SETON HALL L. REV. 807, 813 (2004).

216 Brand, *supra* note 9, at 20 (quoting Juenger, *supra* note 47, at 1204 (footnote omitted)).

217 *See Hague Conference on Private International Law, Commission II, Jurisdiction and Foreign Judgments in Civil and Commercial Matters, Nineteenth Session: Summary of the Outcome of the Discussion in Commission II of the First Part of the Diplomatic Conference 6–20 June 2001, Interim Text*, 77 CHI.-KENT L. REV. 1015, 1028, 1035-37 (2002) [hereinafter *Summary of the Outcome of the Discussion in Commission II*]; Patrick J. Borchers, *The Problem with General Jurisdiction*, 2001 U. CHI. LEGAL F. 119, 137; Clermont, *supra* note 7, at 95–96.

218 *See* Helicopteros Nacionales de Colombia, S.A. v. Hall, 466 U.S. 408 (1984); Perkins v. Benguet Consol. Mining Co., 342 U.S. 437 (1952).

219 *See* Rhodes, *supra* note 215, at 810.

220 *See* Goodyear Dunlop Tires Operations, S.A. v. Brown, 131 S. Ct. 2846, 2857 (2011).

This threshold is inevitably very high. More specifically, the Court held, "For an individual, the paradigm forum for the exercise of general jurisdiction is the individual's domicile; for a corporation, it is an equivalent place, one in which the corporation is fairly regarded as at home."[221]

Even though the Court failed to clarify what "at home" means, and merely cited an article by Professor Lea Brilmayer "identifying domicile, place of incorporation, and principal place of business as 'paradig[m]' bases for the exercise of general jurisdiction," this decision is of great significance for the process of harmonizing jurisdictional rules and reducing the apparent gap between the American and the European approach to general jurisdiction, because it approximates the two ideas.[222] Both Europeans and Americans allow general jurisdiction in the place where the defendant, individual, or corporation, is "at home."[223]

This similarity or convergence does not only occur in the area of general jurisdiction. The analysis that follows shows how the foundational cases for personal jurisdiction decided by the U.S. Supreme Court would be decided similarly by European courts under EC Regulation 44/2001 and the relevant case law.

For instance, *Perkins v. Benguet Consolidated Mining Co.*, where the Supreme Court spelled out the principle of general jurisdiction, would be decided the same way under EC Regulation 44/2001.[224] More specifically, Ohio courts would have jurisdiction over Benguet under articles 2 and 60(1) of EC Regulation 44/2001. Under article 2 of EC Regulation 44/2001, a court has jurisdiction over any defendant who is domiciled within its territory,[225] and under article 60(1), a corporation is considered as domiciled in the place

[221] *Id.* at 2853–54.

[222] *Id.* at 2854 (citing Lea Brilmayer et al., *A General Look at General Jurisdiction*, 66 TEX. L. REV. 721, 728 (1988)).

[223] *See Goodyear*, 131 S. Ct. 2846; *Helicopteros*, 466 U.S. 408; *Perkins*, 342 U.S. 437; Council Regulation 44/2001, *supra* note 143, art. 2 (authorizing the exercise of jurisdiction on any cause of action by the state where the defendant is domiciled); *id.* art. 60 (stating that a legal person is domiciled in the place where it has its principal place of business, central administration, or statutory seat). Before, for a court to be able to exercise doing-business jurisdiction over a corporation, the corporation needed to be considered "present" within the forum state by way of its activities. *See, e.g.*, Phila. & Reading Ry. Co. v. McKibbin, 243 U.S. 264, 265 (1917) ("A foreign corporation is amenable to process to enforce a personal liability, in the absence of consent, only if it is doing business within the State in such manner and to such extent as to warrant the inference that it is present there."); Frene v. Louisville Cement Co., 134 F.2d 511, 515 (D.C. Cir. 1943) ("[I]f, in addition to a regular course of solicitation, other business activities are carried on, such as maintaining a warehouse, making deliveries, etc., the corporation is 'present' for jurisdictional purposes.").

[224] *See* 342 U.S. at 437; discussion *supra*.

[225] Council Regulation 44/2001, *supra* note 143, art. 2.

where its central administration is located.[226] Therefore, because Benguet's central administration was, at the time of the action, located in Ohio, Ohio courts would have jurisdiction over Benguet under articles 2 and 60(1) of EC Regulation 44/2001 as well.

Similar to European jurisdictional law, jurisdiction under American law may be based on consent or agreement. Also as in Europe, the objection for lack of (personal) jurisdiction is waived if not raised by the defendant's first defense.[227] Moreover, by applying the minimum contacts test to see whether an American court has jurisdiction over a nonresident defendant, one obtains the same results he would obtain if he were trying to establish jurisdiction under EC Regulation 44/2001.[228]

Even if European courts do not recognize quasi in rem jurisdiction, in most cases, American quasi in rem jurisdiction cases are decided the same way under American and European jurisdictional law because American courts now apply the minimum contacts analysis to quasi in rem jurisdiction cases.[229] For example, *Shaffer* would be decided the same way under EC Regulation 44/2001.[230] Like the Supreme Court, a European court would also hold that the Delaware court did not have jurisdiction over the nonresident defendants. In fact, because the defendants were not domiciled in Delaware, article 2 of EC Regulation 44/2001 would not apply, and no other provision in the EC Regulation would otherwise confer jurisdiction upon the Delaware courts.

Contracts cases are also decided similarly under American and European jurisdictional law. For example, *Burger King* would be decided the same way under European jurisdictional law.[231] Because the subject matter of the litigation was the failure to perform the franchise agreement that had to be performed partially in Florida, Florida courts would have jurisdiction over the two Michigan defendants under article 5(1)(a) of EC Regulation 44/2001, according to which, "A person domiciled in a Member State may, in another Member State, be sued … in matters relating to a contract, in the courts for the place of performance of the obligation in question."[232]

[226] *Id.* art. 60.
[227] *See* FED. R. CIV. P. 12(b)(2).
[228] *See* discussion *infra*.
[229] *See* IDES & MAY, *supra* note 167, at 66.
[230] *See* Shaffer v. Heitner, 433 U.S. 186 (1977); discussion.
[231] *See* Burger King Corp. v. Rudzewicz, 471 U.S. 462 (1985); discussion *supra*.
[232] Council Regulation 44/2001, supra note 6, art. 5. According to Laura García Gutiérrez:

> As is well-known, notwithstanding the presumptions in Article 5.1.b [of EC Regulation 44/2001, which determines the place of performance of the obligation], as ruled by the European Court of Justice … in *De Bloos*, in deciding whether a case is under international

Hanson v. Denckla would also be decided the same way under the relevant provisions of EC Regulation 44/2001.[233] In *Hanson*, Dora Browning Donner, who lived in Pennsylvania, created a trust with a Delaware trustee. Donner later moved to Florida, where she died. The will was admitted to probate in Florida, and a dispute arose among the beneficiaries of the trust and the beneficiaries under the will. The beneficiaries under the will sued the trustee in Florida, but the U.S. Supreme Court held that the Florida court had no jurisdiction over the trustee, because the Delaware trustee neither engaged in any activity in Florida, nor had any offices there, and thus lacked minimum contacts with Florida. Therefore, the exercise of jurisdiction by the Florida court was inconsistent with due process. Likewise, under EC Regulation 44/2001, Florida courts would not have jurisdiction over the trustee because no provision in the EC Regulation would support this exercise of jurisdiction.

More generally, most tort cases would be decided the same way under American and European jurisdictional law. Under EC Regulation 44/2001, the defendants in *Calder* would be subject to the jurisdiction of California courts.[234] Article 5(3) of EC Regulation 44/2001 allows the plaintiff to sue the defendants in "the place where the harmful event occurred."[235] As explained above, this place includes the place where the event giving rise to the damage occurred, as well as the place where the damage occurred.[236] In *Calder*, the damage occurred in California. Therefore, California would have jurisdiction over the defendants under article 5(3) of EC Regulation 44/2001.[237]

Furthermore, product liability and stream of commerce cases would also be treated similarly under American and European jurisdiction law.[238]

> jurisdiction, the relevant obligation is 'that on which the suit is based', and the 'place of performance of said obligation' shall determine the special jurisdiction. This implies that if the places of performance of the different obligations arising from the franchise contract were to be different, multiple courts would have jurisdiction over these contracts. The inclusion of franchise contracts in the presumptions of Article 5.1.b of the Brussels I Regulation implies that EC legislature would be in favour of concentrating all lawsuits relating to franchise contracts in the place of the 'provision of services', as a special jurisdiction stated in Article 5.1 of the Brussels I Regulation.

Laura García Gutiérrez, *Franchise Contracts and the Rome I Regulation on the Law Applicable to International Contracts*, 10 Y.B. PRIVATE INT'L L. 233, 237 (2008) (footnote omitted) (quoting Council Regulation 44/2011, *supra* note 6, art. 5).

233 *See* 357 U.S. 235 (1958); discussion *supra*.

234 See Calder v. Jones, 465 U.S. 783 (1984); discussion *supra* Part V.A.

235 Council Regulation 44/2001, *supra* note 143, art. 5.

236 *See* discussion *supra* Part IV.C.2.

237 *See* Council Regulation 44/2001, *supra* note 143, art. 5.

238 For an explanation of the "stream-of-commerce" theory, see *supra* text accompanying notes 189–191.

Using reasoning similar to that of the U.S. Supreme Court, a European court would not have permitted the exercise of jurisdiction over the nonresident defendants regional distributor and retailer dealer in *World-Wide Volkswagen.*[239] Under article 16(1) of EC Regulation 44/2001, consumer plaintiffs may sue the "other party to the contract either in the courts of the Member State in which that party is domiciled or in the courts for the place where the consumer is domiciled."[240] Therefore, under EC Regulation 44/2001, the Robinsons might have filed their action before a New York court – the court of the place where they and the "other party to the contract" were domiciled – but not before an Oklahoma court.[241]

It is true that, when exercising jurisdiction, Americans focus on the connection between the defendant and the forum through the minimum contacts test, while Europeans focus on the connection between the forum and the claim or cause of action. However, as the preceding analysis shows, a substantial connection between the claim and the forum is, most of the time, a substantial connection between the defendant and the forum. Therefore, even if it's through different methodological approaches, European and American jurisdictional rules often reach similar results. This should strongly justify and encourage harmonization efforts.

MINOR DIFFERENCES THAT CANNOT PREVENT HARMONIZATION: TAG JURISDICTION AND FORUM NON CONVENIENS

Tag Jurisdiction

Tag or transient jurisdiction is considered an "exorbitant" rule of jurisdiction by most of the legal community, yet this rule still applies in the United States. In *Burnham v. Superior Court of California*, the nine Justices of the Supreme Court, with different rationales but reaching the same conclusion, held that the trial court had personal jurisdiction over a nonresident defendant who had been in the state for three days, doing activities unrelated to the pending action, because he was personally served with process while

[239] World-Wide Volkswagen Corp. v. Woodson, 444 U.S. 286 (1980).
[240] Council Regulation 44/2001, *supra* note 143, art. 16.
[241] *Id.*

voluntarily present within the state.[242] The Court believed that this exercise of personal jurisdiction did not violate the "'traditional notions of fair play

[242] 495 U.S. 604 (1990). Interestingly, however, Justice Brennan, in a concurring opinion, commenting on Scalia's reliance on historical precedents to justify transient jurisdiction, observed:

> [R]eliance solely on historical pedigree ... is foreclosed by our decisions in *International Shoe Co. v. Washington* and *Shaffer v. Heitner*... The critical insight of *Shaffer* is that all rules of jurisdiction, even ancient ones, must satisfy contemporary notions of due process... While our *holding* in *Shaffer* may have been limited to *quasi in rem* jurisdiction, our mode of analysis was not.

Id. at 629–30 (Brennan, J., concurring) (citations omitted). Justice Brennan's minimum contact analysis as applied to transient jurisdiction, however, was so broad as to be meaningless for purposes of making the transient jurisdiction analysis subject to the minimum contacts test. In fact, his test was so broad that persons transitorily present would almost always have the necessary minimum contacts with the forum to satisfy a valid exercise of transient jurisdiction. *See* Robert Taylor-Manning, *An Easy Case Makes Bad Law* – Burnham v. Superior Court of California, *110 S. Ct. 2105 (1990)*, 66 WASH. L. REV. 623, 631–32 (1991).
Perhaps trying to follow the original intent of Justice Brennan, and according to the rationale and continued applicability of the transient jurisdiction doctrine in doubt after *Shaffer*, some courts declined to extend *Shaffer's* reasoning to in personam actions absent clear indication from the Court, while other courts did extend *Shaffer* to in personam actions considering the logic behind it as applicable to both in rem and in personam actions. *Id.* at 629. For instance, in *Harold M. Pitman Co. v. Typecraft Software Ltd.*, the United States District Court for the Northern District of Illinois stated:

> We now hold that, under *Shaffer*, mere service of process upon a defendant transiently present in the jurisdiction does not vest a state with personal jurisdiction over the defendant. Personal service within the jurisdiction is not the litmus test for proper in personam jurisdiction. Rather, the test is whether the defendant has had minimum contacts with the forum "such that maintenance of the suit does not offend traditional notions of fair play and substantial justice."

626 F. Supp. 305, 312 (N.D. Ill. 1986) (quoting Int'l Shoe Co. v. Washington, 326 U.S. 310, 316 (1945)). Also in *Nehemiah v. Athletics Congress of U.S.A.*, the United States Court of Appeals for the Third Circuit held:

> Whether or not our earlier decision in *Pavlovscak* is controlling, we now conclude that due process considerations preclude effecting personal jurisdiction over an unincorporated association merely by in-state service on its agent. It is arguable that the transient presence basis for jurisdiction over any defendant, including an individual, is no longer viable.
>
> ...
>
> ... It is just as unreasonable to request the union to defend the suit in that forum as it would be were it a corporation and service had been made on its officer or employee. Since it is undisputed that mere service on a corporate agent cannot establish personal jurisdiction without a minimum contacts inquiry, we can find no cogent reason not to apply the same principle to an unincorporated association.
>
> ...
>
> We conclude therefore that neither logic nor history supports personal jurisdiction over an unincorporated association solely on the basis of service on its agent within the forum. The district court erred in holding that it was not required to make an inquiry into the quality and nature of contacts between the IAAF and New Jersey to determine whether they satisfied the minimum contacts test of *International Shoe*.

765 F.2d 42, 46–48 (3d Cir. 1985).

and substantial justice.'"[243] The Court in *Burnham* did not indicate that tag jurisdiction could be exercised over domestic and foreign defendants on the basis of the same criteria; it did not say, nor perhaps intend, to have domestic and foreign defendants treated alike with respect to the exercise of tag jurisdiction. However, with no explanation or analysis as to why they were doing this, and despite questions concerning the compliance with international law, lower federal courts and state courts have applied *Burnham* and tag jurisdiction to transnational cases.[244]

Commentators highly criticized tag jurisdiction "[w]ith virtual unanimity."[245] An author observed, "The doctrine was attacked, not on its conceptual basis, but on its inconsistency with modern methods of analysis and its potential for

[243] *Int'l Shoe*, 326 U.S. at 316 (quoting Milliken v. Meyer, 311 U.S. 457, 463 (1940)).

[244] *See* Paul R. Dubinsky, *Is Transnational Litigation a Distinct Field? The Persistence of Exceptionalism in American Procedural Law*, 44 STAN. J. INT'L L. 301, 334 (2008). According to Professor Peter Hay, "The supporters of the Brennan opinion, as well as Justices White and Stevens, should reexamine transient jurisdiction, at least in the limited factual context of casually present international defendants with no or unrelated forum contacts." Peter Hay, *Transient Jurisdiction, Especially over International Defendants: Critical Comments on* Burnham v. Superior Court of California, 1990 U. ILL. L. REV. 593, 603.

[245] Paul C. Wilson, Note, *A Pedigree for Due Process?* Burnham v. Superior Court of California, 56 MO. L. REV. 353, 359 (1991).

Professor Clermont also observes:

> Formerly the most important basis of U.S. jurisdiction, but today far from essential, it is occasionally used to sue foreigners in the United States, even though the resulting judgments would be unlikely to receive recognition or enforcement abroad. Indeed, transient jurisdiction is necessary only when the appropriate bases of jurisdiction are unavailing.

Clermont, *supra* note 7, at 112 (footnote omitted). According to Professor Robert Taylor-Manning:

> Even before its decision in *Burnham*, the Supreme Court encountered difficulty in reconciling the twin demands of interstate sovereignty and constitutional liberty protections. The split in lower courts and of the Supreme Court itself, however, demands reconciliation. Justice Scalia's analysis cannot be reconciled with due process concerns or personal jurisdiction developments since *International Shoe*. Justice Brennan presented an analysis more consistent with Supreme Court decisions since *International Shoe*. Transient jurisdiction should be abandoned and minimum contacts should be applied to individuals in the same manner it is applied to corporations as the standard for all state court jurisdictional assertions. With Justice Brennan's retirement, the outcome of the next transient jurisdiction case before the Supreme Court is less than certain. The only certainty is that, given the confusion created by *Burnham*, the issue will soon arise again.

Taylor-Manning, *supra* note 242, at 640–41 (footnote omitted). Hay also observed:

> Transient jurisdiction presents the same problem. The power concept, the power "myth," may do no harm – indeed it may make some sense – in the interstate context. In an international context, an unqualified, unremitting rule of transient jurisdiction seems quite intolerable and is unfitting. The supporters of the Brennan opinion, as well as Justices

producing unfairness in a highly mobile society."[246] Even the American Law Institute (ALI) reacted to the decision in *Shaffer* by taking an intermediate position on the question of transient jurisdiction. One author noted:

> [The ALI pointed out that the Court in *Shaffer*] rejected the notion that power derived from the mere presence of a thing in a State will always provide that State with a basis to determine interests in the thing. Instead of abolishing the doctrine altogether, however, the [ALI] amended the Restatement (Second) of Conflict of Laws to provide that presence normally would make jurisdiction proper, but not always: A state has power to exercise judicial jurisdiction over an individual who is present within its territory

> White and Stevens, should reexamine transient jurisdiction, at least in the limited factual context of casually present international defendants with no or unrelated forum contacts.

Hay, *supra* note 244, at 602–03 (footnotes omitted). According to Professor Silberman, "[W]hile upholding jurisdiction on the *Burnham* facts, the Court indicated that it has no coherent theory about the relationship of traditional theories of jurisdiction to contemporary notions of due process." Silberman, *supra* note 211, at 570. Silberman also noted:

> Finally, the impact of modern transportation and communication and the innovation of modern procedures to dispose of non-meritorious cases before trial fail to explain the "fairness" of tag jurisdiction. They may indicate why jurisdictional rules generally can be less protective of the convenience of defendants, and may even suggest a rationale for nationwide process, but they in no way provide a rationale for tag jurisdiction itself.

Id. at 575–76 (footnote omitted). Likewise, Professor Scott Irwin noted:

> [T]he question remains as to whether the *Burnham* decision is the "final word" in the transient jurisdiction debate. Is the historical rationale provided by Scalia as clear as his articulation suggests? It is arguable that the answer to this question is clearly in the negative considering the amount of scholarly attention the subject has received.

Scott D. Irwin, Note, Burnham v. Superior Court of California: *The Final Word on Transient Personal Jurisdiction?*, 53 Ohio St. L.J. 613, 628 (1992). Other authors and judges have recognized the abuses that the use of tag jurisdiction may lead to, and they have suggested significant use of the doctrine of forum non conveniens and the reasonableness prong of the minimum contacts test to mitigate such abuses and unfair results. Eric Heichel noted:

> Much of the criticism of the transient presence rule points out that the forum may have no connection with either the defendant or the subject matter of the litigation. To mitigate against the dangers of forcing the defendant to litigate in an inconvenient forum, courts should use the doctrine of forum non conveniens in addition to requiring reasonableness. A court that finds it is a seriously inconvenient forum should dismiss the case and send the parties to another, more convenient, specified forum. With this doctrine courts should refuse jurisdiction over a case that has no contacts with the forum by requiring the plaintiff to bring the action in another forum. Courts are making increasing use of forum non conveniens and can successfully employ it to prevent abuses of the physical presence rule.

Eric P. Heichel, Note, *The Physical Presence Basis of Personal Jurisdiction Ten Years After* Shaffer v. Heitner: *A Rule in Search of a Rationale*, 62 Notre Dame L. Rev. 713, 732–33 (1987) (footnotes omitted).

[246] Wilson, *supra* note 245, at 359 (footnotes omitted).

> unless the individual's relationship is so attenuated as to make the exercise of jurisdiction unreasonable.[247]

Federal and state courts applied tag jurisdiction to internal as well as transnational litigation.[248]

Because *Shaffer* established that the mere presence of property in a state unrelated to the controversy would be insufficient to give that state jurisdiction over the owner of that property,[249] it is hard to understand how the transient presence of the defendant in a state, doing activities unrelated to the controversy, should be enough to give that state jurisdiction over the defendant.[250] Justice Scalia defended transient jurisdiction on the basis of state court decisions, many of which were decided before *International Shoe*, and had no theory with which to replace territorial sovereignty.[251] Justice Brennan

[247] Douglas A. Mays, Note, Burnham v. Superior Court: *The Supreme Court Agrees on Transient Jurisdiction in Practice, but Not in Theory*, 69 N.C. L. REV. 1271, 1285 (1991) (footnotes omitted) (internal quotation marks omitted).

[248] As observed by Professor Paul R. Dubinsky:

> As with *Asahi*, the Court has not revisited the many questions left open in *Burnham*. In the eighteen years since *Burnham*, state and lower federal courts have had to make their own way on transnational transient jurisdiction, with the following options open to them: (1) investigating whether the longstanding historical practice cited by Justice Scalia with respect to tag jurisdiction over domestic defendants exists with respect to foreign defendants; (2) rejecting the historical approach altogether and instead conducting case-by-case determinations as to how reasonableness varies with nationality and residence; (3) declining to extrapolate from either the Scalia or Brennan opinions and, instead, looking to whether international law imposes limits on tag jurisdiction with respect to foreign defendants.
>
> State and lower federal courts have taken none of these paths. Unanimously, they have upheld transient jurisdiction over foreign defendants, and they have done so with unadorned citations to *Burnham* without explaining why they believe *Burnham* requires this result in a transnational setting. In none of these cases has a court acknowledged that *Burnham* is an interstate case, lacking a majority opinion, and that it need not be viewed as a controlling precedent with respect to transnational application of tag jurisdiction. Instead, lower courts' reliance on *Burnham* causes one to wonder whether distinctions between interstate application of tag jurisdiction and transnational application have even been brought to the court's attention by counsel. The response of lower courts to motions challenging tag jurisdiction is similar to their response to motions challenging jurisdiction based on the reasonableness prong of *Asahi*. In both instances, courts are strongly inclined to treat the transnational case as functionally the same as the interstate case.

Dubinsky, *supra* note 244, at 330–31 (footnotes omitted).

[249] Shaffer v. Heitner, 33 U.S. 186 (1977).

[250] See David H. Vernon, *Single-Factor Bases of In Personam Jurisdiction – A Speculation on the Impact of* Shaffer v. Heitner, 1978 WASH. U. L.Q. 273, 302–03.

[251] *See* Burham v. Superior Court, 495 U.S. 604, 609–14 (1990); Taylor-Manning, *supra* note 245, at 635.

criticized Justice Scalia for leaving the protection of constitutional rights to the states, which have little incentive to protect the constitutional rights of nonresidents.[252]

In any event, tag jurisdiction is considered a valid jurisdictional doctrine and has been justified on the basis of the territoriality principle, according to which the court has jurisdiction over people or property located within its territory, even if this presence is only transitory and completely unrelated to the subject of the litigation.[253] However, it is doubtful that a defendant would actually expect to be sued before the court of a state where he is only temporarily visiting for activities unrelated to the controversy brought in that forum.

Civil law systems do not recognize tag jurisdiction or any functional equivalent.[254] However, one may wonder what the purpose is of having tag jurisdiction in transnational litigation on civil and commercial matters if the judgment rendered by an American court with tag jurisdiction over the case is not recognized by the majority of foreign courts. Moreover, American tag jurisdiction is permitted, but not required, by due process. Therefore, the United States is free to join a convention that disallows tag jurisdiction in the transnational litigation context. Of course, a problem would arise if the convention allowed a practice that would violate due process, but that is not the case with tag jurisdiction. Thus, tag jurisdiction should not prevent the harmonization of jurisdictional law governing these types of controversies.[255]

FORUM NON CONVENIENS

Likewise, the doctrine of forum non conveniens should not prevent harmonization. Forum non conveniens is a common law doctrine that allows the court (where an action is filed) the discretion to decline jurisdiction if an adequate alternative and more convenient forum exists for that case. This

[252] *See Burnham*, 495 U.S. at 637; Taylor-Manning, *supra* note 242, at 635.

[253] *See Burnham*, 495 U.S. 604; Pennoyer v. Neff, 95 U.S. 714, 734 (1877), *overruled in part by Shaffer*, 433 U.S. 186.

[254] *See* Schlosser, *supra* note 8, at 31.

[255] In this respect, when writing about the Hague Convention in the year 2000, Professor Clermont wrote:

> The expectation is that this eventual multilateral convention on jurisdiction and the recognition and enforcement of judgments in civil and commercial matters will be similar to the Brussels Convention.
>
> This eventuality means that the United States might soon abandon—on the international level among signatory countries—transient jurisdiction, attachment jurisdiction, and "doing business" as a basis for general jurisdiction.

Clermont, *supra* note 7, at 95 (footnotes omitted).

doctrine was first adopted in Scotland and later developed in other common law countries, which exhibit similarities and differences when compared with the original Scottish version.

In the United States, the term "forum non conveniens" appeared for the first time in 1929 in an article by Professor Paxton Blair. In the article, Blair noted that it was "apparent that the courts of this country have been for years applying the doctrine."[256] Blair also observed that, in applying the forum non conveniens doctrine, American courts considered factors such as these: the availability of witnesses, the burden on the state's citizens, the possible differences between right and remedy, the ability to enforce a judgment when a foreign law governed the dispute, and, most of all, the complexity of the governing foreign law.[257] In other words, when the foreign law applicable to the controversy was too complex, American courts applied the forum non conveniens doctrine to dismiss a case "in the interest of justice."

As described above,[258] the U.S. Supreme Court dealt with the doctrine of forum non conveniens mainly in *Gulf Oil*,[259] *Koster*,[260] and *Piper Aircraft*,[261] but also more recently in *American Dredging Co. v. Miller*.[262] In *American Dredging*, Justice Scalia held that the doctrine "is nothing more or less than a supervening venue provision, permitting displacement of the ordinary rules of venue when, in light of certain conditions, the trial court thinks that jurisdiction ought to be declined."[263] He noted that the doctrine has developed in response to problems with court administration and private litigants that often result from a plaintiff's misuse of venue.[264] Thus, the doctrine serves to discourage plaintiffs from forum shopping.[265] He also noted,

[256] Paxton Blair, *The Doctrine of Forum Non Conveniens in Anglo-American Law*, 29 COLUM. L. REV. 1, 22 (1929). According to John Wilson:

> Blair's thesis was that forum non conveniens should be more widely used to "reliev[e] calendar congestion by partially diverting at its source the flood of litigation by which our courts are being overwhelmed." The cause of the flood, Blair said, was forum shopping, which "merits the unequivocal condemnation of bench and bar."

Wilson, *supra* note 207, at 673 (footnote omitted) (quoting Blair, *supra* at 22).

[257] *See* Blair, *supra* note 256, at 23.

[258] *See* discussion *supra*.

[259] Gulf Oil Corp. v. Gilbert, 330 U.S. 501 (1947), *superseded by statute*, 28 U.S.C. § 1404 (2006), *as recognized in* Am. Dredging Co. v. Miller, 510 U.S. 443 (1994).

[260] Koster v. Lumbermens Mutual Casualty Co., 330 U.S. 518 (1947).

[261] Piper Aircraft Co. v. Reyno, 454 U.S. 235 (1981).

[262] 510 U.S. 443.

[263] *Id.* at 453.

[264] *See id.* at 450.

[265] *See id.* According to John Bies:

"The discretionary nature of the doctrine, combined with the multifariousness of the factors relevant to its application . . . make uniformity and predictability of outcome almost impossible."[266] He thought, however, that this outcome was acceptable because the doctrine serves as a procedural rule rather than as a substantive rule affecting the primary conduct of litigants.[267]

To say the least, this is at odds with our experience and the reality of litigation today. As Professor Kevin Clermont noted, "outcome often turns on forum," and "the fight over forum can be the critical dispute in the case."[268] This means that a "procedural rule" highly affects the conduct of litigants and, ultimately, their substantive rights, thus calling for the application of due process safeguards.

Even though the European Court of Justice made it clear that European law is strongly opposed to the forum non conveniens doctrine, the principles and ideas behind the doctrine are not completely unknown to civil law systems, which occasionally consider whether one forum would be more convenient than another when deciding whether to decline jurisdiction.[269] Articles 27 and 28 of EC Regulation 44/2001 identify the most convenient forum when two cases with the same parties and the same cause of action

> Since the Supreme Court's affirmance of the doctrine of forum non conveniens in *Gilbert*, federal courts have increasingly turned to forum non conveniens as a tool for managing their dockets, particularly in cases brought by foreign plaintiffs. Accompanying this increase in forum non conveniens dismissals has been a concomitant increase in the imposition of conditions on dismissals.

John Bies, Comment, *Conditioning Forum Non Conveniens*, 67 U. CHI. L. REV. 489, 500 (2000).

[266] Am. Dredging, 510 U.S. at 455 (citation omitted).

[267] Id. at 453.

[268] Kevin M. Clermont, *The Role of Private International Law in the United States: Beating the Not-Quite-Dead Horse of Jurisdiction*, *in* 2 PRIVATE LAW, PRIVATE INTERNATIONAL LAW, & JUDICIAL COOPERATION IN THE EU-US RELATIONSHIP 75, 77 (Ronald A. Brand & Mark Walter eds., 2005). Professor Clermont observes:

> Outside the academy, lawyers in the United States expend significant time, energy, and other resources on the process of forum selection. They know that the name of the game is forum-shopping. Few cases reach trial in the U.S. civil litigation system today; after perhaps some initial skirmishing, most cases settle. Yet all cases entail forum selection, be it selection of local venue, interstate shopping, state/federal selection, or international shopping. First, consider the individual case. The plaintiff's opening moves include shopping for the most favorable forum. Then, the defendant's parries and thrusts might include some forum-shopping in return, possibly by a motion for transfer of venue. Forum is worth fighting over because outcome often turns on forum, as I shall document below. When the dust settles, the case does too—but on terms that reflect the results of the skirmishing; thus, the fight over forum can be the critical dispute in the case.

Id. (footnote omitted) (internal quotation marks omitted).

[269] *See* Case C-281/02, Owusu v. Jackson, 2005 E.C.R. I-1383.

(lis pendens, article 27)[270] or when two related actions (related actions, article 28)[271] are pending before different judges.[272] In those cases, even though the ordinary rules of jurisdiction would identify a specific judge as the one with jurisdiction over that case, these two provisions identify a more convenient judge – the court where the same case (article 27) or the related case (article 28) was filed first – the one that better serves the interest of justice.[273] Among the objectives of the EC Regulation 44/2001, recital 15 provides that "[i]n the interests of the harmonious administration of justice it is necessary to minimise the possibility of concurrent proceedings and to ensure that irreconcilable judgments will not be given in two Member States."[274]

The ALI/UNIDROIT Principles of Transnational Civil Procedure adopted the forum non conveniens doctrine as a possible basis for denying jurisdiction.[275] Under principle 2.5, "Jurisdiction may be declined or the proceeding suspended when the court is manifestly inappropriate relative to another more appropriate court that could exercise jurisdiction."[276] This provision would probably be too broad for Europeans. What they would most likely reject is not the outcome – that is, choosing one forum over another because the first is more convenient and better serves the interest of justice. Instead, Europeans would likely reject the lack of criteria and the broad discretion left to judges to decide when one forum is more convenient than another that had been identified as the "natural forum" or "natural judge" by the otherwise applicable provisions.

In contrast to the ALI/UNIDROIT Principle of Transnational Civil Procedure 2.5, the draft of the Hague Convention on Jurisdiction and Recognition and Enforcement of Judgments adopted a provision on forum non conveniens that made an effort to identify the considerations that the court "shall take into account" when deciding whether to grant a motion to dismiss on forum non conveniens grounds:

Article 22 Exceptional circumstances for declining jurisdiction

1. In exceptional circumstances, ... the court may, on application by a party, suspend its proceedings if in that case it is *clearly inappropriate* for that court to exercise jurisdiction and if a court of another State has

[270] Council Regulation 44/2001, *supra* note 6, art. 27.
[271] *Id.* art. 28.
[272] *See* discussion *supra*.
[273] Under article 28, the court seised later may decide to decline the jurisdiction in favor of the court first seised. Here, because the actions are not the same, but merely related, the legislature wanted to leave to the judge's discretion the decision whether to decline or retain jurisdiction over the case. Council Regulation 44/2001, *supra* note 143, art. 28.
[274] *Id.* recital 15.
[275] *See* ALI/UNIDROIT, *supra* note 10, at 762–63.
[276] *Id.*

jurisdiction and is *clearly more appropriate* to resolve the dispute. Such application must be made no later than at the time of the first defence on the merits.

2. The court shall take into account, in particular—

   a) any inconvenience to the parties in view of their habitual residence; *b*) the nature and location of the evidence, including documents and witnesses, and the procedures for obtaining such evidence; *c*) applicable limitation or prescription periods; *d*) the possibility of obtaining recognition and enforcement of any decision on the merits.

3. In deciding whether to suspend the proceedings, a court shall not discriminate on the basis of the nationality or habitual residence of the parties.[277]

The provision was then abandoned, along with much of the rest of the draft convention. However, in view of the increasing amount of transnational litigation, the doctrine of forum non conveniens should be seriously considered and adopted in a text containing uniform jurisdictional rules governing this type of litigation.[278]

A provision on forum non conveniens would greatly enhance efficiency in transnational litigation. Furthermore, European judges would most likely agree with American judges that the forum where witnesses are located is more convenient and that a court that needs to apply a foreign law to the controversy brought before it might not know that law well enough to properly apply it, thus making the forum less convenient for that case. However, Europeans would make, and actually did make, the evaluation as to what is the more convenient forum for each controversy ex ante in EC Regulation 44/2001.[279] The more convenient judge under the Regulation is: the judge of the place where the contract was performed or had to be performed for controversies concerning contracts (article 5(1));[280] the judge of the place where the harmful event occurred or may occur for tort, delict, or quasi-delict controversies (article 5(3));[281] the judge of the place where the branch, agency, or other establishment is located for controversies arising out of the operation of that branch, agency, or establishment (article 5(5));[282] the judge

277 *Summary of the Outcome of the Discussion in Commission II*, *supra* note __, at 1040 (emphasis added). See discussion *supra*, for the author's proposal of a provision on forum non conveniens in transnational litigation.

278 Wilson, *supra* note __, at 662–63.

279 Council Regulation 44/2001, *supra* note 143, art. 5.

280 *Id.*

281 *Id.* art. 5(3).

282 *Id.* art. 5(5).

first seised in cases of lis pendens (article 27);[283] the judge first seised in cases of related actions (article 28);[284] etc.[285] Therefore, the use of the doctrine of forum non conveniens would necessarily be limited in that context.

The adoption of uniform and clear-cut rules to identify the judge with jurisdiction over the case would substantially reduce the need to adopt the doctrine of forum non conveniens. The "convenience" of a forum would be considered in advance when setting forth the criteria for the identification of competent judges. Most of the time, the most convenient forum will be identified when defining the minimum contacts required to establish jurisdiction.[286] When the applicable rule would not be able to identify such a judge, the public policy exception could apply to "adjust" a result that would not be in the best interest of justice.

Thus, the common law doctrine of forum non conveniens should not be an obstacle to the harmonization of jurisdictional law. The United States and Europe should be able to reach a consensus on a provision that, while allowing forum non conveniens dismissals, would also better identify the criteria that courts should apply when granting or denying any such motions. Further, a dismissal on forum non conveniens grounds would be the exception, assuming that the rules identifying the judge with jurisdiction over each case already identify the most convenient forum.

In any event, should Americans and Europeans not reach a consensus on a provision allowing forum non conveniens dismissals, there is no reason why the United States could not join an international convention that forbids dismissals on forum non conveniens grounds in the context of litigation on civil and commercial matters. In fact, American due process merely allows, but does not require, forum non conveniens.

SIMILARITIES PREDOMINATE OVER DIFFERENCES

From the preceding analysis, it is clear that American jurisdictional law and European jurisdictional law share more similarities than differences. They both recognize general jurisdiction and domicile as a "proper" basis for exercising jurisdiction consistent with due process. Whenever the defendant

283 *Id.* art. 27.
284 *Id.* art. 28.
285 *See also* discussion *supra* at 148–149.
286 The same idea was suggested by Professor Clermont, who noted, "The costs of the doctrine [of forum non conveniens] outweigh its benefits; and if the [Hague] treaty also were to narrow general jurisdiction and refine specific jurisdiction, any benefits of forum non conveniens would all but disappear." Clermont, *supra* note 7, at 120.

is not sued before the court of the place where he is domiciled, it is necessary that the defendant's due process rights are guaranteed. The American minimum contacts test and EC Regulation 44/2001 are intended to guarantee these rights. Even though the American test is not codified, while the European provisions are, they lead to the same results – that is, jurisdiction is similarly established or denied in most cases.[287]

Given this shared approach, Americans and Europeans should be able to reach a consensus on what constitutes minimum contacts in various transnational situations – for example, contracts, torts, and property – and codify these contacts in an international convention that would make sure the defendant is "on notice" of the possibility of being sued in a state because of his contacts with it. This convention would only apply to transnational litigation on civil and commercial matters. This harmonization effort would greatly enhance predictability, fairness, and efficiency. The exercise of jurisdiction would be reasonable, forum shopping would be reduced, and consequently, there would be less need to apply the forum non conveniens doctrine for this purpose.

As this analysis shows, due process is the main preoccupation of both American and European jurisdictional law, and the core content of due process is not different in the United States and Europe.[288] Under U.S. law, the required elements of due process are those that "minimize substantively unfair or mistaken deprivations" by enabling persons to contest the basis upon which a state proposes to deprive them of protected interests.[289] At the core of this requirement are notice and a hearing before an impartial tribunal. The concept of due process has been further developed through the idea of "fundamental fairness," as illustrated by case law.[290] Elementary considerations of fairness dictate that individuals should have an opportunity to know which judge has jurisdiction over their case. In Europe this is called the "natural judge," and the right to a "natural," predetermined judge is considered a fundamental right, which is part of the bundle of due process rights to which every individual is entitled.

Despite opinions to the contrary,[291] constitutional analysis is not absent from European jurisdictional law.[292] However, because European jurisdictional law

[287] *See* discussion *supra*.

[288] *See* Juenger, *supra* note 47.

[289] Fuentes v. Shevin, 407 U.S. 67, 81 (1972).

[290] Rogers v. Tennessee, 532 U.S. 451, 460–62 (2001) (stating that the interests in fundamental fairness are considered satisfied "(through notice and fair warning) and the prevention of the arbitrary and vindictive use of the laws").

[291] See the reports of the Hague Convention on jurisdiction and recognition and enforcement of judgments.

[292] *See* Juenger, *supra* note 47, at 1203–04.

is codified, the parties to transnational litigation as well as the judge do not need to run any constitutional analysis to determine whether jurisdiction meets due process requirements in every case. This is because the European legislature ran this analysis when it drafted the rules. This does not mean Europeans do not care about due process; quite the opposite is true. In fact, by clearly and precisely indicating the judge or judges with jurisdiction over specific cases on the basis of specific and reasonable connecting factors, the European legislature intended to ensure that the individual's due process rights were duly implemented.[293]

This approach is shared by most of the constitutions of the EU Member States.[294] The European Court of Justice, when interpreting the jurisdictional rules under EC Regulation 44/2001, observed:

> [I]t must be borne in mind that the Convention is necessarily based on the trust which the Contracting States accord to one another's legal systems and judicial institutions. It is that mutual trust which has enabled a compulsory system of jurisdiction to be established, which all the courts within the purview of the Convention are required to respect ...
>
> It is inherent in that principle of mutual trust that, within the scope of the Convention, the rules on jurisdiction that it lays down, which are common to all the courts of the Contracting States, may be interpreted and applied with the same authority by each of them ...[295]
>
> Similarly, otherwise than in a small number of exceptional cases listed in the first paragraph of Article 28 of the Convention,[296] which are limited to the stage of recognition or enforcement and relate only to certain rules of special or exclusive jurisdiction ... the Convention does not permit the jurisdiction of a court to be reviewed by a court in another Contracting State.[297]

However, in addition to preserving the idea of mutual trusts among the contracting EU Member States, EC Regulation 44/2001 intended to protect the fundamental right (due process) of the individual not to be brought before a judge who is not his natural judge. Article 6 – which resembles article 6 of

[293] The defendant should be able to predict which judge is going to have jurisdiction over his case without any unfair surprise. The identification of the judge should be reasonable and fair.

[294] *See* PIETRO FRANZINA, LA GIURISDIZIONE IN MATERIA CONTRATTUALE: L'ART. 5 N. 1 DEL REGOLAMENTO N. 44/2001/CE NELLA PROSPETTIVA DELLA ARMONIA DELLE DECISIONI 126 (2006).

[295] *See* Case C-351/89, Overseas Union Ins. Ltd. v. N.H. Ins. Co., 1991 E.C.R. I-3342, 3350.

[296] Here, reference is made to the Brussels Convention of 1968, whose provisions are almost identical to the provisions of Council Regulation 44/2001, with very few and minor variations.

[297] Case C-159/02, Turner v. Grovit, 2004 E.C.R. I-3565, 3587–88.

the European Convention for the Protection of Human Rights and Fundamental Freedoms[298] – provides:

> A person domiciled in a Member State may also be sued . . . as a third party in an action on a warranty or guarantee or in any other third party proceedings, in the court seised of the original proceedings, unless these were instituted solely with the object of removing him *from the jurisdiction of the court which would be competent in his case.*[299]

In other words, the defendant has a legitimate expectation to be sued before a certain judge. This expectation is part of his bundle of due process rights, and the EC Regulation is intended to protect such rights by posing clear and well-defined criteria for the identification of the judge with jurisdiction over cases.

European and American jurisdictional law, therefore, agree that the exercise of (personal) jurisdiction must be consistent with due process. However, while European jurisdictional law tries to achieve this result through an ex ante analysis and the identification and codification of the connecting factors pointing to the most "reasonable" and "predictable" judge, American jurisdictional law uses a case-by-case, minimum contacts analysis.[300] Whichever method is used, the result is often the same:[301] The court of a state has jurisdiction over a nonresident defendant when he could reasonably expect to be haled into that forum. Therefore, harmonizing jurisdictional law for transnational litigation on civil and commercial matters is indeed possible.

HARMONIZING CONFLICT OF LAWS RULES AND FINAL REMARKS

The above analysis of civil law and common law conflict of laws rules shows us that, despite a few differences, many similarities exist. Furthermore, these apparent differences disappear once one realizes that American courts tend to adopt the most significant relationship approach, which, most of the time, resembles the approach adopted by Europeans. Moreover, although it is true that there are different ways in which one can identify what the most

[298] Convention for the Protection of Human Rights and Fundamental Freedoms, Nov. 4, 1950, 5 E.T.S. 8, art. 6.

[299] Council Regulation 44/2001, *supra* note 6, art. 6 (emphasis added).

[300] In this respect, it is worth noticing that many American states have so-called "tailored" or "specific acts" long-arm statutes that identify the specific situations over which a court of the state has jurisdiction over a nonresident defendant. The criteria adopted by these statutes strongly resemble the criteria adopted by Council Regulation 44/2001. For examples of long-arm statutes, see IDES & MAY, *supra* note 167, at 87.

[301] *See* discussion *supra*.

significant relationship is, the approaches used by European and American conflict of laws rules are very similar.

Europeans do not completely refuse the governmental interest, or "better law," analysis. Furthermore, there are cases, especially where public policy interests are at stake – such as in marriage, divorce, filiation, and legitimation cases – where Europeans adopt solutions very similar to those adopted by Americans.[302] Public policy considerations, however, rarely find – or should find – application in purely transnational commercial transaction contexts or in various other contexts of transnational litigation on civil and commercial matters.

At the origins of conflict of laws rules, courts identified the laws applicable to the controversies on the basis of very simple and highly predictable connecting factors. The law governing contracts was the law of the place where the contract was made (*lex loci contractus*). The law governing torts or crimes was the law of the place where the tort or the crime was committed (*lex loci delicti*). The law governing property was the law of the place where the property in dispute was situated (*lex rei sitae*). The applicable law also identified the judge with jurisdiction over the case.[303]

The analysis above shows that the systems under consideration have not substantially departed from the original approach, and, in any event, the differences between the two systems seem to be exceptions to a common pattern. These exceptions were adopted as corrective measures to the general rules, to ensure that, as it was in the past, justice prevails over formal rules of conflict of laws when the application of formal rules would be unjust.[304] If we focus on these important similarities, a consensus should be relatively easy to reach, at least as far as uniform rules governing transnational litigation on civil and commercial matters are concerned.

In 1996, the Hague Conference on Private International Law began to work on the draft of an international convention concerning the recognition and enforcement of judgments and the harmonization of jurisdictional rules.[305]

[302] *Id.*

[303] *See* discussion *supra.*

[304] *See* Berman, *supra* note 12, at 46–47.

[305] In fact, the Hague Convention on Recognition and Enforcement of Foreign Judgments in Civil and Commercial Matters had been negotiated throughout the 1960s, but it had remained largely unsuccessful. *See* Convention on the Recognition and Enforcement of Foreign Judgments in Civil and Commercial Matters, Feb. 1, 1971, 1144 U.N.T.S. 249. Even before then, in 1925, the Hague Conference, then consisting of only civil law members, had produced a Convention on the Recognition and Enforcement of Foreign Judgment in Civil and Commercial Matters. This convention never passed the drafting stage either. *See* BAUMGARTNER, *supra* note 211, at 1–3.

The convention had several intentions: (1) identify the grounds of jurisdiction guaranteeing recognition and enforcement under the convention, (2) identify the prohibited grounds of jurisdiction, and (3) provide flexibility for national jurisdiction rules, which could continue to apply.[306] The works were interrupted many times, and in 2001, it was finally clear that there was no consensus on a text adopting uniform jurisdictional bases.[307] Instead, a narrower convention was finally adopted, and was limited to the "exclusive choice of court agreements concluded in civil or commercial matters," with an optional extension of the chapter on recognition and enforcement of judgments given by a court designated in a nonexclusive choice of court agreement.[308] The resulting convention – so far ratified only by Mexico – may seem like a failure when compared to the original ambitious yet feasible project.[309]

The main reasons offered for the failure of this huge project were mostly related to the allegedly different approaches to jurisdiction adopted by common law – that is, American – and civil law – that is, European – systems. The disputes between the Europeans and the Americans overpowered the discussions and strongly affected the negotiations at The Hague, so much so that delegations from other countries often had difficulty presenting their insights and concerns.[310] The apparently irreconcilable differences were found in the American constitutional approach to jurisdiction, the minimum contacts test, doing-business jurisdiction, tag or transient jurisdiction, and the forum non conveniens doctrine.

The approaches and criteria adopted by Americans seemed to be irreconcilable with the approaches and criteria adopted by Europeans. However, as this analysis shows, the approaches and criteria Americans and Europeans adopt are very similar, and, most of the time, reach the same results, despite the different labels. The minimum contacts test that American courts run on a case-by-case basis has already been completed ex ante by Europeans through the identification of the substantial contacts in the provisions of EC Regulation 44/2001 that give courts jurisdiction over the cases. Perhaps, the question should not be what forum is the natural forum, or even the more appropriate

[306] *See Outline: Convention of 30 June 2005 on Choice of Court Agreements*, HAGUE CONF. ON PRIVATE INT'L L., http://hcch.e-vision.nl/upload/outline37e.pdf (last visited Jan. 18, 2012).

[307] *See* RECORDS, *supra* note 54.

[308] *Convention on Choice of Court Agreements*, *supra* note 211.

[309] *See Status Table – 37: Convention of 30 June 2005 on Choice of Court Agreements*, HAGUE CONF. ON PRIVATE INT'L L., http://hcch.e-vision.nl/index_en.php?act=conventions.status&cid=98 (last updated Nov. 19, 2010).

[310] *See* BAUMGARTNER, *supra* note 211, at 5.

one, but rather, which forum is "reasonable" – that is, which forum presents substantial contacts with the controversy.[311]

The substantial contacts or connecting factors that Americans and Europeans use to identify jurisdiction and the law applicable to a controversy are very similar.[312] It would therefore be possible to draft uniform rules of jurisdiction and choice of law rules that, on the basis of the same criteria, identify the judge with jurisdiction over a case and the law applicable to it. These uniform provisions and the criteria adopted would be consistent with due process because they would incorporate the relevant constitutional tests.[313] The controversy and the defendant should present substantial contacts with the forum state to support the idea that the court of that state would have jurisdiction over that controversy.[314] This would make the forum reasonable and predictable for the defendant. Doing-business jurisdiction, if upheld by American courts according to the general guidelines and the high threshold set by the U.S. Supreme Court, is nothing but an articulation of jurisdiction based on the defendant's domicile. In fact, as illustrated above, general or doing-business jurisdiction cases would find similar solutions in the United States and Europe.

As clearly expressed by Professor Clermont, harmonization would bring a fair and advantageous compromise. He noted:

> The Europeans' principal objection to U.S. jurisdictional law is its proclivity to base general jurisdiction on rather thin contacts, namely, allowing any and all causes of action to be brought on the basis of the defendant's physical presence, property ownership, or doing business in the forum. They do not object to specific jurisdiction, as long as a rules-based approach controls its mandatory application.[315]

Tag jurisdiction would most likely be absent from this international convention on conflict of laws as a possible jurisdictional category. However, this should not be a problem for the United States, as has been explained above.[316]

[311] "Substantial contacts" was also adopted as the basis for jurisdiction by principle 2 of the ALI/UNIDROIT Principles of Transnational Civil Procedure. *See* ALI/UNIDROIT, *supra* note __, at 762.

[312] As observed by Professor Juenger, "[F]ourteen hundred years before *International Shoe*, the civil law, unhampered by constitutional doctrine and territorialist dogma, already premised jurisdiction on 'minimum contacts,' and this idea continues to inform current European jurisdictional law." Juenger, *supra* note 47, at 1204.

[313] In favor of regulation of territorial authority to adjudicate, see Clermont, *supra* note __, at 102.

[314] *See* discussion *infra*.

[315] Clermont, *supra* note 7, at 95–96 (footnote omitted).

[316] *See* discussion *supra*. Also, Professor Clermont observed:

Furthermore, forum non conveniens is not an obstacle to harmonization either. As this work illustrates, the notion of a more convenient forum is not unknown to the Europeans, who adopted a similar idea in EC Regulation 44/2001 when dealing with lis pendens and related actions. A general provision on forum non conveniens could be adopted in a global convention on jurisdiction. This provision could contain a nonexhaustive and illustrative list of circumstances that would make a forum more convenient, thus setting the basic guidelines for a decision, which would appear less arbitrary because judges would have less discretion.

According to some authors, Europeans and Americans have differing ideas on what jurisdiction is.[317] However, jurisdiction is the power of the judge to adjudicate cases, and this analysis shows that American and European jurisdictional law began from similar major premises and, most of the time, reach the same results despite their different labels or methodological paths. In fact, as illustrated above, by applying the relevant jurisdictional law provisions under EC Regulation 44/2001 to cases that have been submitted to the U.S. Supreme Court for review of personal jurisdiction issues, the result is usually the same under both European and American law. Thus, uniform rules on jurisdiction over transnational litigation on civil and commercial matters could indeed be adopted.[318]

> Given transient jurisdiction's dubious propriety and general unnecessariness, the United States should be, and seems to be, willing to accept the treaty's prohibition. Perhaps, however, the United States should insist on a new provision for jurisdiction against terrorists and human rights violators, against whom the human rights community has relied on tag jurisdiction.

Clermont, *supra* note 7, at 112 (footnote omitted).

317 *See* Ralf Michaels, *Two Paradigms of Jurisdiction*, 27 MICH. J. INT'L L. 1003, 1011 (2006).

318 For a proposed draft of a uniform convention on jurisdictional law, see discussion *infra*. *See also* Kevin M. Clermont & Kuo-Chang Huang, *Converting the Draft Hague Treaty into Domestic Jurisdictional Law*, *in* A GLOBAL LAW OF JURISDICTION AND JUDGMENTS: LESSONS FROM THE HAGUE 191 (John J. Barceló III & Kevin M. Clermont eds., 2002). The authors adopt the defendant's habitual residence as the basis for general jurisdiction in title 2, section 201. *Id.* at 200. Given that "general jurisdiction confers broad power to adjudicate any claim against the defendant, without taking into consideration the relation between the particular case and the forum, the basis for this jurisdiction requires a strong nexus between the defendant and the forum." *Id.* at 201. The authors then suggest a series of bases of specific jurisdiction. For instance, with reference to contracts, "A state has personal jurisdiction over a defendant as to a claim in contract if the claim arose from the defendant's transacting business in that state." *Id.* at 205. "Transacting business" was chosen as a basis for personal jurisdiction in cases dealing with contracts in order "to provide flexibility." *Id.* at 207. The proposed provision "uses the restrictive phrase 'arose from' to ensure a close connection." *Id.* In regard to torts, title 2, section 202(b) provides, "A state has personal jurisdiction over a defendant as to a claim in tort if: (1) the act or omission causing injury occurred in that state; or (2) the injury occurred in that state and the defendant purposefully directed other activities relating to the

Harmonization should be pursued when the means to do so exist, and there are no real obstacles. International conventions on service of process,[319] the abolition of legalization,[320] and the taking of evidence abroad[321] are perfect examples of how the original differences existing among the countries did not prevent harmonization,[322] how exorbitant rules adopted by some countries could be set aside in favor of harmonization,[323] and how the international community as a whole could highly benefit from these instruments. Through the adoption of standardized forms, these conventions have introduced cheaper and faster mechanisms that can be adopted in transnational litigation, thus eventually enhancing international judicial cooperation and improving transnational litigation.

However, jurisdictional law still needs to be harmonized. This is not an easy task, as the "failure" of the Hague Convention on Jurisdiction and Recognition and Enforcement of Judgments proved. Nevertheless, this is not an

tortuous injury to that state." *Id.* at 205. "This jurisdictional basis for specific jurisdiction in tort has long been deemed appropriate in the United States." *Id.* at 210; *see also* RESTATEMENT (SECOND) OF CONFLICT OF LAWS § 36(1) (1971).

[319] Hague Service Convention, *supra* note __.

[320] Convention Abolishing the Requirement of Legalisation for Foreign Public Documents, *supra* note 6.

[321] Hague Evidence Convention, *supra* note 6.

[322] As it has been observed:

> Until the Convetion [on the service abroad] was implemented, the contracting nations followed widely divergent practices for serving judicial documentrs across international borders, some of which did not ensure any notice, much less timely notice, and therefore often produced unfair default judgments. Particularly controversial was a procedure, ommon among civil-law countries, called notification au parquet, which permitted delivery of process to a local official who was then ordinarily supposed to transmit the document abroad through diplomatic or other channels. Typically, service was deemed complete upon delivery of the document to the official whether or not the official succeded in transmitting it to the defendant and whether or not the defendant otherwise received notice of the pending lawsuit.
>
> The United States delegation ot the Convention objected to notification au parquet as inconsistent with the requirements of due process of law under the Federal Constitution. The head of the delegation has derided its [i]njustice, extravagance, [and] absurdity...
>
> In response to this and other concerns, the Convention prescribes the exclusive means for service of process emanating from one contracting nation and culminating in another. As the Court observes, the Convention applies only when the document is to be transmit[ted] ... for service abroad; it covers not every transmission of judicial documents abroad, but only those transmissions abroad that constitute formal service.

BORN, *supra* note 29, at 829 (footnote omitted) (internal quotation marks omitted).

[323] For a definition of "exorbitant rules" and information on notification *au parquet*, see *supra* text accompanying note 14.

impossible task, especially if we limit it to areas where harmonization would not only be highly beneficial, but also very feasible. Countries will have to accept compromises to reach a consensus on a uniform set of rules and a uniform text. However, this work shows that the bases for a reasonable compromise exist and that international commercial transactions and legal systems in general would greatly benefit from uniform conflict of laws rules. Also, ratifying countries could finally have their judgments more easily recognized and enforced abroad, and have the other countries renounce their exorbitant rules too.

An international convention on conflict of laws rules could adopt very simple, easily predictable, and alternative connecting factors – the recurring connecting factors that have been adopted by the various legal systems and proved successful there.[324] As this analysis shows, the connecting factors that legal systems adopt are very similar. The new uniform conflict of laws rules would leave to judges the power to depart from them only under exceptional circumstances when it would be unjust or against the fundamental principles and public policy of that system to apply them.

The convention could identify such exceptional circumstances, which would call for governmental interest analysis or for the identification of the better law. This would be possible through the application of each country's fundamental principles of policy (or rules of mandatory application) and *ordre public*. In other words, rules of mandatory application and *ordre public* would be the vehicle through which a state would be able to pursue its own governmental interest or to select the better law to apply to the controversy. However, departures from the general rules for reasons of *ordre public* should be the exception, especially considering that transnational litigation on civil and commercial matters should not be the place where public policy exceptions – which are usually concerned with family, succession, administrative matters, etc. – apply.

In any event, there cannot be a fundamental public policy or *ordre public* that needs to be considered every time a conflict of laws problem arises. Furthermore, although governmental interests and public policies may change throughout the years, they rarely change significantly, especially over limited periods of time. This will give the systems some further stability.

This chapter does not suggest a reversion to the vested rights approach under the First Restatement, an approach that proved to be inadequate to

[324] Alternative factors would be adopted to ensure a certain level of flexibility. *See* BAUMGARTNER, *supra* note 211, at 27.

meet the needs of justice.[325] Rather, this chapter suggests the adoption of a uniform and flexible system, based on a pluralistic approach, which would still be able to achieve uniformity of solutions and harmonization, while preserving the real differences.

In such a system, public policy as an escape device would be used cautiously. As Professor Carter observed:

> [P]ublic policy should not be invoked in private international law merely because it could, or would, be invoked in the *forum* if the same facts had been presented in a purely domestic context—unless, of course, the internal law of the *forum* is the *lex causae*. Locally acceptable inhibitions and prejudices are not always appropriate in a transnational context. The automatic injection of standards applicable in a domestic situation into a transnational situation may be seen, at best as an exercise in mechanical jurisprudence, and at worst as blatant judicial chauvinism.
>
> Secondly, and more generally, the initial reaction to any attempted invocation of public policy should be, if not hostile, at least one of guarded suspicion. As Cardozo J[.] said in *Loucks v. Standard Oil Co.* over 70 years ago: "The courts are not free to enforce a foreign right at the pleasure of the judges, to suit the individual notion of expediency or fairness. They do not close their doors unless help would violate some fundamental principle of justice, some prevalent conception of good morals, some deep-rooted tradition of the commonweal." These are oft-quoted words, but, when resort has been had to public policy, oft-disregarded words. The message that they embody is nevertheless salutary and benign.[326]

Care must be taken to ensure:

> Public policy [, the] "unruly horse" [,] is not allowed to wreak havoc in international pastures. To vary the metaphor—indulgence in "palm tree" justice is as undesirable in private international law as it is in internal law.
>
> The penultimate objective must largely lie in judicial restraint. But this, although to be welcomed, can be no more than a palliative of uneven consistency.[327]

Well-defined conflict of laws rules would help avoid the risk of arbitrary decisions. Conflict of laws rules should be framed in such a way that there would be no need to refer to public policy to avoid unfairness and injustice. Carter suggests that rigid rules with a narrowly and appropriately defined

[325] *See* discussion *supra*.

[326] Carter, *supra* note 70, at 2 (footnotes omitted) (quoting Loucks v. Standard Oil Co. of N.Y., 120 N.E. 198, 202 (N.Y. 1918)).

[327] *Id.* at 9–10 (internal quotation marks omitted).

scope, or flexible rules with a sufficiently broad scope, should be adopted, and that rigid rules of broad scope should be avoided, because they give rise to the need to refer to public policy.[328] An international convention might set forth general rules which would embrace the approach adopted by the original conflict of laws rules, preserving and encouraging a strong interaction between choice of law and jurisdictional law rules.

The rules of this international convention would identify the law applicable to the controversy, and the judge with jurisdiction over it, based on a single set of connecting factors, which would make the selection of the applicable law and of the jurisdiction over the case highly predictable, fair, and efficient. Public policy would be invoked only under exceptional circumstances, thus avoiding the application of locally acceptable inhibitions and prejudices to transnational controversies. These rules would be specifically adopted for international controversies, and thus, would often be different from the rules adopted for domestic controversies. The presumption of applying the same rules to national as well as transnational controversies by definition must be wrong. There should be a separate regulation for transnational controversies and an international agreement upon those rules, which would eventually enhance the quality of the rules themselves.[329] This is what happened with the EC Regulations.[330]

However, as shown above, the EC Regulations still contain many useless repetitions of similar connecting factors used to identify the judge with jurisdiction over the case and the law applicable to it. Such repetitions could easily be avoided by adopting a uniform and single set of criteria whenever possible.

[328] *Id.* at 10.

[329] Hence, not only the quality of the international rules, but also the quality of the internal rules would be enhanced. "The exercise of specifying which of the constitutional forums are the more convenient, efficient, and otherwise desirable would do a great service to U.S. law. In addition, learning more about foreign thinking on jurisdictional matters could have only a salutary effect on the shape of U.S. law." Clermont, *supra* note 7, at 116.

[330] As noted by Professor Clermont:

> The Brussels Convention takes only the best of the civilian tradition regarding jurisdiction...
>
> On the prohibited side, each member state gave up its exorbitant jurisdiction, but only as against domiciliaries of other member states. So, France gave up jurisdiction based on the plaintiff's French nationality. England, too, is now a signatory and has relinquished transient and attachment jurisdiction. Furthermore, the Convention not only prohibits exorbitant jurisdiction, but also makes mandatory the permissible bases of jurisdiction. Accordingly, England abandoned its judicial practice of sometimes declining jurisdiction on expressly discretionary grounds, but again only when the Convention applies.

Id. at 92–93 (footnotes omitted).

There are multiple interactions between jurisdictional law and choice of law connecting factors that cannot be ignored. As in the past, courts still often recognize this strong interaction between the two sets of rules. For instance, dissenting in *Shaffer* and linking choice of law and jurisdictional law considerations, Justice Brennan observed:

> I recognize that the jurisdictional and choice-of-law inquiries are not identical. But I would not compartmentalize thinking in this area quite so rigidly as it seems to me the Court does today, for *both inquiries* are often closely related and to a substantial degree *depend upon similar considerations.*[331]

Furthermore, concurring in *Burnham*, Justice Brennan again noted that there is "an interaction among rules governing jurisdiction, *forum non conveniens*, and choice of law."[332]

Similar to Justice Brennan in his dissent in *Shaffer*, Justice Black, dissenting in *Hanson v. Denckla*, noted, "True, the question whether the law of a State can be applied to a transaction is different from the question whether the courts of that State have jurisdiction to enter a judgment, but *the two are often closely related and to a substantial degree depend upon similar considerations.*"[333] Justice Stevens, concurring in *Allstate Insurance Co. v. Hague*, observed:

> I question whether a judge's decision to apply the law of his own State could ever be described as wholly irrational. For judges are presumably familiar with their own state law and may find it difficult and time consuming to discover and apply correctly the law of another State. The forum State's interest in the fair and efficient administration of justice is therefore sufficient, in my judgment, to attach a presumption of validity to a forum State's decision to apply its own law to a dispute over which it has jurisdiction.[334]

[331] Shaffer v. Heitner, 433 U.S. 186, 224–25 (1977) (Brennan, J., concurring in part and dissenting in part) (emphasis added) (citation omitted) (internal quotation marks omitted).

[332] Burnham v. Superior Court of California, 495 U.S. 604, 634 n.9 (1990) (Brennan, J., concurring) (citations omitted).

[333] 357 U.S. 235, 258 (1958) (Black, J., dissenting) (emphasis added).

[334] 449 U.S. 302, 326 (1981) (Stevens, J., concurring) (footnote omitted). Other case law adopted the same unified approach to choice of law and jurisdictional rules. In *Alton v. Alton*, rather than begin with the in rem nature of the proceedings and deduce the application of the forum law to the case, the Third Circuit began with a decision to apply forum law and inferred that their choice of law could be guaranteed only through an in rem proceeding based on domicile, the traditional test for presence of the marital res. 207 F.2d 667, 674 (3d Cir. 1953), *vacated*, 347 U.S. 610 (1954). As observed by Carol Bruch Myers:

> Striking down an attempt by the Virgin Islands legislature to base divorce on other grounds, the court of appeals majority apparently failed to recognize the distinction

Not only judges, but also authoritative scholars have recognized and praised this interaction between jurisdictional rules and choice of law rules.[335]

A proposed unifying theory for jurisdiction and choice of law rules recognizes that "[t]he selection of a forum has a determinative and inescapable

> between judicial jurisdiction and application of forum law. Consequently, Judge Goodrich used reasoning appropriate to a choice of law decision, although the issue was one of jurisdiction: "We think that adherence to the domiciliary requirement is necessary if our states are really to have control over the domestic relations of their citizens."
> As Judge Hastie suggested, the court's concern could have been met instead by a requirement that the law of the place of domicile be applied in divorce cases, regardless of the jurisdictional base. Indeed, such a choice of law rule would secure application of the same law as jurisdiction based on domicile, yet allow in personam adjudications where convenience to the parties would be better served.
> Under current practice, an in personam jurisdictional base is necessary for resolution of the property and financial aspects of a divorce.

Carol Bruch Myers, *At the Intersection of Jurisdiction and Choice of Law*, 59 CALIF. L. REV. 1514, 1522–23 (1971) (footnotes omitted) (quoting *Alton*, 207 F.2d at 676). In cases dealing with the Internet, when "U.S. law *may* apply, the judges seem to assume that U.S. law *should* apply, even without any sustained discussion of other possible outcomes." Paul Schiff Berman, *Towards a Cosmopolitan Vision of Conflict of Laws: Redefining Governmental Interests in a Global Era*, 153 U. PA. L. REV. 1819, 1823 (2005). Additionally, the decision in *GlobalSantaFe Corp. v. Globalsantafe.com*, which involved two American corporations and a Korean individual, yielded a "vision of choice of law that . . . is founded solely on jurisdictional power and a race to the courthouse." *Id.* at 1829; *see also* GlobalSantaFe Corp. v. Globalsantafe.com, 250 F. Supp. 2d 610 (E.D. Va. 2003). In *GlobalSantaFe Corp.*, the United States District for the Eastern District of Virginia never questioned that the Anticybersquatting Consumer Protection Act (ACPA) was the only possible relevant legal regime. Indeed, the court assumed that the ACPA's legal reach was limited solely by the scope of the court's jurisdiction, and not by any choice of law considerations. 250 F. Supp. 2d 610; Berman, *supra* at 1828. While constitutional limitations on the choice of law are by no means settled, important considerations certainly include the expectancies of the parties and the fairness of governing the defendants' acts and behavior by rules of conduct created by a given jurisdiction. *See, e.g.*, Home Ins. Co. v. Dick, 281 U.S. 397 (1930); RESTATEMENT (SECOND) OF CONFLICT OF LAWS § 6 (1971). These same factors bear upon the propriety of a state's exercising jurisdiction over a legal dispute. "At the minimum, the decision that it is fair to bind a defendant by a State's laws and rules should prove to be highly relevant to the fairness of permitting that same State to accept jurisdiction for adjudicating the controversy." *Shaffer*, 433 U.S. at 225 (Brennan, J., concurring in part and dissenting in part).

335 *See* Albert A. Ehrenzweig, *A Proper Law in a Proper Forum: A "Restatement" of the "Lex Fori Approach,"* 18 OKLA. L. REV. 340 (1965). Professor Silberman also observed:

> Any real due process or "reasonableness" test for jurisdiction would need to take the impact of choice of law into account, and the Supreme Court has given little indication of either its willingness or competence to do so. . . Choice-of-law rules need to be fashioned which neutrally weigh the interests of competing states, and ways of ensuring that neutrality must be found.

Silberman, *supra* note 211, at 595. Professor Currie, for instance, believed that the forum courts were instruments of state policy, and thus, they had to apply forum laws whenever legitimate interests were present. *See* CURRIE ET AL., *supra* note 86.

influence on the result in the case before it, an effect that cannot be nullified by the forum's decision to apply rules that parallel some other sovereign's rules of local law."[336] The identification of the forum selects an entire decision-making regime and "[d]eciding that the forum's exercise of judicial jurisdiction is constitutional also decides that it is constitutional for the forum to determine the result in the case."[337] "[T]he power to decide carries with it the power to select the rules that will inform that decision."[338] Therefore, there is a necessary interrelation between the two sets of rules, and a unified approach to them would ensure consistency and logical and efficient solutions.

The rules that have been adopted and proven successful in the participating states would form the basis for the provisions in this convention. This convention would not adopt any exorbitant rules, like tag jurisdiction.

Not long ago, I spoke with a colleague about my idea of harmonizing civil procedure rules. He listened and then said: "Well, you have to consider that institutions perform the same functions, and civil procedure systems have been adopted to solve disputes. They cannot be that different after all." I thought he captured the issue well. When trying to harmonize legal provisions, the goal of such provisions should always be kept in mind, as well as the final goal of legal systems, which is to solve disputes in a just, efficient, and speedy way, whether or not this has been expressly stated by rules or case law.

As indicated by Aristotle, laws perform similar functions for society, and the purpose of things is part of their nature.[339] Behind this idea was the teleological image of the world striving for perfection, where "is" and "ought" were connected, and the correct laws could be deduced from the nature of things.[340] These thoughts, initially rejected, were revived during the twentieth century, and once it could be shown that not only problems but also their solutions were similar, "a return to a minimal version of Natural law or at least *ius gentium*, based on the Artistotelian notion of function, seemed possible."[341]

We comparativists often forget this when we focus on differences rather than similarities. If we had the goal of the provisions we were analyzing in mind, there would be more works on "convergences" rather than on

336 Harold G. Maier & Thomas R. McCoy, *A Unifying Theory for Judicial Jurisdiction and Choice of Law*, 39 AM. J. COMP. L. 249, 255 (1991) (footnote omitted).

337 *Id.* at 257.

338 *Id.* at 281.

339 *See* Ralf Michaels, *The Functional Method of Comparative Law*, *in* THE OXFORD HANDBOOK OF COMPARATIVE LAW 339, 346 (Mathias Reimann & Reinhard Zimmermann eds., 2006).

340 *Id.*

341 *Id.*

"divergences," and more "professional awareness." Professional awareness is hard to achieve, but it is the key factor in achieving harmonization.

I also thought my colleague's comment was brilliant in its simplicity. It made me think that we do not need exceptionally complicated theories to support harmonization. All we need is a careful study and analysis of the systems under consideration, one that would look beyond the surface of what seem like irreconcilable differences and rediscover common origins and shared roots as well as functional equivalences that still exist today.

The common goal of legal systems is to solve disputes in a just, efficient, and speedy way. Therefore, legal systems' rules must share significant similarities. Where they do not, one of these systems must be adopting the less efficient or less fair solution, unless the different approach or method is justified by a real public policy reason requiring a different approach. Harmonization would be an excellent tool in the hands of the legislatures, but professional awareness must be increased to reach this very important goal.

*****

An International Convention on Conflict of Laws Rules: A Draft Proposal

SECTION I

SCOPE AND APPLICATION

ARTICLE I

This Convention shall apply to conflict of laws issues arising in transnational litigation on civil and commercial matters.

The scope of this Convention is intentionally limited to transnational litigation on civil and commercial matters, considering it an area where harmonization is especially needed – uniform rules would reduce the costs of litigation and enhance predictability and fairness – and is possible – civil law and common law systems share many similarities and public policy issues preventing the application of the otherwise applicable uniform rules should not arise except under exceptional circumstances. The expression "civil and commercial matters" resembles the one used in the various EC Regulations, as well as in the Hague Conventions governing procedural issues; for example, the Hague Convention on the Taking of Evidence Abroad and the Hague Convention on the Service of Process Abroad. If the Convention applies to "civil and commercial matters," this means that it does not apply to tax, customs and administrative issues, family law, competition, arbitration, social security, bankruptcy, or wills and succession.

ARTICLE II

Any law indicated by this Convention as the law applicable to the controversy shall be applied, whether or not it is the law of a country that has ratified the Convention.

Any judge indicated by this Convention as the judge with jurisdiction over a case shall have jurisdiction over the case, whether or not it is the judge of a country that has ratified the Convention.

The Convention provides that even when the connecting factors it adopts lead to the application of a law or to the identification of a competent judge of a country that has not ratified the Convention, this selection will be valid. This selection mechanism enhances predictability and efficiency, and it encourages countries to ratify the Convention.

SECTION II

GENERAL JURISDICTION

ARTICLE III

Subject to this Convention, individuals having their domicile, or corporations having their statutory seat, central administration, or principal place of business in a country that has ratified the Convention may, whatever their nationality, be sued in the courts of that country.

Individuals or corporations doing continuous, systematic, and substantial activities in a country that has ratified the Convention, whatever their nationality, may also be sued in that country.

Domicile as a basis of jurisdiction is consistent with due process and the defendant can reasonably anticipate being haled into court there for any cause of action. This makes the exercise of jurisdiction consistent with due process.

The formal concept of "domicile" is expanded to include the idea of "domicile in fact." When doing continuous, substantial, and systematic activity in a place, the individual or corporation will be considered as if he or it were domiciled there for purposes of jurisdiction. The exercise of jurisdiction by the courts of that place will be consistent with due process, because by reason of the activities – commercial or not – that the defendant is carrying out in that place, the defendant could reasonably expect to be haled into court there over any cause of action, including those that are not related to the activities carried out in that place. When jurisdiction is based on the domicile or domicile in fact of the defendant, the defendant may be sued on any cause of action. No relationship between the activity carried out by the defendant and the cause of action is necessary for a valid exercise of jurisdiction under the Convention.

SECTION III

RIGHTS IN REM

ARTICLE IV

The title or possession of real estate shall be governed by the law of the country where the real estate is located.

The judge with jurisdiction over a dispute involving the title or possession of real estate shall be the judge of the country where the real estate is located.

The principle, according to which actions over title or possession of real estate should be brought before the court of the place where the real estate is located and governed by the law of the same place, was originally adopted by Roman law and then by common law. The place where the real estate is located is an "exclusive" forum, that is, the controversies under this Article shall be brought before the judge where the real estate is located. No other forum will be considered proper.

SECTION IV

PENDENT PARTY JURISDICTION

ARTICLE V

A person domiciled in a country may also be sued: (1) where he is one of a number of defendants, in the courts of the place where any one of them is domiciled, provided that the claims are so closely connected that it is expedient to hear and determine them together to avoid the risk of irreconcilable judgments resulting from separate proceedings; (2) as a third party in an action on a warranty or guarantee or in any other third party proceedings in the court seised in the original proceedings, unless these were instituted solely with the object of removing him from the jurisdiction of the court which would be competent in his case; (3) on a counterclaim arising from the same contract or facts on which the original claim was based in the court in which the original claim is pending; and (4) in matters relating to a contract, if the action may be combined with an action against the same defendant in matters relating to rights in rem in real estate, in the court of the country in which the property is situated.

This Article provides for the possibility of bringing claims arising out of the same transaction or occurrence as the main claim before the same judge, including those that would not otherwise fall within the jurisdiction of that judge. This is intended to enhance judicial efficiency and fairness as well as avoid any res judicata problems. For this type of jurisdiction to be properly exercised, there must be a fairly strict connection between the claims against the original and the additional party or parties.

SECTION V

LIS PENDENS AND RELATED ACTIONS

ARTICLE VI

Where proceedings involving the same cause of action and between the same parties are brought in the courts of different countries, any court other than the court first seised shall of its own motion stay its proceedings until such time as the jurisdiction of the court first seised is established. Where the jurisdiction of the court first seised is established, any court other than the court first seised shall decline jurisdiction in favor of that court.

When related actions are pending in the courts of different countries, any court other than the court first seised may stay its proceeding. Where these actions are pending at first instance, any court other than the court first seised may also, on the application of one of the parties, decline jurisdiction if the court first seised has jurisdiction over the action in question and its law permits the consolidation thereof. For the purposes of this Article, actions are deemed to be related when they are so closely connected that it is expedient to hear and determine them together in order to avoid the risk of irreconcilable judgments resulting from separate proceedings.

In cases of lis pendens, any court other than the court first seised shall decline jurisdiction in favor of the court first seised that has declared to have jurisdiction over the case. This is intended to enhance efficiency and avoid the risk of irreconcilable judgments.

The court will determine, in its own discretion, whether two or more actions are "related." In this case, any court other than the court first seised will have discretion to decline jurisdiction in favor of the court first seised. When deciding to decline jurisdiction, courts will consider, inter alia, the status of the proceedings – that is, the court will consider whether the status of the proceeding pending before the court first seised is such to allow a thorough examination of the issues involved in the second proceeding – the interests of the parties in consolidating the actions, and any delay or any other prejudice that the defendant or the other parties may suffer.

SECTION VI

CONTRACTUAL OBLIGATIONS

ARTICLE VII

A contract shall be governed by the law chosen by the parties. By their choice, the parties can select the law applicable to all or only part of the contract. Notwithstanding the above choice, where all other elements relevant to the situation at the time of the choice are located in a country other than the country whose law has been chosen, the choice of the parties shall not prejudice the application of the provisions of the law of the other country that cannot be derogated from by agreement.

The parties may choose the judge with jurisdiction over their contractual obligations by agreement entered into before or after the event of default occurred, if all the parties are pursuing a commercial activity. Such jurisdiction shall be exclusive unless the parties have agreed otherwise.

The choice as to the applicable law, or the judge with jurisdiction over a contractual dispute, or both, shall be: (1) in writing or evidenced in writing; (2) in a form that accords with practices the parties have established between themselves; or (3) in matters involving international trade or commerce, in a form that accords with a usage of which the parties are or ought to have been aware, and that in such trade or commerce is widely known to, and regularly observed by, parties to contracts of the type involved in the particular trade or commerce concerned.

The parties' choice of the applicable law or of the judge with jurisdiction over the case shall be preserved, except where this choice is clearly intended to circumvent the public policy provisions of the country with which the contract is mostly connected. The choice of the judge with jurisdiction over the case shall be exclusive unless the parties have agreed otherwise. This is intended to address the issue of forum-selection clauses and the power that courts may have to disregard such clauses when deciding motions to transfer the case to another forum. The parties' choice shall be clearly indicated and proven according to the provision of this Article.

ARTICLE VIII

In the absence of the parties' choice, the law applicable to the contract shall be the law of: (1) the place of contracting; (2) the place of performance; (3) the place of subject matter of the contract; (4) the domicile, residence, place of incorporation, or place of business of the parties; or (5) the place with which the defendant and the case are more closely connected. The same connecting factors will be applied to identify the judge with jurisdiction over the case.

This Article adopts a "methodological pluralism" approach in order to identify the law that is more closely connected to the parties and the case, which is consistent with due process.

SECTION VII

NONCONTRACTUAL OBLIGATIONS

ARTICLE IX

The law applicable to noncontractual obligations shall be the law that the parties have selected by agreement, entered into before the event giving rise to the damage or after the damage occurred, if all the parties are pursuing a commercial activity.

The judge with jurisdiction over noncontractual disputes may be the judge whom the parties have selected by agreement, entered into either before or after the event giving rise to the damage occurred, if all the parties are pursuing a commercial activity. Such jurisdiction shall be exclusive unless the parties have agreed otherwise.

The choice shall be expressed or demonstrated with reasonable certainty by the circumstances of the case and shall not prejudice the rights of third parties.

Notwithstanding that provided by the preceding paragraph, where all the elements relevant to the situation at the time when the event giving rise to the damage occurs are located in a country other than the country whose law has been chosen, the choice of the parties shall not prejudice the application of provisions of the law of the country that cannot be derogated from by agreement.

Parties have the right to choose the law governing their noncontractual obligations as well as the judge with jurisdiction over any case concerning such obligations.

The forum selection clause shall be exclusive unless the parties have agreed otherwise.

ARTICLE X

In the absence of the parties' choice, the law applicable to noncontractual obligations shall be: (1) the law of the country where the damage occurred;

(2) the law of the country where the event giving rise to the damage occurred; (3) the law of the country where both parties are domiciled, habitually reside, have their place of incorporation, or have their place of business; (4) the law of the country with which the defendant and the case are manifestly more closely connected; or (5) the law of the country with which the parties and the case are manifestly more closely connected. The same connecting factors will be applied to identify the judge with jurisdiction over the case.

This provision adopts a methodological pluralism approach in order to identify the law and the judge that are more closely connected to the parties and the case, which is consistent with due process.

ARTICLE XI

The law applicable to noncontractual obligations arising out of damage caused by a product shall be the law that the parties have selected by agreement entered into before the event giving rise to the damage.

The judge with jurisdiction over noncontractual disputes may be the judge whom the parties have selected by agreement entered into before the event giving rise to the damage. Such jurisdiction shall be exclusive unless the parties have agreed otherwise. The choice shall be in writing or evidenced in writing.

ARTICLE XII

In the absence of the parties' choice, the law applicable to noncontractual obligations arising out of damage caused by a product shall be: (1) the law of the country where the individual sustaining the damage had his or her habitual residence when the damage occurred; (2) the law of the country where the manufacturer had his habitual residence or statutory seat, central administration, or principal place of business when the damage occurred; or (3) the law of the country with which the parties and the case are manifestly more closely connected.

A consumer may bring proceedings against the other party to a contract either in the courts of the country in which that party is domiciled or in the courts of the place where the consumer is domiciled.

Proceedings may be brought against a consumer by the other party to the contract only in the courts of the country where the consumer is domiciled.

The slightly different regimes under Articles XI and XII are provided considering the consumer as the weakest part in the relationship.

SECTION VIII

FORUM NON CONVENIENS

ARTICLE XIII

Jurisdiction may be declined or the proceedings suspended when the court is manifestly inappropriate relative to another more appropriate court that could exercise jurisdiction. When deciding whether a forum is more convenient than another, the judge may take into account the following factors: (1) the relative ease of access to sources of proof; (2) the availability of compulsory process for attendance of unwilling witnesses, and the cost of obtaining attendance of willing witnesses; (3) the administrative difficulties that follow for courts when litigation is piled up in congested centers instead of being handled at its origin; (4) jury duties; and (5) a local interest in having localized controversies decided in the local forum.

Forum non conveniens is a possible ground for denying jurisdiction that would otherwise be proper under this Convention. The list of considerations that a court may make when deciding whether to deny jurisdiction on forum non conveniens grounds is nonexhaustive. However, the considerations that a court may make when deciding to deny jurisdiction on forum non conveniens grounds should closely resemble the factors listed in this Article.

SECTION X

TAG JURISDICTION

ARTICLE XIV

Jurisdiction cannot be exercised solely on the basis of proper service of process made upon an individual temporarily and voluntarily present within a country when such presence is unrelated to the object of the litigation.

Tag jurisdiction is not allowed.

SECTION XI

PUBLIC POLICY OF THE FORUM

ARTICLE XV

The application of a provision of the law of any country specified by this Convention may be refused only if such application is manifestly incompatible with a fundamental public policy (*ordre public*) of the forum.

This "escape device" should be used only under exceptional circumstances that indicate the presence of a fundamental public policy of the forum that needs to be preserved.

SECTION XII

RECOGNITION AND ENFORCEMENT OF JUDGMENTS

ARTICLE XVI

The judgment rendered by a judge with jurisdiction over the case as identified by the above provisions shall be recognized and enforced in the countries that have ratified this Convention by appropriate procedures provided by the same countries.

The procedure for recognition and enforcement of judgments shall be provided by the domestic law of the forum that should recognize and enforce judgments.

5

Subject Matter Jurisdiction[1]

INTRODUCTION

Federal courts may only exercise that jurisdiction conferred on them by Article III, §2 of the U.S. Constitution, and that which an implementing statute vests in them. Such statutes may not exceed the Article III grant of power, but they may vest less than the whole of that power. Article III, §2 lists nine categories of cases and controversies that may be heard by a federal court, the most important of which is "cases, in law and equity, arising under this Constitution, the laws of the United States, and treaties made, or which shall be made, under their authority."[2] In accord with that provision, 28 U.S.C. §1331 provides, "The district courts shall have original jurisdiction of all civil actions arising under the Constitution, laws, or treaties of the United States."[3] The simple phrase "arising under" has led to a complex web of doctrinal developments, driven almost exclusively by Supreme Court decisions. Here I examine how the Court's common law method operates in this jurisdictionally significant context.

A CLAIM-CENTERED, FUNDAMENTAL PRINCIPLES APPROACH TO ARISING-UNDER JURISDICTION

The generally accepted model of arising-under jurisdiction presumes that a case arises under federal law if federal law creates the claim for relief, the so-called Holmes "creation test." Under this approach, the creation test

[1] *See also* Simona Grossi, *A Modified Theory of the Law of Federal Courts: The Case of Arising-Under Jurisdiction*, 88 Wash. L. Rev. 3 (2013).

[2] U.S. Const., Art. III, §2.

[3] 28 U.S.C. §1331.

represents the primary vehicle for determining jurisdiction.[4] According to this view, there are two limited exceptions to the creation test: one that extends jurisdiction to some nonfederal claims that include an essential federal ingredient, and one that excludes jurisdiction over federally created claims that are essentially governed by state or local law or in which the presumed intent of Congress to create jurisdiction is otherwise rebutted.[5]

While it is sometimes thought that the creation test represents the earliest approach to arising under, this is by no means clear. In their recent study, Professors Ann Woolhandler and Michael Collins show that federal courts in the nineteenth century exercised jurisdiction in numerous cases well beyond the contours of the creation test.[6] This phenomenon occurred both before and after the adoption of the Act of 1875, in which Congress vested federal courts with general federal question jurisdiction.[7] Indeed, not a single case references anything akin to a creation test prior to 1916, when the Supreme Court's opinion in *American Well Works Co. v. Layne & Bowler Co.*[8] made a cryptic allusion to such a possibility. Rather, the vast body of early cases adopted a more inclusive and holistic approach to arising-under jurisdiction, one that in no way depended on the source of the claim or right asserted. As I will show below, the decision in *American Well Works* fits well within that established jurisprudence.

The 1900 decision in *Shoshone Mining Co. v. Rutter*[9] provides an apt example of the holistic approach to arising-under jurisdiction. *Shoshone* involved a dispute over the entitlement to a mining claim on federally owned lands. A federal statute required any person who disputed another party's application for a mining claim to file an "adverse suit" in "a court of competent jurisdiction" within thirty days of having filed the adverse claim with the register of land. Either local custom or state property law would usually determine entitlement to the property. At best, any potential federal issue remained in the background. As a consequence, the Supreme Court concluded that such adverse claims did not necessarily arise under federal law:

[4] Grable & Sons Metal Products, Inc., v. Darue Engineering & Manufacturing, 545 U.S. 308, 312 (2005); Gunn v. Minton, 133 S.Ct. 1059, 1064–1065 (2013).

[5] *Gunn*, 133 S.Ct. at 1064–1065; Mims v. Arrow Financial Services, LLC, 132 S.Ct. 740, 744 (2012); *Grable*, 545 U.S. at 311-313, 317 n. 5; 15 JAMES WM. MOORE ET AL., MOORE'S FEDERAL PRACTICE §103.31[3] (2013); CHARLES ALAN WRIGHT ET AL., FEDERAL PRACTICE AND PROCEDURE, §3562 (3d ed. 2013).

[6] Ann Woolhandler & Michael G. Collins, *Federal Question Jurisdiction and Justice Holmes*, 84 Notre Dame L. Rev. 2151 (2009) (hereinafter Woolhandler & Collins, *Justice Holmes*).

[7] *Id.*

[8] 241 U.S. 247 (1916).

[9] 177 U.S. 505 (1900).

> Inasmuch, therefore, as the "adverse suit" to determine the right of possession may not involve any question as to the construction or effect of the Constitution or laws of the United States, but may present simply a question of fact as to the time of the discovery of mineral, the location of the claim on the ground, or a determination of the meaning and effect of certain local rules and customs prescribed by the miners of the district, or the effect of state statutes, it would seem to follow that it is not one which necessarily arises under the Constitution and laws of the United States.[10]

Shoshone is often described as an exception to the creation test, but that description is inaccurate. At the time *Shoshone* was decided, there was no creation test. *American Well Works* was still sixteen years in the future. It is also not clear that the federal statute at issue in *Shoshone* created a cause of action. Most importantly, however, the rationale adopted by the *Shoshone* Court did not focus on the source of the plaintiff's right to sue, but rather on whether the adverse suit called for the "construction or effect" of federal law. As such, *Shoshone* does not represent an exception to a rule, but an application of the broader core principle.

The Court took a similar principled approach in *Shulthis v. McDougal*.[11] There, the plaintiff filed a lawsuit in a federal circuit court seeking to quiet title to a tract of land located on an Indian reservation. The defendants filed a motion to dismiss the action for lack of subject matter jurisdiction. In response, the plaintiff argued that the case was one arising under federal law since the ownership of the tract was ultimately traceable to a grant from the federal government. In resolving the jurisdictional question, the Court explained that the key consideration was whether the dispute involved "the validity, construction, or effect of" federal law:

> A suit to enforce a right which takes its origin in the laws of the United States is not necessarily, or for that reason alone, one arising under those laws, for a suit does not so arise unless it really and substantially involves a dispute or controversy respecting the validity, construction, or effect of such a law, upon the determination of which the result depends.[12]

Applying that principle in mind, the Court rejected plaintiff's attempt to premise jurisdiction solely on the federal source of his claimed right of ownership. Instead, the Court explained that for a case to fall within the scope of statutory arising-under jurisdiction, it was not enough that federal law be the source of the rights sought to be enforced.[13]

[10] *Id.*, at 509.
[11] 225 U.S. 561 (1912).
[12] *Shulthis*, 225 U.S. at 569.
[13] *Id.*, at 568–569.

We now come to *American Well Works*[14]; however, the presumption that the Court there endorsed the creation test as the true measure of arising-under jurisdiction is erroneous. *American Well Works* involved a suit by an individual who claimed that his business had been damaged by the defendant's disparagement of his patent and by the defendant's threat to sue him and his customers for patent infringement. The Court explained that the plaintiff's claim involved no controversy over a question of federal law, including patent law. The fact that the narrative of the case somehow involved a patent was not enough to make the case one arising under patent law. Rather, the case involved no more than a state-created disparagement of business claim in which patent law played no role. Hence, federal question jurisdiction was lacking.

This result in *American Well Works* was fully consistent with *Shoshone* and *Shulthis*, since the case did not involve "a controversy respecting the validity, construction, or effect of" federal law.[15] However, Justice Holmes, writing for the *American Well Works* Court, wrapped his conclusion in an epigram: "[a] suit arises under the law that creates the cause of action."[16] Given the precedents then extant, this pithy statement was both too broad and too narrow, for it failed to take measure of the role of the federal question in the case under consideration, a role that, according to established precedent, was wholly independent of the source of the right sought to be enforced.

That *American Well Works* had not endorsed a "creation test" was made clear five years later, in *Smith v. Kansas City Title & Trust Co.*[17] There, the plaintiff, a shareholder in the defendant trust company, sued the trust seeking to enjoin it from purchasing bonds that had been issued under the terms of a federal statute that the plaintiff claimed to be unconstitutional. Since the trust was only authorized to purchase "legal" bonds, the plaintiff claimed that the planned purchase of the federal bonds represented a breach of fiduciary duty, a claim created by state law. Notwithstanding, the Court held that the case was one arising under federal law:

> In the instant case the averments of the bill show that the directors were proceeding to make the investments in view of the act authorizing the bonds about to be purchased, maintaining that the act authorizing them was constitutional and the bonds valid and desirable investments. The objecting shareholder avers in the bill that the securities were issued under an unconstitutional law, and hence of no validity. It is therefore apparent that

14 241 U.S. 247 (1916).
15 *Shulthis*, 225 U.S. at 569.
16 *Id.*, at 260. *See also* Woolhandler & Collins, *Justice Holmes*, *supra* note 6, at 2171–2178.
17 255 U.S. 180 (1921).

> the controversy concerns the constitutional validity of an act of Congress which is directly drawn in question. The decision depends upon the determination of this issue.[18]

The decision in *Smith* did not create a novel approach to jurisdiction. In fact, as Woolhandler and Collins have amply demonstrated, *Smith* reflected a standard exercise of federal question jurisdiction that was well recognized in the nineteenth and early twentieth centuries.[19]

Justice Holmes dissented, and took his epigram a step further by insisting on the exclusivity of the creation principle: "a suit cannot be said to arise under any other law than that which creates the cause of action."[20] But quite clearly, the majority, following the standard jurisprudence, rejected this view. In fact, the majority neither referenced *American Well Works* nor responded to Justice Holmes's solo dissent. The majority was not alone in disagreeing with Holmes. In the ensuing year, the creation test would play but a minor role at best in the Court's arising-under jurisprudence. Indeed, it did not rise to prominence in that jurisprudence until the Court's decision in *Franchise Tax Board v. Construction Laborers Vacation Trust* in 1983.[21]

According to Woolhandler and Collins, Holmes's creation test formula might have been the result of "[Holmes's] collapsing of the concepts of primary and remedial rights as part of his predictive view of law."[22] Similarly, Professor Lumen Mulligan argues:

> Despite the fact that early federal question jurisdictional practice took a rights-inclusive view, Justice Holmes specifically eschewed rights, unadorned with causes of action, as a meaningful, stand-alone legal category. His position on this score flows from his famous "bad man" theory of law – the view that law is best understood not from a moral vantage point, but from that of the bad man who cares only to know the predictable judicial responses to his conduct. That is to say, Justice Holmes, generally speaking, focused solely upon the enforcement aspect of law, which in the civil context corresponds to causes of action and not rights per se.[23]

Mulligan's point is that Holmes's endorsement of a cause-of-action-centric test was both out of step with the then current jurisprudential developments in

[18] *Id.*, at 201.
[19] *See* Woolhandler & Collins, *Justice Holmes*, *supra* note 6, at 2171–2178.
[20] 255 U.S. at 214.
[21] 463 U.S. 1 (1983). The creation test did, however, hold a prominent position in the first edition of Hart & Wechsler's casebook, perhaps paving the way to its eventual inclusion in the Court's arising-under jurisprudence. *See* HART & WECHSLER, *supra* note 18 (Chapter 1), at 752.
[22] *See* Woolhandler & Collins, *Justice Holmes*, *supra* note 6, at 2187.
[23] Lumen N. Mulligan, *You Can't Go Holmes Again*, 107 Nw. U. L. Rev., 240 (2012).

cases such as *Shoshone* and *Smith*[24] and insufficient to fully embrace the full range of jurisdictional possibilities that had been and continue to be recognized by the Court.[25] Mulligan's solution is to include "rights" as part of the jurisdictional equation and, in so doing, create a presumption in favor of the exercise of arisingunder jurisdiction. I agree with Mulligan's conclusion but not with his solution.

Holmes may have indeed adopted the creation test to conform to his badman theory of law, and his creation-centric approach to jurisdiction is certainly inconsistent with the full range of jurisdictional possibilities. The true mistake Holmes made, however, was in assuming that the cause-of-action component of his equation somehow defined the scope of jurisdiction, which is not necessarily so. Mulligan's solution is simply to add the component of "rights" to the jurisdictional equation, but this solution invites a similar mechanical approach to jurisdiction by adding yet another incomplete test to the inquiry.

My approach is different. Instead of immersing myself in the debate over what constitutes a cause of action, I would rather focus the jurisdictional inquiry on what constitutes a "claim." Under the Federal Rules of Civil Procedure (and under the modern law of res judicata or preclusion), a claim is defined by reference to the facts that establish a legal right to relief. To paraphrase Holmes, a claim arises only under the sovereign law that creates it. But some claims are hybrid, their component parts being created by more than one sovereign. Such claims arise under the laws of all contributing sovereigns, regardless of which created the cause of action, which

24 The core principle that guided the analysis in cases like *Shoshone* and *Shulthis* did not focus on the distinction between causes of action and rights, but rather on the claim, which is a composite of rights and remedies.

25 Mulligan's analysis was prompted by the Supreme Court's recent decision in Mims v. Arrow Financial Services, LLC., 132 S.Ct. 740 (2012). Mulligan praises that opinion for breaking with the Holmes's cause-of-action-centric tradition and for recasting the standard §1331 test as one that looks to both the cause of action and the right. Although Mulligan's interpretation of the *Mims* decision is attractive, I don't think that that opinion can carry the weight of his conclusions. The distinction between causes of action and rights was certainly not necessary to the holding in *Mims*, and the decision in *Mims* is just as consistent with the Holmes creation test as it is with Mulligan's more inclusive approach to federal arising-under jurisdiction. At most, the *Mims* decision supports the proposition that when federal law creates the cause of action and establishes the rule of decision, there is a strong presumption in favor of federal jurisdiction; however, in a sense, this is really a reiteration of the creation test. In addition, the language from *Mims* that Mulligan relies on is, by his own admission, "inconsistent" and "unclear," suggesting that the Court was not aware that it was making the sophisticated move that Mulligan attributes to it. Further evidence that *Mims* did not change the jurisprudential landscape can be found in *Gunn v. Minton*, where the Court returned to the cause-of-action-centric position, treating it as the primary vehicle for establishing arising under jurisdiction.

created the right, or which created the controlling legal principle. The Holmesian error was not in Holmes's collapse of causes of action and rights into a single concept – which is essentially to say "a claim upon which relief can be granted" – but in his failure to see that the unification did not dictate the narrow jurisdictional test he ultimately endorsed.

Mulligan falls into a similar trap by drawing a bright line between causes of action and rights. Unlike Holmes, Mulligan would allow jurisdiction in cases falling on either side of the line. And such an approach can be used to validate a wider range of the Court's arising-under jurisprudence. But it also invites a mechanical distinction between claims created by federal law and claims that merely include a federal ingredient. In fact, Mulligan's test would not validate decisions such as *Smith*, where neither the cause of action nor the right was a creature of federal law. Rather, federal law was simply an element of the plaintiff's state-created claim. Yet, despite the absence of both a federal cause of action and a federal right, the Court nonetheless found jurisdiction because the plaintiff's claim turned on a question of federal law. My approach would fully support the decision in *Smith*.

With a proper reading of the foundational arising-under cases – e.g., *Shoshone, Shulthis, Smith* and *American Well Works* (properly understood) – and with a clearer understanding of what constitutes a claim upon which a relief can be granted, my approach focuses on the nature of the plaintiff's claim, asking whether the resolution of the plaintiff's claim depends on the validity, construction or effect of federal law.

GULLY REDISCOVERED

Congress first vested the lower federal courts with general "arising-under" jurisdiction in the Act of March 3, 1875 ("Act of 1875"),[26] thereby giving them "the vast range of power which had lain dormant in the Constitution since 1789. These courts ceased to be restricted tribunals of fair dealing between citizens of different states and became the primary and powerful reliances for vindicating every right given by the Constitution, the laws, and treaties of the United States."[27] The available evidence suggests that Congress, in passing the Act of 1875, thought that it was vesting lower federal courts with the

[26] Act of Mar. 3, 1875, ch. 137, §1, 18 Stat. 470.

[27] FELIX FRANKFURTER & JAMES MCCAULEY LANDIS, THE BUSINESS OF THE SUPREME COURT: A STUDY IN THE FEDERAL JUDICIAL SYSTEM 65 (1928).

complete range of Article III arising-under jurisdiction.[28] As one sponsor of the measure explained, the Act gives the federal judiciary "precisely the power which the Constitution confers – nothing more, nothing less."[29] Significantly, at that time, the enforcement of federal rights was often dependent on common law and state-created remedies.[30] Hence, hybrid "federal-ingredient" claims would not have been considered unusual or even distinct from a jurisdictional perspective.

The Court offered a typical description of the arising-under standard in *Starin v. City of New York*:[31]

> The character of a case is determined by the questions involved. If from the questions it appears that some title, right, privilege, or immunity, on which the recovery depends, will be defeated by one construction of the constitution or a law of the United States, or sustained by the opposite construction, the case will be one arising under the constitution or laws of the United States, within the meaning of that term as used in the act of 1875; otherwise not.[32]

By the first half of the twentieth century, the fundamental principles of statutory arising-under jurisdiction were sufficiently familiar and so well settled that in 1936, the Court in *Gully v. First National Bank in Meridian*[33] could describe them with confident clarity:

> How and when a case arises "under the Constitution or laws of the United States" has been much considered in the books. Some tests are well established. To bring a case within the statute, a right or immunity created by the Constitution or laws of the United States must be an element, and an essential one, of the plaintiff's cause of action. The right or immunity must be such that it will be supported if the Constitution or laws of the United

[28] In Franchise Tax Board v. Construction Laborers Vacation Trust, 463 U.S. 1 (1983), the Court observed:

> The statute's "arising under" language tracks similar language in art. III, § 2 of the Constitution, which has been construed as permitting Congress to extend federal jurisdiction to any case of which federal law potentially "forms an ingredient," see *Osborn v. Bank of the United States*, 9 Wheat. 738, 823 (1824), and its limited legislative history suggests that the 44th Congress may have meant to "confer the whole power which the Constitution conferred."

Id., at 8, n.8. *See also* Michael G. Collins, *The Unhappy History of Federal Question Removal*, 71 IOWA L. REV. 717, 723 & n.32–34 (1986) (citing sources).

[29] 2 Cong. Rec. 4986–4987 (1874) (remarks of Sen. Carpenter).

[30] *See* Woolhandler & Collins, *Justice Holmes*, *supra* note 6, at 2157–2170.

[31] 115 U.S. 248 (1885).

[32] *Id.* at 257.

[33] 299 U.S. 109 (1936) (citations omitted).

> States are given one construction or effect, and defeated if they receive another. A genuine and present controversy, not merely a possible or conjectural one, must exist with reference thereto, and the controversy must be disclosed upon the face of the complaint, unaided by the answer or by the petition for removal. Indeed, the complaint itself will not avail as a basis of jurisdiction in so far as it goes beyond a statement of the plaintiff's cause of action and anticipates or replies to a probable defense.[34]

As the *Gully* Court recognized, it was established early on that a federal court could not exercise original or removal arising-under jurisdiction unless the plaintiff's complaint revealed a claim that required resolution of a federal question.[35] A federal defense raised by the defendant would not suffice.[36] Nor would it be sufficient for the plaintiff to anticipate such a defense.[37] The explanation for this rule was that a federal court should be able to assess jurisdiction at the outset by examining the pleadings then before it.[38]

Beyond this "well-pleaded complaint" rule, the approach to federal jurisdiction was directed more toward a flexible assessment of the nature of the federal issue presented and the role that issue played as an element of the jurisdiction-invoking claim. As noted above, this jurisdictional formula had deep roots in the nineteenth century[39] and was also fully supported by precedent from the early twentieth century.

The facts of *Gully* were simple and informative. First National Bank agreed to assume the debts of an insolvent national banking association. Among those debts were taxes owed to the State of Mississippi. When Gully, the state tax collector, sued First National Bank in state court to collect those debts, First National Bank removed the case to federal court on the theory that it was one arising under federal law since federal law authorized states to tax national banking associations. In concluding that federal jurisdiction did not exist, the Supreme Court first explained that Gully's claim was built on a contract that was governed by Mississippi law. While the defendant argued that a federal controversy existed because the validity of a tax imposed on a nationally chartered bank was ultimately a question of federal law, the Court disagreed,

[34] *Id.*, at 112–113 (citations omitted).

[35] Metcalf v. City of Watertown, 128 U.S. 586 (1888).

[36] Tennessee v. Union & Planters' Bank, 152 U.S. 454 (1894).

[37] Louisville & Nashville R.Co. v. Mottley, 211 U.S. 149 (1908).

[38] *Metcalf*, 128 U.S. at 589–590.

[39] McCain v. City of Des Moines, 174 U.S. 168, 180 (1899); Starin v. City of New York, 115 U.S. 248, 257 (1885); St. Joseph & G.I.R. Co. v. Steele, 167 U.S. 659, 662 (1897); Walker v. Collins, 167 U.S. 57, 59 (1897); Ex Parte Lennon, 166 U.S. 548, 553–554 (1897); *see also* Woolhandler & Collins, *Justice Holmes*, *supra* note 52, at 2171–2178.

explaining that federal law played absolutely no role in the resolution of the plaintiff's claim.[40]

The *Gully* Court noted that the key element in the federal question jurisdiction analysis was the nature of the claim presented:

> This Court has had occasion to point out how futile is the attempt to define a "cause of action" without reference to the context. To define broadly and in abstract "a case arising under the Constitution or laws of the United States" has hazards of a kindred order. What is needed is something of that common-sense accommodation of judgment to kaleidoscopic situations which characterizes the law in its treatment of problems of causation. One could carry the search for causes backward, almost without end. Instead, there has been a selective process which picks the substantial causes out of the web and lays the other ones aside. As in problems of causation, so here in the search for the underlying law. If we follow the ascent far enough, countless claims of right can be discovered to have their source or their operative limits in the provisions of a federal statute or in the Constitution itself with its circumambient restrictions upon legislative power. To set bounds to the pursuit, the courts have formulated the distinction between controversies that are basic and those that are collateral, between disputes that are necessary and those that are merely possible. We shall be lost in a maze if we put that compass by.[41]

Thus, up through *Gully*, the only jurisdictional bright-line rule that the Court had endorsed was the well-pleaded complaint rule, and the Court's jurisprudence drew no distinction between claims created by federal law and state-law claims that included an essential federal ingredient. That aside, the law of federal question jurisdiction was governed by a claim-centered, arising-under jurisdictional theory that focused on the nature of the claim and the role that federal law played within that claim.

Given the lyrical language of the *Gully* opinion, one might be tempted to think that the standard is open-ended and indeterminative. But that is far from the case. In fact, *Gully* offers clear guidance as to the key question that should inform the arising-under jurisdiction analysis. That question asks whether the "right or immunity [is] such that it will be supported if the Constitution or laws of the United States are given one construction or effect, and defeated if they receive another."[42] In other words, the goal is to determine whether resolution of the plaintiff's claim turns on a question of federal law. This test, although precise in its focus, is not mechanical since it realistically acknowledges the kaleidoscopic range of possibilities in which such a federal question might arise.

[40] 299 U.S., at 115–116.

[41] *Id.*, 117–118 (citations omitted).

[42] *Id.* at 112.

Gully can be seen as a nearly perfect exemplar of both the classic and modified versions of legal process previously described. In terms of the principle of institutional settlement, the opinion assigns courts a role that is appropriate and consistent with congressional intent, namely the determination of whether a particular claim falls within the broad sweep of jurisdiction vested in the federal courts by the Constitution and by Congress. Certainly one gets no sense that *Gully* invites the judiciary to engage in anything but a legitimate judicial function. Further, *Gully* cannot be described as formalistic in any sense. Rather, it invites a flexible but principled assessment of jurisdiction that cannot be measured by any simple bright-line or mechanical rule, but that should nonetheless lead to results that are premised on predictable and nonsubjective questions and conclusions. By focusing its attention on the claim, the *Gully* Court establishes a principle that respects the individual claims of right. This approach is consistent with the full range of structural concerns that animate the Constitution, including a balanced approach to federalism, separation of powers and individual rights. Finally, the analysis is premised on a rational explanation of a durable legal principle – one that had been used effectively for at least sixty years before *Gully* – that focuses on the nature of the claim.

THE MECHANICAL APPROACH TO ARISING-UNDER JURISDICTION

As I explained earlier, one of the critical factors in the legal process method is the requirement of reasoned elaboration. And as Professor Fallon pointed out, the legal process scholarly agenda requires a careful examination and critique of doctrine.[43] The following discussion is premised on both of these principles. It provides a relatively detailed examination of five major cases, all of which stray from the legal process path in one way or another, and all of which suffer from lack of reasoned elaboration.

Franchise Tax Board v. Construction Laborers Vacation Trust

Gully remained the foundational federal question case for several decades, without any apparent deviation from the approach endorsed there.[44] Indeed, it

[43] Fallon, *Reflections*, *supra* note 12 (Chapter 1), at 977.

[44] *See, e.g.*, Phillips Petroleum Co. v. Texaco, Inc., 415 U.S. 125, 128 (1974); Oneida Indian Nation of N.Y. State v. Oneida County, New York, 414 U.S. 661, 675 (1974); Skelly Oil Co. v. Phillips Petroleum Co., 339 U.S. 667, 672 (1950). PAUL M. BATOR, PAUL J. MISHKIN, DAVID L. SHAPIRO, HERBERT WECHSLER, HART AND WECHSLER'S THE FEDERAL COURT AND THE FEDERAL SYSTEM 884 (2d ed. 1973); JOHN J. COUND, JACK H. FRIEDENTHAL, ARTHUR R. MILLER, CIVIL PROCEDURE CASES AND MATERIALS 190 (2d ed. 1974).

has been cited and relied on by the Supreme Court and lower courts up to the present time.[45] However, the Supreme Court's approach to federal question jurisdiction began to diverge from *Gully*'s path in 1983 with the decision in *Franchise Tax Board v. Construction Laborers Vacation Trust*.[46] There, the California Franchise Tax Board sought a levy on funds held in trust for three construction workers by the Construction Laborers Vacation Trust ("CLVT"). The Tax Board claimed a right to the funds based on the members' failure to pay the state income tax. When the trustee refused to meet the Tax Board's demands, the Tax Board filed an action in California state court seeking damages for the amount of the taxes owed and a declaration that its right to those funds was not preempted by the federal Employment Retirement Income Security Act of 1974 (ERISA). CLVT removed the case to federal court on the theory that the plaintiff's action for declaratory relief arose under federal law. The plaintiff filed a motion to remand. The trial court denied that motion and on the merits ruled that ERISA did not preempt the State's claims. The Court of Appeals affirmed on the jurisdictional question, but reversed on the merits. Tax Board appealed to the Supreme Court. The Court addressed only the jurisdictional issue.

The Court's jurisdictional inquiry focused largely on the claim for declaratory relief. As the Court explained, the decision in *Skelly Oil Co. v. Phillips Petroleum Co.*[47] had held that the Federal Declaratory Judgment Act did not expand the scope of federal arising-under jurisdiction. Although the immediate action was filed under the California Declaratory Judgment Act, the Court ruled that the standard applicable under *Skelly Oil* would also apply to actions filed under state declaratory judgment statutes. Under *Skelly Oil*, federal question jurisdiction is satisfied only if one of the parties to the declaratory relief action could have filed a coercive suit against the opposing party that itself would arise under federal law consistently with the well-pleaded complaint rule. Hence, if the party filing for declaratory relief does no more than seek a declaration that its claimed right is not preempted by federal law, the case does not arise under federal law for purposes of §1331, since in a suit by that party to enforce that right, the federal preemption question would be raised by the defendant as a defense to the action. But if the declaratory judgment defendant would have a coercive federal preemption claim against

[45] Vaden v. Discover Bank, 556 U.S. 49, 78 (2009); Grable & Sons Metal Products, Inc. v. Darue Engineering, 545 U.S. 308, 321(2005); Christianson v. Colt Industries Operating Corp., 486 U.S. 800, 808 (1988); Merrell Dow Pharmaceuticals Inc. v. Thompson, 478 U.S. 804, 820 (1986) (Brennan, J., dissenting).

[46] 463 U.S. 1 (1983).

[47] 339 U.S. 667 (1950).

the declaratory judgment plaintiff,[48] then the case will in fact arise under federal law.[49]

Although the Tax Board's claim for declaratory relief did seek a declaration that its claim was not preempted by federal law, there was something more to the case. As the Court explained:

> Federal courts have regularly taken original jurisdiction over declaratory judgment suits in which the declaratory judgment defendant brought a coercive action to enforce its rights, that suit would necessarily present a federal question. Section 502(a)(3) of ERISA specifically grants trustees of ERISA-covered plans like CLVT a cause of action for injunctive relief when their rights and duties under ERISA are at issue, and that action is exclusively governed by federal law. If CLVT could have sought an injunction under ERISA against application to it of state regulations that require acts inconsistent with ERISA, does a declaratory judgment by the State "arise under" federal law?[50]

Given that CLVT had a claim for coercive relief under ERISA – the mirror image of the plaintiff's "defensive" claim for declaratory relief – the obvious answer would seem to be "yes." However, the Court concluded otherwise:

> We have always interpreted what *Skelly Oil* called "the current of jurisdictional legislation since the Act of March 3, 1875," with an eye to practicality and necessity.... There are good reasons why the federal courts should not entertain suits by the States to declare the validity of their regulations despite possibly conflicting federal law. States are not significantly prejudiced by an inability to come to federal court for a declaratory judgment in advance of a possible injunctive suit by a person subject to federal regulation. They have a variety of means by which they can enforce their own laws in their own courts, and they do not suffer if the preemption questions such enforcement may raise are tested there. The express grant of federal jurisdiction in ERISA is limited to suits brought by certain parties as to whom Congress presumably determined that a right to enter federal court was necessary to further the

[48] *See, e.g.*, Osborn v. Bank of the United States, 22 U.S. 738 (1824).

[49] *Franchise Tax Board*, 463 U.S. at 19 ("Federal courts have regularly taken original jurisdiction over declaratory judgment suits in which, if the declaratory judgment defendant brought a coercive action to enforce its rights, that suit would necessarily present a federal question.")

[50] *Id.*, at 19–20. Section 502(a)(3) of ERISA provided:

> [A civil action may be brought] by a participant, beneficiary, or fiduciary (A) to enjoin any act or practice which violates any provision of this subchapter or the terms of the plan, or (B) to obtain other appropriate equitable relief (i) to redress such violations or (ii) to enforce any provision of this subchapter..."

29 U.S.C. §1132(a)(2).

> statute's purposes. It did not go so far as to provide that any suit *against* such parties must also be brought in federal court when they themselves did not choose to sue.[51]

The Court also held that the Tax Board's suit to enforce tax levies was not subject to the complete preemption doctrine, since such tax proceedings were "not of central concern" to ERISA.[52]

While the Court's introductory discussion of the law of federal question jurisdiction suggested a relatively traditional approach to the topic, the Court's application of the traditional standards was, to say the least, novel. Clearly, CLVT qualified as a declaratory judgment defendant with a coercive claim that presented a substantial federal question, namely, whether the State's action was preempted by ERISA. Thus, under *Skelly Oil*, and as the Court itself had just explained, the case presented a substantial federal issue consistent with the well-pleaded complaint rule as applied in actions for declaratory relief.

However, the Court's analysis ignored this factor and instead took a surprising turn driven by the open-ended policy considerations of "practicality and necessity." The passage quoted above provides the Court's entire discussion of the relevant policy. Essentially, the Court reasoned that federal jurisdiction was lacking since the State could vindicate its rights in state court and since Congress had not expressly given the State access to the federal forum. The fact that Congress clearly wanted ERISA-preemption claims litigated in federal courts seemed irrelevant. Nor did the Court credit the fact that Congress had vested parties such as CLVT with a right to a federal forum.

Judged against the classic and modified legal process method, the *Franchise Tax Board* opinion is deficient in several respects. As already noted, it abandoned a well-established and durable principle in service of a vague policy judgment seemingly designed to resolve the specific case before it. In addition, the Court's opinion betrayed the principle of reasoned elaboration given the empty space that fell between the Court's description of arising-under standards and the Court's ultimate and inexplicable conclusion that those standards had not been satisfied. Finally, jurisdiction was denied in the face of

[51] 463 U.S. at 20–21 (emphasis in original). *See also id.*, at 27 ("Nevertheless, CLVT's argument that appellant's second cause of action arises under ERISA fails for the second reason given above. ERISA carefully enumerates the parties entitled to seek relief under §502; it does not provide anyone other than participants, beneficiaries, or fiduciaries with an express cause of action for a declaratory judgment on the issues in this case. A suit for similar relief by some other party does not 'arise under' that provision.")

[52] *Id.*, at 25–26.

clear congressional intent to the contrary and in violation of the principles of institutional settlement and separation of powers.

Merrell Dow Pharmaceuticals Inc. v. Thompson

In 1986, the Court in *Merrell Dow Pharmaceuticals Inc. v. Thompson*[53] took *Franchise Tax Board*'s "practicality and necessity" approach a step further. There, two sets of parents, residents of Canada and Scotland respectively, sued Merrell Dow, a drug manufacturer, claiming that their children had suffered birth defects caused by a drug manufactured by the defendant and ingested by the mothers while pregnant. The suit was filed in an Ohio state court and removed to federal court by the defendant. The defendant argued that the case arose under federal law because one of the six claims asserted by the plaintiffs relied on an alleged violation of the labeling standard imposed by the Federal Food, Drug, and Cosmetic Act (FDCA), the violation of which was said to create a presumption of negligence under state law.[54] The plaintiffs filed a motion to remand, arguing that no federal question was presented in their suit. The defendants responded by filing a motion to dismiss on *forum non conveniens* grounds. The district court denied plaintiffs' motion to remand but granted the defendant's motion to dismiss. The court of appeals, addressing only the jurisdictional issue, reversed in a one-page opinion, concluding that federal law was not necessarily implicated in the plaintiffs' suit and that, as a consequence, the case did not arise under federal law.[55] The question before the Supreme Court was whether the plaintiffs' claim arose under federal law for purposes of §1331.

Adopting the policy-driven approach endorsed by the Court three years earlier in *Franchise Tax Board*, the focus of the majority opinion was less on the nature of the action, as had been the focus of the court of appeals, and more on the "dictates of sound judicial policy" that, in the majority's view, should justify the exercise of federal jurisdiction:

> We have consistently emphasized that, in exploring the outer reaches of §1331, determinations about federal jurisdiction require sensitive judgments about congressional intent, judicial power, and the federal system.... In *Franchise Tax Board*, we forcefully reiterated this need for prudence and restraint in the jurisdictional inquiry: "We have always interpreted what

[53] 478 U.S. 804 (1986).

[54] Although alienage jurisdiction was satisfied under §1332(a)(2), the case could not be removed under §1441 since Merrell Dow was a resident of the forum state. 28 U.S.C. §1441(b).

[55] Thompson v. Merrell Dow Pharmaceuticals, Inc., 766 F.2d 1005 (6th Cir. 1985).

> *Skelly Oil* called 'the current of jurisdictional legislation since the Act of March 3, 1875' ... with an eye to practicality and necessity."[56]

And thus, according to the Court,

> the "increased complexity of federal legislation and the increased volume of federal litigation," as well as "the desirability of a more careful scrutiny of legislative intent," are precisely the kind of considerations that should inform the concern for "practicality and necessity" that *Franchise Tax Board* advised for the construction of §1331 when jurisdiction is asserted because of the presence of a federal issue in a state cause of action.[57]

In concluding that there was no federal question jurisdiction in this case, the most significant factor to the Court was the untested assumption that Congress had not intended to create a private right of action to enforce the FDCA. From this assumption, the Court further assumed that Congress also intended to preclude the exercise of federal jurisdiction over state law claims premised on a violation of an FDCA standard.[58] In response to the petitioner's argument that the claim included a substantial federal question,[59] the Court replied that:

> the congressional determination that there should be no federal remedy for the violation of this federal statute is tantamount to a congressional conclusion that the presence of a claimed violation of the statute as an element of a state cause of action is insufficiently "substantial" to confer federal-question jurisdiction.[60]

Thus, in *Merrell Dow*, a judicially imposed policy judgment, driven by case-management concerns and mechanically applied, operated as a determinative measure of substantiality. In fact, the Court attributed a variety of meanings to the word "substantial," further enhancing the scope of its discretion to reject federal jurisdiction in these cases. "Substantial," said the Court, could connote meaningful within the context of the pending case,[61] important to the

[56] 478 U.S. at 810.
[57] *Id.*, at 811–812 (citation omitted).
[58] *Id.*, at 812.
[59] The petitioner contended that "the case represents a straightforward application of the statement in *Franchise Tax Board* that federal-question jurisdiction is appropriate when 'it appears that some substantial, disputed question of federal law is a necessary element of one of the well-pleaded state claims.'" *Id.*, at 813 (quoting *Franchise Tax Board*, 463 U.S. at 13).
[60] 478 U.S. at 814.
[61] *Id.* (quoting Shulthis v. McDougal, 225 U.S. 561, 569–570 (1912) ("A suit to enforce a right which takes its origin in the laws of the United States is not necessarily, or for that reason alone, one arising under those laws, for a suit does not so arise unless it really and substantially involves a dispute or controversy respecting the validity, construction or effect of such a law, upon the determination of which the result depends. This is especially so of a suit involving rights to land acquired under a law of the United States. If it were not, every suit to establish title

federal system in a way that transcended the pending case,[62] or nonfrivolous as a matter of substantive law.[63] The federal issue presented in *Merrell Dow* was insubstantial under any of these standards, and proof of that insubstantiality required no resort to the Court's newly crafted policy judgment. Instead, the Court could simply have asked and answered a simple question: Was the case one that was truly about federal law?

In order to answer this question, a little background might be helpful. The lawyer who represented the two sets of parents in *Merrell Dow* had previously filed a virtually identical suit against the company in the same federal district court, invoking that court's diversity jurisdiction, but representing different (also foreign) plaintiffs. The district court dismissed that case on *forum non conveniens* grounds. The lawyer, with new foreign clients in hand, then sued Merrell Dow in an Ohio state court, asserting essentially the same claims. Merrell Dow, quite plainly, wanted this new iteration of the case in the same federal court that had earlier dismissed on *forum non conveniens* grounds. Since 28 U.S.C. §1441(b) precluded removal on diversity grounds – Merrell Dow being a citizen of Ohio for purposes of diversity – the only possibility was removal as a federal question case. So the fight over jurisdiction was really a fight over *forum non conveniens*.

The focus on *forum non conveniens* helps explain why the plaintiffs, who invoked federal law in their complaint, argued against jurisdiction, while the defendant, who denied the legitimacy of their "federal claim," argued that federal question jurisdiction was satisfied. It's true that the plaintiffs' complaints raised a potential violation of the FDCA, but what isn't apparent from the *Merrell Dow* decision is that the federal issue was frivolous from the outset and more a product of the imagination of the lawyers representing Merrell Dow than anything else. The text of the FDCA addresses itself to interstate and intrastate transactions. It does not (at least on its face) purport to apply to drugs manufactured and sold outside the United States. The drugs at issue in *Merrell Dow* were, in fact, manufactured and sold outside the United States (though that wasn't revealed on the face of the complaint). *Merrell Dow* nonetheless argued, however, that the case presented a significant question

to land in the central and western States would so arise, as all titles in those States are traceable back to those laws")).

[62] *Id.*, at 814. ("We simply conclude that the congressional determination that there should be no federal remedy for the violation of this federal statute is tantamount to a congressional conclusion that the presence of a claimed violation of the statute as an element of a state cause of action is insufficiently "substantial" to confer federal-question jurisdiction.")

[63] *Id.*, at 817. ("Although it is true that federal jurisdiction cannot be based on a frivolous or insubstantial federal question . . . .).

of whether the FDCA applied beyond the U.S. borders. But the plaintiffs had made no such claim; rather, their complaints seemed to be based on the prayer that no one would notice that the statutory standard they invoked was inapplicable under the circumstances presented. Given the foregoing, the oddest thing about the *Merrell Dow* case is that the Court granted certiorari.

Returning to the question of whether this was a case that could be heard by a federal court, the dissent, authored by Justice Brennan, questioned the logic of the majority's reasoning:

> Why should the fact that Congress chose not to create a private federal *remedy* mean that Congress would not want there to be federal *jurisdiction* to adjudicate a state claim that imposes liability for violating the federal law? Clearly, the decision not to provide a private federal remedy should not affect federal jurisdiction unless the reasons Congress withholds a federal remedy are also reasons for withholding federal jurisdiction.[64]

In the dissent's view, the majority had not even considered that question:

> [T]he Court has not examined the purposes underlying either the FDCA or §1331 in reaching its conclusion that Congress' presumed decision not to provide a private federal remedy under the FDCA must be taken to withdraw federal jurisdiction over a private state remedy that imposes liability for violating the FDCA. Moreover, such an examination demonstrates not only that it is consistent with legislative intent to find that there is federal jurisdiction over such a claim, but, indeed, that it is the Court's contrary conclusion that is inconsistent with congressional intent.[65]

As to the last point, the dissent observed that Congress had vested U.S. district courts with exclusive jurisdiction over administrative actions arising under the FDCA, strongly suggesting that the exercise of jurisdiction in cases such as this would be consistent with congressional intent as to the proper scope of federal question jurisdiction.[66] The dissent further explained:

> Congress passes laws in order to shape behavior; a federal law expresses Congress' determination that there is a federal interest in having individuals or other entities conform their actions to a particular norm established by that law.... It is the duty of courts to interpret these laws and apply them in such a way that the congressional purpose is realized. As noted above, Congress granted the district courts power to hear cases "arising under" federal law in order to enhance the likelihood that federal laws would be interpreted more

[64] *Id.*, at 818, 825–826 (Brennan, J., dissenting) (emphasis in original).
[65] *Id.*, at 830.
[66] *Id.*, at 831.

> correctly and applied more uniformly. In other words, Congress determined that the availability of a federal forum to adjudicate cases involving federal questions would make it more likely that federal laws would shape behavior in the way that Congress intended.
>
> By making federal law an essential element of a state-law claim, the State places the federal law into a context where it will operate to shape behavior: the threat of liability will force individuals to conform their conduct to interpretations of the federal law made by courts adjudicating the state-law claim. . . . Consequently, the possibility that the federal law will be incorrectly interpreted in the context of adjudicating the state-law claim implicates the concerns that led Congress to grant the district courts power to adjudicate cases involving federal questions in precisely the same way as if it was federal law that "created" the cause of action. It therefore follows that there is federal jurisdiction under §1331.[67]

The views of the dissent are well taken. The majority opinion replaced the fundamental inquiry into the nature of the federal issue and the role of that issue within that lawsuit with an abstract policy judgment based on a presumed congressional intent, an intent that was never examined by the Court. The dissent, on the other hand, returned the analysis to durable principles of general applicability, more consistently with *Gully* and with the Court's obligation to exercise the jurisdiction intentionally vested in it by Congress – and thus more consistently with legal process.

Christianson v. Colt Industries Operating Corp.

In 1988, the Court added another consideration to the arising-under analysis. In *Christianson v. Colt Industries Operating Corp.*,[68] the plaintiff sued his former employer in a federal court, claiming violations of sections 1 and 2 of the Sherman Act and state law tortious interference with his business relationships. The defendant responded by arguing that its conduct was justified by a need to protect its trade secrets, and by filing a variety of counterclaims based on the plaintiff's alleged misappropriation of one of defendant's patent specifications. The precise question before the Supreme Court was whether either the Seventh Circuit or the Federal Circuit had appellate jurisdiction over this case. The answer to that question depended on whether the case arose under patent law within the meaning of 28 U.S.C. §1338, for if it did, then appellate jurisdiction would lie exclusively in the Federal Circuit. The Court held that the case was not one arising under patent law. In so ruling, the Court explained:

[67] *Id.*, at 827–828.
[68] 486 U.S. 800 (1988).

> Nor is it necessarily sufficient that a well-pleaded claim alleges a single theory under which resolution of a patent-law question is essential. If "on the face of a well-pleaded complaint there are … reasons completely unrelated to the provisions and purposes of [the patent laws] why the [plaintiff] may or may not be entitled to the relief it seeks," *Franchise Tax Board*, 463 U.S., at 26, then the claim does not "arise under" those laws. Thus, a claim supported by alternative theories in the complaint may not form the basis for §1338(a) jurisdiction unless patent law is essential to each of those theories.
>
> Framed in these terms, our resolution of the jurisdictional issue in this case is straightforward. Petitioners' antitrust count can readily be understood to encompass both a monopolization claim under §2 of the Sherman Act and a group-boycott claim under §1. The patent-law issue, while arguably necessary to at least one theory under each claim, is not necessary to the overall success of either claim.[69]

The *Christianson* Court further limited the scope of federal question jurisdiction by adding yet another mechanical test, specifically, the alternative theories test.[70] In adopting this approach, the Court did not define or even consider the difference between separate claims, separate theories on the same claim, and the possibility of having original jurisdiction over some claims (and/or theories) and supplemental jurisdiction over others. Moreover, the Court's reliance on *Franchise Tax Board* as establishing an alternative-theories test was completely misplaced, since the Court in *Franchise Tax Board* neither adopted nor alluded to any such test. Rather, the language from *Franchise Tax Board* that the *Christianson* Court relied on was simply used as an explanation as to why the complete preemption doctrine did not apply to that case.[71] This obvious misreading of a precedent certainly flies in the face of the principle of reasoned elaboration.

69 *Id.*, at 810 (citations omitted).

70 The Court, indeed, explained that "arising under" means precisely the same thing under §1331 and §1338. *Id.* at 808.

71 *See Franchise Tax Board*, 463 U.S., at 25–26:

> Against this background, it is clear that a suit by state tax authorities under a statute like §18818 does not "arise under" ERISA. Unlike the contract rights at issue in *Avco*, the State's right to enforce its tax levies is not of central concern to the federal statute. For that reason, as in *Gully*, on the face of a well-pleaded complaint there are many reasons completely unrelated to the provisions and purposes of ERISA why the State may or may not be entitled to the relief it seeks. Furthermore, ERISA does not provide an alternative cause of action in favor of the State to enforce its rights, while §301 expressly supplied the plaintiff in *Avco* with a federal cause of action to replace its preempted state contract claim. Therefore, even though the Court of Appeals may well be correct that ERISA precludes enforcement of the State's levy in the circumstances of this case, an action to enforce the levy is not itself preempted by ERISA.

Id.

The combination of *Franchise Tax Board*, *Merrell Dow*, and *Christianson* fragmented the jurisdictional inquiry and abandoned the principled approach endorsed in *Gully* and its predecessors, making it increasingly difficult to honor the institutional authority of Congress to vest federal courts with general arising-under jurisdiction.

In deciding these cases, the Court had clearly strayed from the path set by *Gully*. Practicality and necessity, speculation about an ersatz congressional intent, and mechanical tests had come to replace the fundamental inquiry into the federal nature of the plaintiff's claim. In this sense, the Court's emerging jurisprudence sacrificed the interest of the individual in service of the interest of the federal judicial system. At the same time, the Court was slowly developing a doctrine that would give federal judges a potential veto over cases that would otherwise have fallen within their "arising-under" jurisdiction.

Merrell Dow, in addition to abandoning *Gully*, generated a major conflict among the lower federal courts. Circuit courts became split on the critical question of whether federal courts could exercise federal jurisdiction on state-law claims that include an essential federal ingredient in the absence of an express or implied right of action to enforce the federal standard.[72] The Court finally granted certiorari in *Grable & Sons Metal Products, Inc. v. Darue Engineering & Manufacturing*,[73] in an effort to resolve this conflict.[74]

Grable & Sons Metal Products, Inc. v. Darue Engineering & Manufacturing

In *Grable*, the Internal Revenue Service (IRS) seized real property owned by Grable to satisfy Grable's federal tax delinquency. The IRS gave Grable notice of the seizure by certified mail and Grable received actual notice. After the property was sold to Darue, Grable did not exercise its statutory right to redeem it. Five years later, Grable sued Darue in a quiet title action in a state court claiming that Darue's title "was invalid because the IRS had failed to

[72] *Compare* Flood v. Braaten, 727 F.2d 303 (3rd Cir. 1984) (finding arising-under jurisdiction under Parental Kidnaping Prevention Act (PKPA) despite absence of private right of action); Hickey v. Baxter, 833 F.2d 1005 (4th Cir. 1987) (accord); McDougald v. Jenson, 786 F.2d 1465 (11th Cir.), *cert. denied*, 479 U.S. 860 (1986) (accord); Heartfield v. Heartfield, 749 F.2d 1138 (5th Cir. 1985) (accord); *with* Rogers v. Platt, 814 F.2d 683 (1987) (arriving at the opposite conclusion post-*Merrell Dow*). *See also* Ormet Corp. v. Ohio Power Co., 98 F.3d 799 (4th Cir. 1996) (no private right of action required to establish federal ingredient jurisdiction post-*Merrell Dow*); *but see* Seinfeld v. Austen, 39 F.3d 761, 764 (7th Cir. 1994) (private right of action required to establish federal ingredient jurisdiction post-*Merrell Dow*).

[73] 545 U.S. 308 (2005).

[74] *Id.* at 312 & n. 2.

notify Grable of the seizure in the exact manner required by [26 U.S.C.] §6335 (a)."[75] That section provided that written notice had to be "given by the Secretary to the owner of the property [or] left at his usual place of abode or business."[76] The defendant removed the case to federal court asserting jurisdiction under §1331 since the quite-title claim depended on the interpretation and application of the federal notice statute. The district court denied Grable's motion to remand, and a judgment was entered for Darue, the court having concluded that the notice given to Grable was "in substantial compliance" with §6335(a). The court of appeals affirmed.

The question presented to the Supreme Court was whether the state-created quiet title claim contained a federal ingredient sufficient to justify the exercise of federal question jurisdiction. The Court explained that the mere presence of a federal ingredient in a state law claim is not itself sufficient to satisfy statutory "arising-under" standard. Rather,

> the question is, does a state-law claim necessarily raise a stated federal issue, actually disputed and substantial, which a federal forum may entertain without disturbing any congressionally approved balance of federal and state judicial responsibilities.[77]

In adopting this approach, the Court also made it clear that *Merrell Dow* was not to be read as requiring a private right of action in order to establish "arising-under" jurisdiction.[78] While it thus aligned itself with the lower courts that had similarly held, the *Grable* Court did not return to *Gully*'s durable principle. Instead, it remained focused on the details of a doctrine that seems designed to serve the federal judiciary's interest at the expense of the legitimate interests of individual claimants in choosing a federal forum.

Applying this test to the case, the Court found that Grable's claim was one arising under federal law, largely because of the federal system's interest in the dispute.

> The meaning of the federal tax provision is an important issue of federal law that sensibly belongs in a federal court. The Government has a strong interest in the "prompt and certain collection of delinquent taxes," and the ability of the IRS

[75] *Id.*, at 311.
[76] 26 U.S.C. §6335(a)
[77] 545 U.S. at 314.
[78] In the Court's words:

> Accordingly, *Merrell Dow* should be read in its entirety as treating the absence of a federal private right of action as evidence relevant to, but not dispositive of, the "sensitive judgments about congressional intent" that §1331 requires.

Id., at 318.

> to satisfy its claims from the property of delinquents requires clear terms of notice to allow buyers like Darue to satisfy themselves that the Service has touched the bases necessary for good title. The Government thus has a direct interest in the availability of a federal forum to vindicate its own administrative action, and buyers (as well as tax delinquents) may find it valuable to come before judges used to federal tax matters. Finally, because it will be the rare state title case that raises a contested matter of federal law, federal jurisdiction to resolve genuine disagreement over federal tax title provisions will portend only a microscopic effect on the federal-state division of labor.[79]

On the positive side, the *Grable* Court eliminated the conflicts caused by *Merrell Dow* with respect to the role of the private right of action in the determination of arising-under jurisdiction. On the negative side, however, *Grable* did nothing to clarify *Merrell Dow*'s multiple usages of the word "substantial," for it did precisely the same thing, varying the meaning of substantial between important to the pending litigation,[80] and important in a way that transcended that litigation.[81] In addition, the *Grable* Court endorsed and amplified the policy-driven approach introduced by the Court in *Franchise Tax Board* and thus made the potential veto into an integral component of the arising-under analysis. This component, which ostensibly focuses on the presumed intent of a silent Congress, cannot be identified or measured other than through the subjective, ad hoc judgment of the courts, a judgment having nothing to do with the nature of the federal issue and its role in the individual's claim, nor with the actual intent of Congress to provide a federal forum for federal questions.

The inconsistency between the Grable approach, on the one hand, and, the classic and modified legal process method on the other is palpable. The veto principle is neither durable nor of general application, as it calls for ad hoc determinations while providing no guidance as to how those determinations should be made. It is also inconsistent with the separation of powers principle since it allows courts to ignore the actual intent of Congress.

Empire Healthchoice Assurance, Inc. v. McVeigh

The arising-under saga continued in *Empire Healthchoice Assurance, Inc. v. McVeigh*,[82] where a private healthcare provider for federal employees brought an action against a former enrollee's estate, seeking reimbursement of

[79] *Id.*, at 315.
[80] *Id.*, at 310 & 312.
[81] *Id.*, at 315.
[82] 547 U.S. 677 (2006).

insurance benefits on the ground that the enrollee had recovered damages for his injuries in a state-court tort action. The question presented was whether the action for reimbursement arose under federal law for purposes of §1331. The plan itself was subject to the Federal Employees Health Benefits Act of 1959 (FEHBA) and was a product of negotiations with a federal agency. However, neither FEHBA nor any federal regulation addressed the question of reimbursement, nor was there any dispute as to the interpretation of any federal statute or rule on which the healthcare provider's contractually based reimbursement claim depended. Nonetheless, the suit was filed in federal court invoking §1331 jurisdiction. The district court granted the defendant's motion to dismiss for lack of subject matter jurisdiction and the Second Circuit affirmed.

The Supreme Court likewise affirmed. It first held that neither federal common law[83] nor FEHBA[84] created a cause of action for reimbursement. Indeed, the Court's resolution of these questions strongly suggested that there was no federal issue whatsoever relevant to the reimbursement claim. Yet, the Court engaged in an extensive essential federal ingredient analysis and, in the end, came up with a test to interpret the *Grable* test. In the course of so doing, it made it clear that the essential federal ingredient test is designed to reach on a "special and small category" of cases.[85] As the Court explained:

> This case is poles apart from *Grable*. The dispute there centered on the action of a federal agency (IRS) and its compatibility with a federal statute, the question qualified as "substantial," and its resolution was both dispositive of the case and would be controlling in numerous other cases. Here, the reimbursement claim was triggered, not by the action of any federal department, agency, or service, but by the settlement of a personal-injury action launched in state court, and the bottom-line practical issue is the share of that settlement properly payable to Empire.
>
> *Grable* presented a nearly "pure issue of law," one "that could be settled once and for all and thereafter would govern numerous tax sale cases." In contrast, Empire's reimbursement claim, McVeigh's counsel represented without contradiction, is fact-bound and situation-specific.[86]

The approach adopted by the *Empire* Court raises several problems. First, as a general matter, the *Empire* Court's treatment of the specific facts of *Grable* as suggesting additional doctrinal limitations on the scope of federal-ingredient jurisdiction misperceives the role of the facts in the development of the law

[83] *Id.*, at 691–693.
[84] *Id.*, at 693–699.
[85] *Id.*, at 699.
[86] *Id.*, at 700–701 (citations omitted).

and confuses the particular application of a rule with the rule itself. Certainly, the absence of a federal agency in the background of the case has no necessary bearing on the substantiality of the federal issue presented. Second, given that the category of federal question cases is inherently "special and small," the inclusion of that phrase suggests another unprincipled contraction of the federal-ingredient category further disserving the intent of Congress. On what principled ground, and by whose authority, must that category be small? Finally, the distinction drawn by the Court between pure questions of law and questions of fact fails to recognize the important role of federal courts as finders of fact in vindicating federal rights and obligations. As the Court had previously observed in *England v. Louisiana State Bd. of Medical Examiners*, factfinding is a critical component of a federal district court's exercise of federal question jurisdiction:

> Limiting the litigant to review here would deny him the benefit of a federal trial court's role in constructing a record and making fact findings. How the facts are found will often dictate the decision of federal claims. "It is the typical, not the rare, case in which constitutional claims turn upon the resolution of contested factual issues." "There is always in litigation a margin of error, representing error in factfinding."[87]

It is also fair to say that *Empire* failed to satisfy the reasoned elaboration principle, in that the Court's discussion has virtually nothing to do with resolving the federal question before it. The discussion wanders into the law of arising under when no such journey was required by the claims presented to it. Instead, all that the Court had to do was rule that no federal question was presented in the case, or on that basis dismiss the petition on the ground that certiorari was improvidently granted.

In the wake of *Grable* and *Empire*, lower federal courts have engaged in diverse and increasingly complex forms of analysis stemming from the varying

[87] 375 U.S. 411, 416–417 (1964) (citations omitted). *See also*, Osborn v. Bank of the United States, 22 U.S. 738, 821–822 (1824) ("A cause may depend on several questions of fact and law. . .. [I]f the circumstance that other points are involved in it, shall disable Congress from authorizing those Courts of the Union to take jurisdiction of the original cause, it equally disables Congress from authorizing those Courts to take jurisdiction of the whole cause, on appeal, and thus will be restricted to a single question in that cause; and words obviously intended to secure to those who claim rights under the constitution, laws, or treaties of the United States, a trial in the federal Courts, will be restricted to the insecure remedy of an appeal upon an insulated point, after it has received that shape which may be given to it by another tribunal, into which he is forced against his will."); William Cohen, *The Broken Compass: The Requirement That a Case Arise "Directly" Under Federal Law*, 115 U.Pa. L. Rev, 890, 892–893 (1967); Paul J. Mishkin, *The Federal "Question" in the District Courts*, 53 Colum. L. Rev. 157, 170–172 (1953).

interpretations of those cases.[88] For example, some courts created their own multifactor tests to measure the scope of the *Grable/Empire* standard.[89] Others attempted to avoid the full implications of that standard by compressing the *Grable* four-part test.[90] Although the *Grable* Court focused much of its substantiality analysis on whether the federal issue was dear to the federal system, lower federal courts did not approach this issue uniformly. Some followed *Grable* strictly, sometimes completely ignoring the importance of the role of the federal issue in the pending litigation.[91] Others considered the absence of a federal agency in the case as being a significant limiting factor.[92] Others required that the federal issue present an almost pure question of law, implicitly discarding the important fact-finding role of federal courts.[93] Several others enforced the alternative-theory principle elaborated in *Christianson*.[94] Still others focused on the inherent importance (or unimportance) of the federal issue presented,[95] or on the role that issue played within the context of

88 For a rare case in which all of the *Grable* and *Empire* factors seem to have been satisfied, see Gilmore v. Weatherford, 694 F.3d 1160 (10th Cir. 2012).

89 Thus, in Mikulski v. Centerior Energy Corp., 501 F.3d 555 (6th Cir. 2007) (*en banc*), cert. denied, 553 U.S. 1031 (2008), the court adopted a four-part test to measure the *Grable* substantiality prong:

> (1) whether the case includes a federal agency, and particularly, whether that agency's compliance with the federal statute is in dispute; (2) whether the federal question is important (i.e., not trivial); (3) whether a decision on the federal question will resolve the case (i.e., the federal question is not merely incidental to the outcome); and (4) whether a decision as to the federal question will control numerous other cases (i.e., the issue is not anomalous or isolated).

Id., at 570.

90 Immunocept, L.L.C. v. Fulbright & Jaworski, L.L.P, 504 F.3d 1281 (Fed. Cir. 2007); Air Measurement Tech., Inc. v. Akin Gump Strauss Hauer & Feld, L.L.P., 504 F.3d 1262 (Fed. Cir. 2007).

91 McCormick v. Excel Corp., 413 F.Supp.2d 967, 970 (E.D.Wis. 2006).

92 Gilmore v. Weatherford, 694 F.3d 1160, 1174 (10th Cir. 2012).

93 Gilmore v. Weatherford, 694 F.3d 1160, 1174 (10th Cir. 2012); Bender v. Jordan, 623 F.3d 1128, 1130 (D.C. Cir. 2010); Alade v. Barnes-Jewish Hosp., Inc., 2012 WL 2598091, 5 (E.D.Mo. 2012); Yellen v. Teledne Continental Motors, Inc., 832 F.Supp.2d 490, 497–498 (E.D.Pa. 2011); McAdams v. Medtronic, Inc., 2010 WL 3909958, 2. (S.D.Tex. 2010).

94 In re Oxycontin Antitrust Litigation, 821 F.Supp. 2d 591, 599 (S.D.N.Y. 2011); Blakenship v. Bridgestone Americas Holding, Inc., 467 F.Supp. 2d 886, 898 (C.D.Ill. 2006); Whittington v. Morgan Stanley Smith Barney, 2012 WL 4846484, 4 (W.D.C.V. 2012).

95 Immunocept, L.L.C. v. Fulbright & Jaworski, L.L.P, 504 F.3d 1281 (Fed. Cir. 2007); Air Measurement Tech., Inc. v. Akin Gump Strauss Hauer & Feld, L.L.P., 504 F.3d 1262 (Fed. Cir. 2007); Dixon v. Coburg Dairy, Inc., 369 F.3d 811, 818 (4th Cir. 2004); Bowdrie v. Sun Pharmaceutical Industries Ltd., 2012 WL 5465994, 4 (E.D.N.Y. 2012); West Virginia ex rel. McGraw v. Eli Lilly & Co., 476 F.Supp. 2d 230, 234 (E.D.N.Y. 2007); Beechwood Development Group, Inc. v. Konersman, 517 F.Supp.2d 770, 775 (D.S.C., 2007).

the pending case.[96] Some even held that the federal issue must be embodied in a federal statute.[97] Still others demanded that resolution of the federal issue be applicable to a broad range of future cases.[98] And others indicated that "jurisdiction is disfavored for cases that . . . involve substantial questions of state as well as federal law."[99] In addition, some treated *Empire*'s admonition that cases satisfying the *Grable* standard should represent a "special and small" category as creating an additional presumption against the exercise of federal question jurisdiction.[100] Taking all of these approaches together, and considering their inherent malleability, the law of federal question jurisdiction became anything but principled and seemingly rested within the hands of each individual federal court judge. In short, *Gully*'s elegant compass, with its point pinned on the "true north" of congressional intent and the role played by the federal issue in the claim presented, has been replaced by a maze of multi-pronged tests that mask the essential inquiry with rhetoric of policy, pragmatics, ersatz intent, and speculations.

Gunn v. Minton: A Case Study

We now come to the Supreme Court's latest foray into the thicket of arising-under jurisdiction. Vernon Minton filed a federal patent infringement action (the "Patent Litigation") against the National Association of Securities Dealers, Inc. (the "NASD"), assisted by attorney Jerry W. Gunn and other lawyers. Minton alleged that the NASD had infringed his U.S. patent for TEXCEN, a telecommunications network and software program. Minton's company had leased TEXCEN to R.M. Stark & Co. ("Stark") more than one year before he applied for the patent for that invention. At the time of the

96 New York City Health and Hospitals Corp. v. WellCare of New York, Inc., 769 F.Supp.2d 250, 257 (S.D.N.Y. 2001).

97 In re Countrywide Financial Corp. Mortf. Marketing and Sales Practices Litigation, 2008 WL 5450351, 4 (S.D.Cal 2008).

98 Alade v. Barnes-Jewish Hosp., Inc., 2012 WL 2598091, 5 (E.D.Mo. 2012); Yellen v. Teledne Continental Motors, Inc., 832 F.Supp.2d 490, 497–498 (E.D.Pa. 2011); McAdams v. Medtronic, Inc., 2010 WL 3909958, 2. (S.D.Tex. 2010); Alcarmen v. Citibank N.A., 2009 WL 1330803, 3 (N.D. Cal. 2009).

99 Bender v. Jordan, 623 F.3d 1128, 1130 (D.C. Cir. 2010)

100 Gilmore v. Weatherford, 694 F.3d 1160, 1171 (10th Cir. 2012); Alade v. Barnes-Jewish Hosp., Inc., 2012 WL 2598091, 5 (E.D.Mo. 2012); Yellen v. Teledne Continental Motors, Inc., 832 F.Supp.2d 490, 497–498 (E.D.Pa. 2011); Baum v. Keystone Mercy Health Plan, 826 F.Supp. 2d 718, 720 (E.D.Pa. 2011); McAdams v. Medtronic, Inc., 2010 WL 3909958, at 2. (S.D.Tex. 2010); J. Kaz, Inc. v. Brown, F.Supp.2d, 2010 WL 2024483, at 3 (W.D.Pa. 2010); In re Countrywide Financial Corp. Mortf. Marketing and Sales Practices Litigation, 2008 WL 5450351, at 4 (S.D.Cal 2008).

lease, Minton assured Stark that TEXCEN was a finished product and never suggested that the purpose of the lease was experimentation. NASD moved for summary judgment arguing that the technology that formed the basis of Minton's patent had been the subject of a commercial lease – the lease to Stark – more than a year before Minton applied for the patent. According to NASD, the "on sale bar" would thus apply and preclude Minton from acquiring a patent on the technology. The district court granted NASD's summary judgment motion. Minton's attorneys then filed a motion for reconsideration, raising the new argument that the "experimental use" that negated the "on sale bar." The district court, however, denied reconsideration. Minton appealed and the Federal Circuit affirmed the district court's judgment.[101]

Minton then filed a legal malpractice suit before a Texas state court against Gunn and the attorneys who represented Minton in the patent litigation. He alleged that by failing to raise the experimental use doctrine in a timely fashion, his lawyers had been negligent and caused him to lose the case. The lawyer defendants filed motions for summary judgment, challenging the causation element of Minton's malpractice claim. They argued that the experimental use exception did not apply to the commercial lease at issue and that their alleged failure to timely plead and brief the exception therefore could not have caused Minton any harm. The trial court granted the defendants' summary judgment motions and entered a take-nothing judgment on all Minton's claims. Minton appealed to the Court of Appeals for the Second District of Texas.[102] While that appeal was pending, the Federal Circuit decided *Air Measurement Tech., Inc. v. Akin Gump Strauss Hauer & Feld, L.L.P.*[103] and *Immunocept, L.L.C. v. Fulbright & Jaworski, L.L.P.*,[104] each of which addressed the precise question presented in *Gunn v. Minton*.

In *Air Measurement*, the question was whether a state-created legal malpractice case for negligent representation in a previous patent prosecution and litigation could be removed to federal court as a suit arising under the patent laws within the meaning of §1338. The Federal Circuit held that it could. The court first explained that the patent law issue was embedded in the malpractice claim:

> Because [the suit underlying the malpractice claim] is a patent infringement action against ... defendants, the district court will have to adjudicate, hypothetically, the merits of the infringement claim. Because proof of patent infringement is necessary to show [plaintiff] would have prevailed in the prior

[101] Petitioner's Brief on the Merits, *Gunn v. Minton*, 2012 WL 5884814, at 3–5.
[102] *Id.*, at 5–6.
[103] 504 F.3d 1262 (Fed. Cir. 2007).
[104] 504 F.3d 1281 (Fed. Cir. 2007).

> litigation, patent infringement is a "necessary element" of [plaintiff's] malpractice claim and therefore apparently presents a substantial question of patent law conferring §1338 jurisdiction.[105]

The court also found that the federal ingredient was actually disputed.[106] The federal issue was also deemed substantial because "it [was] a necessary element of the malpractice case."[107] The only question remaining was then whether the federal issue was substantial and, if so, whether the exercise of jurisdiction would upset the traditional division of labor between federal and state courts. In what the court described as the "federalism" analysis required by *Grable*, it then revisited substantiality from a different perspective:

> There is a strong federal interest in the adjudication of patent infringement claims in federal court because patents are issued by a federal agency. The litigants will also benefit from federal judges who have experience in claim construction and infringement matters.[108]

Finally, as to the last *Grable* prong, the court simply noted:

> Congress considered the federal-state division of labor and struck a balance in favor of this court's entertaining patent infringement. For us to conclude otherwise would undermine Congress's expectation.[109]

The *Immunocept* case, decided by the Federal Circuit on the same day as *Air Measurement*, involved another patent-based legal malpractice claim. The court again found arising-under jurisdiction satisfied. As was true in *Air Measurement*, the plaintiff's malpractice claim included an essential federal ingredient that was the subject of an actual dispute between the parties.[110] Having so concluded, the court addressed the last two prongs of the *Grable* test jointly – combining the "substantiality" of the federal essential ingredient with what the Federal Circuit again described as the federalism component of *Grable*:

> Because patent claim scope defines the scope of patent protection, we surely consider claim scope to be a substantial question of patent law....
>
> Claim scope determination is a question of law that can be complex in that it may involve many claim construction doctrines. Litigants will benefit from federal judges who are used to handling these complicated rules.

[105] 504 F.3d at 1269 (internal citations omitted).
[106] *Id.*, at 1272.
[107] *Id.*
[108] *Id.*
[109] *Id.*
[110] 504 F.3d at 1285.

> Additionally, Congress' intent to remove non-uniformity in the patent law, as evidenced by its enactment of the Federal Courts Improvement Act of 1982, is further indicium that §1338 jurisdiction is proper here.[111]

In this compressed discussion, the court said three things: the federal issue presented in the case was important as a matter of patent law; the issue was one that called for the expertise of federal judges from which litigants would benefit; and the exercise of jurisdiction under the circumstances was consistent with congressional intent. In concluding that there was federal question jurisdiction, the court did not consider at all the potential for distortion of the traditional division of labor between federal and state courts. One could say, however, that the court implicitly found that the potential to distort was absent because the litigation involved patent law, a quintessential federal question over which Congress intentionally and expressly vested federal courts with exclusive jurisdiction.

Air Measurement and *Immunocept* can be seen as almost perfect exemplars of the classic and modified legal process method. Each is premised on durable jurisdictional principles of general applicability, which each court applied consistently with the full range of constitutional structure in mind, including the right of individual claimants to seek a federal forum under standards consistent with congressional intent. The courts' analysis also provides a straightforward, reasoned elaboration in that the conclusions reached logically proceed from the principled premise on which they are based. It almost goes without saying (but I have to say it!) that both cases are consistent with the claim-centered approach to jurisdiction developed in Part I.B of this article and, hence, consistent with *Gully*.

In his then pending case before the Texas Court of Appeals, Minton now argued, based on *Air Measurement* and *Immunocept*, that his legal malpractice action belonged to the exclusive jurisdiction of federal courts. The state court disagreed and held that Minton's state law malpractice claims did not "arise under" federal law. Specifically, the Court of Appeals' majority found that the third and fourth prongs of the *Grable* test had not been satisfied.[112]

In so ruling, the state court declined to follow the Federal Circuit's decisions in *Air Measurement* and *Immunocept*, explaining that those rulings were not binding on it. The appellate court further observed that, in its view, the Federal Circuit had misapplied United States Supreme Court precedent by disregarding the "federalism" component of the *Grable* test and by misapplying the substantiality requirement.[113]

Minton appealed to the Texas Supreme Court. The Texas high court, relying on *Grable*, found that Minton's legal malpractice claim fell within

[111] *Id.*, 1285–1286.

[112] 301 S.W. 3d 702, 709 (Tex. Ct. App. 2009).

[113] *Id.*

the exclusive jurisdiction of the federal courts. Having found that the first and second prongs of *Grable* were satisfied, the court addressed the third prong:

> Following *Grable*, other courts have deemed federal patent issues substantial when the determination of the patent issues establishes the success or failure of an overlying state-law claim. Similarly, to succeed on his state-based legal malpractice claim, Minton must establish that Gunn was required to raise the experimental use exception because it was a legally and factually viable defense to the on-sale bar and that Gunn's failure to do so proximately caused Minton to lose his federal patent infringement litigation.[114]

On the fourth prong of the *Grable* test, which the Texas Supreme Court described as "perhaps the most important,"[115] the court explained:

> Although we recognize that legal malpractice claims traditionally fall under the domain of state courts, we conclude that federal courts may decide this malpractice case without upsetting the jurisdictional balance between federal and state courts. ... In conducting the federalism analysis required under *Grable*, the Federal Circuit has recognized that federal courts also have a strong interest in having federal patent law applied uniformly. Not only does the federal government have an interest in the uniform application of patent law, but so do litigants involved in patent law disputes.[116]

The dissent pointed out that under *Grable*, for the essential federal ingredient to be "actually disputed," there must be a controversy as to the "validity, construction, or effect" of the federal issue.[117] In the dissent's view, the essential federal ingredient represented by the experimental use exception was not actually disputed, in that the doctrine's meaning and scope were well established[118] and the parties did not dispute either of them, but simply argued as to whether the exception was available as a defense in the Patent Litigation.[119] Hence, the dispute centered on a mere question of fact.[120] Therefore, because *Gunn*, unlike *Grable*, presented a question of fact rather than an "almost purely legal issue, one whose resolution would both be dispositive in that case, and 'controlling in numerous other cases,'"[121] the essential federal ingredient in *Gunn* was not substantial enough to confer exclusive federal question jurisdiction. Moreover, said the dissent, unlike *Grable*, *Gunn* did

114 Gunn v. Minton, 355 S.W.3d 634, at 643–644 (Tex. 2011) (internal citations omitted).
115 *Id.*, at 644.
116 *Id.*, at 644–645 (internal citation omitted).
117 *Grable*, 545 U.S. at 315 n. 3 (quoting Shulthis v. McDougal, 225 U.S. 561, 570 (1912)).
118 355 S.W. 3d, at 650 (Guzman, J., dissenting).
119 *Id.*
120 *Id.*
121 *Id.*, at 651.

not center "on the action of a federal agency (IRS) and its compatibility with a federal statute."[122] Thus, the federal issue presented did not require uniformity of interpretation and its decision would not result in precedent that controls numerous other cases. In addition, the federal ingredient in *Gunn*, the experimental use exception, was "a creature of federal common law, not of any statute"[123] and, as the Supreme Court had indicated, "it is hardly apparent why a proper 'federal–state balance' would place such a nonstatutory issue under the complete governance of federal law, to be declared in a federal forum."[124] Finally, as to the fourth prong of the *Grable* test, the dissent concluded that the exercise of jurisdiction over a legal malpractice case would upset the legally mandated balance between federal and state jurisdiction.[125]

The majority opinion of the Texas Supreme Court adhered to a claim-centered approach similar to the one adopted in *Gully*. In addition, while the court's opinion did address the importance of the federal issue to the federal system, it did so by carefully balancing federalism and supremacy interests. The majority also adopted a more inclusive approach to the principle of structural interpretation by addressing the importance of the federal issue to the individual claim of right. In doing so, the majority's approach fully embraced the classic and modified legal process method.

In contrast, the dissent adopted a hypertechnical and mechanical doctrinal approach that seemed far removed from any durable principle capable of application to a wide range of cases. The dissent insisted on applying a litany of tests on the misguided assumption that those tests should replace the essential inquiry into the federal nature of the claim.

On October 5, 2012, the Supreme Court granted *certiorari* in *Gunn v. Minton* (No. 11-1118) on the following question:

> Did the Federal Circuit depart from the standard this Court articulated in *Grable & Sons Metal Products, Inc. v. Darue Eng'g & Mfg.*, 545 U.S. 308 (2005), for "arising-under" jurisdiction of the federal courts under 28 U.S.C. §1338, when it held that state law legal malpractice claims against trial lawyers for their handling of underlying patent matters come within the exclusive jurisdiction of the federal courts? Because the Federal Circuit has exclusive jurisdiction over appeals involving patents, are state courts and federal courts strictly following the Federal Circuit's mistaken standard, thereby magnifying its jurisdictional error and sweeping broad swaths of state law claims – which

[122] *Id.*
[123] *Id.*, at 651.
[124] *Id.*
[125] *Id.*, at 651–652.

> involve no actual patents and have no impact on actual patent rights – into the federal courts?[126]

Thus, the issue presented in *Gunn* was whether a state-based malpractice claim that requires the resolution of a federal patent law question arises under federal law for purposes of §1338.

Before we analyze the Supreme Court's decision in that case, let's address the issue under the standards established by *Gully* and through the lens of an appropriate reading of legal process method.

Gunn through the unified claim-centered approach

When deciding whether a case arises under federal law, the essential question should be whether the plaintiff's claim depends on the construction, validity, or effect of federal law.[127] Resolving this question does not require the application of any multipronged or mechanical test. Nor does this question require a distinction between causes of action created by federal law and state causes of action that include an essential federal ingredient. In both circumstances, the relevant litigation unit is the claim. Hence, the jurisdictional analysis requires nothing more than a careful assessment of the claim and a sound judgment as to the role that the federal question plays in the resolution of that claim. It would be difficult to improve on Justice Cardozo's earlier quoted admonition in *Gully*:

> What is needed is something of that common-sense accommodation of judgment to kaleidoscopic situations which characterizes the law in its treatment of problems of causation. One could carry the search for causes backward, almost without end. Instead, there has been a selective process which picks the substantial causes out of the web and lays the other ones aside. As in problems of causation, so here in the search for the underlying law. If we follow the ascent far enough, countless claims of right can be discovered to have their source or their operative limits in the provisions of a federal statute or in the Constitution itself with its circumambient restrictions upon legislative power. To set bounds to the pursuit, the courts have formulated the distinction between controversies that are basic and those that are collateral, between disputes that are necessary and those that are merely possible. We shall be lost in a maze if we put that compass by.[128]

[126] 133 S.Ct. 420 (2012); *see* Petition for Certiorari, 2012 WL 826572, at i.

[127] Louisville & Nashville Railroad Company v. Mottley, 211 U.S. 149 (1908); Tennessee v. Union & Planters' Bank, 152 U.S. 454 (1894).

[128] 299 U.S. at 117–118 (internal citations omitted).

The only policy reflected in Justice Cardozo's analysis is one of careful judgment in determining whether the role played by the federal question in the claim is sufficiently important to justify the exercise of jurisdiction. Thus, the entire analysis focuses on a durable principle, and no mechanical test or formula can improve on that. Rather, as indicated by Justice Cardozo, a mechanical approach carries the risk of creating doctrinal labyrinths which there is no exit.

One could argue that the approach offered by Justice Cardozo in *Gully* is too broad and too vague, and that the tests and the doctrinal formulas later endorsed by the Supreme Court in cases such as *Franchise Tax Board*, *Merell Dow*, *Christianson*, *Grable*, and *Empire* were necessary to give content and contour to the general principles and foundations identified in *Gully*. Yet history belies this. Decades before *Gully*, the Court had established that the focus of arising-under jurisdiction analysis was on the plaintiff's claim and on the federal question substantially involved in that claim, and there had been no indication that this formula was not working or that it had caused a flood of litigation in the federal courts. As explained in *Shulthis*, if the plaintiff's claim depended on the "construction, validity or effect"[129] of federal law, that claim gave rise to a true controversy on federal law which, as such, deserved a federal forum. The standard may have been simple, but it was not vague.

Any additional inquiry is a distraction from these fundamental questions and could lead to results inconsistent with the underlying durable principle and with congressional intent. For example, to ask simply whether a claim has been created by federal law is to misstate the inquiry. The issue is not one of creation or of the source of the right being sued upon, but rather pertains solely to the nature of claim. This approach is fully consistent with the classic and modified legal process model. It reflects the entire range of structural considerations that ought to be included in a legal process methodology. It renders to federal courts that which is truly federal in nature (federalism and supremacy), it respects the judgment of Congress (separation of powers), and it measures the scope of jurisdiction from the perspective of the individual's claim of right (individual rights).

Likewise, to speak in terms of an "essential federal ingredient" adds an additional layer of complexity to the analysis by suggesting that a different line of inquiry is needed to assess the availability of federal question jurisdiction in that particular context. Instead, the proper question is simply whether the plaintiff's claim truly involves the construction, validity or effect of federal law. Certainly this is the approach that was applied in *Smith*, and the one that was endorsed in Justice Frankfurter's oft-quoted description of federal question jurisdiction:

[129] Shulthis v. McDougal, 225 U.S. 561, 570 (1912).

> Almost without exception, decisions under the general statutory grants have tested jurisdiction in terms of the presence, as an integral part of plaintiff's cause of action, of an issue calling for interpretation or application of federal law. E.g., *Gully v. First National Bank*, 299 U.S. 109. Although it has sometimes been suggested that the "cause of action" must derive from federal law, see *American Well Works Co. v. Layne and Bowler Co.*, 241 U.S. 257, it has been found sufficient that some aspect of federal law is essential to plaintiff's success. *Smith v. Kansas City Title & Trust Co.*, 255 U.S. 180. The litigation-provoking problem has been the degree to which federal law must be in the forefront of the case and not collateral, peripheral or remote.[130]

Once it is established that the plaintiff's claim requires the determination of a federal question, the natural consequence should be that that question may be addressed by a federal court. True, federal courts are courts of limited jurisdiction. However, they were created in part to ensure uniformity in the interpretation and application of federal law. Any artificial limitation on the access to federal courts undermines that purpose. Also, if a nonfrivolous federal question appears in the case, exercising arising-under jurisdiction over that question cannot by definition upset the congressionally mandated balance between federal and state courts in the absence of an express congressional direction to the contrary. Whether the exercise of federal question jurisdiction upsets the congressionally mandated balance is a question for Congress ultimately to decide, and Congress is fully capable of doing that. Indeed, one wonders how a court can ever know whether some exercise of federal question jurisdiction would upset that balance other than through sheer speculation. Moreover, it is unclear on what legitimate basis a federal court judge should have the authority to force cases involving basic and necessary federal questions into state courts.

Thus, the way out of the maze created by the modern approach to federal question jurisdiction is to be found in the claim-centered approach as exemplified in *Gully* and not in some further elaborations of *Grable* or any of the other recent jurisdictional cases. Indeed, the second, third, and fourth prongs of *Grable* are all suspect. Given that the jurisdictional analysis must be carried out solely by reference to the plaintiff's complaint, the *Grable* Court's requirement that the federal issue be actually disputed is impossible to apply, for no actual dispute can be assessed by reference to only one side of the controversy. Hence, a lower federal court's effort to determine whether a federal issue is

[130] Textile Workers Union of America v. Lincoln Mills of Alabama, 353 U.S. 448, 470 (1956) (Frankfurter, J., dissenting).

actually disputed in a case is misplaced and completely inconsistent with the well-pleaded complaint rule.

The third *Grable* inquiry – the substantiality of the federal issue – is redundant. Establishing the existence of a true and colorable controversy on the construction, validity or effect of federal law should create the strongest possible presumption in favor of federal jurisdiction. No independent inquiry into substantiality need be required. In fact, learning from the struggles of and the diverging approaches of the lower courts, and from *Gully* and *Smith*, a federal issue should be considered "substantial" if it is meaningful within the context of the litigation, i.e., colorable and essential within that proceeding. And, certainly, if a federal question plays an important role in the case, the strongest presumption should be that there is a federal forum available to hear that claim. Thus, the last *Grable* inquiry – the possible veto – is illegitimate. In fact, in light of the strong presumption in favor of jurisdiction when a federal question is truly presented, only a clear signal from Congress to the contrary should provide a sufficient rebuttal.

The answer to the issue presented by *Gunn* should now be easy. In *Gunn*, the malpractice litigation was truly about patent law. In fact, if Minton's lawyers did not properly raise the experimental use exception in the Patent Litigation, Minton will prevail on his legal malpractice claim. To make that determination, it would be necessary to interpret and apply the standards of patent law to the facts relevant to Minton's malpractice claim. Thus, the controversy over the federal issue is neither collateral nor merely possible. Rather, the controversy over the proper interpretation and application of the experimental use exception is basic and necessary to the resolution of Minton's claim. This is a quintessential question for federal courts. Having established this proposition, any additional analysis required by *Grable* would be either redundant or illegitimate. Moreover, any contrary conclusion on the jurisdictional issue would simply be wrong since Congress has in no way suggested that jurisdiction should be unavailable for the adjudication of such federal issues. Quite the opposite: by giving exclusive federal question jurisdiction over patent law claims and patent law counterclaims,[131] Congress has expressed a clear mandate that patent law issues should be welcomed by and adjudicated in federal courts and only in federal courts.[132]

[131] The "Holmes Group Fix," contained in Pub. L. No. 112-29, §19; 28 U.S.C. §1338.

[132] Apropos to that mandate, leaving disputes over federal law such as that presented in *Gunn* to state courts would pose the risk of inconsistent interpretations and applications of a body of law that Congress wanted exclusively decided by federal courts. Patent lawyers would have to be aware of the federal interpretation of patent law and of individual state courts' interpretation of that law under which they could be subject to malpractice. This complexity would certainly have an impact on the litigation of patent issues in federal courts

The *Gunn* Court arrived at a different conclusion, not under a different interpretation of *Gully*, but under an approach that draws a bright-line distinction between causes of action created by federal law and state law claims containing an essential federal ingredient. This approach essentially ignores *Gully* and turns a blind eye to congressional intent in an apparent effort to reduce the federal courts' caseload.

THE SUPREME COURT'S MECHANICAL SOLUTION IN GUNN

The *Gunn* Court began its analysis by admitting that its arising-under jurisprudence had come to resemble a "Jackson Pollock" canvas.[133] However, as the Court explained, *Grable* was designed to "bring some order to this unruly doctrine,"[134] and, in the Court's view, resolution of the issue in *Gunn* required nothing more than a straightforward application of the four-prong *Grable* test, a myopic paint-by-numbers approach to jurisdiction under which a judge may never look at much less consider the picture as a whole.

In applying that test, the Court acknowledged that the "resolution of the federal patent question [was] 'necessary' to Minton's case"[135] and that the patent-law issue was "the central point of dispute."[136] The third and fourth prongs of the *Grable* test, however, proved fatal to Minton's quest for exclusive federal jurisdiction.[137]

On the question of substantiality, the Court noted:

> In reaching the opposite conclusion [that the federal issue in the case was substantial], the Supreme Court of Texas focused on the importance of the issue to the plaintiff's case and to the parties before it. As our past cases show, however, it is not enough that the federal issue be significant to the particular parties in the immediate suit; that will *always* be true when the state claim "necessarily raise[s] a disputed federal issue, as *Grable* separately requires. The substantiality inquiry under *Grable* looks instead to the importance of the issue to the federal system as a whole.[138]

The Court followed up on this observation by explaining that in *Grable*, the "Federal Government" had a "strong interest" in the resolution of the federal issue there presented.[139] Hence, the exercise of jurisdiction there was in order.

[133] 133 S.Ct. at 1065.
[134] *Id.*
[135] *Id.*
[136] *Id.*
[137] *Id.* at 1066–1068.
[138] *Id.* at 1066 (citations omitted).
[139] *Id.*

I have several concerns with the *Gunn* Court's treatment of substantiality. First, the artificial distinction between cases satisfying the creation test and cases satisfying the essential federal ingredient test is a relatively recent phenomenon, traceable largely to *Merrell Dow*. Certainly, the Court in *Smith* did not create a novel jurisdictional doctrine.[140] Prior to *Merrell Dow*, there was a unified arising-under theory fully captured by the decision in *Gully*. That theory focused on the importance of the federal issue to the plaintiff's claim, an approach that seemed completely consistent with the congressional intent to create a federal forum for the resolution of claims premised on questions of federal law. Also, there is no evidence that Congress wanted the courts to adopt a narrower construction of arising-under jurisdiction in federal-ingredient cases. Hence, this distinction, however useful it may be in reducing the federal courts' caseload, is nothing more than a creature of judicial imagination.[141]

Federal courts were created by Congress and vested with federal question jurisdiction for the benefit of litigants, not for the benefit of the federal system or federal judges. The notion that federal question jurisdiction should turn on the interest of the federal government or on the interest of the federal system (whatever that may mean), or in federal judges' perception as to the burden of their caseload, is wholly inconsistent with this principle. This notion, first introduced in 1986 in *Merrell Dow* and further developed in *Grable* and *Empire*, seems to be more in service of the judiciary's interest in docket management than it is faithful to congressional intent. Indeed, given that the purpose of federal question jurisdiction is to serve litigants who assert claims premised on federal law, this newly created principle flies in the face of congressional intent and the structural principles of separation of powers and the protection of individual claims of right.[142]

The Supreme Court is of course free to change doctrine. As I previously noted, courts retain an important role in statesmanship. But nothing in the Court's recent federal question jurisprudence suggests that its abandonment of *Gully*'s durable principle and a claim-centered approach to jurisdiction is a

[140] *See* Woolhandler & Collins, *Justice Holmes*, *supra* note 6, at 2153 (essential federal ingredient cases "were perhaps the paradigm 'arising under' cases" in the nineteenth century).

[141] *See* F. Andrew Hessick III, *The Common Law of Federal Question Jurisdiction*, 60 Ala. L. Rev. 895 (2009).

[142] Congress has consistently indicated its intent to open the doors of federal courts to a wide range of federal question cases. *See* 28 U.S.C. §§1338(a)(extending patent arising under jurisdiction to patent law counterclaims); 1367(a) (broad supplemental jurisdiction over claims and parties in federal question cases); 1441(c) (removal of federal question cases that have been joined with otherwise non-removable claims); 1454 (authorizing removal of actions in which any party asserts a claim for relief arising under patent or copyright law).

product of statesmanship. Rather, given the workability of the established principles, the exercise of jurisdiction would seem to call for an exercise of judicial craftsmanship, a skill that is sorely lacking in the Court's recent federal question jurisprudence.

The *Gunn* Court also thought that the federal issue presented there was not substantial because it was "posed in a merely hypothetical sense: *If* Minton's lawyers had raised a timely experimental-use argument, would the result in the patent infringement proceeding have been different?"[143] It is true that the resolution of this question would not have altered the judgment already rendered in the patent litigation. However, this "hypothetical" issue was, as the Court noted, essential to Minton's claim and, if he prevailed on it, he would be entitled to significant monetary damages from his former attorneys. In addition, this hypothetical patent law decision, if resolved by the state courts, would necessarily have an effect on patent law attorneys practicing in that state, for they would have to adjust their patent litigation practices to the patent law interpretations rendered by the courts of the state in which they practice. One might think that this collateral consequence would be of interest to the "federal system," but the Court offers no elaboration, reasoned or otherwise, of why it did not matter.

The Court, borrowing from *Empire* and measuring the case before it against a mechanical test rather than a durable principle, also noted that "[t]he present case is 'poles apart from *Grable*,' in which … resolution of the federal question 'would be controlling in numerous other cases.'"[144] This is a curious observation, since the federal issue in *Grable* was not important enough for the Supreme Court to review on *certiorari*. Instead, the Supreme Court left that question to the lower courts. One also wonders how a federal district court, measuring arising-under jurisdiction from the perspective of the plaintiff's complaint, could possibly determine whether the federal issue presented is going to be controlling in numerous other cases. Certainly, the Court has offered no workable method through which a federal court can assess this impact other than by looking at the court's own caseload, which often will not fully reflect the importance of an issue on a national basis.

The Court also observed that the "fact-bound and situation-specific" nature of the federal issue weighted against the exercise of federal question jurisdiction.[145] However, as the Court noted in *Osborn v. Bank of the United States*, "[a] cause may depend on several questions of fact and law."[146] Thus, the

[143] 133 S.Ct. at 1067.
[144] *Id.*
[145] *Id.* at 1068.
[146] 22 U.S. 738, 821 (1824).

Gunn Court's narrow view of the role of federal court jurisdiction as one pertaining only to the interpretation of law overlooks the important factfinding role of federal trial courts[147] and again fails to account for a federal court's role in providing a *federal* forum for the vindication of individual claims of right.

Finally, the Court's treatment of the fourth *Grable* prong was peculiar. The Court suggested that because the third prong was not satisfied, the fourth wasn't either, essentially rendering the fourth prong meaningless.[148] The Court did observe, however, that the states have a special interest in policing members of licensed professions. As to the legal profession, the Court noted that the states'

> interest . . . in regulating lawyers is especially great since lawyers are essential to the primary governmental function of administering justice and have historically been officers of the courts.[149]

Yet the Court did not explain why a state would have a paramount interest in ensuring the competence of lawyers litigating patent law issues in federal courts. Nor did the Court consider the countervailing federal interest in the competence of those lawyers, who are, after all, members of the federal bar. The Court's reasoning here is illogical in that a state's general interest in regulating the practice of law does not establish a specific interest in regulating the practice of law in federal courts exercising exclusive federal jurisdiction. Also, the Court fell into the trap of treating federalism as a narrow concept reflecting only the "states' rights" side of the equation. Hence, the opinion on this point runs afoul of the principles of structural interpretation and reasoned elaboration.

*****

As it stands right now, after the decision in *Gunn*, the essential federal ingredient test requires (at a minimum): (1) an essential federal ingredient embedded in a state law claim, that is (2) actually disputed, (3) substantial – i.e., (i) an issue of law, (ii) important to the federal system, and (iii) controlling numerous other cases – and (4) such that assigning it to federal courts would not distort the appropriate balance of federal and state judicial responsibilities as envisioned by the courts. In addition to the above, however, one must also take into account the other factors that the lower courts continue to apply.

Under the standards established in *Gunn*, it will be a very rare federal-ingredient case indeed that qualifies for statutory arising-under jurisdiction.

[147] *See infra*, text accompanying note 87.

[148] 133 S.Ct. at 1068.

[149] *Id.* (quoting *Goldfarb v. Virginia State Bar*, 421 U.S. 773, 792 (1975).

To put it differently, it would be very easy for a busy federal judge to apply *Gunn* in a way that finds jurisdiction to be lacking. Yet, if a case truly presents a federal issue that is at the forefront of a state-created claim, it should be the exceptional circumstance under which jurisdiction is denied.

As Justice Brennan observed in his *Merrell Dow* dissent:

> Congress passes laws in order to shape behavior; a federal law expresses Congress' determination that there is a federal interest in having individuals or other entities conform their actions to a particular norm established by that law. . . . It is the duty of courts to interpret these laws and apply them in such a way that the congressional purpose is realized. . . . Congress granted the district courts power to hear cases "arising under" federal law in order to enhance the likelihood that federal laws would be interpreted more correctly and applied more uniformly. In other words, Congress determined that the availability of a federal forum to adjudicate cases involving federal questions would make it more likely that federal laws would shape behavior in the way that Congress intended.
>
> By making federal law an essential element of a state-law claim, the State places the federal law into a context where it will operate to shape behavior: the threat of liability will force individuals to conform their conduct to interpretations of the federal law made by courts adjudicating the state-law claim. . . . Consequently, the possibility that the federal law will be incorrectly interpreted in the context of adjudicating the state-law claim implicates the concerns that led Congress to grant the district courts power to adjudicate cases involving federal questions in precisely the same way as if it was federal law that "created" the cause of action.[150]

To be sure, if Congress expressly precludes the exercise of jurisdiction, a court must conform to that express intent. There might also be other circumstances indicating a congressional intent to limit jurisdiction over particular federal questions, or to give courts discretion as to whether a particular form of jurisdiction should be exercised.[151] But whether there are such circumstances should not be dependent on an artificial, judicially created four-part test. That artificial test allows judges to ignore congressional intent and to reject federal jurisdiction at the expense of allowing a plaintiff to have her federal claim heard in a federal court.

CONCLUDING REMARKS

The current law of federal question jurisdiction is just another example of the problems generated by the proliferation of doctrines and tests apparently

[150] *Merrell Dow*, 478 U.S. at 827–828 (Brennan, J. dissenting).

[151] *See, e.g.*, 28 U.S.C. §1367(c) (giving federal courts discretion with respect to hearing certain supplemental jurisdiction claims).

intended to provide guidance to lower courts and perhaps cabin their discretion. However, this proliferation of doctrines and tests ends up, as the Court itself has admitted, creating a Jackson Pollock canvas, cluttering the analysis, at least in the context of federal question jurisdiction, with irrelevancies and illegitimate considerations that stray far from the durable principles that should instead guide the courts. The results are often confusing, rarely helpful and frequently inconsistent with the fundamental principles that they purport to apply.

The Supreme Court's decision in *Gunn* represents the Supreme Court's most recent statement on the law of arising-under jurisdiction in the context of a federal question embedded in a state law claim. The decision appears inconsistent with virtually all classic and modified legal process principles. As to the principle of structural interpretation, the Court overplays federalism by failing to take into account other countervailing interests such as federal supremacy, actual congressional intent, and individuals' congressionally vested right to access a federal forum on claims that truly raise federal issues – issues as to which a federal court may be more expert and fairer than its state counterpart.

The Court's decision also challenges the institutional settlement principle by adopting what is in essence a procedural test that will lead to ad hoc and unpredictable results. In addition, the *Gunn* opinion's freestyle interpretation of federal statutes represents a type of antiformalism that borders on legal realism and allows the judicially perceived interests of the "federal system" to trump a wider spectrum of legitimate and constitutionally demanded interests, including the actual intent of Congress. *Gunn* is also inconsistent with the rule of law principle, for it designs a completely unpredictable and unworkable procedure that allows federal courts to divest themselves of cases that would otherwise sensibly fall within the scope of arising-under jurisdiction. Next, as I have already explained, several passages of the opinion fail to satisfy any sensible standard of reasonable elaboration. But most importantly, the major flaw with the *Gunn* opinion, as with several of the Court's other recent procedural decisions,[152] is its mechanical test-driven approach to doctrine that operates contrary to the valid, durable principles and fails to provide any real guidance to lower courts and litigants in the application of the law. This myopic

[152] For an analysis of this phenomenon in related contexts, see Chapters II and III, *supra*; Allan Ides & Simona Grossi, *Puporseful Availment Trap*, Federal Courts Law Review, 7 Fed. Cts. L. Rev. 118 (2013); Allan Ides, *A Critical Appraisal of the Supreme Court's Decision in J. Mcintyre Machinery, Ltd. v. Nicastro*, 45 Loy. L.A. L. Rev. 341 (2012); Allan Ides, *The Standard for Measuring the Validity of a Federal Rule of Civil Procedure: The Shady Grove Debate between Justices Scalia and Stevens*, 86 Notre Dame Law Review 1041 (2011).

test-driven approach is not only inappropriate but it is inefficient, for it requires continuous interventions by the Court to revisit its earlier pronouncements that have proven themselves inadequate and theoretically ungrounded.[153]

While there is clearly a need for the Court to again visit the statutory arising-under topic, one would be naïve to believe that the next visit will suddenly rescue certainty from this sea of confusion. In the meantime, the level of unpredictability and unfairness will likely remain high. While it may often be healthy that reasonable minds differ, this is not true with respect to the standards that govern the access to the federal courts. These standards, particularly for federal question cases, should be clear, fair, and true to the underlying intent of Congress, rather than subject to the unfettered discretion of courts that may be interested in reducing their caseload.

[153] An apt example of this phenomenon can be seen in the law of personal jurisdiction where the Court seems unable to find a transcendent, theoretical principle to meaningfully guide the analysis. Thus, on March 4, 2013, the Supreme Court granted certiorari in *Walden v. Fiore* (No. 12-574), yet another case involving personal jurisdiction. 133 S.Ct. 1493. This happened less than two years after the Court decided two other personal jurisdiction cases, Goodyear Dunlop Tires Operations, S.A. v. Brown, 131 S. Ct. 2846 (2010), and J. McIntyre Machinery, Ltd. v. Nicastro, 131 S. Ct. 2780 (2011).

6

A Look Abroad: Is the Supreme Court's Decision-Making Process Unique?

Allan Ides, my colleague from Loyola Law School Los Angeles, and I have prepared the following questionnaire to test the reactions of a selected group of civil law judges, lawyers, and scholars to the U.S. Supreme Court's modern common law method. What follows is the questionnaire and the responses collected.

While these responses may not be definitive and do not purport to give a complete picture of the foreign countries under examination, they do offer a very informative contrast to the U.S. Supreme Court's modern common law approach. They provide a variety of perspectives and insights that cannot be distilled into a single formula or interpretation. Thus, the reader is free to engage each of these responses in a manner that opens a wide range of possibilities.

There do, however, seem to be some commonalities among the responses. Ironically, the civil law codification proves more capable of adjusting to unforeseen possibilities than the modern common law case law method. This may be in part due to the civil law focus on the plaintiff's right to sue in a natural forum, such as the plaintiff's home forum, versus the common law focus on the defendant's right to be sued in its most convenient forum. In addition, the doctrinal boxes created by the case-by-case method tend to foreclose possibilities, while the civil law codification, and the absence of a rigid *stare decisis*, has the opposite effect.

As a consequence, at times, the civil law response to the law of jurisdiction seems more consistent with due process than the common law one. Also, the U.S. courts might deny jurisdiction when there would be no unfairness to the defendant, but yet the plaintiff would be denied of the forum to which he is otherwise entitled.

*****

I. Preliminary Information

This study is intended to examine how the highest courts—Supreme Court or Constitutional Court—of an array of countries would solve the issues in the fact-patterns presented below.

The goal is not to catalogue substantive outcomes, but to examine the decision-making method employed by these courts, both in general and in two specific contexts.

Please fill in the following questionnaire and send it by e-mail to simona.grossi@lls.edu and allan.ides@lls.edu.

II. Background Information

a. Please identify yourself, your professional position, and the country on which your answers will be based.
b. Briefly describe the highest court (or courts) of your country and indicate its (or their) function within your legal system.

III. Judicial Decision Making

The modern common law method in the U.S. can be described as follows: begin with a rule, interpret that rule, and then develop a series of multiprong tests through which to apply that interpretation.

For example, in the U.S., the law of jurisdiction begins with the text of the Due Process Clauses of the U.S. Constitution, which provide that no person shall be deprived of "life, liberty or property, without due process of law." Interpreting this rule, the U.S. Supreme Court has held that jurisdiction is proper when it is consistent with the "traditional notions of fair play and substantial justice"; that is, when the defendant's connections with the forum state are such that they create a reasonable expectation of suit in the forum.

This interpretation embraces two broad jurisdictional categories: the traditional bases of jurisdiction, such as domicile or consent, and a more encompassing category directed toward nonresidents of the forum, known as the "minimum contacts" test.

In application, the minimum contacts test has evolved into further subcategories—activities in state, contractual relations with a resident of the state, suits arising out of injuries caused by products sold in the state, and out-of-state activities having an effect in the state. Each of these subcategories has unique, fact-specific requirements, but they all share some elements. The common elements include the quantity and quality of the contacts, and the relationship between those contacts and the plaintiff's claim.

The U.S. Supreme Court has added yet another layer to the jurisdictional analysis, one that can defeat jurisdiction even when all of the above specific and common requirements have been satisfied. This so-called "reasonableness" inquiry requires a court to balance the plaintiff's choice of forum, any significant litigation-based burdens imposed on the defendant, and the interest of the judicial system in providing a fair and efficient resolution of the dispute.

To be clear, this reasonableness inquiry has nothing to do with the defendant's reasonable expectations of suit in the forum. Rather, it presumes that jurisdiction would otherwise be satisfied under the connecting factors and reasonable expectations formula, but nonetheless allows a court to decline jurisdiction in accord with the independent reasonableness inquiry.

In short, there is a rule, an interpretation of that rule, and further interpretations creating increasingly specialized tests to control and sometimes limit the scope of the underlying principle as applied.

a. Have you observed a similar phenomenon in your judicial system? If so, please identify the area(s) of law in which this has occurred. (Please do not limit yourself to questions involving jurisdiction.)
b. If you have observed this phenomenon, does it sometimes occur that the judicially developed tests limit the principles that the tests purport to articulate?

IV. Jurisdiction

a. Hypo

Assume that a foreign manufacturer's product is sold in your country through an agent not from your country, and that this product injures an individual domiciled there. Assume also that the foreign manufacturer did not directly market its product in your country but instructed its agent to market the product wherever it could be sold.

b. U.S. Theoretical Premise

See Part III above.

c. The U.S. Supreme Court's Solution

The U.S. is divided into fifty states, each of which possesses a range of independent sovereignty. In a case based on facts similar to those above, the U.S. Supreme Court held that the court of the State where the party was injured could not exercise jurisdiction over the foreign manufacturer, because although the manufacturer had targeted the U.S. market, it had not specifically targeted the State where the product was sold and the injury occurred. The Court held that under the circumstances the exercise of jurisdiction would violate the due process rights of the foreign manufacturer.

d. Your System's Solution

(i) Would your country exercise jurisdiction over the foreign manufacturer on a claim against it by the injured party?

(ii) On which provisions and/or case law do you base your answer? If your highest court has addressed this or a similar issue, please describe how the court solved it.

(iii) If you need additional facts to answer this question, please indicate which type of facts you would need and why.

(iv) Additional Comments

Express any additional comment you may have on the solutions offered by your system and the U.S. system.

V. Justiciability

a. Hypo

The mother of an illegitimate child brought an action on behalf of her child to enjoin the discriminatory application of a law providing that "any parent who shall wilfully desert, neglect or refuse to provide for the support and maintenance of his or her child, shall be guilty of a misdemeanor, and upon conviction, shall be punished by imprisonment for not more than two years." The statute applied solely to the parents of legitimate children and imposed no duty of support on the parents of illegitimate children. In her complaint, the mother alleged that the father of her illegitimate child had refused to provide support for the child, and that although she made application to the local prosecuting attorney for enforcement of the statute against the father of her child, the prosecuting attorney refused to take action for the express reason that the fathers of illegitimate children were not within the scope of the law. The mother claimed that the law denied her child equal protection of the law. Assume that this claim was valid. The government challenged the mother's right to bring the claim.

b. U.S. Theoretical Premise

In the United States, three separate issues must be decided in determining whether a party can pursue a claim. First, the party must be the "real party in interest." Second, the party must state a claim upon which relief can be granted. Third, the party must satisfy the "justiciability" doctrine.

> The real party in interest is the party who owns the right sought to be enforced or who is authorized to represent such a party. Next, to state a claim upon which relief can be granted, the party must show that she has properly alleged the violation of a legally recognized right. Finally, to satisfy justiciability, the party must show that she has standing, that her claim is ripe, and that the claim has not become moot. As to standing, the party must show

that she or the party she represents has suffered a concrete injury, that this injury was caused by the defendant, and that the judiciary may properly redress it. Ripeness requires that the party show that she has already suffered injury or will immediately do so. Finally, mootness requires that the claim remain "alive" during the entire course of the litigation.

c. The U.S. Supreme Court's Solution

In a case based on similar facts, the U.S. Supreme Court held that the mother could not bring this claim. The Court did not hold that the mother was not the real party in interest since she clearly could represent the interests of the child; nor did the Court hold that the mother had failed to state a claim upon which relief could be granted. Rather, the Court's ruling was based on the standing component of justiciability. The Court identified the child's injury as the lack of support from the father, and concluded that this injury would not necessarily be "redressed" by the relief that the plaintiff sought, for the father's prosecution would not necessarily lead to the father's future payment of support.

d. Your System's Solution

(i) How would the courts of your country resolve the question of whether the mother should be allowed to proceed with her claim?

(ii) On which provisions and/or case law do you base your answer? If your highest court has addressed this or a similar issue, please describe how the court solved it.

(iii) If you need additional facts to answer this question, please indicate which type of facts you would need and why.

(iv) Does your legal system require the same range of considerations to determine whether a party can bring a claim? Are those considerations statutory or constitutional?

(v) Additional Comments

Express any additional comment you may have on the solutions offered by your system and the U.S. system.

BELGIUM

WILLEM VERRIJDT
Law Clerk (Référendaire) *in the Belgian Constitutional Court and PhD Student at KU Leuven*

II.b Briefly describe the highest court (or courts) of your country and indicate its (or their) function within your legal system.

There are three "highest" courts:

- The Court of Cassation (Hof van Cassatie, Cour de cassation): the highest court in the pyramid of ordinary jurisdiction (civil law, criminal law, social law, commercial law), competent to annul decisions rendered in second instance (mostly by a court of appeal), after which it sends the case to another jurisdiction of the same level for a new examination on the merits.
- The Council of State (Raad van State, Conseil d'Etat): the highest administrative court (established in 1946), competent for annulling administrative decisions. Depending on the subject matter, it acts as a first instance judge, or as an appeal judge or a cassation judge for lower administrative jurisdictions.
- The Constitutional Court (Grondwettelijk Hof, Cour constitutionnelle): competent for constitutional review of formal legislation (established in 1984), in two procedures: (1) an annulment procedure, after a petition for annulment filed within a delay of six months after the legal provision's official publication, initiated by a legislator, a government, or any natural or legal person possessing an interest in the annulment; (2) a preliminary references procedure, answering validity questions (no interpretation questions) asked by other judges, including the Court of Cassation and the Council of State, which are in principle obliged to refer such a question raised by one of the parties to the Constitutional Court.

Two remarks:

- Formal legislation's constitutionality can only be examined by the Constitutional Court, whereas all ordinary and administrative judges are competent to review whether formal legislation respects international law, EU law, or the ECHR.

- Yet, the Constitutional Court has developed two distinct techniques to review indirectly whether formal legislation respects international or supranational norms: (1) by combining them with the principle of equality and non-discrimination in the articles 10–11 of the Constitution; (2) by combining them with "analogous" human rights provisions in the Constitution.

III. JUDICIAL DECISION MAKING

(a) Have you observed a similar phenomenon in your judicial system? If so, please identify the area(s) of law in which this has occurred. (Please do not limit yourself to questions involving jurisdiction.)

You describe a decision-making process in three steps. Belgian decision-making processes (or, at least, the way they are described) tend to have only two steps: the legal norm and its interpretation. The concept of "tests" is not in use. I see several reasons for this:

1) The three-step type of judicial decision making is to be expected when the applicable legislation is not very detailed and "technical," but rather makes use of vague and broadly defined concepts. These broad concepts are then judicially molded so as to fit the first couple of factual situations the judge needs to assess, yet these first factual applications will then survive as "tests."

Civil law countries tend to have more legal norms; these norms tend to be more detailed and "technical," leaving less room for interpretation.

2) We still use rather old concepts of interpretation: linguistic interpretation (merely analyzing the text), teleological interpretation (looking at the legislator's goal), etc. An interpretation should, in principle, not be "extensive" or "restrictive" in the sense that it reads content into the legal provision or that it reads content out of it. A nuance: whereas extensive interpretation *praeter legem* is accepted, an interpretation *contra legem* is prohibited, as this would clearly violate the separation of powers.
3) The three-step decision-making will probably be absent in areas with a strong "principle of legality" (e.g. criminal law and tax law). The principle of legality is strongly connected to the principle of legal certainty, which implies that everyone should be able to base his or

her behavior on the applicable legislation without being surprised by its subsequent application.

This does not mean, however, that the "tests" are absent from Belgian law; it only means that there is only little room for them. Furthermore, when "tests" exist, they are not rigid: jurisprudence applying vague norms can easily change due to changing circumstances or better insights. New jurisprudence, replacing the old one, can easily develop. There is no *stare decisis*: prior interpretations by higher courts are not formally binding; the only reason why lower judges tend to follow higher courts' interpretations is that they don't like seeing their judgments being quashed.

In Belgium, not a lot of fields of law allow for this type of decision making; legislation often tends to be rather technical and detailed. I can only imagine two major fields:

- Human rights and unwritten legal principles. However, I should stress that judicial development in this field will often not really take place within the Belgian Judiciary, because Belgian constitutional rights are interpreted as being analogous to the European and international human rights, which implies that the Belgian Courts will "develop" Belgian human rights jurisprudence by simply following the developments in ECtHR and ECJ jurisprudence. These supranational courts tend to be very extensive in interpreting their reference provisions, for which they are often criticized in the legal doctrine (lack of legitimacy of courts, and *a fortiori* lack of legitimacy of supranational courts), but once these supranational Courts have developed these (criticized) interpretations, they will be followed by the Belgian judges.
- Civil tort law. The provisions concerning civil tort law are very summarily laid down in the articles 1382-1386*bis* of the Civil Code (Burgerlijk Wetboek), and the more detailed rules have all been developed by the judges applying these provisions. Article 1382 CC simply states that "Elke daad van de mens, waardoor aan een ander schade wordt veroorzaakt, verplicht degene door wiens schuld de schade is ontstaan, deze te vergoeden." (Each human action causing damage to another, obliges the one responsible for the damage to compensate it.) The jurisprudence has derived from that phrasing that three concepts are essential: "fault" (article 1383 is about negligence, but the principles are the same), "damage," and "causal link between fault and damage." Throughout the decades, a lot of jurisprudence has filled in these concepts, and currently, the text books about general tort law (i.e., not discussing the more specific regimes of damages, such as product liability) need many hundreds of pages in order to summarize this jurisprudence.

Furthermore, there is no legislation whatsoever about damages caused by the government. Before 1920, the Court of Cassation ruled that the judge is incompetent to judge executive action, because of the separation of powers ("*juger l'administration, c'est encore administrer*"). In 1920, it accepted that damages are due for executive actions or executive negligence, in 1991 it accepted the principles of damages for faults or negligence by the Judiciary, and only in 2006 it accepted that damages are due for faults or negligence by the legislature. The government's liability is now a field of law of its own, fully governed by jurisprudence, which largely consists of applying the same principles to official bodies than the ones applied to human actions and human negligence.

(b) If you have observed this phenomenon, does it sometimes occur that the judicially developed tests limit the principles that the tests purport to articulate?

This is not likely to happen, for the following reasons:

- There is no real distinction between "interpretation" and "subsequent tests";
- Judicial interpretations "changing" the text of the legislation will most often be "extensive";
- - The most common interpretation technique being the "teleological interpretation," it is not likely that an interpretation goes against the goal of the rule it is trying to interpret;
- Topical exceptions will soon be set aside by better jurisprudence.

It is, however, always possible that a judicial concept will not be able to apply to its full extent, because of the fact that it must be balanced against other, conflicting principles.

IV. JURISDICTION

(d)(i) Would your country exercise jurisdiction over the foreign manufacturer on a claim against it by the injured party?

Yes. A distinction needs to be made concerning whether the foreign manufacturer is based in another EU Member State or in a country not belonging to the EU, but in both cases, Belgian courts have jurisdiction.

(ii) On which provisions and/or case law do you base your answer? If your highest court has addressed this or a similar issue, please describe how the court solved it.

- For situations with no link to EU law (i.e., import from a "third country"), this situation is governed by article 97 of the Belgian Conflict of Legislation Act of 16 July 2004. This detailed act stipulates, for almost all matters of private, commercial, or social law, when the Belgian judge has jurisdiction and which legislation he should apply (e.g., Belgian law or foreign law).

The given hypothesis is most likely to be a B2C-situation (if not, article 96 of the same Act applies and the Belgian judge will probably still have jurisdiction), and the plaintiff will most likely be a consumer.

Article 97, § 1 sets two alternative criteria: the Belgian judges have jurisdiction if

(1) the Belgian consumer has contracted with the foreign company while being *domiciled* in Belgium AND while at that time being present in Belgium [in this case, it is not relevant where the goods were or should be delivered];

OR

(2) the goods were or should have been delivered to a consumer who was a *resident* [domicile is not necessary] in Belgium when he ordered the goods, provided that prior to the order the company has made publicity in Belgium.

Article 97 § 3 adds that an agreement making the judge of another country competent is only valid if it dates after the conflict has arisen.

This is the general jurisdiction rule for B2C-contracts. This rule applies to product liability, as there is no *lex specialis* for this matter.

I should add that it is not necessary to direct the claim against the foreign producer: the applicable Act on Product Liability (25 February 1991), which is based on an EU directive, renders the company that imports goods into the European Union *in solidum* liable together with the producer (article 4, § 1). This means that the consumer can choose to claim full damages from the importer (also before the Belgian judge) or from the producer, and that the division of the damage between the producer and the importer is a matter to be resolved between them later, without the consumer's involvement. If the identity of one of both is unknown, the retailer is equally *in solidum* liable (article 4, §2).

- For situations with a link to EU law (i.e., goods manufactured in another member State), article 16.1 of the Brussels I Regulation (22 December 2000, no. 44/2001) applies, according to which the consumer has the choice: he can either bring his action before the judge of his Member State or before the judge of the producer's Member State.

(iii) If you need additional facts to answer this question, please indicate which type of facts you would need and why.

The only fact that I added to the hypothesis is to specify that this case probably concerns a consumer (i.e., someone who has not bought the product in his professional capacity) in his relation with a producer.

(iv) Additional comments. Express any additional comment you may have on the solutions offered by your system and the U.S. system.

For both Belgium and the EU, I should add that "the due process rights" of the manufacturer play no role in this regard (i.e. insofar as jurisdiction is concerned). Product liability is a matter of consumer protection, and the rules on jurisdiction and applicable legislation reflect this.

In neither situation (link with EU law or not) is it relevant whether the manufacturer has "targeted" the Belgian market. For Belgian law, the importer is liable *in solidum*, and in EU law, the consumer has a free choice of jurisdiction.

The solution given by the US Supreme Court might violate article 6 ECHR, which encompasses a right of effective access to the competent judge. If the Judiciary first develops a principle establishing jurisdiction, and then disapplies that same principle in a B2C-relation, the ECtHR might rule that the legal framework provokes legal uncertainty.

V. JUSTICIABILITY

(d)(i) How would the courts of your country resolve the question of whether the mother should be allowed to proceed with her claim?

I must first mention [the relevance of this intermezzo is explained under (v)] that the action that the plaintiff in the hypothesis wants to pursue, does, in Belgium, not (entirely) fall under the jurisdiction of the ordinary courts. She will have to start the action before the ordinary courts, immediately admitting[1] that the applicable legislation does not grant her that right because the law only concerns legitimate children, yet adding that this distinction between legitimate and illegitimate children violates articles 10 and 11 of the

[1] She can also choose, for tactical reasons, not to admit this. The defendant will then make this submission, and subsequently, the mother may still ask for a preliminary reference to the CC.

Constitution (the principle of equality and nondiscrimination), *juncto* article 22 of the Constitution and article 8 ECHR (the right to respect for privacy and family life). The judge, who does not have jurisdiction to rule on questions of constitutionality of legislation, will then have to suspend the procedure and submit the case to the Constitutional Court (preliminary reference). The Constitutional Court will then state a *lacuna legis* (a lack of legislation for the relevant category of persons). This judgment allows the referring judge to refuse the application of the legal provision at hand; in case of a *lacuna legis*, this refusal to apply will probably (if the CC has ruled that the lacuna is "self-repairing", i.e., that no legislative action is required in order to extend the legal right to the category not mentioned in the law) come down to extending the law's scope to illegitimate children.

As to the "justiciability," I should mention that, although the Belgian terminology is different, and although the rules are classified differently, their superficial content appears to be rather similar.

The basic distinction concerns the case's admissibility and the case's merits. The merits are only examined after it is stated that the complaint is admissible (which does not exclude that the admissibility and the merits are examined in one and the same judgment). The likeliness that the case will lack foundation on the merits does not influence the prior examination of the admissibility (see v).

As to the merits, all discriminations between legitimate and illegitimate children are to be seen as clear violations of articles 8 and 14 because of the ECtHR's *Marckx v. Belgium* judgment (1979). Belgian judges refuse to apply legislation violating the rules set out in the *Marckx* judgment. There is no doubt that this part of the mother's action (i.e., the discrimination in the legal provisions at hand) would be well founded.

As to the admissibility, the problem found by the Supreme Court comes closest to the Belgian admissibility criterion of "interest"; however, as far as Belgian law is concerned, this criterion should *in casu* not lead to the case's inadmissibility (see iv): the child's interest (the mother is only the representative) is actual, personal, and legitimate.

(ii) On which provisions and/or case law do you base your answer? If your highest court has addressed this or a similar issue, please describe how the court solved it.

The requirement of interest is laid down in articles 17 and 18 of the Code of Civil Procedure (*Gerechtelijk Wetboek*):

> "Art. 17. De rechtsvordering kan niet worden toegelaten, indien de eiser geen hoedanigheid en geen belang heeft om ze in te dienen.
>
> Art. 18. Het belang moet een reeds verkregen en dadelijk belang zijn.

> De rechtsvordering kan worden toegelaten, indien zij, zelfs tot verkrijging van een verklaring van recht, is ingesteld om schending van een ernstig bedreigd recht te voorkomen."

(Art. 17. The action is inadmissible if the plaintiff does not possess quality and interest to start the action.

Art. 18. The interest must be acquired and immediate.

The action can nevertheless be allowed if – even when initiated to obtain the declaration of a right – it pursues the prevention of the violation of a seriously endangered right.)

Such rules of procedure are interpreted neither restrictively nor extensively. The interpretation is "teleological." The judge must also take into account article 6, §1 ECHR: the Strasbourg Court sanctions judicial interpretations amounting to an "excessive formalism," which hinders the use of the right of access to court.

(iii) If you need additional facts to answer this question, please indicate which type of facts you would need and why.

As far as Belgian law is concerned, the question can be answered with the data provided.

(iv) Does your legal system require the same range of considerations to determine whether a party can bring a claim? Are those considerations statutory or constitutional?

In order to file an admissible complaint, the following general admissibility criteria are essential:

- "Personality" (the plaintiff and the defendant both have to be either natural persons or legal persons);
- "Legal competence" (i.e., mental ability to express a free will);
- "Interest" (the plaintiff must pursue an amelioration of his current legal position);
- "Quality" (only the one entitled to the material right at issue is able to claim it before the Courts; representation is, however, possible).

The criterion that is most linked to the hypothesis described above, is the criterion of "interest". The interest must be:

- "Actual": the interest must already exist, and an *actio ad futurum* is therefore inadmissible.
- "Personal and immediate": the case should concern the plaintiff's material or moral goods; an *actio popularis* is not allowed, except in environmental matters. This does not exclude representation.

- "Legitimate": if the interest goes against the *ordre public*, or public morality, the action is inadmissible.

These criteria are statutory, but need interpretation by the courts. Article 6, §1 ECHR (due process) is, however, always present "at the background", i.e., as a tool for interpretation. The Belgian Constitution, dating back to 1831, is rather silent concerning due process rights, but article 6, §1 ECHR is applied on a daily basis by the Belgian courts.

(v) Additional comments. Express any additional comment you may have on the solutions offered by your system and the U.S. system.

In the hypothesis, the Supreme Court seems to have declared an action inadmissible for reasons that have to do with the merits. This mixing up of admissibility and merits would be really uncommon in Belgium: they are only mixed up if the procedural rule itself is being challenged for being unconstitutional or unconventional.

Another distinction – and this is why I mentioned the jurisdiction issue under (i) – is the distinction between *contentieux objectif* and *contentieux subjectif*. The vast majority of cases concern "subjective rights,", i.e., claims from one person against another person (which might be the government) based on the text of a legal provision granting the plaintiff a right. *Contentieux objectif*, in its turn, does not deal with establishing a "right," but with examining whether a governmental (statutory, reglementory, individual) decision respects higher norms. *Contentieux objectif* leads to the annulment or the disapplication of the lower norm for violation of the higher norm. Actions for *contentieux objectif*, which are always directed against an official body, are admissible if the petitioner shows an "interest" in the annulment or disapplication. This interest might be a procedure concerning a subjective right, e.g., a subsequent action for damages against the government.

Whereas subjective rights must always be examined by an ordinary judge (article 144 Constitution), the *contentieux objectif* may or may not fall under his jurisdiction. Concerning statutory provisions: (1) if the reference norm is a norm of international law, the ordinary judge ruling upon the subjective right, is also competent for examining the legal provision's conventionality; (2) if the reference norm is in the Constitution, only the Constitutional Court has jurisdiction.

I mentioned the jurisdiction issue under (i) because in the case of the mother claiming support for her illegitimate child, the subjective right is examined by the ordinary court, but only after the Constitutional Court, in a judgment of *contentieux objectif*, has removed the hurdle of the discrimination.

In the hypothesis described above, it seems that the Supreme Court has mixed up *contentieux objectif* and *contentieux subjectif*: it declared a case concerning *contentieux objectif* inadmissible because, in the event that the *contentieux objectif* claim (the discriminatory nature of the law) would be founded, it remained uncertain that the subsequent *contentieux subjectif* (the claim for support) would be founded (presumably for reasons laid down in the legislation on support?). It doesn't work like this in Belgium: the Constitutional Court will declare the preliminary reference admissible if there is a chance that the answer will be relevant in the case pending before the referring judge. This judge, who is then to apply child support legislation to the case of the illegitimate child, might of course subsequently find that one of the criteria in that legislation is not met, but this does not influence the *prior* jurisdiction of the Constitutional Court.

BRAZIL

ALEXANDRE FREITAS CÂMARA

Rio de Janeiro Court of Appeals Judge since 2008; Professor Emeritus and Head of the Civil Procedure Department at Rio de Janeiro Judicial School

II. BACKGROUND INFORMATION

a) My name is Alexandre Freitas Câmara. I have been a judge at Rio de Janeiro Court of Appeals since 2008. Before that, I was a private attorney for twenty years. I am also professor emeritus and head of the Civil Procedure Department at Rio de Janeiro Judicial School (a body that belongs to the Judiciary of Rio de Janeiro State and has two main goals: training people who want to become judges (in a three-years course) and providing continuous education for those who are already judges. Besides that, I am a member of the Brazilian Institute of Procedural Law, the Iberian-American Institute of Procedural Law, and the International Association of Procedural Law.

b) Brazilian Supreme Court (*Supremo Tribunal Federal*) is not a Constitutional Court in the European way, but a Court that was inspired by the U.S. Supreme Court. It has a full bench of eleven judges, called *Ministros*. To become a *Ministro* one has to be born in Brazil and be at least 35 years old. At the age of 70 years old, every *Ministro* is forced to retire.

The Supreme Court has three kinds of jurisdiction, including jurisdiction over some cases that are originally filed there and both criminal and civil cases.

Among criminal cases, it is possible to cite those in which the defendant is a member of the National Congress or the president of the Republic. Among civil cases, we can find those where the parties are members of the Brazilian Republic and a foreign state.

The Brazilian Supreme Court also has original jurisdiction over cases about the constitutionality of a bill. In these cases, the Court acts like the European Constitutional Courts, analyzing the constitutionality of a bill in an "objective proceeding" (i.e., in a procedure where no subjective interests are examined). Among these Constitutional proceedings there are two that are most important: the "action for the declaration of unconstitutionality" and the "action for the declaration of constitutionality."

The second kind of jurisdiction of the Brazilian Supreme Court is dedicated to examine and decide *ordinary appeals*. There are some criminal and civil cases in which the ordinary appeal is decided by the Supreme Court. For example, this could be a criminal case if the crime is considered political. It is also what happens when the appeal goes against a decision rendered in *habeas corpus* originally decided by the Superior Court of Justice (which is the second most important Brazilian Court).

Finally, there is a third kind of jurisdiction. The Supreme Court has jurisdiction on *extraordinary appeals*, which can be used against the final decisions of any judge or Court when there is a constitutional issue to be examined.

III. JUDICIAL DECISION MAKING

Brazil operates under civil law. According to the civil law tradition, there are two kinds of issues that a judge (or a court) has to solve: factual issues and legal issues.

Factual issues are solved by an evaluation of the evidence. Judges are free to attribute value to evidence, but their decisions on this matter must be grounded, meaning that the judge must disclose the foundations of his decision, revealing how he evaluated the evidence.

Legal issues are solved by the interpretation of the rules. Everything starts with the Constitution, where the main foundations of the legal system are seen. It is in the Constitution that we can find the due process of law clause (article 5, LV: "no one shall be deprived of liberty or property without due process of law"). Below the Constitution there are many bills and acts (the most important are the Codes – Civil, Criminal, Civil Procedure, Criminal Procedure, Taxes and Consumers – which are the bases for deciding the majority of the cases).

Precedents are also used as a base to shape judicial persuasion. Although few precedents are binding (only some of Supreme Court's decisions are binding precedents), judges usually cite persuasive precedents of the Superior Courts in their sentences.

There are four Superior Courts in Brazil: the Labor Superior Court, the Military Superior Court, the Electoral Superior Court, and the Superior Court of Justice (with a residual jurisdiction, judging cases that are not labor, military, or electoral).

When judging an extraordinary appeal, the Supreme Court does not solve factual issues, but rather only legal issues. The facts are received and accepted by the Supreme Court as the inferior Court has said they happened. The Supreme Court's function is only to examine if the legal solution of the case was correct and, if not, to adjust the sentence.

Courts and judges interpret rules and principles. They often limit the rules or principles that could be considered applicable to the case. It is allowed to be done in some cases, especially when it is necessary to balance principles (Dworkin's influence on Brazilian decisionmaking process is remarkable).

To offer an example: there was a civil case about fatherhood recognition some years ago where an interesting sentence was rendered by the Supreme Court. There had been a first proceeding in which it was decided that the defendant was not the plaintiff's father. This sentence became *res iudicata*. Some years later, it became possible to go on DNA exams. The plaintiff again sued the defendant, pleading for a sentence that would declare the existence of the father–son relationship between the parties. The defendant replied to this civil action with one main argument: there is *res iudicata* and it is not possible to examine this issue again. The Brazilian Supreme Court decided that it was necessary to balance two principles: on one hand there was the "security principle" represented by *res iudicata*. On the other hand, the "principle of human dignity" represented by the right to know, with certainty, who is one's father. In this sentence, the Supreme Court limited the "security principle" and allowed the second proceeding (RE 363889/DF, reported by *Ministro* Dias Toffoli, decided on June 2, 2011, http://redir.stf.jus.br/paginadorpub/paginador.jsp?docTP=TP&docID=1638003).

IV. JURISDICTION

Taking into consideration the hypo described in the questionnaire, it is possible to say that Brazilian Courts would exercise jurisdiction over the foreign manufacturer on a claim suited by the injured party.

Brazilian Civil Procedure Code explicitly establishes that Brazilian Judiciary has jurisdiction on civil cases based on facts that happened in Brazil (art. 88, III, of the Brazilian Civil Procedure Code: the Brazilian judicial authority has jurisdiction whenever the claim is originated from a fact that occurred or from an act that was done in Brazil).

It was not possible to find any decision rendered by the Brazilian Supreme Court or by the Brazilian Superior Court of Justice in an equivalent case. But there are some similar cases that can be brought into consideration.

In a recent decision, the Brazilian Superior Court of Justice examined a claim brought by a Brazilian insurance company against an Argentinean vehicle motors manufacturer. They had executed – in Argentina – an insurance contract to protect a consumer against recalls (and the consumer was an Argentinean trucks manufacturer with an agency in Brazil). After a recall, the insurance company had to pay damages to the consumer and then sued the motors manufacturer to be reimbursed.

The Superior Court of Justice decided that the Brazilian Judiciary had jurisdiction in the case just because the fact (the recall) happened in Brazil (Brazilian Superior Court of Justice, REsp 1308686/SP, reported by *Ministro* Ricardo Villas Bôas Cueva, decided on April 11, 2013, https://ww2.stj.jus.br/revistaeletronica/Abre_Documento.asp?sSeq=1223987&sReg=201101773558&sData=20130417&formato=PDF).

It is important to say that Brazilian jurisdiction in these cases (and including all cases mentioned in article 88 of the Brazilian Civil Procedure Code) is concurrent with other jurisdictions. This was once noted by the Brazilian Supreme Court (CR 4707 AgR/United Kingdom of Great Britain and Northern Ireland, reported by *Ministro* Rafael Mayer, decided on June 23, 1988, http://redir.stf.jus.br/paginadorpub/paginador.jsp?docTP=AC&docID=324369). In a hypo such as the one in the questionnaire it would be possible to bring the claim in Brazil, but our legal system recognizes (and allows the enforcement) of a sentence rendered in another country, such as the country where the manufacturer is domiciled.

V. JUSTICIABILITY

Brazilian Courts would resolve the question of whether the mother should be allowed to proceed with her claim differently. Here it would be possible to proceed.

First of all, it is necessary to make clear that according to Brazilian Law there is no possibility of considering a child either legitimate or illegitimate. Brazilian Constitution says that any kind of discrimination among children is forbidden (article 227, paragraph 6: "Children, had by married couples or not, or adopted, have the same rights and qualifications, and any discriminatory designation related to parenthood is forbidden") and since our Constitution took into effect (October 5, 1988), there is no more difference between children of a married couple and children of an unmarried couple. So, in Brazil there is no adjective that can be connected to the noun "child" when one is speaking about legal status. This is considered an explicit manifestation of equality principle.

According to Brazilian regulations, every parent has the duty to pay alimony for child's support. So, in a case like that of the hypo, the father could be sued and, if there is evidence that he has the means to pay alimony, there would be a judgment against him.

In Brazil, there are also three issues that must be decided in determining whether a party can pursue a claim. And they are very similar to what can be found in the U.S. system.

First of all, it is necessary to be the "real party in interest." In the Brazilian legal system, this is called "legitimacy of the party." A party is considered legitimate if it proves it is the owner of the right sought to be enforced. When this party is a minor, it is represented by one of the parents. It must also identify the defendant as being responsible for the injury that the plaintiff says that has happened or that is about to happen (defendant's legitimacy).

Furthermore, ripeness is necessary (in the Brazilian system, this is called "procedural interest"). There is procedural interest when it is necessary to bring a suit and the party chooses the right procedural track to claim protection of his or her rights. This procedural interest must remain throughout the proceeding (similar to U.S. mootness). So, if the procedural interest disappears during the proceeding (for instance, the plaintiff claims for the possession of a good and during the proceeding this good is destructed by a fire), the proceeding must end.

Finally, there is a need for what we call in Brazil "legal possibility of the claim." In other words, the judge or the Court must verify if the plaintiff does not claim something forbidden by Brazilian Law.

Just to show an example, there is a prohibition, predicated on Brazilian Civil Code, to sue a defendant because he did not pay a gambling debt (Civil Code, article 814). If a plaintiff seeks a judgment condemning the defendant to pay this sort of debt, the ongoing of the proceeding is not allowed.

All these questions are statutory, and they can be found in Brazilian Civil Procedure Code (art. 267, VI: "proceeding must not go on if there is a lack of one of the following requisites: legal possibility, legitimacy of the parties and procedural interest").

BRAZIL

DANIEL MITIDIERO

Professor of Law, Federal University of Rio Grande do Sul (UFRGS), Brazil; JSD, Universidade Federal do Rio Grande do Sul; Visiting Scholar, Università degli Studi di Pavia, Italy

with the collaboration of

GUILHERME RECENA COSTA

JD, cum laude, Federal University of Rio Grande do Sul (UFRGS); LLM, University of Sao Paulo (USP); JSD Candidate (2015), University of Sao Paulo (USP); LLM Candidate (2013–2014), Yale Law School (YLS)

II.b Briefly describe the highest court (or courts) of your country and indicate its (or their) function within your legal system.

Brazil's judicial organization encompasses three autonomous *specialized* federal court hierarchies (according to subject-matter: electoral, military, and labor courts) and an *ordinary* court system (encompassing both state and federal courts) – *see* Art. 92, Federal Constitution ("FC").

Each specialized court system has its own Superior Court (namely, Superior Labor Court; Superior Electoral Court; Superior Military Court).

Courts of ordinary nature (state and federal) – i.e., not integrated into any of the specialized court systems – are subject to the appellate jurisdiction of both the Superior Court of Justice [Superior Tribunal de Justiça – STJ] (Art. 105, FC) and the Supreme Federal Court [Supremo Tribunal Federal – STF] (Art. 103, FC).

Both the STJ and the STF may be viewed as Supreme Courts – i.e., Courts sitting at the top of judicial hierarchy, having the last word on questions of law. Apart from their original jurisdiction on special types of claims (as opposed to appellate jurisdiction), the STJ hears appeals on questions of law relating to federal statutory provisions; the STF hears appeals on questions of law of constitutional nature. (This distinction is somewhat artificial and is not without practical problems in distinguishing statutory and constitutional claims. The STF usually requires that a lower decision represent a *direct violation* to the Constitution to hear a case; an *indirect violation*, i.e., a violation to a provision that, on statutory level, materializes or furthers constitutional provisions would not satisfy. The latter would be under the STJ's appellate jurisdiction.)

Together, the STJ and the STF, as Supreme Appellate Courts (the former, for statutory matters; the latter, for constitutional matters), exercise functions similar to the French *Cour de Cassation* or the German *Bundesgerichtof* – i.e., to settle case law on specific questions of law. Although Brazil, as a civil law jurisdiction, does not traditionally adopt a *stare decisis* system, growing importance has been given to court precedents as a source of law and, in recent reforms, certain rulings and maxims have been given binding effect on lower courts.

Lastly, the STF also serves as a Constitutional Court by ruling on claims relating to the abstract validity of statutes vis-à-vis the Constitution (European model of Constitutional Courts – e.g., German *Bundesverfassungsgericht*). As such, Brazil has incorporated both the American model (via appeals in concrete cases) and the European model (via a direct and abstract claim to strike down unconstitutional statutory provisions) of judicial review of legislative statutes.

III. JUDICIAL DECISION MAKING

(a) Have you observed a similar phenomenon in your judicial system? If so, please identify the area(s) of law in which this has occurred. (Please do not limit yourself to questions involving jurisdiction.)

As a civil law system, Brazilian Courts (including its Supreme Courts) begin with the legislative text. It is interpreted so as to "extract" a general norm or maxim, which is then applied to the case at hand.

Due to the codification of legal rules, reasoning is more deductive and abstract in nature when compared to common law jurisdictions. As a result, increasingly specialized tests to control and sometimes limit the scope of the underlying principle are not common – courts tend rather to rely on the statutory provisions themselves or broad reformulations found in previous case law.

However, jurisdictional issues (on an international level) tend to be an exception. Although no *forum non conveniens* doctrine is known, as such, under Brazilian law, some discretion is left to courts on the matter. In this case, courts do apply a "test" through which they may take into account, according to the principles of *interest* and *effectiveness*, the importance of the claim to the Brazilian Judiciary and the possibility of its effective enforcement in order to establish their own jurisdiction. (As a leading case showing this discretion and application of the "test," the STJ held that Brazilian courts had interest in hearing a claim for damages filed by a French national with

Brazilian citizenship against the Federal Republic of Germany based on World War II crimes (based on the country's strict stance on human rights protection), ordering the claim to be served, although anticipating Germany could present a defense based on its sovereign immunity – (RO. 64/SP, Rel. Ministra Nancy Andrighi, Terceira Turma, *julgado em* 13/05/2008, DJe 23/06/2008)).

IV. JURISDICTION

(d)(i) Would your country exercise jurisdiction over the foreign manufacturer on a claim against it by the injured party?

Yes. Under article 88, III, of the Brazilian Civil Procedure Code, national courts have *concurrent* jurisdiction (i.e., not exclusive, meaning that also foreign courts may rule on the issue and the award may be recognized and enforced in Brazil) over claims that originate from "facts occurred or acts practiced in Brazil." This provision, combined with broad consumer legislation (Art. 12, Consumer Protection Code) holding manufacturers (national or foreign) liable for their products, even if they are not in privity with the victim, would allow for the claim to be brought against the manufacturer in Brazil.

(II) On which provisions and/or case law do you base your answer? If your highest court has addressed this or a similar issue, please describe how the court solved it.

Article 12, Consumer Protection Code; Article 88, III, Civil Procedure Code.

V. JUSTICIABILITY

(d)(i) How would the courts of your country resolve the question of whether the mother should be allowed to proceed with her claim?

In principle, Brazilian courts would allow the mother to proceed with the claim.

(ii) On which provisions and/or case law do you base your answer? If your highest court has addressed this or a similar issue, please describe how the court solved it.

Article 733, §1º, Civil Procedure Code; Article 19, Statute nº. 5.478/1968. The STJ has consolidated, in its case law, that imprisonment of debtors who do not provide child support or alimony is enforceable (maxim n. 309).

. . .

(iv) Does your legal system require the same range of considerations to determine whether a party can bring a claim? Are those considerations statutory or constitutional?

The Brazilian legal system requires that the claimant show standing and interest. However, the concept of standing does not encompass the discretionary notion that the claimant's injury must be "properly redressed"; if a legal remedy is available to the parties – e.g., imprisonment of those who do not provided child support – judges will apply the codified law and not question how effective the measure will be. (However, to enforce certain types of judgments – e.g. *faciendi* obligations – judges enjoy some discretion to determine alternative measures in order to achieve the sought result: imposing fines on the debtor, determining execution via third parties, etc. – articles 461 and 461A, Civil Procedure Code.)

BRAZIL

PROF. DR. SIDNEI BENETI

Justice of the High Court of Justice of Brazil (Tribunal Superior de Justiça) – SAFS, Q 6, L. 1, T. III – Ed. Min. II, 8th Floor – 70095-900 – Brasilia – Brazil – E-Mail: sidneibeneti@stj.jus.br; benetigm@gmail.com – Phone: ±55-61-33197004; Cel: ±55-11-996591791

II(b). II.b Briefly describe the highest court (or courts) of your country and indicate its (or their) function within your legal system.

Brazil, like some continental system countries (Italy, Spain, Portugal, Germany, Austria), follows the model of having a Constitutional Court (Supremo Tribunal Federal) for constitutional claims (and also some special cases, e.g., penal issues against the president of the Republic, ministers, senators and representatives); four High Courts of Justice (Superior Tribunal de Justiça, for civil and criminal cases; a Tribunal Superior do Trabalho, for labor cases, Tribunal Superior Eleitoral, for electoral matters, and a Superior Tribunal Militar, for military cases. The cases come to the high courts (Superior Tribunal de Justiça, Tribunal Superior do Trabalho, Tribunal Superior Eleitoral, or Superior Tribunal Militar). As a federation, Brazil observes two branches of jurisdiction, like the United States, a state branch (trial judges and state supreme courts: Tribunais de Justiça Estaduais) and a federal branch (federal trial judges and federal regional courts: Tribunais Regionais Federais). Constitutional cases from both state and federal branches can apply to the Constitutional Court (Supremo Tribunal Federal).

III. JUDICIAL DECISION MAKING

a. Have you observed a similar phenomenon in your judicial system? If so, please identify the area(s) of law in which this has occurred. (Please do not limit yourself to questions involving jurisdiction.)

As a civil law country, Brazil follows the system of interpretation of law similar to other countries of the same family (e.g., Italy, Portugal, Spain, Germany). A Brazilian judge considers a case and will try to insert it in a considered rule of law stablished by one of the Brazilian Codes (e.g., Código Civil, Código Penal, Código de Processo Civil, Código de Processo Penal), getting some help from the precedents of the Courts.

It is mandatory for Brazilian courts to decide each case openly and in writing the reasons for the opinions. The discretionary power of a Brazilian judge to refuse to decide a case is not permitted (even in the high courts and the Supreme Constitutional Court).

Recently, however, the procedural system has permitted a few special kinds of appeals that provide increasing powers to some highly qualified strong precedents of the high courts. This change was designed in order to deal with the huge problem of mass litigation in the country (e.g., consumer law, tax claims, public officers rights, pensions, etc.) and it has been passed by special legislation that allows justices of the high courts, when cases of "mass litigation"are detected, to choose a "pilot" case to be decided and to stay proceedings of similar cases at the trial and intermediate (federal and state) courts. The Supremo Tribunal Federal (Constitutional Court) has recently been allowed to render binding final decisions that are considered leading cases and that must be observed by all the judges in the country.

In such a context, we can consider that, in certain circumstances, the Brazilian system is leaning toward a precedent system, in spite of its being part of the continental system (code system).

b. If you have observed this phenomenon, does it sometimes occur that the judicially developed tests limit the principles that the tests purport to articulate?

As explained above, the Brazilian system in general does not follow a "tests" system in order to allow precedents. But, as also explained above, there has been a slow movement toward the importance of precedents in the construction of a strong jurisprudence, and thus some "tests" have been observed in the qualification of the cases, particularly by the high courts.

Some of the criteria in the case selection by the high courts at present times can be similar to "tests" (e.g., qualification of questions as "fact" or "contract interpretation" are similar to a "test" typical of the common law model).

IV. JURISDICTION

d. (i) Would your country exercise jurisdiction over the foreign manufacturer on a claim against it by the injured party?

There are two possibilities for this, both under federal law (and excluding state legislation), as follows: a) if the case deals with general rules for compensation or b) if the case is placed under the consumer protection law.

(a) In the first case (general compensation rules, e.g., the plaintiff is not characterized as a consumer), according to federal procedural law, the claim against the agent domiciled in Brazil has to be filed at the state court (excluding federal jurisdiction) of its domicile in Brazil (Civil Procedural Code, arts. 88 and 94), and the claim against the foreign defendant should be filed at the foreign jurisdiction. If both are filed, a cause to stop the Brazilian procedure is not recognized (no *lis pendens* – Código de Proc. Civil, art. 90).
(b) In the second case, when dealing with consumer law, Brazilian procedural law provides for the claim to be filed at the state court of the domicile of the consumer (plaintiff).

Legislation does not differentiate between national and foreign defendants. In the case of a Brazilian consumer injured by a product, the consumer can opt for the court of his own domicile, even if the seller or the producer is domiciled abroad. Depending on the individual charge of liability of the seller or the producer, the consumer will opt to file the claim against one or both of them. Brazilian federal consumer law is very protective toward the consumer, even in some cases where a product has been sold by a seller that is in fact responsible by the damage to the product (because Brazilian legislation recognizes the responsibility of the producer, including in the case of the responsibility of the seller of his product, remaining to the producer the possibility to claim against the seller). We can conclude that in such a case, the claim could be filed in Brazil against both the agent and the manufacturer.

However, in spite of the possibility, injured consumers do not typically make a claim against a foreign manufacturer in Brazil: it can be very expensive to call in the foreign party, the foreign party most likely also has a branch in the Country; or the consumer finds it sufficient to bring suit against the seller in Brazil alone.

(ii) On which provisions and/or case law do you base your answer? If your highest court has addressed this or a similar issue, please describe how the court solved it.

The solution above is a result of the Brazilian Consumer Code (Law 8070, September 1990, arts. 3, 6, VIII, 12, 13, 18, and 101, I). The Brazilian Consumer Code is a federal law, valid for all Brazilian states. The Brazilian Constitution also provides nationwide protection of consumers (Federal Constitution, arts. 5, XXXII and 170, V).

(iii) If you need additional facts to answer this question, please indicate which type of facts you would need and why.

No other additional facts are required.

(iv) Additional comments. Express any additional comment you may have on the solutions offered by your system and the U.S. system.

There are two remarks: a) There is no possible conflict between state law and federal law in such a case. There is no kind of "state sovereignty" concerning tort law, consumer law, and procedural law in Brazil. b) Another important difference between the systems of the United States and Brazil results from the strong rule of consumer protection in Brazil regarding the determination of competent jurisdiction for a consumer law case.

V. JUSTICIABILITY

d. (i) How would the courts of your country resolve the question of whether the mother should be allowed to proceed with her claim?

The first point consists in the right of the mother to proceed with the claim. At this point the answer is positive, because the mother represents her child, no matter if the child is illegitimate or legitimate.

However, the mother will not succeed in her penal claim because of the lack of an essential requirement of the Brazilian Penal Code (art. 244), which consists in the voluntary, formal recognition of the child by his father or by judicial decision brought about through a claim for recognition or paternity.

The absence of that requirement (previous recognition of the paternity of the child) makes it impossible to subsume the case into the crime of material abandon of the child (CP, art. 244); thus, the penal claim would be rejected because of the impossibility of characterization of the legal description of the crime established by the penal law.

Brazilian system ignores the concept of "justiciability," taken into consideration by the U.S. Supreme Court doctrine, that has oriented the decision of the criminal case; however, in a certain way, the lack of characterization of the crime of material abandon of child (CP, art. 244) leads to the same solution given by the U.S. Supreme Court.

(ii) On which provisions and/or case law do you base your answer? If your highest court has addressed this or a similar issue, please describe how the court solved it.

Penal Code, art. 244. There is no precedent decided by the Brazilian Superior Court, but it is sure that such a penal claim would be unacceptable.

(iii) If you need additional facts to answer this question, please indicate which type of facts would you need and why.

No additional facts are necessary.

(iv) Does your legal system require the same range of considerations to determine whether a party can bring a claim? Are those considerations statutory or constitutional?

A claim could be brought by the mother through the public prosecutor's office if she had previously obtained from a family court the recognition of the paternity of her child.

(v) Additional comments. Express any additional comment you may have on the solutions offered by your system and the U.S. system.

There are no additional comments.

GERMANY

CLAUDIA MAYER

Assistant Professor at the Chair for Private Law, Civil Procedure, and Private International Law of Professor Dr. Wolfgang Hau, University of Passau

II.b Briefly describe the highest court (or courts) of your country and indicate its (or their) function within your legal system.

In the German Federal Court system there are five Supreme Federal Courts (courts of final appeal/courts of last instance): Our highest court in civil matters or rather matters of ordinary jurisdiction is the Federal Court of Justice (*Bundesgerichtshof*) located in Karlsruhe. Besides there is the Federal Administrative Court (*Bundesverwaltungsgericht*) located in Leipzip, the Federal Finance Court (*Bundesfinanzhof*) located in Munich, the Federal Labour Court (*Bundesarbeitsgericht*) located in Erfurt and the Federal Social Court (*Bundessozialgericht*) located in Kassel.

1. TASK OF THE SUPREME FEDERAL COURTS

The task of these Supreme Federal Courts is best described by drawing on the official information of the Federal Court of Justice:[1]

With a few exceptions, the Federal Court of Justice acts as a court of appeal. Its principal task is to ensure uniformity of the law through clarification of fundamental questions of law and development of the law. It will not undertake fact finding of its own but will confine itself to reviewing the legal assessment of a case by the lower courts. The facts established by these courts are binding on the Federal Court of Justice, unless such findings are affected by a procedural error at the lower court pointed out in the statement of grounds for appeal. Evidence will therefore not normally be heard by the Federal Court of Justice.

[1] The following citations refer to the website of the Federal Court of Justice http://www.bundesgerichtshof.de/EN/FCoJ/TaskOrganisation/taskOrganisation_node.html.

2. THE FEDERAL CONSTITUTIONAL COURT AND THE EUROPEAN COURTS

Apart from the Federal Court of Justice, there are four other supreme federal courts (courts of final appeal/courts of last instance): the Federal Administrative Court (*Bundesverwaltungsgericht*), the Federal Finance Court (*Bundesfinanzhof*), the Federal Labour Court (*Bundesarbeitsgericht*), and the Federal Social Court (*Bundessozialgericht*).

Above these Supreme Federal Courts stands the Federal Constitutional Court (*Bundesverfassungsgericht*), also located in Karlsruhe, which plays a special role within the German court system. Its task is to monitor compliance of all state actions, including judgments of the courts of final appeal over the constitution. "In what is known as judicial review proceedings, it examines laws and, in case of complaints of unconstitutionality, other acts of state such as court rulings for their constitutionality. In that case, however, appellants must assert that a violation of their constitutionally guaranteed rights has occurred. The interpretation and application of so-called ordinary law – i.e., rules and regulations of a nonconstitutional nature – lie outside the purview of constitutional jurisdiction. Individuals can only lodge a constitutional complaint if they have exhausted all remedies before the lower courts up to the courts of final appeal.

As European unification proceeds, the Luxembourg-based European Court of Justice (ECJ) is gaining increasing importance. In accordance with Article 234, 3rd paragraph of the EC Treaty, the Federal Court of Justice, as the court of last instance in matters of ordinary jurisdiction, will refer questions concerning the interpretation of Community Law to the ECJ for decision.

Finally, in order to enforce the rights laid down in the Convention for the Protection of Human Rights and Fundamental Freedoms of 4 November 1950, cases can be taken to the European Court of Human Rights (ECHR) in Strasbourg."

III. JUDICIAL DECISION MAKING

a. *Have you observed a similar phenomenon in your judicial system? If so, please identify the area(s) of law in which this has occurred. (Please do not limit yourself to questions involving jurisdiction.)*
b. *If you have observed this phenomenon, does it sometimes occur that the judicially developed tests limit the principles that the tests purport to articulate?*

Generally, the approach of German courts in the judicial decision-making process is similar. According to Article 20 (3), Basic Law for the Federal Republic of Germany (*Grundgesetz*), "the judiciary [is bound] by law and justice." Therefore, courts must base their decisions on (written) statutory law. It is their task to interpret the law and – where the legal terms are vague and open to interpretation – also to develop the law. Vague legal concepts are not uncommon in German legislation (e.g., §138 German Civil Code: Legal transaction contrary to public policy/usury; or §242 German Civil Code: Performance in good faith); when the exact meaning is not obvious, it is the courts that give guidance as to its meaning. The Courts of last instance in particular serve this function. In consequence, within the scope of vague legal concepts, the judiciary has developed categories and case groups in order to make the relevant statutory provision manageable in each single case.

Now, if a new case does not fall within one of the established categories, the judiciary may develop new categories; it can also conclude that the new case can be distinguished from other cases falling within one category and thus can be excluded from the established categories. That way, developed categories can also be limited to certain aspects.

Although the German courts of last instance have the power to interpret vague legal concepts and thus ensure uniformity of the law or rather its uniform application, no lower court is – by law – bound by this interpretation in a different/new case.[2] Every lower court can deviate from the decisions of the highest courts (except the Federal Constitutional Court) and give its own interpretation of vague statutory provisions. In practice, however, the parties are able to challenge such a decision on appeal and will likely be successful unless the highest court changes its opinion (e.g., with regard to a more convincing interpretation by the lower court)

IV. JURISDICTION

I. *Manufacturer domiciled in other EU Member State*

1. Individual buyer is a trader

If the manufacturer is domiciled in another EU Member State and the product is sold to another trader in Germany, the jurisdiction is determined by Regulation (EC) No 44/2001 (OJ 2001 L 12/1) (Brussels I Regulation).

[2] Only the lower court to which a case is remitted on appeal is bound by the higher court's decision.

I presume that the sales contract is made between the manufacturer, represented by the agent, and the individual. If the individual is a trader (not a consumer), jurisdiction for a claim based on the contract is governed by Article 5 No 1 (b) Regulation No 44/2001, which states:

> "A person domiciled in a Member State may, in another Member State, be sued:
>
> 1.(a) in matters relating to a contract, in the courts for the place of performance of the obligation in question;
>
> (b) for the purpose of this provision and unless otherwise agreed, the place of performance of the obligation in question shall be: in the case of the sale of goods, the place in a Member State where, under the contract, the goods were delivered or should have been delivered …"

Therefore, the German courts would exercise their jurisdiction for contractual claims.

If the individual bases its claims on a tortious act Article 5(3) provides jurisdiction for the courts in the jurisdiction of which the tortious act was committed or the result/injury occurred.

> "Article 5:
>
> A person domiciled in a Member State may, in another Member State, be sued:
>
> 3. in matters relating to tort, delict or quasi-delict, in the courts for the place where the harmful event occurred or may occur."

2. *Individual buyer is a consumer*

If the German buyer is a consumer, Article 15 ff. Regulation No 44/2001 contain *lex specialis* provisions for jurisdiction in matters relating to a contract. Article 16 allows a consumer to sue the manufacturer at his home courts if one of the matters listed exhaustively in Article 15 is concerned.

> Article 15 reads:
>
> "1. In matters relating to a contract concluded by a person, the consumer, for a purpose which can be regarded as being outside his trade or profession, jurisdiction shall be determined by this Section, without prejudice to Article 4 and point 5 of Article 5, if:

> (a) it is a contract for the sale of goods on instalment credit terms; or
> (b) it is a contract for a loan repayable by instalments, or for any other form of credit, made to finance the sale of goods; or
> (c) in all other cases, the contract has been concluded with a person who pursues commercial or professional activities in the Member State of the consumer's domicile or, by any means, directs such activities to that Member State or to several States including that Member State, and the contract falls within the scope of such activities. (emphasis added)
>
> (...)"
>
> Article 16 reads:
>
> "1. A consumer may bring proceedings against the other party to a contract either in the courts of the Member State in which that party is domiciled or in the courts for the place where the consumer is domiciled. (...)"

Article 15 (1) (c) contains a contested provision similar to the U.S. Supreme Court's solution. The meaning of the term "a person who ... directs such activities to that Member State" was determined by the ECJ in joint cases decided on 7 December 2010. The essence of this holding was that it is necessary that one can determine the trader's intention to win consumers of that Member State as customers; he must be willing to contract with consumers of that State.

In Joined Cases C-585/08 (Pammer/Reederei Karl Schlüter) and C-144/09 (Hotel Alpenhof/Heller), the ECJ held:

> In order to determine whether a trader whose activity is presented on its website or on that of an intermediary can be considered to be "directing" its activity to the Member State of the consumer's domicile, within the meaning of Article 15(1)(c) of Regulation No 44/2001, it should be ascertained whether, before the conclusion of any contract with the consumer, it is apparent from those websites and the trader's overall activity that the trader was envisaging doing business with consumers domiciled in one or more Member States, including the Member State of that consumer's domicile, in the sense that it was minded to conclude a contract with them.
>
> The following matters, the list of which is not exhaustive, are capable of constituting evidence from which it may be concluded that the trader's activity is directed to the Member State of the consumer's domicile, namely the international nature of the activity, mention of itineraries from other Member States for going to the place where the trader is established, use of a language or a currency other than the language or currency generally used in the Member State in which the trader is established with the possibility of making and confirming the reservation in that other language, mention of

telephone numbers with an international code, outlay of expenditure on an Internet referencing service in order to facilitate access to the trader's site or that of its intermediary by consumers domiciled in other Member States, use of a top-level domain name other than that of the Member State in which the trader is established, and mention of an international clientele composed of customers domiciled in various Member States. It is for the national courts to ascertain whether such evidence exists.

Therefore, in the hypothetical case of the survey, in my opinion, Article 15(1)(c) would be applied in the affirmative by German courts according to the interpretation by the ECJ. Thus, the individual buyer (consumer) is able to sue before his home courts.

A similar result would be obtain in a B2C contract, if the manufacturer is domiciled outside the EU, but has a branch, agency or other establishment in one of the Member States. In disputes arising out of the operations of the branch, agency or establishment, the manufacturer is deemed to be domiciled in that State, if the other party to the contract is a consumer (Article 15(2) Regulation No 44/2001).

Article 15(2):

2. Where a consumer enters into a contract with a party who is not domiciled in the Member State but has a branch, agency or other establishment in one of the Member States, that party shall, in disputes arising out of the operations of the branch, agency or establishment, be deemed to be domiciled in that State.

Where a consumer brings a tort action, jurisdiction is determined by Article 5(3) Regulation No 44/2001. In this respect there is no difference with regard to whether the plaintiff is a consumer or a trader.

II. MANUFACTURER DOMICILED IN A NON-EU MEMBER STATE

If the manufacturer is domiciled outside the EU, Regulation No 44/2001 is not applicable. In this case, the German rules on venue are also applied with regard to the international jurisdiction of German courts (dual functionality of the rules on venue). Jurisdiction would thus be established either by §29 or §32 of the German Code of Civil Procedure (*Zivilprozessordnung*):

§29: Specific jurisdiction of the place of performance:

(1) For any disputes arising from a contractual relationship and disputes regarding its existence, the court of that location shall have jurisdiction at which the obligation is to be performed that is at issue.

(...)

§32: Specific jurisdiction for tort:

For complaints arising from tort, the court in the jurisdiction of which the tortious act was committed shall have jurisdiction.

III. ADDITIONAL COMMENTS

With the entry into force of the new Brussels Ia Regulation (EU) No 1215/2012 (OJ 2012 L 351/1) in 2015 the scope of the regulation will partly be extended to third country defendants. According to Article 18(1) Regulation No 1215/2012 "a consumer may bring proceedings against the other party to a contract either in the courts of the Member State in which that party is domiciled or, regardless of the domicile of the other party, in the courts for the place where the consumer is domiciled." This applies, however, only for contractual claims. The jurisdictional provisions for claims based on tortious acts remain unchanged (Article 7(2) equals Article 5(3) Regulation No 44/2001). In matters relating to tort, delict or quasi-delict a manufacturer, thus, can only be sued in the courts for the place where the harmful event occurred, when he or she is domiciled in a EU Member State.

V. JUSTICIABILITY

d. Your System's Solution.

I. *Criminal Law*

In German Criminal Law, the Public Prosecution Office is obligated to start criminal proceedings against a suspect as soon as there are factual indications that a criminal offence has occurred. §152 German Code of Criminal Procedure (*Strafprozessordnung*) reads:

§152: Indicting Authority; Principle of Mandatory Prosecution

(1) The public prosecution office shall have the authority to prefer public charges.
(2) Except as otherwise provided by law, the public prosecution office shall be obliged to take action in relation to all prosecutable criminal offences, provided there are sufficient factual indications.

§158 German Code of Criminal Procedure provides that information of a criminal offence or an application for criminal prosecution (where necessary according to a criminal provision) may be filed orally or in writing with the public prosecution office, with authorities and officials in the police force, and with the Local Courts.

The mother of the illegitimate child would thus be able to provide the Public Prosecution Office with the information concerning the father's offense [nonpayment of child support, see §170 German Criminal Code (*Strafgesetzbuch*); according to German civil law, the father of an illegitimate child is obligated to pay maintenance, see §1615l German Civil Code] and the Public Prosecution Office would be obligated to take actions.

Section 170 German Criminal Code: Nonpayment of child support, etc.

(1) Whosoever evades a statutory maintenance obligation so that the necessities of the person entitled to maintenance are endangered or would be endangered without the assistance of others, shall be liable to imprisonment not exceeding three years or a fine.
(2) Whosoever is obliged to provide maintenance to a pregnant woman and withholds this maintenance in an inappropriate manner and thereby causes a termination of the pregnancy, shall be liable to imprisonment not exceeding five years or a fine.

II. CONSTITUTIONAL LAW

If the Public Prosecution Office terminates the proceedings or even refuses to start proceedings, the person affected can, under certain circumstances, compel proceedings:

§171 German Criminal Code: Notification of the Applicant

If the public prosecution office does not grant an application for preferring public charges, or after conclusion of the investigation it orders the proceedings to be terminated, it shall notify the applicant, indicating the reasons. The decision shall inform the applicant, if he is at the same time the aggrieved person, of the possibility of contesting the decision and of the time limit provided therefor (§172 subsection (1)).

§172 German Criminal Code: Proceedings to Compel Public Charges

(1) Where the applicant is also the aggrieved person, he shall be entitled to lodge a complaint against the notification made pursuant to Section 171 to the official superior of the public prosecution office within two weeks after

receipt of such notification. On the filing of the complaint with the public prosecution office the time limit shall be deemed to have been observed. Time shall not start to run if no instruction was given pursuant to Section 171, second sentence.

(2) The applicant may, within one month of receipt of notification, apply for a court decision in respect of the dismissal of the complaint by the official superior of the public prosecution office. He shall be instructed as to this right and as to the form such application shall take; the time limit shall not run if no instruction has been given. The application shall be inadmissible where the sole subject of the proceedings is a criminal offence which may be prosecuted by the aggrieved person by way of a private prosecution, or where the public prosecution office has dispensed with preferring public charges in accordance with Section 153 subsection (1), Section 153a subsection (1), first and seventh sentences, or Section 153b subsection (1); the same shall apply in the cases referred to in Sections 153c to 154 subsection (1), as well as in Sections 154b and 154c.

(3) The application for a court decision must indicate the facts that are intended to substantiate preferment of public charges as well as the evidence. The application must be signed by an attorney; legal aid shall be governed by the same provisions as in civil litigation. The application shall be submitted to the court competent to decide.

(4) The Higher Regional Court shall be competent to decide on the application. . . .

However, in cases – comparably to the hypothetical case – where the law does not criminalize a certain behavior the Public Prosecution Office may not start criminal proceedings. A complaint according to § 172 German Criminal Code would not be successful.

In such a situation, a person affected by the termination of proceedings can only – under even stricter conditions – lodge a constitutional complaint with the Federal Constitutional Court. Such a complaint is only admissible if the complainant is (1) herself, (2) directly, and (3) currently affected by a state action. If the state action is a law that is allegedly too lenient according to the complainant, these conditions are very difficult to establish. Moreover, the complainant must prove that one of her constitutionally guaranteed fundamental rights (Article 1-20 Basic Law for the Federal Republic of Germany (*Grundgesetz*)) – in the hypothetical case, probably Article 3: Equality before the law – is violated by the law.

It must be established that due to the violation of the Equal Protection Clause of Article 3 Basic Law the legislator is obliged to change the existing law or enact a new law that satisfies the constitutional guarantee.

GERMANY

DR. CLEMENS A. FEINÄUGLE

Coordinator of Scientific Research and Senior Research Fellow, Max Planck Institute, Luxembourg, for International, European, and Regulatory Procedural Law (reporting on Germany)

In collaboration with

ADRIANI DORI

LL.M., Research Fellow, Max Planck Institute, Luxembourg, for International, European and Regulatory Procedural Law (contributed to Section IV of the questionnaire)

II.b Briefly describe the highest court (or courts) of your country and indicate its (or their) function within your legal system.

Germany has a centralized system of constitutional review: the Federal Constitutional Court reviews court decisions but also acts for the legislature in light of the German constitution. It is separate and without, e.g., a link of appeal, from the so-called specialized jurisdiction, made up of five Federal Supreme Courts that deal with cases coming from the fields of criminal/civil law, administrative law, social security law, tax law, and labor law.

III. JUDICIAL DECISION MAKING

(d)(1) Have you observed a similar phenomenon in your judicial system? If so, please identify the area(s) of law in which this has occurred. (Please do not limit yourself to questions involving jurisdiction.)

The German legal order is a civil law system. Courts interpret and apply written statutory laws. More general clauses can lead to an interpretation that creates more precise rules for specific groups of cases to make the general clause applicable in a specific case.

One example would be Section 138 (1) of the German Civil Code, which says that "a legal transaction which is contrary to public policy is void." The underlying idea of this section is to protect the weaker party of a contract.

To make the section effective in that sense, the Federal Supreme Court has developed specific constellations in which a transaction would be contrary to public policy, such as an abuse of a monopoly, over-indebtedness of family members as a consequence of incurring guarantees, or a strong imbalance between performance and consideration.

More frequently, however, such a technique is used by the Federal Constitutional Court. The different human rights in a constitution are traditionally phrased in a short manner without much text. A constitution has to be open to a dynamic interpretation necessary to give due regard to new developments and changes in state and society.

One case before the German Federal Constitutional Court concerned Article 12(1) of the German Constitution, which says that "all Germans shall have the right to freely choose their occupation or profession, their place of work and their place of training." The Court interpreted this language and developed a so-called three-level theory that differentiates between three kinds of restrictions of the freedom and that prescribes differing requirements of justification for the restrictions: On the first level, there are rules regulating the *exercise* of a profession, i.e., those that concern an employee in his/her job – for such rules limiting the freedom of occupation, it suffices to be justified in light of this constitutional freedom if there are reasonable considerations of the public interest for the limitation. On the second level, there are the so-called *subjective* rules regulating the *access* to a profession, making such access dependent on the presence of specific qualifications and skills in the person of the applicant.

Since this is a severe limitation, as it can block access to a profession altogether for the applicant, the justification in light of this constitutional freedom is more demanding and means that the required qualifications have to be necessary in the interest of an important public good (e.g., the requirement of a specific certificate in order to guarantee the quality of the work in the craft sector). On the third level, there are *objective* rules regulating the *access* to a profession, making such access dependent on requirements that are independent of the person of the applicant. Since this is the strongest limitation, as the applicant has no influence on the requirements, the establishment of such requirements is only justified in light of this constitutional freedom if they are necessary to prevent a severe and proven danger for an eminently important public good (e.g., public health).

(ii) If you have observed this phenomenon, does it sometimes occur that the judicially developed tests limit the principles that the tests purport to articulate?

I cannot see that this has happened.

IV. JURISDICTION

(d)(i) Would your country exercise jurisdiction over the foreign manufacturer on a claim against it by the injured party?

German courts could in general exercise jurisdiction over the non-EU manufacturer for contractual or noncontractual claims brought by the injured consumer (for details, please see the answer to question (ii)).

(ii) On which provisions and/or case law do you base your answer? If your highest court has addressed this or a similar issue, please describe how the court solved it.

The rules of international jurisdiction of German courts over consumer contracts are provided for in Arts. 15–17 of Council Regulation (EC) No 44/2001 of 22 December 2000 on jurisdiction and the recognition and enforcement of judgments in civil and commercial matters (Brussels I Regulation).

In order to answer the question on the international jurisdiction over manufacturers not domiciled in the EU, we must distinguish depending on the contracting party of the German consumer:

Assuming that the contracting party was a manufacturer not domiciled in the EU, contractual claims against the latter can be brought in Germany under Article 15 (2) Brussels I Regulation, which holds that a party who is not domiciled in a Member State but has a branch, agency, or other establishment in one of the Member States shall, in disputes arising out of the operations of the branch, agency, or establishment, be deemed to be domiciled in that State.

Assuming that the contract has been executed between the German consumer and the agent, German courts could exercise jurisdiction over the foreign manufacturer for product liability or noncontractual liability for defective goods or claims arising from a tort according to Art 5 (3) of the Brussels I Regulation. Due to the personal scope of the Brussels I Regulation, however, the manufacturer must be domiciled in an EU Member State (Art. 4). According to Article 4 (1) and Recital 9 of the Regulation, a defendant not domiciled in a EU Member State is in general subject to national rules of jurisdiction applicable in the territory of the Member State of the court seized. By applying German procedural law, German courts could only exercise jurisdiction over a non-EU manufacturer under Section 32 of the German code of civil procedure.

(iii) If you need additional facts to answer this question, please indicate which type of facts you would need and why.

In order to be able to address the questions, we would need to know whether the manufacturer and the agent are domiciled in a EU Member State. We would also need to know who the contracting party of the German consumer is.

(vi) Additional comments. Express any additional comment you may have on the solutions offered by your system and the U.S. system.

The recent recast of the Brussels I Regulation (Art. 18 (1) of the Regulation No 1215/2012 of the European Parliament and of the Council of 12 December 2012 on jurisdiction and the recognition and enforcement of judgments in civil and commercial matters) extended the scope of the Brussels I Regulation to cases involving third-country defendants. After the new Regulation enforced in 2015, consumers will be able to sue their contracting party regardless of the latter's domicile in the courts of the Member State in which the consumer is domiciled (new Article 18). However, the jurisdictional grounds of Article 5 (3) (new Article 7(2)), which foresees that claims in respect of torts (and thus also in respect of product liability) may be brought in the courts of the place where the harmful event occurred or may occur, have not been extended to cover third state domiciled defendants.

V. JUSTICIABILITY

(d)(i) How would the courts of your country resolve the question of whether the mother should be allowed to proceed with her claim?

Assuming that that law indeed denies the mother equal protection, any (lower) court in Germany should try to interpret the law in conformity with the constitution. This could mean that the law is – by way of analogy – also applied to illegitimate children. If such an interpretation is not possible, e.g., because the legislative materials explicitly state that illegitimate children should be excluded, the courts would have to halt proceedings and refer the question of constitutionality of the law for a preliminary ruling to the Federal Constitutional Court.

(ii) On which provisions and/or case law do you base your answer? If your highest court has addressed this or a similar issue, please describe how the court solved it.

The obligation of a court to interpret the law in conformity with the constitution is recognized in the case law of the Federal Constitutional Court (see, e.g., the decision in Volume 86 of the official collection of decisions of the German Federal Constitutional Court (page 322)): The respect for the legislator requires to take into consideration as much as possible the intention of the legislator. The Constitutional Court held, however, that this interpretation of the law in conformity with the constitution had to stop where it would run counter to the wording of the law and to the clear intention of the legislator (see, e.g., volume 110, page 226(267)).

. . .

(iv) Does your legal system require the same range of considerations to determine whether a party can bring a claim? Are those considerations statutory or constitutional?

Before a civil court, the mother would have to prove similar aspects to arrive at the admissibility of the case, such as an interest in bringing proceedings (which is, however, easily accepted in cases of actions for performance), the authorization to present the child, etc. Most of these considerations are laid down in the statutory law.

GREECE

NIKOLAOS M. KATIFORIS

Lecturer, University of Athens, Greece,
Faculty of Law

II.b Briefly describe the highest court (or courts) of your country and indicate its (or their) function within your legal system.

Areios Pagos is the civil and criminal Supreme Court of Greece. Following the example of the French Cour de Cassation, the review exercised by Areios Pagos is traditionally strictly limited to points of law. Starting from its foundation in 1838, Areios Pagos has gradually developed a highly significant role in both securing the uniformity of law and in adjusting legal norms to current situations.

III. JUDICIAL DECISION MAKING

a. Have you observed a similar phenomenon in your judicial system? If so, please identify the area(s) of law in which this has occurred.(Please do not limit yourself to questions involving jurisdiction.)

Article 559 No. 1 of the Greek Code of Civil Procedure has provided for a ground for cassation "when a substantial law rule has been violated, including those that involve the interpretation of judicial acts, whether a statute law or a custom, a rule of Greek law or of foreign law, a rule of internal or of international law."

The abovementioned phenomenon is observed in almost all areas of law, as Areios Pagos, by reviewing the legal qualification given to facts, particularly in the course of the application of the abstract concepts most often contained in several rules of substantial law, e.g., good faith, force majeure, important reason, good morals, abuse of rights, public policy etc., has exercised more effective control over the lower courts, despite the difficulties of exact distinctions which have quite often emerged.

b. If you have observed this phenomenon, does it sometimes occur that the judicially developed tests limit the principles that the tests purport to articulate?

The principle of the proportionality has been recently limited by Areios Pagos, which refuses to review the issue of whether the definition of a certain amount as compensation by a lower court is considered as "proportionate" or not.

IV. JURISDICTION

d(i). Would your country exercise jurisdiction over the foreign manufacturer on a claim against it by the injured party?

Yes.

(ii) On which provisions and/or case law do you base your answer? If your highest court has addressed this or a similar issue, please describe how the court solved it.

The international jurisdiction of the Greek civil courts is regulated through: (a) International law (especially international – mostly bilateral – treaties concerning the jurisdiction, recognition, and enforcement of foreign titles), (b) European law (esp. the Council Regulations 44/2001 and 2201/2003) and (c) domestic law (especially C.C.Pr.).

According to Art. 3 I C.C.Pr., the Greek Civil Courts have jurisdiction over Greeks and foreigners, if a Greek Court has territorial competence. It is therefore said that in Greek Law, international jurisdiction is the resultant of all territorial competences.

According to the above, the Greek Courts have international jurisdiction, e.g., if a tort has occurred in Greece (Art. 3 I, 35 C.C. Pr., Art. 5.3 Reg. 44/2001), regardless of whether the defendant is domiciled in Greece.

(iii) If you need additional facts to answer this question, please indicate which type of facts you would need and why.

(iv) Additional comments. Express any additional comment you may have on the solutions offered by your system and the U.S. system.

According to the decision of the ECG *Shevill v. Press Alliance* SA, based on the phrase "place where the harmful event occurred," in Art. 5.3 Reg. 44/2001, the victim of libel by a newspaper distributed in several states may sue for damages against the publisher either before the courts of the State of the place where the publisher of the defamatory publication is established, which have jurisdiction to award damages for all the harm caused by the defamation (which is more convenient for the alleged wrongdoer), or before the courts of each Member State in which the publication was distributed and where the victim claims to have suffered injury to his reputation, which have jurisdiction to rule solely in respect of the harm caused in the forum State (which again is burdensome) [so-called *mosaic theory*].

V. JUSTICIABILITY

d(i) *How would the courts of your country resolve the question of whether the mother should be allowed to proceed with her claim?*

(ii) *On which provisions and/or case law do you base your answer? If your highest court has addressed this or a similar issue, please describe how the court solved it.*

(iii) *If you need additional facts to answer this question, please indicate which type of facts would you need and why.*

(iv) *Does your legal system require the same range of considerations to determine whether a party can bring a claim? Are those considerations statutory or constitutional?*

Art. 68 C.C.Pr. provides that judicial protection can be granted to persons claiming to have a direct legal interest.

Legal interest entails the main legally provided guideline to the judge concerning the acceptance of the standing to sue.

Standing to sue is one of the procedural prerequisites and, if it is lacking, the court will not proceed to the merits of the case, but will dismiss the action as "inadmissible."

The question of whether the mother should be allowed to proceed with her claim should be resolved in the context of the fundamental principle of equality, as Art. 4 I of the Greek Constitution provides that "All Greeks are equal before the law." Consequently, given that the Greek functional independent judge is obliged not to apply laws that are contrary to the Constitution (Art. 93 IV of the Constitution), the specific judge should apply the said provision as far as the illegitimate children are concerned as well, *mutatis mutandis*.

GREECE

CHAROULA APALAGAKI

Professor of Civil Procedure Law, Law Faculty, Aristotles University of Thessaloniki[1]

II.b Briefly describe the highest court (or courts) of your country and indicate its (or their) function within your legal system.

The organization and the competence of the Greek courts are outlined by the Greek Constitution that has been in force since 1975 and that was revised in 1986 and 2001. The judicial jurisdiction is divided into administrative, civil, and penal matters (see Art. 93 of the Constitution). The determination of each dispute's category is determined by the legislature, which in turn is bound by the order of the Constitution. All the courts, regardless of their particular jurisdiction, are organized in courts of first and second instance and the Supreme Court in each group of disputes. The Supreme Court in Civil Matters, the Areios Pagos (so named according to the Supreme Court in Ancient Greece), is divided into more Senates. The number and the competence of each Senate are defined by the Plenum of the Areios Pagos (according to Law 1756/1988, as revised by Law 3346/2005), every year. The most recent definition of the internal organization of Areios Pagos has been resolved in Plenum session Number 20/2012 (published in the Government Gazette Number 2186/2012) and shall remain in force for the year 2012–2013. According to this latter resolution of the Plenum, seven Senates are established. Four are competent to hear civil matters and the remaining three are

[1] Recently, the law faculty has been included into the 150 top faculties worldwide. The lesson of civil procedure law is obligatory for law faculty students and the classes are divided into three semesters. Over the fifth semester, the students attend the main body of the so-called recognition proceedings (or the General Part of the Civil Procedure Law); in the seventh semester, they continue with appeals law and enforcement methods; finally, in the eighth and last semester, they work on specific complicated issues of civil procedure law in general. Charoula Apalagaki, has been a member of the law faculty since 1982, garnering significant practical experience as a lawyer before the Greek Supreme Court in Civil Matters (Areios Pagos).

competent for penal matters. Each Senate is made up of seven judges and one vice president. The president of the Supreme Court has a rather administrative role and leads the Session of the Plenum (in both civil and administrative matters). The prosecutor of the Supreme Court is responsible for the supervision of the penal jurisdiction and of all the prosecutors. Although the function of the Supreme Court is divided into civil and penal matters, the judges of the courts (first and second instance) hear both civil and criminal cases. In the more significant geographical areas of Athens/Piraeus/Thessaloniki (i.e., the biggest Greek cities), the judges are competent solely either for civil or criminal matters.

The simultaneous engagement of the same judges in both procedures (civil and criminal) still complies with the Constitutional Provision for the division between civil and penal courts.

The Courts of First Instance in civil matters are Peace Courts located even in smaller areas. The Peace Courts are normally competent for civil matters, which don't exceed the amount of 20,000 euros and exceptionally in some other cases. Recently the competence of the Peace Courts has been expanded by Law No. 4055/2012 in cases of nonvoluntary jurisdiction (with a more administrative function, such as, for instance, the provision of heritage cerficates or the provisional arrangement of the administration of legal entities). Additionally, the Peace Courts have to resolve the insolvency of individual persons. Currently, Greece has 301 Peace Courts.

Furthermore, the Civil Procedure Code provides the competence of the First Instance Courts for disputes between 20,001 and 250,000 euro (see Art. 14 of the Greek Civil Procedure Code), and the multimember (three-member) First Instance Courts, for disputes of material interest exceeding the amount of 250,000 euros (see Art. 14 and 18 of the Greek Civil Procedure Code). The First Instance Court with only one justice presiding is additionally competent to hear the appeals against the decrees of the Peace Courts. Currently, Greece has 64 First Instance Courts (single or tri-member).

The Appeals Courts (single or three member) are located in the geographically larger areas of the Country (there are currently 21). The Appeals Courts are competent to hear appeals against the Courts of First Instance; the single-member Appeal Courts are competent to hear appeals against the judgments of the single-seat Courts of First Instance, whereas the tri-seat Appeals Courts are competent to hear appeals against the judgments of the tri-seat Courts of First Instance.

The Supreme Court in Administrative matters (Conseil d' Etat) is competent as Court of First Instance for all appeals against administrative acts of higher interest and as the Revision Court in order to judge the revisions against decisions of the Administrative Appeals Courts. Administrative Courts are also distinguished in first and second Instance (see Art. 95 of the Greek Constitution).

Finally, the Supreme Court of Audit is competent for the financial accounts of the State and the State-owned entities as well for the pension resolutions.

The Greek Constitution does not allow for Special Courts. We have two exceptions. The first is the court designated to judge the malus claims against judges, and the second is the Supreme Court, which resolves disputes between the Supreme Court in Civil Matters (Areios Pagos) and the Supreme Court in Administrative Matters (Conseil d' Etat), regarding the constitutionality of a particular law or legal provision.

Greece does not have a Constitutional Court. All the courts, regardless of their jurisdiction and competence are entitled to review the constitutionality of any legal provision (see Art. 93 par. 4 of the Greek Constitution).

Courts and judges are independent from the government and the Parliament (see Art. 26 and 87 of the Greek Constitution).

Since 1993, lawyers interested in joining the judicial branch have to take special examinations and attend a special academic program in the Judges Academy, located in Thessaloniki (the second-largest city in Greece).

The independence of the judges is limited by the Appointment of the Presidents of all Supreme Courts, by the Government Council, following a hearing of the candidates by the Greek Parliament (see Art. 90 of the Constitution).

III. JUDICIAL DECISION MAKING

(a) Have you observed a similar phenomenon in your judicial system? If so, please identify the area(s) of law in which this has occurred. (Please do not limit yourself to questions involving jurisdiction.).

The Greek legal and judicial system belongs to the Group of the Continental legal systems. That means that the judge does not create law, but hears each separate case and applies the law in force. Of course, the real meaning of each particular legal provision becomes effective through its application by the court. So even if the continental legal systems are primarily defined by legislation and not court decisions (case law), the interpretation of the legal provisions – which is governed by certain principles (proportionality principle, compliance to the Constitution) – by the courts is the tool for the real implementation of the specific legal provisions.

So the jurisprudence delivers, besides the law, a very crucial source of the current legal frame. The courts, even those of First Instance, are not bound by precedent and are permitted to freely give another solution (this is aligned with the notion of the independency of the judges). But, since the parties mostly rely on precedent, mainly the precedent of the Supreme Courts), the First Instance or the Appeals Court, follow the precedent set by the Supreme Court.

Precedent has obtained practically the range and the force of legislation. Greece is a member of the European Union and a member of the Convention of the Human Rights (in force in Greece since 1994). The jurisprudence of both the European Court, seated in Luxemburg and the European Court for the Human Rights, seated in Strasburg, is considered to be an intergral part of our domestic legal frame.

All the obligations undertaken by the Greek State, through bilateral or multilateral conventions, have to be applied taking priority over the domestic legislation (Art. 28 of the Greek Constitution); thus in many occasions, the Greek courts of lower levels overturn Supreme Court decisions in order to satisfly the international legal obligations of Greece.

So it is not only the legislative branch, but also the courts that have the power to interpret a rule and to restrict or to expand the real meaning of the law. For instance, the Greek Supreme Court in civil matters considered for a very long time that the right to property did not include standard financial interests or general rights of proprietary nature, which meant in turn that they were not guaranteed by the Constitution. But under the influence of the jurisprudence of the Court of Human Rights, the Plenum of the Supreme Court changed this view in 1998 (Decision Number 40).

(b) If you have observed this phenomenon, does it sometimes occur that the judicially developed tests limit the principles that the tests purport to articulate?

Since the judge has the power to implement the relevant legal provision in each dispute, sometimes the solution given by the court seems to violate the scope of the legal framework and to be far removed from the spirit of the law. Usually the courts disregard the provisions of procedural law.

The delays noted in the rendering of judgments remain an open issue for Greece. Every amendment of the procedural law becomes void and null, since the courts cannot practically adopt all these amendments. That means that although the justice is expected to provide effective solutions, the results are rather disappointing. Recently, we have had two expanded revisions of the Civil Procedure Code (Law 3994/2011 and 4055/2012) and a further revision is under discussion.

IV. JURISDICTION

(d)(i) *Would your country exercise jurisdiction over the foreign manufacturer on a claim against it by the injured party?*

(ii) *On which provisions and/or case law do you base your answer? If your highest court has addressed this or a similar issue, please describe how the court solved it.*

(iii) *If you need additional facts to answer this question, please indicate which type of facts you would need and why.*

Both Greek law and the European Union law grant a high level of protection to consumers. The basis of our internal legislation is the Council Directive 93/13/1993 and Laws 2251/1994 as revised by Law 3587/2007. The special legislation in force for consumer protection includes not only friendly provisions for the claims and the rights of the consumers, but also special procedural provisions that enable the plaintiff to file a suit in his own country and domicile.

Regarding the European legislation according to Art. 16 par. 2 of the Regulation 44/2001, which regulates the matters of the international jurisdiction and the enforcement of judgments among the EU member states, it provides that disputes between consumers and the manufacturers or other commercial entities are to be resolved solely by the country of the consumer's domicile. So the definition of the forum is connected not to the domicile of the defendant but of the plaintiff.

The same solution is adopted by the Greek courts regarding its jurisdiction. The residence of the plaintiff consumer can be the appropriate forum for both the contractual claim (Art. 33 of the Civil Procedure Code) or the tort (Art. 35 of the same code). It is a common understanding for the Greek legal provisions that the protection of the weak parties – for instance consumers, employees, etc. – dictates that these groups should be enabled to have simple access to the court and to bring their cases in the place of their residence, or of their countries. According to the same jurisprudence, even jurisdiction clauses, concluded between consumers and the manufacturer, should not exclude the right of the consumer to bring his case before the courts of his residence

V. JUSTICIABILITY

(d)(i) *How would the courts of your country resolve the question of whether the mother should be allowed to proceed with her claim?*

(ii) *On which provisions and/or case law do you base your answer? If your highest court has addressed this or a similar issue, please describe how the court solved it.*
(iii) *If you need additional facts to answer this question, please indicate which type of facts would you need and why.*
(iv) *Does your legal system require the same range of considerations to determine whether a party can bring a claim? Are those considerations statutory or constitutional?*
(v) *Additional Comments. Express any additional comment you may have on the solutions offered by your system and the U.S. system.*

According to Greek law, illegitimate offspring have the same rights against their physical parents as the legitimate. The relevant provision of Greek law regarding children focuses on the protection of their lives, education, and prosperity, both within the penal and civil law legal frame.

Both parents are responsible for the welfare of their children and are required to abstain from any actions that may be harmful to their lives or situation (see Art. 306 of the Penal Code). Either parent is entitled to take or to initiate all legal proceedings that protect the rights and the interests of the child. The omission to pay the alimentation by the responsible party is considered to be a penal action (see Art. 358 of the Penal Code).

Illegitimate children enjoy the same protection by their parents (Art. 1515), but each of them is entitled to act separately (see mainly Art. 619 of the Greek Civil Procedure Code) against the other parent or any other third party, and undertake or initiate all the legal measures concerning the monetary or personal welfare of the children.

GREECE

EVANGELIA ASIMAKOPOULOU

LLM PhD Candidate at the Aristotle University of Thessaloniki Attorney at Law

II. b. The highest court for civil cases in the Greek legal system is called Areios Pagos. It examines only legal matters, after a claim by the litigant for the refutation of a court decision. This means that this court does not examine all the facts and how they were considered by the lower courts, Courts of First Instance or Courts of Appeal, which examine both the material and legal matters of a case. The legal reasons on which a claim for refutation can be based are strictly and exclusively cited in article 559 of the Greek Civil Procedure Code. The decision of the High Court, concerning this specific legal matter, is binding only for the court whose decision was examined. For all the other courts, this decision is not officially binding, but functions in a way as "binding" case law.

III. JUDICIAL DECISION MAKING

a. There is nothing akin to "reasonableness" in the Greek civil procedure system.

There is a similar provision in the general part of the Greek Civil Procedure Code, in the chapter on general procedural clauses, which requires the respect, during the process, of good faith and sound morals on the part of the litigants (article 116 of Greek Civil Procedure Code), but this provision is a general clause without any sanction and it is not examined as a separate prerequisite of the process.

However, Greece, as a member state of the Treaty of Rome, which was voted under the auspices of the Council of Europe for the protection of human rights (European Convention of Human Rights, [ECHR]), is legally obliged, under Article 28 of the Greek Constitution, to interpret and implement every provision of Greek civil procedure under the principle of the provision 6 par. 1 of the above treaty of ECHR, which orders the exercising of litigation under the scope of the due process.

On the other hand, in the field of civil law, there is the general clause of good faith and sound morals and customary practice (Articles 173, 200, 288 of the Greek Civil Procedure Code), as a rule of interpretation for all the obligations and contracts between individuals; this clause is binding for the court in the implementation of the law and the interpretation of declarations, etc.

Furthermore, the Greek Civil Procedure Code includes a provision that requires the respect of good faith and good morals as a prerequisite to the demand of a right; however, this is examined by the courts only after an objection by the litigants (Article 281 of the Greek Civil Code).

In conclusion, it can be said that the Greek legal system, not just in civil law but also in civil procedure law, is based strictly, with very few exceptions that are not within the scope of this survey, on the relationship between the parties of a contract or the relationship between the litigants. Concerning all the other given elements of the U.S. system, the judicial decision making is of course based on a specific rule, the interpretation of this rule, the analysis of the facts strictly as they were presented by the litigants, and the application of the rule to the specific facts.

IV. JURISDICTION

(d)(i)&(ii). The international jurisdiction of the Greek courts is exercised when there is a local jurisdiction of any Greek court on the pending case (Article 3 of the Greek Civil Procedure Code).

In this specific case, the Greek courts would exercise jurisdiction according to a combination of Articles 3 and 35 of the Greek Civil Procedure Code. Article 3 is cited above.

Article 35 regulates the local jurisdiction of a court for a tort in the place where the tort took place or in the place where the consequences of this tort were felt. In this given case, this would be appreciated as a tort from the manufacturer, and the court would exercise the international jurisdiction according to all the above reasons (see also Multi Member Court of First Instance of Athens 6010/2012, published on the website of NOMOS).

V. JUSTICIABILITY

At first, it must be clarified that the Greek civil procedure system distinguishes between the procedural prerequisites of the process and the substantial prerequisites of the case.

The procedural prerequisites of the case, such as the ability to be a litigant (Article 62 of the Greek Civil Procedure Code), the ability of court performance (Article 63 of the Greek Civil Procedure Code), the international and local jurisdiction (Articles 3 and 22 and the following of the Greek Civil Procedure Code), the jurisdiction according the value of the matter of the case (Article 7 and the following of the Greek Civil Procedure Code), and the legitimate interest of the case (Article 68 of the Greek Civil Procedure Code).

The substantial prerequisites have to do with the right that is examined, the elements of which must be clearly and specifically represented by the claimant. Actually, the legitimate interest lies between the fields of procedural and substantial prerequisites because, in some cases, the court has to examine the right that is demanded in order to answer if there is the legitimate interest as a procedural prerequisite.

(i) As from the scope of procedural prerequisite, the mother could raise this claim on behalf of her minor child, because she has the legal authorization (Article 1510 of Greek Civil Code, because the substantial authorization is regulated by the civil law) to represent her child, according to Article 63 of Greek Civil Procedure Code that regulates the ability of performance for an underage child by its legal representatives.

However, the mother has only the right of the performance of the litigation. The litigant of the process is the child (Article 62 of Greek Civil Procedure Code; see also Areios Pagos 1005/2006 publ. Elliniki Dikaiosini 2006, p. 1352; Areios Pagos 2182/2009 publ. Nomiko Vima 2010, p. 1726; Sinle Member Court of First Instance Athens 313/2011 publ. in the website of NOMOS). This means that the claim could be raised by the mother on behalf of her child, as a procedural prerequisite, but all the other substantial facts and the legitimate interest would be examined only according to the legal status of the child. (The above answer applies also to the questions under (ii) and (iii)).

(iv) Except all the above that is cited in the introduction, the extra consideration that is claimed is the specific and explicit presentation of the facts of the case by the litigants. Nothing else can be taken into account by the court (see Articles 106 and 216 of Greek Civil Procedure, and simply as an example, Plenary Session of Areios Pagos 15/2012 publ. in the website NOMOS; Areios Pagos 220/2012 publ. in the website NOMOS).

All the considerations of determination are statutory and not constitutional, as provided in the Greek Civil Procedure Code. There is only one general provision in the Greek Constitution that provides a general clause of the right of every person to access to justice (Article 20 of the Greek Constitution).

Every single provision of the Greek Civil Procedure Code is determined under the scope of this provision. So, it could be said, taking into account the legal effect of constitutional rights in every legal relationship (Article 25 of the Greek Constitution), that the entire legal procedural system is interpreted under this clause but that generally the prerequisites and the procedure is regulated by the statutes of Greek civil procedure.

HUNGARY

PÉTER GÁRDOS

PhD, Attorney at Law

II. b) The Hungarian judicial system consists of four levels: local courts, regional courts, high courts and the Curia. The Curia has two major roles: it functions as the third level in certain legal disputes and has the obligation to maintain the unity of jurisprudence.

III. JUDICIAL DECISION MAKING

The situation is slightly different in Hungary than in the example you gave. The starting point is necessarily the same: the rule provided by the Parliament is often too abstract and therefore requires interpretation. However, as Hungary does not have a precedent system in the way it exists in the U.S., the courts are free to reinterpret the rule in each and every case. This is even more so as judgments are not reported in their entirety, only the very brief summary of the most important cases are published, such deviation in interpretation is usually difficult to realize. Tort law may serve as a good example. The law provides that "all damage" shall be reimbursed. The courts have to interpret in each case what "all" means. The published cases show that courts tend to apply different tests: the so-called remoteness test, the weakness of causal link test, etc.

IV. JURISDICTION

Jurisdiction in non-contractual cases is based on, among other factors, the place where damage has occurred. If the product injures the buyer in Hungary, Hungarian courts will have jurisdiction. This is based on Law Decree 13 of 1979 in private international law. The same rule can be found in Council Regulation (EC) No 44/2001 of 22 December 2000 on jurisdiction and the recognition and enforcement of judgments in civil and commercial matters. The provisions on product liability are further to be found in Act X of 1993, which implements Council Directive 85/374/EEC on the approximation of the laws, regulations, and administrative provisions of the Member States concerning liability for defective products.

V. JUSTICIABILITY

Before answering your question, it is important to note that Hungarian law gives a clear answer to the question you raise. The Act on Family Law and the new Civil Code, which will replace the current act as of 15 March 2014, provide that the father is obliged to provide support for the child.

If we assume that there is no such provision, the starting point shall be that the Hungarian Constitution provides for equal treatment. If the law provides that only fathers of legitimate children are obliged to provide support for the child, it is highly unlikely that the courts could find valid legal bases to oblige fathers of illegitimate child to provide similar support.

However, the courts would have the right to suspend the procedure and turn to the Constitutional Court to ask whether the legislation that discriminates against illegitimate children is constitutional. If the Constitutional Court finds the law to be unconstitutional, it has the right to repeal the law and order Parliament to pass a new law in line with the constitutional requirements.

HUNGARY

PROF. DR. ZSUZSA WOPERA

Director of the Institute of European and International Law, University of Miskolc, Faculty of Law, Department of Civil Procedure, Hungary

II. BACKGROUND INFORMATION

1.1. *Judicial system of Hungary*

At the base of the Court pyramid, there are the *municipal and district courts*, called *local courts*. The six district courts operate in Budapest; the municipal courts are located in major cities. Altogether, there are more than 100 (exactly 111) in Hungary.

At the next level, there are the *tribunals* (formerly: county courts). There are 19 counties in Hungary; therefore, there are 19 *tribunals* and the *Capital Tribunal* in Budapest. Tribunals are first instance courts (in civil actions where the litigated amount is above 30 000 000 HUF) and operate as appeal courts too.

Since 2005, five *regional courts of appeal* have been operating in Hungary exclusively as appeal courts. They are seated in Budapest, Debrecen, Győr, Pécs, and Szeged. These courts have competence to render judgment on legal remedy submitted against the decision of local courts or tribunals. The regional Court of appeal reexamines the facts of the case and reaches its own conclusions. In most cases, it is possible to contest the decision by appealing in cassation to the Curia.

The highest court of Hungary is the *Curia* (formerly known as the *Supreme Court*), which hears the appeal submitted against the decisions of the upper courts and exclusively adjudges petitions for revision in law.

The following courts shall proceed in the first instance in civil procedures:

- local courts (municipal courts, district courts) and
- tribunals (Capital Tribunal of Budapest).

The following courts shall proceed in the second instance:

a) *tribunals* in cases falling within the jurisdiction of local courts (municipal courts, district courts),
b) *regional courts of appeal* in cases falling within the jurisdiction of tribunals and Capital Tribunal of Budapest,
c) the *Curia* in cases falling within the jurisdiction of regional courts of appeal (CCP Section 233/A), and also in the cases referred to in CCP Subsection (3) of Section 235 ("leap frog" appeal – see further on).

The Curia shall proceed in cases of review (revision).

The basic source of Hungarian law of Civil Procedure is the Act III of 1952 on Code of Civil Procedure (hereafter: CCP).

1.2. *The functions of the Curia (Supreme Court)*

To satisfy the requirements of administering justice efficiently with regard to the principle of rule of law, to realize the principle of independency of the judiciary, to ensure the uniformity of passing judgments and to enforce the Fundamental Law of Hungary (formerly: the Constitution), the Parliament adopted Act CLXI of 2011 on the Organization and Administration of Courts of Hungary.

We define the functions of the Curia according to this Act.

The Curia shall be the supreme judicial body.

(1) The Curia shall
  a) rule on the legal remedy submitted against the decision of the tribunal or the regional court of appeal,
  b) rule on petitions for review (revision proceeding),
  c) adopt an obligatory uniformity decision applicable for courts,
  d) analyze jurisprudence in cases where a final decision has been adopted, including exploring and examining the jurisprudence of courts,
  e) publish court rulings and decisions or authoritative rulings,
  f) adopt decisions on the conflict of local ordinances with other legislation and their annulment,
  g) adopt decisions on establishing a local government's neglect of its statutory legislative obligation, and
  h) proceed in other cases referred to its jurisdiction.

Ad a) The Curia as a Court of Appeal (exceptional function)

The Curia shall proceed in the second instance in cases falling within the jurisdiction of regional courts of appeal (CCP Section 233/A) and also in the cases referred to in CCP Subsection (3) of Section 235 ("leap frog" appeal).

CCP Section 233/A: An appeal may be filed against a final decision passed in the second instance, against which, according to the rules of the first instance proceeding, an appeal may be lodged, and against a second instance ruling rejecting the appeal ex officio.

If the decision was rendered in the first instance by the tribunal, the parties represented by legal counsel may lodge a joint request enclosed with the appeal against the decision with a motion to have the appeal – suggesting the infringement of any substantive law – transferred directly to the Curia. In action relating to rights in property the parties may request to have the case transferred to the Curia if the amount disputed is in excess of 500,000 forints. This appeal shall be decided without a formal hearing, under the provisions of review proceedings; therefore, the Curia shall render its decision relying on the documents made available. The decision of the Curia may not be subject to further judicial review ("leap frog" appeal).

Ad b) The Curia as a Court of Revision (determinative judicial function)

There are two types of extraordinary remedies in Hungarian Civil Procedure: reopening of a case (retrial) and revision (review proceeding). The reopening of a case is a review in facts; the revision is a review in law. As these extraordinary petitions break through *res iudicata* they can be lodged only under special, restricted conditions.

The submission of an extraordinary petition doesn't suspend the enforcement of the contested judgment, but the reviewing court can – on the request of the interested party – suspend the enforcement until the final decision is delivered.

The *reopening of a case* (retrial) and the reopening procedure is a special review procedure concerning only legally binding judgments and other decisions of the same effect (e.g., default judgment) (CCP Sections 260–269).

Revision (review proceeding) can be sought only if the final judgment is unlawful, and this unlawfulness affects the merits of the case. Only final judgments can be contested before Curia in a revision procedure. A motion for the review of a final judgment or a final ruling adopted on the merits of the case may be submitted to the Curia – on the grounds of infringement – by the party, the intervener, or any person to whom any provision of the decision may be of concern, against the appropriate section (CCP Sections 270–275).

Ad c) The Curia operates as a unifying court (not judicial (judging) function)

The Curia shall make legal standardisation decisions, shall conduct jurisprudence analyses in cases completed on a final and absolute basis, and shall publish authoritative court rulings and authoritative court decisions.

A law standardization procedure shall be instituted if *a)* it is necessary to adopt a law standardization decision or to alter or to repeal a previously adopted law standardization decision in the interest of the further development of jurisprudence or the maintenance of standard practices in the administration of justice, or *b)* a justice administration chamber of the Curia wishes to depart from the ruling of another justice administration chamber of the Curia published as an authoritative court ruling or from a published authoritative court decision on a legal issue.

At the Curia, criminal, combined civil and business, and combined administrative and labur law standardization councils shall operate. The law standardization council shall be headed by the president, vice president, division head or deputy division head of the Curia. The law standardization council shall be made up of a chair and four further members, and the members shall be selected by the chair of the law standardization council.

Ad d) The Curia operates as a jurisprudence analyzing court (not judicial – judging – function)

It is the duty of the jurisprudence analysis task force to analyse practices in the administration of justice. The topics to be investigated shall be determined by the president of the Curia annually, after due consultation with the divisions of the Curia.

The jurisprudence analysis task force shall prepare a summary opinion on the result of their investigation. The completed summary report shall be debated by the division of the Curia competent with reference to the subject matter thereof and, in the event of their agreement, the findings of the opinion shall be published by the head of the task force on the website of the Curia.

Ad e) The Curia operates as a unifying Court (not judicial –
Judging – function)

If the Curia's jurisprudence council passed a ruling concerning a wide strata of society or a ruling of particular significance from the viewpoint of public interests that also extends to theoretical issues, the chair of the council shall, without delay after the ruling has been committed to writing, notify the competent division head. The division head shall present the ruling to the authoritative publication council, which shall decide, if warranted by the circumstances, on the publication thereof as an authoritative court ruling.

Ad f) and g) Nonlitigious Proceedings Aimed at the Reviewing of Local Ordinances and Due to Omissions Related to the Statutory Legislative Obligations of Local Municipalities

A so-called municipal chamber operates at the Curia. The municipal chamber shall consist of three judge members. It is the duty of the municipal chamber to conduct nonlitigious proceedings aimed at the reviewing of unlawful local ordinances and nonlitigious proceedings instituted due to omissions related to the statutory legislative obligations of local municipalities.

This nonlitigious proceedings aimed at the reviewing of local ordinances may be initiated against a local municipality by the metropolitan or county government bureau exercising the powers of supervision in respect of the local municipality on the basis of a motion satisfying the criteria and within the time limit determined in the Act on local municipalities.

Nonlitigious proceedings instituted due to omissions related to the statutory legislative obligations of local municipalities shall be governed by the rules relating to nonlitigious proceedings aimed at the reviewing of unlawful local ordinances subject to the differences set forth under the present sub-title.

Concerning the study, we have to focus on the revision (review proceeding) because this is the determinative judicial function of the Curia in the field of civil and commercial matters.

*****

III. JUDICIAL DECISION MAKING

I have not experienced the phenomenon described under III. The rules of jurisdiction are mandatory; they do not allow this kind of measuring (balancing) of the judge.

IV. JURISDICTION

(d)(i)&(ii)

Hungary has been member of the EU since May 1 2004, so the rules of jurisdiction fall under the regime of the Council Regulation (EC) 44/2001 on jurisdiction and the recognition and enforcement of judgments in civil and commercial matters.

Solving the hypothetic case will depend on whether the defendant's seat or domicile is in a Member State or outside of the EU.

A) If the defendant (foreign manufacturer) has a seat in one of the Member States of EU, the Hungarian court has to apply the Regulation.

According to Article 3 (1) of the Regulation, "Persons domiciled in a Member State may be sued in the courts of another Member State only by virtue of the rules set out in Sections 2 to 7 of this Chapter."

Section 4 of the Brussels I regulation determines the special rules of jurisdiction over consumer contracts. According to Article 16 of Section 4, a consumer may bring proceedings against the other party to a contract either in the courts of the Member State in which that party is domiciled or in the courts for the place where the consumer is domiciled.

So if the injured consumer is domiciled in Hungary, the Hungarian Court (including the Curia) has jurisdiction in the case of a lawsuit arising from that consumer contract.

B) According to Article 4 of the Regulation that defines the personal scope of the Regulation: "1. If the defendant is not domiciled in a Member State, the jurisdiction of the courts of each Member State shall (...) be determined by the law of that Member State. 2. As against such a defendant, any person domiciled in a Member State may, whatever his nationality, avail himself in that State of the rules of jurisdiction there in force, and in particular those specified in Annex I, in the same way as the nationals of that State."

So, in the hypothetical case in which the foreign manufacturer has no domicile (or seat) in the EU, the rules of jurisdiction are determined by the law of the Member State.

In Hungary, the Law Decree 13 of 1979 on the Private International Law regulates the rules of jurisdiction. The general rule is that the Hungarian courts have jurisdiction if the seat (in the case of legal persons) or the habitual residence (in case of natural persons) of the defendant is in Hungary.

According to Section 60 of the Law Decree on Private International Law, the Hungarian court has jurisdiction in the case of a lawsuit arising from a consumer contract initiated by the consumer if the place of living or residence of the consumer is in Hungary and if the individual contracting with the consumer acting in its professional or business capacity: (a) acts in Hungary or targets its activity carried out elsewhere to Hungarian consumers, or (b) has a branch or representative office in Hungary or is considered to be established in Hungary as independent entrepreneur.

Furthermore, according to Section 60 of the Law Decree on Private International Law, the parties of a legal dispute may submit themselves to the jurisdiction of a country, except in an exclusive or disqualified jurisdiction. The submission must not result in that consumer being sued in the courts of a country other than that which the place of living or residence of the consumer is or in that a consumer be restrained from bringing a lawsuit in the courts of a country in which the place of living or residence of the consumer is, except where the submission is dated after the legal dispute arose.

V. JUSTICIABILITY

1. *The applicable substantive civil, family law and civil procedure law*

Under Hungarian Law any support or maintenance claim commence against the parents of legitimate children. The parent of illegitimate child has no support or maintenance obligation for his/her biological children.

If the mother has an illegitimate child, she must first file an action to settle the family status of her child. She must bring an action for the establishment of paternity. According to the New Civil Code of Hungary (Act V of 2013 on Code of Civil Law, Section 4:104), the mother files this action against the father on behalf of her child (as her child's represent) and in her own name.

If the father, or the person against whom the action is taken is not alive, or his whereabouts are unknown, the guardian appointed by the court shall be named as the defendant. Any relative in direct line shall, in such cases, have the right to intervene on behalf of either party (Section 295 (2) of CCP).

This action for the establishment of paternity may be combined – before the same court – with an action for child support; furthermore, a claim for child support may be presented subsequently in an action for establishing paternity pending before the court of the first instance (Section 295–296 of CCP).

If paternity was established by a court decision, the father has an obbligation of support when the judgment becomes final.

2. *The applicable substantive criminal law and criminal procedure law*

The Hungarian Law knows the crime of "omission of support,"[1] but the perpetrator of this crime could be the legitimate parent alone. This crime is prosecuted *ex officio*, so while the mother cannot commence this criminal procedure, she can denounce the father of her child to the police because of the omission of support.

[1] Omission of support

(1) The person who fails to perform his obligation of support based on a legal rule and prescribed in an executable authority decision through his own fault, commits a misdemeanor, and shall be punishable with imprisonment up to two years, labor in the public interests, or a fine.

(2) The punishment shall be imprisonment of up to three years for a felony if the omission of the support exposes the entitled party to serious deprivation.

(3) The perpetrator shall not be punishable, or his punishment may be mitigated without limitation, if he satisfies his obligation before the passing of the sentence of first instance (Section 196 of Act IV of 1978 of the Criminal Code).

Under Hungarian law in this case, the State can provide maintenance instead of the debtor and can claim reimbursement from the debtor of benefits provided to the creditor instead of maintenance.

However, the crime of omission of support is committed even if the creditor (the child) does not suffer a loss because the State can provide maintenance instead of the debtor. In any event, prosecuting the father does not redress an omission of support.

3. *Answers*

(i) As I made clear above, the mother can bring an action in order to establish paternity and demand child support. Failing this procedure, she has no legal way to commence any civil or criminal procedures against the biological father of her child.

(ii) I described above on which provisions my answer is based. There is no way that this similar issue can reach the highest court of Hungary because the lower courts will dismiss this claim and inform the party that she has to bring an action for the establishment of paternity foremost.

(iii) I do not need additional facts.

(iv) Yes, the Hungarian Code of Civil Procedure under Section 3 (1) defines that "The court shall initiate proceedings in connection with civil disputes when so requested. Such request – unless otherwise provided for by law – may only be submitted by a party to the dispute." This is the "real party of interests" component of Hungarian civil procedure law. The "standing, the ripeness and the mootness components" are the same in Hungarian Law.

These considerations are statutory, based on the Sections of CCP (3, 122 (1)) and Sections of Act IV of 1952 on Family Law (Sections 35–45). However, these provisions have a constitutional basis, according to Article XVI[2] of the Fundamental Law of Hungary (April 25, 2011).

[2] Article XVI

(1) Every child shall have the right to the protection and care required for his or her proper physical, mental, and moral development.

(2) Parents shall have the right to choose the type of upbringing they deem fit for their children.

(3) Parents shall be obliged to look after their children. This obligation shall include the provision of schooling for their children.

(4) Adult children shall be obliged to look after their parents if they are in need.

APPENDIX

Revision Proceeding in Details

1. THE ESSENCE OF REVISION

While reopening always concerns the factual bases of a case, a revision never does. Revision is aimed at correcting mistakes in law, either substantive or procedural ones, subordinated to the primary object of the unification and development of the law.

Revision in law is an extraordinary appeal from final judgments and other rulings of the merits of non-contentious cases.

2. COMPOSITION OF THE COURT

Revision falls within the jurisdiction of the Curia. In revision proceedings, the Curia shall proceed in a panel composed of three professional judges. Where so justified in view of the complexity of the case, the Curia may decide to proceed in a panel of five professional judges.

Legal representation is mandatory in proceeding before Curia for persons lodging a petition for revision (adjoining-petition for revision).

3. OBJECT OF REVISION

Revision can be sought only if the final judgment in unlawful and this unlawfulness affects the merits of the case.

A motion for the revision of a final judgment or a final ruling adopted on the merits of the case may be submitted to the Curia – on the grounds of infringement – by the party, the intervener, or by any person to whom any provision of the decision may be of concern, against the appropriate section.

4. SUBJECTS OF REVISION

Only final judgment (and in non-contentious proceeding/e.g., in execution procedure/orders given on the merits of the case) can be contested before the Curia in a revision procedure, provided they became legally binding on appeal.

A petition for revision may be filed against an order for the refusal of the statement of claim without issuing any writ of summons, and dismissing the action.

In the petition the party shall determine

- the challenged decision,
- the reasons for revision and
- an expressed request concerning the decision of the Curia.

Judicial revision may not be requested:

a) against any decision in the first instance that has become final and enforceable, unless it is permitted by law (e.g., in actions for supervision of administrative actions);
b) if the party did not exercise his right to appeal and the court of the second instance sustained the decision of the first instance under appeal by the other party;
c) against the part of a final decision pertaining only to payment of interest and the bearing of court costs, except if the appeal was lodged against these provisions of the decision in the first instance;
d) against the part of a final decision pertaining only to deadlines for performance or payment by installments;
e) if the decision was rendered by the Curia;
f) against any judgment for the annulment or dissolution of marriage, as regards the annulment or dissolution;
g) against any judgment to rebut the presumption of fatherhood – in the part rebutting the presumption of fatherhood – if fatherhood is assumed by any person subject to the father's full-fledged consent after the presumption of fatherhood has been rebutted, or if fatherhood was established by final court decision, or if the child's mother is married subsequently and the mother's spouse is to be recognized as the child's father;
h) against a ruling for the approval of a settlement;
i) against a ruling on the grant of probate;

j) in capital government debt consolidation procedures, against the ruling ordering debt consolidation;
k) against court decisions rendered in connection with the issue of visas;
l) where precluded by law.

No revision may be requested in respect of actions relating to property rights where the value disputed in the petition for revision is below 3 million HUF (~ 10,000 euros).

5. FILING OF THE REVISION PETITION

The petition for revision shall be submitted to the court having rendered the decision in the first instance within 60 days from the time of publication of the decision, or shall be sent by registered mail containing a copy for each party involved in the action, plus two. No application for continuation will be accepted upon failure to meet the deadline for submission of the petition for review past 30 days from the last day of the deadline, even if the party was unaware of having missed the deadline, or if the obstacle was not eliminated in due time.

The petition for revision shall specify the decision that is the subject of the petition for review, furthermore, it shall demonstrate – in addition to the infringement – the party's request to have the decision modified as to extent, showing also the reasons.

The petition for review shall have attached the legal counsel's power of attorney, unless it was made available previously (CCP Section 272).

If the time limit for the submission of petitions for revision expired with respect to all parties, or if the petition for revision has been submitted by all parties, the court of the first instance shall forward it together with the documents of the case to the Curia without delay, and shall send a copy of the petition for revision to the court having rendered the final decision with a notice of the opening of the procedure. If enforcement has already been ordered, or if suspension of the enforcement has been requested, the petition for revision shall be forwarded upon receipt without delay.

A petition for revision shall *have no suspensory effect* concerning the enforcement of the decision; however, the Curia has powers to suspend enforcement upon request, under special circumstances. In adopting a ruling for the suspension of enforcement the court shall – first and foremost – take into consideration as to whether the original state can be restored following enforcement, or whether the damage caused by the lack of enforcement outweighs the loss the suspension of enforcement is likely to entail.

6. LIMITS OF CONSIDERATION OF CASE

The Curia shall have powers to revision a final decision *only within the limits of the petition for revision or the adjoining-petition for revision*, unless it decides to dismiss the action of its own motion, or if the court that rendered the decision had not been properly formed, or if a judge who should have been disqualified by law took part in rendering the decision.

The opposing party can submit two types of defense: *counterpetition for revision* and *adjoining-petition for revision*. The provisions of submission these two types of defense are the same than the counterappeal and the adjoining-appeal in the appellate procedure.

No changes are allowed in the petition for revision; however, it may be withdrawn before the Curia renders its decision, or – if a hearing is held – until it retires for returning a decision.

7. COURT POWER; GROUNDS FOR REVERSAL OF JUDGMENT; CASSATIONAL COURT RULINGS; BINDING POWER OF THE RULINGS

The Curia shall decide the petition for revision without a formal hearing, except if either of the parties has requested a hearing, or if the Curia is of the opinion that a hearing is necessary. In the case of petition for revision submitted against a ruling requesting a hearing is not an option.

A request for hearing shall be made by the petitioner in the petition for revision, or within eight days of receipt of the opposing party's adjoining-petition for revision, and by the opposing party within eight days of receipt of the petition for revision. No application for continuation will be accepted upon failure to meet these deadlines.

In revision procedures, no taking of evidence shall be performed. The Curia shall render its decision concerning the petition for revision relying on the documents available.

A) The Curia *discontinues the action* with an order if a cause of termination exists and in addition sets aside the first instance judgment totally or partly affected by this cause. The ground of discontinuance are, e.g., the plaintiff has withdrawn his claim or the parties jointly file for dismissal of the action. [CCP Section 275 (2)]
B) The Curia *repeals the final judgment* and remits the case to the first or to the second instance court for retrial if the first instance court was not duly formed or a judge whom a cause for exclusion exists participated in passing the judgment. [CCP Section 275 (2)]

C) If the decision reviewed is found in compliance with the relevant legislation the Curia *keeps the judgment in force*, so the petition is groundless. [CCP 275 (3)]

D) If a decision is found unlawful, except the breach of procedural regulations had no impact on the merits of the case, the Curia shall *repeal the unlawful decision* in whole or in part, and if the facts needed for a decision can be ascertained, it shall render a new decision instead, or in any other cases it shall instruct the competent court of the first or second instance to retrial the case and to render a new decision.

If the Curia has ordered the competent court of the first or second instance to retrial the case and to render a new decision, it shall also convey mandatory instructions in its ruling of abolishment.

In this case, it shall only determine the amount of the costs of the revision procedure, whereas the decision as to the bearing of such costs lies with the court rendering the new decision.

If the Curia orders the court of the second instance to reopen the case, its decision shall be delivered to the parties by the court of the second instance, in other cases by the court of the first instance, and shall take measures – consistent with the decision – for having the enforcement procedure terminated or restricted, or for having the suspension of the enforcement procedure lifted.

If the case is retrialed, the hearing shall be opened by reciting the decision of the Curia, and shall continue according to the relevant provisions applicable to the court hearing the case [CCP 275 (5)-(7)].

ITALY

FERRUCCIO AULETTA

Professore ordinario di Diritto processuale civile,
Università degli Studi di Napoli, Federico II, Italia

II.b Briefly describe the highest court (or courts) of your country and indicate its (or their) function within your legal system.

Gli organi di vertice del sistema italiano sono rappresentati dalla Corte costituzionale e dalla Corte di cassazione.

La Corte costituzionale, ai sensi dell'art. 134 Cost., giudica: 1) «sulle controversie relative alla legittimità costituzionale delle leggi e degli atti, aventi forza di legge, dello Stato e delle Regioni»; 2) «sui conflitti di attribuzione tra i poteri dello Stato e su quelli tra lo Stato e le Regioni, e tra le Regioni»; 3) «sulle accuse promosse contro il Presidente della Repubblica, a norma della Costituzione».

Rispetto all'attività giurisdizionale, assume rilevanza la prima funzione della Corte. Fermo infatti il dovere del giudice di merito e di legittimità di cercare, quando sia possibile, un'interpretazione costituzionalmente orientata della norma da applicare (cfr. da ultimo Corte cost. [ord.], 19 dicembre 2012, n. 304, in www.cortecostituzionale.it; e Corte cost. [ord.], 07-03-2012, n. 44, *ibidem*), quando tale interpretazione non sia rinvenibile, il sindacato di costituzionalità è devoluto esclusivamente alla Corte costituzionale.

Per tale funzione la Corte non può essere adita in via diretta dall'interessato, ma soltanto in via "incidentale" (o, se si preferisce, "indiretta"). Ciò avviene a seguito di un atto di rimessione, posto in essere dall'autorità giurisdizionale – compresi gli arbitri rituali (cfr. Corte cost., 28-11-2001, n. 376, *ibidem*) – dinanzi alla quale pende il giudizio, previo esame della rilevanza e della non manifesta infondatezza della questione di legittimità costituzionale, rilevata d'ufficio o sollevata da una delle parti (cfr. art. 1, L. costituzionale 9 febbraio 1948, n. 1; ed art. 23, L. 11 marzo 1953, n. 87).

La Corte di Cassazione è l'organo giurisdizionale supremo. Le sue attribuzioni risultano dall'art. 65 del R.D. 30 gennaio 1941, n. 12 (Ordinamento giudiziario). Secondo questa norma la Corte è «organo supremo della giustizia, assicura l'esatta osservanza e l'uniforme interpretazione della legge, l'unità del diritto oggettivo nazionale» (cd. funzione nomofilattica). La Corte di Cassazione, inoltre, assicura «il rispetto dei limiti delle diverse giurisdizioni». La Corte ha sede a Roma ed ha giurisdizione su tutto il territorio dello Stato.

Si tratta di un giudice di legittimità, al quale è proponibile un'impugnazione a critica vincolata (per i motivi di ricorso cfr., per le controversie civili, l'art. 360 c.p.c. e l'art. 111, 7°co., Cost.; avverso le decisioni del Consiglio di Stato o della Corte dei Conti il ricorso è tuttavia ammesso soltanto per motivi inerenti alla giurisdizione, cfr. art. 111, 8°co., Cost.). Di conseguenza, la decisione nel merito è consentita soltanto quando non siano necessari ulteriori accertamenti di fatto (cfr., sempre per le controversie civili, l'art. 384, 2°co., c.p.c.).

III. JUDICIAL DECISION MAKING

(a) Have you observed a similar phenomenon in your judicial system? If so, please identify the area(s) of law in which this has occurred. (Please do not limit yourself to questions involving jurisdiction.)

Il sistema normativo italiano – fermo il ruolo delle norme costituzionali, talora anch'esse immediatamente precettive – è fondato su norme di dettaglio. Non si assiste, dunque, alla posizione e successiva specificazione di regole generali, né le autorità giudiziarie applicano il sistema dei *multi-prong tests* al fine di applicare e specificare la regola generale.

L'applicazione di regole generali può tuttavia divenire necessaria, ma con funzioni differenti.

Un primo caso è rappresentato dal ricorso ai principi generali dell'ordinamento per colmare una lacuna normativa (lacuna apparente, vista la presunzione di completezza dell'ordinamento). In tal caso si può risalire, attraverso il meccanismo dell'*analogia iuris*, ai principi generali dell'ordinamento, al fine di ricavare la regola applicabile al caso concreto non espressamente disciplinato.

Un secondo caso consiste nell'applicazione dei cd. "principi informatori della materia", vale a dire i principi a cui il legislatore si è ispirato nel dettare la disciplina di una determinata materia. Questi principi possono essere invocati come un limite non superabile dal giudice, come avviene nel giudizio di equità reso dal giudice di pace ai sensi dell'art. 113 c.p.c. (cfr. Cass. civ., sez. III, 14-07-2011, n. 15460, sulla scia di Corte costituzionale 6 luglio 2004, n. 206; v. ora l'art. 339, 3°co., c.p.c., che nel testo vigente, come sostituito dall'art. 1 del decreto legislativo 2 febbraio 2006, n. 40, parla di principi *regolatori* della materia).

Nei due casi appena descritti – *analogia iuris* e *principi informatori della materia* – non si assiste alla specificazione di un principio generale; piuttosto si ricorre a questo o per colmare una lacuna dell'ordinamento o per verificarne l'osservanza.

Un' ipotesi simile al meccanismo esposto *sub* III. si potrebbe invece rinvenire, nell' ordinamento italiano, con riferimento alle cd. "norme elastiche" (o "concetti giuridici indeterminati" o "clausole generali"). Si può pensare al concetto di "buona fede" di cui all'art. 1337 c.c. (cfr. Cass. civ., sez. III, 08-10-2008, n. 24795, in *Giust. civ.*, 2010, I, 149; v. anche Cass. civ., sez. II, 01-04-2008, n. 8449, in *Giust. civ.*, 2009, I, 1069); o, in materia di lavoro, al concetto di "giusta causa" di licenziamento *ex* art. 2119 c.c. (o di proporzionalità della sanzione disciplinare *ex* art. 2106 c.c., cfr. Cass. civ., sez. lav., 31-01-2012, n. 1403, in *Notiziario giurisprudenza lav.*, 2012, 190); o ancora, in materia di concorrenza, alla definizione di "mercato rilevante" (cfr. C. Stato, sez. VI, 20-05-2011, n. 3013, in *Giur. comm.*, 2012, II, 615).

(b) If you have observed this phenomenon, does it sometimes occur that the judicially developed tests limit the principles that the tests purport to articulate?

Per la concreta applicazione delle cd. "norme elastiche" (o "concetti giuridici indeterminati" o "clausole generali") non si utilizzano *tests* a tal fine preordinati, ma si compie una valutazione *ad hoc* in relazione al singolo caso. È rispetto al caso concreto che si compie la specificazione della clausola generale e la valutazione della sua applicabilità. In particolare, l'opera della Corte di cassazione rispetto a tali norme si manifesta, in quanto giudice di legittimità, nel controllo sulla corretta specificazione (o, meglio, sul riempimento) della norma elastica, sulla base di una censura per violazione di legge *ex* art. 360, n. 3, c.p.c.; ma entro certi limiti è consentita la censura anche per insufficiente o contradditoria motivazione (art. 360, n. 5, c.p.c.).

Per un caso concreto, basti il seguente, in tema di "giusta causa" di licenziamento: «Cass. civ., sez. lav., 12-08-2009, n. 18247. La giusta causa di licenziamento, quale fatto «che non consenta la prosecuzione, anche provvisoria, del rapporto», configura una norma elastica, in quanto costituisce una disposizione di contenuto precettivo ampio e polivalente destinato ad essere progressivamente precisato, nell'estrinsecarsi della funzione nomofilattica della corte di cassazione, fino alla formazione del diritto vivente mediante puntualizzazioni, di carattere generale ed astratto; a tale processo non partecipa, invece, la soluzione del caso singolo, se non nella misura in cui da essa sia possibile estrarre una puntualizzazione della norma mediante una massima di giurisprudenza; ne consegue che, mentre l' integrazione giurisprudenziale della nozione di *giusta causa* a livello generale ed astratto si colloca sul piano normativo, e consente, pertanto, una verifica di legittimità sotto il profilo della violazione di legge, l' applicazione in concreto del più specifico canone integrativo, così ricostruito, rientra nella valutazione di fatto devoluta al giudice di merito, e non è censurabile in sede di legittimità se non per vizio di motivazione insufficiente o contraddittoria».

IV. JURISDICTION

(d)(i) Would your country exercise jurisdiction over the foreign manufacturer on a claim against it by the injured party?

Sì.

(ii) On which provisions and/or case law do you base your answer? If your highest court has addressed this or a similar issue, please describe how the court solved it.

Si devono distinguere due ipotesi, ma in entrambe si può affermare la giurisdizione italiana.

A) Se si tratta di una controversia tra persone domiciliate nel territorio di uno Stato membro dell'Unione Europea, trova applicazione il Regolamento CE n. 44/2001 del Consiglio, del 22 dicembre 2000, concernente la competenza giurisdizionale, il riconoscimento e l'esecuzione delle decisioni in materia civile e commerciale (o, qualora sia ancora applicabile in ragione dello Stato coinvolto, v. la Convenzione di Bruxelles del 1968, di cui anche *infra*).

L'art. 5, n. 3, del Reg. 44/2001 afferma che in materia di illeciti civili dolosi o colposi, la persona domiciliata nel territorio di uno Stato membro può essere convenuta «davanti al giudice del luogo *in cui l'evento dannoso è avvenuto* o può avvenire». Lo stesso criterio opera se si tratta di azione di risarcimento del danno nascente da reato (cfr. art. 5, n. 4, Reg. cit.; se si tratta di consumatore, v. invece gli artt. 15 e spec. 16, n. 1, Reg. cit., che consente di attribuire la competenza giurisdizionale al giudice del luogo in cui è domiciliato il consumatore).

Ipotesi B): Se non ricorre il requisito soggettivo di applicazione del Reg. 44/2001 (e sempre che non ricorra una convenzione bilaterale tra gli Stati interessati), si applicano le norme di diritto internazionale privato dettate dalla L. 31 maggio 1995, n. 218.

In particolare, ai sensi dell'art. 3, 2°co., L. 218/1995, in combinato disposto con le norme della Convenzione di Bruxelles del 1968 da esso richiamate, nel caso di specie sussisterebbe la giurisdizione italiana. Risulta infatti applicabile il criterio di competenza giurisdizionale fissato dall'art. 5, n. 3, della Convenzione, che consente, in «materia di delitti o quasi-delitti», di adire il giudice del luogo in cui l'evento dannoso è avvenuto.

Infine, è utile evidenziare che nella fattispecie concreta proposta il difetto di giurisdizione dovrebbe essere eccepito dal convenuto; in mancanza si consoliderebbe la giurisdizione italiana (cfr. art. 4, 1°co., L. 218/1995).

(iii) If you need additional facts to answer this question, please indicate which type of facts you would need and why.

(iv) Additional comments. Express any additional comment you may have on the solutions offered by your system and the U.S. system.

Le riflessioni compiute sono ovviamente condizionate dalla differente forma di governo.

V. JUSTICIABILITY

(d)(i) How would the courts of your country resolve the question of whether the mother should be allowed to proceed with her claim?

Nell'ordinamento italiano l'obbligo di mantenimento del genitore è subordinato al riconoscimento del figlio (cfr. art. 261 c.c.; e art. 258 c.c.). Ne discende che per poter attribuire rilevanza penale alla condotta è necessario, in primo luogo, che vi sia stato il riconoscimento del figlio naturale da parte del genitore. Così sorto l'obbligo di mantenimento, la sua violazione può integrare il reato di "Violazione degli obblighi di assistenza familiare", previsto dall'art. 570 c.p.

Se, quindi, si trattasse di un figlio naturale riconosciuto, si potrebbe configurare nell' ordinamento italiano il reato di cui all'art. 570 c.p. (perseguibile a querela della persona offesa e punito con la reclusione fino a un anno o con la multa da euro 103 a euro 1.032).

La valutazione compiuta dalla Corte Suprema degli Stati Uniti, che nel caso di specie ha ritenuto non sussistente la "justiciability", non sembra poter trovare riscontro presso il giudice italiano. In particolare, il riferimento della Corte Suprema all'inidoneità della misura a garantire il futuro adempimento del padre non precluderebbe la sanzionabilità della condotta già tenuta (sia dal punto di vista penale, sia per i danni civili, materiali ed eventualmente morali). In una fattispecie come quella esposta resterebbero distinti il profilo civilistico da quello penalistico.

Dal punto di vista del diritto civile, la madre – sempre che il padre abbia riconosciuto il figlio naturale – potrebbe agire per il credito di mantenimento (v. anche la recente unificazione dello *status* di figlio ad opera della L. 10 dicembre 2012, n. 219, che ha in più parti modificato il codice civile).

Dal momento che questa prestazione ha natura fungibile, potrà procedere, dopo aver ottenuto la condanna del genitore inadempiente, all'espropriazione forzata. Per le prestazioni future, visto che l'obbligazione di mantenimento si concretizza in una prestazione di durata a carattere periodico, potrà richiedere un sequestro *ex* art. 156 c.c. a garanzia dei crediti di mantenimento futuri (cfr. Cass. civ., sez. I, 02-02-2012, n. 1518, in *Foro it.*, 2012, I, 1467). Il sequestro può, in tal modo, rappresentare il mezzo per garantire l'adempimento futuro del padre, vista l'inapplicabilità dell'art. 614 bis c.p.c., che contempla uno strumento compulsivo volto a garantire l'attuazione di un *facere* "infungibile".

Resta invece distinto il profilo penale, fondato sulla già ricordata fattispecie delittuosa di cui all'art. 570 c.p.

(ii) On which provisions and/or case law do you base your answer? If your highest court has addressed this or a similar issue, please describe how the court solved it.

Vedi la risposta al punto precedente ed in particolare, tra gli interventi della giurisprudenza, Cass. pen., sez. VI, 28-03-2012, n. 15952, che esamina le condizioni affinché la fattispecie dell'art. 570 c.p. sia applicabile al padre naturale; e la già citata Cass., sez. I, 02-02-2012, n. 1518, che contiene utili spunti in tema di sequestro *ex* art. 156 c.c. ed espropriazione forzata.

(iii) If you need additional facts to answer this question, please indicate which type of facts would you need and why.

(iv) Does your legal system require the same range of considerations to determine whether a party can bring a claim? Are those considerations statutory or constitutional?

Per le azioni civili operano le note condizioni dell'azione: la legittimazione ad agire, l'interesse ad agire e la possibilità giuridica (intesa come l'esistenza di una norma che tuteli la posizione giuridica vantata).

Rispetto alla valutazione di *justiciability*, alcuni elementi – *standing* e *ripeness* – sono in parte coperti dalla nostra valutazione sull'interesse ad agire, inteso come: a) manifestazione di bisogno di tutela giudiziale; b) e come idoneità del provvedimento richiesto al fine di reintegrare la posizione giuridica lesa attraverso il tipo di tutela richiesta. Se l'interesse ad agire è inteso nei modi appena descritti, esso è in grado di coprire anche il profilo del "mootness", perchè, quale condizione dell'azione, l'interesse ad agire deve sussistere al momento della decisione del giudice.

ITALY

CHIARA MASTRACCHIO

PhD Student, Università degli Studi di Roma, La Sapienza, Italy, Attorney at Law

II.b. Briefly describe the highest court (or courts) of your country and indicate its (or their) function within your legal system.

Le Corti Supreme dell'ordinamento italiano sono la Corte di Cassazione e la Corte Costituzionale.

La Corte di Cassazione è l'organo posto al vertice dell'ordinamento giudiziario italiano ordinario.

Si tratta di un unico ufficio giudiziario[1], che costituisce l'ultimo grado di giudizio per la giurisdizione ordinaria (dopo il Tribunale – organo di primo grado- e la Corte d'Appello – organo di secondo grado), deputato al controllo della *sola legittimità*, senza poter conoscere i fatti storici della causa.

Le funzioni della Corte di Cassazione sono indicate dall'art. 65 l. ord. giud. (r.d. 30 gennaio 1941 n. 12), a norma del quale "la Corte Suprema di Cassazione, quale organo supremo della giustizia, assicura l'esatta osservanza e l'uniforme interpretazione della legge, l'unità del diritto oggettivo nazionale, il rispetto dei limiti delle diverse giurisdizioni; regola i conflitti di competenza e di attribuzioni, ed adempie gli altri compiti ad essa conferiti dalla legge".

La funzione di garantire "l'esatta osservanza e l'uniforme interpretazione della legge" ha le sue radici nel pensiero di Piero Calamandrei ed è quella che ha creato maggiori difficoltà interpretative[2].

[1] Dal 1923, data della unificazione della Corte di Cassazione; fino a tale data esistevano invece cinque Corti di cassazione, distribuite in diverse città del territorio nazionale. V. per tutti C. CONSOLO, *Spiegazioni di diritto processuale civile*, III, Torino 2012, 372 ss.; N. PICARDI, *L'unificazione della Corte di cassazione*, *Riv. trim. dir. proc. civ.* 2012, 721 ss., 739.

[2] La letteratura italiana al riguardo è vastissima; oltre alla classica opera di P. CALAMANDREI, *La Cassazione civile*, Firenze 1920, si considerino, tra i tanti, M. TARUFFO, *Il Vertice ambiguo, Saggi sulla cassazione civile*, Bologna 1991; A. PANZAROLA, *La Cassazione civile giudice del merito*, Torino 2005; e da ultimo G. F. RICCI, *Il giudizio civile di cassazione*, Torino 2013.

Si ritiene comunemente che la Corte da un lato sia l'organo della "*nomofilachia*" (dal greco νόμος- φυλαξ), e debba in tale qualità controllare che i giudici di grado inferiore (i giudici *di merito*) abbiano correttamente interpretato ed applicato la legge; dall'altro debba garantire che l'*interpretazione* della legge sia *uniforme* su tutto il territorio nazionale, in modo da assicurare il rispetto del principio di eguaglianza sancito dall'art. 3 della Costituzione italiana.

Attraverso lo svolgimento di queste funzioni, si soddisfano esigenze di tutela di *coerenza dell'ordinamento* (si parla in proposito di tutela dello *ius constitutionis*); le decisioni della Corte di cassazione, infatti, pur non avendo efficacia vincolante per i giudici di grado inferiore, hanno una notevole efficacia persuasiva, ed è molto probabile che la interpretazione di una norma di diritto operata dalla Corte sia seguita dagli altri giudici nella risoluzione delle controversie in cui si ripresenti la necessità di applicare quella norma.

D'altro canto, la Corte decidendo sul ricorso proposto dalla parte rende *giustizia nel caso concreto*, eliminando eventuali errori che si sono verificati nelle precedenti fasi del giudizio (si parla in proposito di tutela dello *ius litigatoris*)[3].

Alla Corte di cassazione le parti possono proporre ricorso contro le sentenze dei giudici ordinari emesse in grado di appello ed in unico grado, sebbene esclusivamente per i motivi previsti dalla legge [elencati dall'art. 360 del codice di procedura civile italiano: motivi attinenti alla giurisdizione, questioni relative alla competenza – ma solo in alcuni casi[4], violazione-falsa applicazione di norme di diritto e di contratti o accordi collettivi nazionali di lavoro, nullità della sentenza o del procedimento e omesso esame circa un fatto decisivo per il giudizio che è stato oggetto di controversia tra le parti[5]].

Si tratta di un potere espressamente previsto anche dalla Costituzione, che all'art. 111 comma 7 stabilisce che "contro le sentenze ... è sempre ammesso ricorso in cassazione per violazione di legge".

[3] Quale dei due interessi debba prevalere o prevalga concretamente è questione discussa in dottrina, e riflette le idee di ciascun interprete in relazione al ruolo che la Corte ha o dovrebbe avere; il tema è complesso e non è qui possibile affrontarlo compiutamente. Recentemente sul punto G. VERDE, *Jus litigatoris e jus constitutionis*, in *Il difficile rapporto tra giudice e legge*, Napoli 2012, 11 ss.

[4] Ossia, come dice la norma, "quando non è prescritto il regolamento di competenza".

[5] Questo ultimo motivo di ricorso è stato modificato dalla l. n. 134 del 7 agosto 2012. Anteriormente a tale modifica il motivo era così formulato: "omessa, insufficiente o contraddittoria motivazione circa un punto decisivo della controversia, prospettato dalle parti o rilevabile d'ufficio". Su tale intervento si veda B. SASSANI, *Legittimità, "nomofilachia" e motivazione della sentenza: l'incontrollabilità in cassazione del ragionamento del giudice*, *www. judicium.it.*

Proposta l'impugnazione contro la sentenza, la Corte, se ritiene che l'impugnazione sia fondata, accoglie il ricorso e "cassa" la sentenza, ossia annulla la sentenza impugnata e di norma[6] rinvia la causa ad un giudice dello stesso grado di quello che aveva pronunciato la sentenza (es: il giudice di appello); il giudice del rinvio deve attenersi al principio di diritto enunciato dalla Corte ed applicarlo ai fatti di causa, in modo da giungere ad una decisione nel merito.

La Corte è inoltre l'organo davanti a cui sono impugnabili le decisioni di giudici appartenenti a *diversi ordini giurisdizionali* ("speciali", per distinguerli dalla giurisdizione ordinaria).

Dinanzi alla Corte possono infatti essere impugnate le decisioni dei giudici tributari, amministrativi e contabili, sebbene le pronunce di ultima istanza dei giudici amministrativi (Consiglio di Stato) e contabili (Corte dei Conti) possano essere impugnate con ricorso per cassazione *solo per motivi attinenti alla giurisdizione* (così prescrive l'art. 111 ultimo comma della Costituzione).

A questo va aggiunto che la giurisprudenza della Corte di cassazione, muovendo dall'art. 111 comma 7 della Costituzione, che come detto prevede che "contro le sentenze e contro i provvedimenti sulla libertà personale, pronunciati dagli organi giurisdizionali o speciali, è sempre ammesso il ricorso in cassazione *per violazione di legge*", fin dal 1953[7] ha elaborato il concetto di "sentenza in senso sostanziale", consentendo il ricorso avverso tutti quei provvedimenti che, pur avendo forma diversa dalla sentenza statuiscano su diritti soggettivi o status (e quindi presentino i caratteri della *decisorietà*) e non siano in altro modo impugnabili o riesaminabili. (quindi abbiano i connotati della *definitività*).

Il ricorso avverso tali provvedimenti è chiamato *ricorso straordinario* in cassazione.

Nel 2006, tra l'altro, il legislatore italiano ha preso atto di tale orientamento giurisprudenziale ed ha previsto, all'art. 360 ultimo comma c.p.c. che ai provvedimenti diversi dalla sentenza per cui è ammesso il ricorso per cassazione *per violazione di legge* si applichi il primo comma del medesimo articolo – che indica i motivi di ricorso-, in tal modo consentendo il ricorso straordinario per tutti i motivi per cui è ammesso quello ordinario.

[6] È possibile – difatti- che la Corte cassi la sentenza impugnata ma senza rinvio (si tratta dei casi indicati dall'art. 382 comma 3 del codice di procedura civile: difetto assoluto di giurisdizione, improponibilità della domanda ed improseguibilità del processo. È poi possibile che la Corte accolga il ricorso e decida la causa "nel merito", applicando cioè il principio di diritto ai fatti di causa, così come ricostruiti nel giudizio di merito; il che può accadere solo quando "non sono necessari ulteriori accertamenti di fatto" (l'ipotesi è prevista dall'art. 384 del c.p.c.).

[7] Con la pronuncia a S.U. n. 2593.

L'effettivo adempimento dei compiti assegnati dalla legge alla Corte è da diverso tempo in crisi, soprattutto a causa dell'enorme numero di ricorsi proposti annualmente[8], tanto che il legislatore italiano è intervenuto recentemente più volte introducendo strumenti in diversi modi diretti a ridurre la possibilità di accesso alla Corte.

La Corte Costituzionale è l'organo deputato al giudizio di legittimità costituzionale delle leggi e degli atti aventi forza di legge dello Stato e delle Regioni; ma tra le sue funzioni vi è anche quella di giudicare sui conflitti di attribuzione tra poteri dello Stato e tra lo Stato e le Regioni, sui giudizi di accusa al Presidente della Repubblica per le ipotesi di alto tradimento e di attentato alla Costituzione, e sull'ammissibilità del referendum abrogativo[9].

III. JUDICIAL DECISION MAKING

III.a Un fenomeno analogo a quello indicato sembra riscontrabile, ad esempio:

1) nella interpretazione che la Corte di Cassazione ha fornito dell'istituto del *ricorso incidentale*.

Il ricorso incidentale in cassazione (art. 371 c.p.c.) è uno strumento che consente al soccombente parziale su *domanda* di impugnare la sentenza nella parte in cui gli ha dato torto ed al soccombente su *questione* pregiudiziale di rito o preliminare di merito, pur vittorioso nel merito, di riproporre tali questioni dinanzi alla Corte.

La Corte di Cassazione ritiene che il ricorso incidentale che ha ad oggetto questioni pregiudiziali di rito (giurisdizione compresa) o preliminari di merito che siano state oggetto di decisione esplicita o implicita (se possibile) nel giudizio di merito sia *necessariamente condizionato*[10], cioè possa essere esaminato (sempre, e non solamente nel caso in cui lo richieda la parte) unicamente in caso di positiva valutazione sulla fondatezza del ricorso principale.

2) nella interpretazione fornita dell'art. 269 comma 3 c.p.c.

Il codice di procedura civile italiano prevede che se il convenuto intende chiamare in causa un terzo deve farne menzione nel primo atto difensivo

[8] La crisi della Cassazione è da tempo avvertita e segnalata dalla dottrina, come dagli stessi magistrati della Suprema Corte e l'eccessivo numero dei ricorsi, se non è la sola, è sicuramente una delle cause principali "dei disservizi dell'istituto" (così G.F. RICCI, *Il giudizio civile*, cit., 38).

[9] Così per tutti P. RESCIGNO, *Corso di diritto pubblico*, Bologna 2012, 461 ss.

[10] Così Cass. sez. un. 6 marzo 2009 n. 5456, in *Riv. dir. proc.*, 2010, 191 ss. con nota di A. PANZAROLA, *Sul condizionamento de jure del ricorso incidentale per cassazione del vincitore nel merito.*

(la comparsa di risposta) e chiedere al giudice lo spostamento dell'udienza; ai sensi dell'art. 269 comma 3 del codice "il giudice *provvede* con decreto a fissare la data della nuova udienza".

La Corte ha ritenuto che "In tema di chiamata in causa di un terzo su istanza di parte, al di fuori delle ipotesi di litisconsorzio necessario di cui all'art. 102 c.p.c., *è discrezionale il provvedimento del giudice di fissazione di una nuova udienza* per consentire la citazione del terzo, chiesta tempestivamente dal convenuto ai sensi dell'art. 269 c.p.c., come modificato dalla l. 26 novembre 1990 n. 353; conseguentemente, qualora sia stata chiesta dal convenuto la chiamata in causa del terzo, in manleva o in regresso, il giudice può rifiutare di fissare una nuova prima udienza per la costituzione del terzo, motivando la propria scelta sulla base di esigenze di economia processuale e di ragionevole durata del processo"[11].

Il fenomeno si inserisce nel tema più generale del potere discrezionale del giudice, che la dottrina italiana ha osservato non da ora essere fenomeno in espansione[12], sia pure in contesti e con finalità differenti (si pensi al potere discrezionale del giudice nei confronti delle clausole generali come "buona fede" o "giusta causa"). In questo quadro sembra potersi collocare anche un recente intervento del legislatore italiano attuato con la l. 7 agosto 2012 n. 134, che ha introdotto nel codice di procedura civile quello che è stato subito definito il "filtro in appello"[13].

Si tratta dell'art. 348 *bis*, a norma del quale "Fuori dei casi in cui deve essere dichiarata con sentenza l'inammissibilità o l'improcedibilità dell'appello, l'impugnazione è dichiarata inammissibile dal giudice competente quando non ha una ***ragionevole probabilità*** di essere accolta"[14].

[11] Cass. civ. s. u. 23 febbraio 2010 n. 4309, in Foro It. 2010, I, 1794, con nota critica di R. CAPONI, D. DALFINO, A. PROTO PISANI, G. SCARSELLI, *In difesa delle norme processuali*.

[12] Così N. PICARDI, *Manuale del processo civile*, Milano 2013, 124 ss.

[13] E che fa seguito ad un precedente intervento legislativo (l. n. 69 del 2009) operato sul giudizio di cassazione, con la introduzione di quello che è conosciuto come "filtro in cassazione". Questa legge ha inserito nel codice di procedura civile l'art. 360 *bis*, che prevede un "filtro" al ricorso per cassazione, consistente in ciò, che il ricorso è inammissibile: "1) quando il provvedimento impugnato ha deciso le questioni di diritto in modo conforme alla giurisprudenza della Corte e l'esame dei motivi non offre elementi per confermare o mutare l'orientamento della stessa; 2) quando è manifestamente infondata la censura relativa alla violazione dei principi del giusto processo". Con la stessa legge è stata introdotta una nuova sezione della Corte di cassazione civile (sezione VI) che ha lo specifico compito di verificare se il ricorso è ammissibile, e solo in tal caso "inviarlo" ad una delle cinque sezioni civili competenti per le singole materie (es: responsabilità civile, controversie di lavoro, controversie tributarie).

[14] Cfr. A. PANZAROLA, *Tra "filtro" in appello e "doppia conforme": alcune considerazioni a margine della l. n. 134 del 2012, Il giusto processo civile* 2013, 89 ss. il quale evidenzia come il filtro attribuisca al giudice di appello un ampio potere discrezionale. Potere che, come insegna

III. b *If you have observed this phenomenon, does it sometimes occur that the judicially developed tests limit the principles that the tests purport to articulate?* V. quanto detto *retro sub* III a

IV. JURISDICTION

IV d. (i) *Would your country exercise jurisdiction over the foreign manufacturer on a claim against it by the injured party?*

Si.

IV d. *(ii) On which provisions and/or case law do you base your answer? If your highest court has addressed this or a similar issue, please describe how the court solved it.*

La giurisdizione italiana non è universale ed incontra dei limiti "esterni"[15] ogni volta in cui la giurisdizione appartiene ad un *giudice sovranazionale* ovvero ad un *giudice di un altro Stato,* appartenente o meno all'Unione Europea.

Le norme che regolano i limiti "esterni" della giurisdizione civile italiana con riferimento alla *giurisdizione di altri Stati* sono contenute principalmente in regolamenti comunitari e nella legge italiana di riforma del sistema di diritto internazionale privato (l. 218/1995).

Queste normative sono ispirate al principio per cui la giurisdizione può essere esercitata solo in ordine a situazioni che presentano un particolare legame con l'ordinamento, legame che si pone come un *titolo di giurisdizione,* e che fa sorgere in capo al giudice adito il potere-dovere di giudicare.

Fatta tale premessa, per rispondere al quesito sottoposto occorre distinguere a seconda che il produttore sia o meno appartenente ad uno Stato dell'Unione Europea.

Ipotesi 1: Il produttore appartiene ad uno Stato membro dell'Unione Europea.

N. PICARDI, *Manuale,* cit., 125, si caratterizza per essere in posizione intermedia tra il potere assoluto –illimitato ed insindacabile – ed il potere vincolato. Si tratta di un potere limitato "in quanto il giudice nel momento della scelta tra le diverse opzioni è ancora condizionato da tutta una serie di vincoli, alcuni introdotti da regole legislative e deontologiche, altri da precedenti e da prassi, altri ancora da tradizioni e tecniche risalenti"; "sindacabile" perché il modo in cui il giudice ha esercitato il proprio potere è controllabile in sede di impugnazione, ed a tal fine gioca un ruolo decisivo l'obbligo di motivazione dei provvedimenti giurisdizionali.

[15] Cfr. N. PICARDI, *Manuale,* cit., 52 ss.

Se il produttore appartiene (*rectius*: è domiciliato[16]) in uno Stato membro dell'U.E., la normativa applicabile è quella del REG. CE 22. 12. 2000 n. 44/2001, concernente la competenza giurisdizionale, il riconoscimento e l'esecuzione delle decisioni in materia civile e commerciale.

Il *foro generale* posto da tale normativa comunitaria è quello enunciato all'art. 2 comma 1: le persone domiciliate in uno Stato membro sono convenute – a prescindere dalla loro nazionalità- davanti ai giudici di questo Stato.

Applicando tale regola, lo Stato italiano *non* avrebbe giurisdizione sul produttore straniero (che sia domiciliato in un altro Stato membro).

Tuttavia, accanto al foro generale –applicando il quale non sussisterebbe la giurisdizione del giudice italiano- si rinvengono nel regolamento 44/2001 anche *fori speciali* ad esso alternativi [il rapporto tra tali fori è di regola-eccezione: Corte di Giustizia 27 ottobre 1998, causa C-51/97, Réunion européenne, punto 16; causa C- 440/97 GIE, punti 23 e 24, entrambe riferite alla Convenzione di Bruxelles 27 settembre 1968, sostituita poi dal REG. 44/2001].

La individuazione del foro speciale applicabile tra quelli previsti nel regolamento dipende dalla qualificazione che si attribuisca alla azione esercitata.

Si può ritenere infatti che si tratti

a) di azione di *responsabilità extracontrattuale* nei confronti del produttore. Troverebbe applicazione l'art. 5 n. 3 REG. 44/2001, in base a cui il soggetto domiciliato in uno Stato membro può essere convenuto davanti ai giudici di un altro Stato "in materia di illeciti civili dolosi o colposi". Precisamente può essere convenuto "davanti al giudice del luogo in cui l'evento dannoso è avvenuto o può avvenire".

In base a tale norma, dunque, l'acquirente – in ipotesi domiciliato in Italia- potrebbe agire nei confronti del produttore straniero (ad es. tedesco) *davanti ai giudici italiani* (i giudici dello Stato in cui si è verificato il danno);

b) di controversia in materia di contratti conclusi con i *consumatori*, disciplinati dalla sezione 4 del Reg. 44/2001.

Nella fattispecie indicata, il soggetto che ha subìto un danno potrebbe essere considerato un consumatore (a tal fine sarebbe necessario che egli abbia

[16] I criteri per stabilire se un convenuto è o meno domiciliato in uno Stato membro sono stabiliti dagli artt. 59 e 60 del REG. 44/2001 e riguardano sia le persone fisiche che gli enti, dotati o meno di personalità giuridica, di carattere associativo e non. V. F. MOSCONI - C. CAMPIGLIO, *Diritto internazionale privato e processuale*, Torino 2010, 57.
Il Reg. 44/2001 sarà sostituito, a partire dal gennaio 2015, dal Reg. 1215 del 2012.

acquistato il bene "per un uso che possa considerarsi estraneo alla sua attività professionale": così l'art. 15 del REG. 44/2001. Per la definizione di contratto concluso con un consumatore v. Corte di Giustizia C. E. 20 gennaio 2005, causa C-464/01, Gruber).

In tal caso, potrebbe ritenersi che la fattispecie rientri nella situazione descritta dall'art. 15 lett. c, ossia che si tratti di un contratto "concluso con una persona le cui attività commerciali o professionali si svolgono nello Stato membro in cui è domiciliato il consumatore o sono dirette, *con qualsiasi mezzo*, verso tale Stato membro o verso una pluralità di Stati che comprende tale Stato membro, purché il contratto rientri nell'ambito di dette attività" (corsivo mio).

Si potrebbe ritenere che si tratti di un contratto concluso con un produttore le cui attività commerciali si sono svolte - per il tramite dell'agente straniero- in una serie di Stati membri, tra cui quello italiano.

In questa ipotesi si prevede all'art. 16 del citato Regolamento che l'azione del consumatore contro l'altra parte del contratto possa essere proposta davanti ai giudici dello Stato membro in cui è domiciliata l'altra parte o *davanti ai giudici del luogo in cui è domiciliato il consumatore.*

In entrambe le ipotesi individuate – *sub* a) e *sub* b)- si tratta di *fori facoltativi*, che si aggiungono al foro generale indicato all'art 2 del REG. 44/2001 (v. *supra*), che consentirebbero al consumatore di agire davanti ai giudici del proprio Stato membro (l'Italia).

Ipotesi 2: Il produttore non appartiene ad un paese membro dell'Unione Europea.

Lo stesso art. 4 del REG. 44/2001 stabilisce che "se il convenuto non è domiciliato nel territorio di uno Stato membro, la competenza è disciplinata, in ciascuno Stato membro, dalla legge di tale Stato, salva l'applicazione degli articoli 22 e 23[17]".

La legge italiana applicabile è la l. 31 maggio 1995 n. 218, di riforma del sistema italiano di diritto internazionale privato; l'ambito della giurisdizione italiana è delimitato dall'art. 3, a norma del quale la giurisdizione sussiste "se il convenuto è domiciliato o residente in Italia o vi ha un rappresentante che sia autorizzato a stare in giudizio a norma dell'art. 77 del codice di procedura civile o negli altri casi in cui è prevista dalla legge".

In base a questa norma, il produttore straniero che ha il proprio domicilio-sede in uno Stato estero *non* potrebbe essere convenuto davanti ai giudici italiani.

[17] Sono i casi di competenza giurisdizionale esclusiva – tra cui non rientra la fattispecie in esame- e di proroga della competenza.

Il medesimo articolo stabilisce tuttavia che la giurisdizione italiana sussiste in base ai criteri stabiliti dalle sezioni 2, 3, 4 del titolo II della Convenzione di Bruxelles 27 settembre 1968 e successive modifiche in vigore per l'Italia *anche se il convenuto non è domiciliato nel territorio di uno Stato contraente*.

Il riferimento alla Convenzione di Bruxelles è stato tradizionalmente letto dalla dottrina come riferimento al Reg. CE 44/2001; tuttavia la Corte di Cassazione italiana (Cass. S. U. 21 ottobre 2009 n. 22239) ha ritenuto che il richiamo debba interpretarsi letteralmente, e sia dunque relativo alla sola Convenzione di Bruxelles.

In ogni caso – sia che si intenda come richiamo al Regolamento, sia che si intenda come richiamo alla Convenzione- anche qualora il convenuto sia domiciliato in uno Stato non appartenente all'Unione Europea, potrebbe trovare applicazione il foro facoltativo di cui si è detto *sub* a) e l'acquirente *potrebbe agire davanti ai giudici italiani*[18]. Più problematico sarebbe invece radicare la giurisdizione se l'azione si qualificasse come *sub* b), avendo per tale aspetto il Reg. 44/2001 ampliato la tutela del consumatore rispetto alla Convenzione, che non contiene una norma come quella dell'art. 15 lettera c del Reg. 44/2001.

(iii) If you need additional facts to answer this question, please indicate which type of facts you would need and why.

Non occorrono ulteriori fatti.

(iv) Additional comments

Non ci sono commenti.

V. JUSTICIABILITY

IV(i) *How would the courts of your country resolve the question of whether the mother should be allowed to proceed with her claim?*

In una situazione analoga a quella descritta nel questionario, ossia se una legge prescrivesse l'obbligo di mantenimento solamente verso i figli legittimi, qualora la madre del figlio illegittimo agisse in sede civile chiedendo la condanna del padre, un giudice civile italiano da un lato potrebbe ritenere che si tratti di una tutela non accordabile, perché non prevista dalla legge[19];

[18] Troverebbe applicazione l'art. 5 n. 3 della Convenzione secondo cui in materia di delitti o quasi delitti il convenuto domiciliato in uno Stato contraente può essere citato dinanzi al giudice del luogo in cui l'evento dannoso è avvenuto.

[19] E' come se, ad esempio, si fosse richiesto al giudice di dichiarare lo scioglimento del matrimonio prima della introduzione in Italia, della l. 898/1970. Egli non avrebbe potuto accordare la tutela richiesta, proprio per la mancanza di una legge che riconosceva tale diritto.

dall'altro, visti i profili di incostituzionalità di una normativa di tal genere, per le discriminazioni che crea tra figli legittimi e non e quindi per la violazione del principio di eguaglianza, verosimilmente solleverebbe una questione di legittimità costituzionale dinanzi alla Corte costituzionale.

In Italia, tuttavia, una norma costituzionale (l'art. 30) sancisce l'obbligo di mantenere, istruire ed educare i figli anche se nati fuori dal matrimonio, disposizione interpretata tra l'altro da una parte della dottrina nel senso di ritenere che l'obbligo sorga per il solo fatto della procreazione[20]; recentemente, inoltre, una legge ordinaria, la n. 219 del 2012, ha compiuto un importante passo avanti nel processo di parificazione dei figli nati dal matrimonio ovvero al di fuori di esso, rendendo unico lo *status* di figlio.

(ii) On which provisions/or case law do you base your answer? If your highest court has addressed this or a similar issue, please describe how the court solved it.

V. IL PUNTO PRECEDENTE

(iii) If you need additional facts to answer this question, please indicate which type of facts would you need and why.

Non occorrono ulteriori fatti

(iv) Does your legal system require the same range of considerations to determine whether a party can bring a claim? Are those considerations statutory or constitutional?

Il problema della tutela di diritti che si assumono lesi da una legge incostituzionale si è posto, ad esempio, in relazione alla adozione di misure cautelari (in particolare, di provvedimenti di urgenza *ex* art. 700 cod. proc. civ.): il caso è quello di chi richiede l'emissione di un provvedimento d'urgenza per la tutela di una situazione soggettiva che non è ancora assurta a livello di "diritto soggettivo", ma che lo sarebbe se una legge ordinaria fosse dichiarata incostituzionale. Ci si è chiesti come debba operare il giudice in una situazione di questo tipo. Da un lato difatti c'è la necessità di provvedere in via urgente, dall'altro la competenza esclusiva della Corte costituzionale a pronunciarsi sulla (il)legittimità della legge. Del resto se il giudice adottasse la misura urgente, è stato notato (da ultimo cfr. A. PANZAROLA, *I provvedimenti di urgenza dell'art. 700 c.p.c.*, in *I procedimenti cautelari*, a cura di A. CARRATTA, Bologna 2013) come la questione di legittimità verrebbe privata del requisito della *rilevanza*, e dunque sarebbe destinata ad una pronuncia di inammissibilità da parte della Corte. La soluzione suggerita dalla Corte costituzionale (C. Cost., 18 giugno 1997, n. 183; 10 gennaio 2000, n. 4, in *Foro it.*, 2000, I, 1754; 12 ottobre 1990, n. 440, in *Giur. cost.*, 1990, 2652; Id., 27 gennaio 1995, n. 30, ivi, 1995, 331 ss.) è quella di ammettere che il giudice della cautela possa pronunciarsi in via interinale (proprio per far fronte alle esigenze di urgenza sottese alla richiesta misura cautelare) e rimettere la questione alla Corte, salvo poi pronunciarsi definitivamente (seppure sempre in via cautelare) dopo la chiusura dell'incidente di costituzionalità.

[20] Cfr. C.M. BIANCA, *Diritto civile*, II, *La famiglia. Le successioni*, Milano 2005, 345.

Nell'ordinamento giuridico italiano il diritto di agire in giudizio è costituzionalmente garantito dall'art. 24 della Costituzione, a norma del quale "tutti possono agire in giudizio per la tutela dei propri diritti e interessi legittimi".

Premesso ciò, anche nel sistema italiano perché il giudice possa emettere un provvedimento di merito è necessario che sussistano determinati presupposti; la dottrina[21] è solita parlare di "condizioni dell'azione", e vi ricomprende la *legittimazione* e l'*interesse ad agire*.

È legittimato ad agire colui che *si afferma* titolare del diritto per cui si chiede tutela.

La norma di riferimento è l'art. 81 del codice di procedura civile, il quale afferma che "fuori dei casi espressamente previsti dalla legge nessuno può far valere, nel processo, in nome proprio un diritto altrui". Da questa norma si ricavano due nozioni: 1) quella di legittimazione *straordinaria*, che si verifica quando un soggetto agisce nel processo *in nome proprio ma per far valere un diritto altrui* (un esempio è quello dell'azione surrogatoria prevista dall'art. 2900 del codice civile: il creditore di un soggetto – a sua volta creditore di un terzo- agisce in giudizio per far valere il credito che il suo debitore-creditore vanta nei confronti del terzo); 2) quella di legittimazione *ordinaria*, in cui un soggetto agisce in nome proprio per fa valere un proprio diritto.

La legittimazione ad agire discende dal solo fatto che al momento della proposizione della domanda un soggetto *affermi* di essere titolare del diritto dedotto in giudizio; se all'esito del processo egli risulterà non titolare del diritto, la sua domanda sarà rigettata *nel merito*, e non perché il soggetto non era legittimato ad agire[22].

[21] V. per tutti N. PICARDI, *Manuale*, cit., 151 ss.

[22] Così F. P. LUISO, *Diritto processuale civile*, Milano 2009, I, 214 ss. Si riporta una parte della motivazione di una recente sentenza della Corte Suprema di Cassazione (29.01.2013 n. 2046): "In proposito occorre osservare che dalla dottrina e dalla giurisprudenza di legittimità più recenti si ritiene che le *condizioni dell'azione* - possibilità giuridica, interesse ad agire, legittimazione ad agire e contraddire - debbano essere accertate in relazione non alla loro sussistenza effettiva ma *alla loro affermazione con l'atto introduttivo del giudizio*, nell'ambito di una preliminare valutazione formale dell'ipotetica accoglibilità della domanda e, così configuratele, possa parlarsi di condizioni la cui sussistenza deve essere accertata con riferimento al momento della proposizione della domanda stessa; diversamente, l'accertamento non dell'ipotetica titolarità dell'azione ma dell'effettiva titolarità del rapporto controverso, così da lato attivo come da quello passivo, attiene al merito della causa, investendo i concreti requisiti di accoglibilità della domanda e, quindi, la sua fondatezza. In tale sistematica, la legittimazione o titolarità dell'azione costituisce una condizione dell'azione stessa che si concretizza, dal lato attivo, nel diritto potestativo di ottenere dal giudice una decisione di merito e si risolve nel potere di promuovere il giudizio, inteso ad una sentenza, dichiarativa o costitutiva o di condanna, sul rapporto giuridico sostanziale dedotto ad oggetto di controversia indipendentemente dalla sussistenza o meno dell'effettiva titolarità attiva del rapporto stesso in capo all'attore, dacchè si determina in base alla sola affermazione di questi della sua titolarità

La legittimazione straordinaria va distinta dalla *rappresentanza*, perché il rappresentante è colui cha agisce *in nome e per conto* del rappresentato. In questo caso gli effetti dell'attività svolta dal rappresentante si producono direttamente nella sfera giuridica del rappresentato.

La rappresentanza è necessaria nel processo civile quando la persona "non ha il libero esercizio dei diritti che si fanno valere nel processo" (art. 75 codice di procedura civile); un esempio di rappresentanza è proprio quello dei *genitori che agiscono in rappresentanza del figlio minore*.

L'*interesse ad agire* (che dovrebbe corrispondere allo *standing* statunitense) è richiesto espressamente dall'art. 100 del codice di procedura civile, secondo cui "per proporre una domanda o per contraddire alla stessa è necessario avervi interesse".

La dottrina italiana insegna che l'interesse ad agire sussiste ogni volta in cui l'accoglimento nel merito della domanda può apportare una qualche utilità all'attore; di conseguenza non c'è interesse ad agire, e la domanda non può essere decisa nel merito, quando anche se la domanda fosse accolta, la parte che l'ha proposta non ne otterrebbe alcun vantaggio.

Oltre alla legittimazione e all'interesse, chi agisce in giudizio deve chiedere la tutela di una *situazione sostanziale che possa essere tutelata in via giurisdizionale*; nel caso in cui la situazione sostanziale dedotta in giudizio non possa essere tutelata davanti ad alcun giudice (né ordinario né speciale, come ad es. il giudice amministrativo), si parla di *improponibilità oggettiva* della domanda[23].

In relazione al requisito *mootness*, un istituto del processo civile italiano che potrebbe essere considerato analogo è quello della *cessazione della materia del contendere*[24].

della posizione soggettiva attiva dedotta, onde, per verificarne la sussistenza, si deve avere riguardo solo a quanto dallo stesso affermato, prescindendosi dalla veridicità o meno di tale affermazione. In altri termini, l'accertamento della legittimazione attiva deve rivolgersi alla coincidenza, dal lato attivo, tra il soggetto che propone la domanda ed il soggetto che nella domanda stessa è affermato titolare del diritto. Onde, ove di tale coincidenza risultasse il difetto, rimarrebbe ex actis accertato che, indipendentemente dalla rispondenza al vero dei fatti allegati, comunque l'ipotetico diritto azionato non apparterrebbe a colui che agisce e ciò non può che comportare una pronunzia di inammissibilità dell'azione per difetto di titolarità attiva o passiva della stessa (e pluribus, da ultimo, Cass. 29 dicembre 2011 n. 29830; Cass. 15 dicembre 2010 n. 25344; Cass. 25 giugno 2010 n. 15352; Cass. 6 marzo 2008 n. 6132; Cass. 26 gennaio 2006 n. 1507; Cass. 27 giugno 2005 n. 13738)" (corsivo mio).

[23] Seppure la questione è stata ricondotta in passato al difetto assoluto di giurisdizione; cfr. N. PICARDI, *Manuale*, cit., 67.

[24] Su cui cfr., *ex multis*, A. PANZAROLA, voce *Cessazione della materia del contendere (dir. proc. civ.)*, in *Enc. dir.*, vol. Agg. VI, Milano, 2002.

La cessazione della materia del contendere *non* è prevista dalla legge, che tra le ipotesi di chiusura del processo prima della (e senza la) decisione disciplina la rinuncia agli atti del processo (art. 306 codice di procedura civile) e la estinzione per inattività delle parti (art. 307), ma è stata introdotta dalla giurisprudenza (una delle prime pronunce è quella della Corte di Cassazione 19. 01. 1954 n. 92) ed è considerata ormai "diritto vivente".

La cessazione della materia del contendere è stata ravvisata in una molteplicità di ipotesi, quali:

1) l'integrale adempimento o, più in generale, il completo soddisfacimento della pretesa dell'attore (Cass. 29 aprile 1974 n. 1218; Cass. 9 luglio 1997 n. 6226); 2) il riconoscimento dell'avversa pretesa (Cass. 29 aprile 1974 n. 1216; Cass. 9 maggio 1975 n. 1809; Cass. 12 dicembre 1975 n. 4151); 3) la successione di leggi (Cass. 8 luglio 1960 n. 1813); 4) lo scioglimento consensuale del contratto di cui è stata chiesta la risoluzione per inadempimento (Cass. 14 novembre 1977 n. 4923); 5) la morte di uno dei coniugi nel processo di separazione personale (Cass. 12 maggio 1981 n. 1442; Cass. 3 febbraio 1990 n. 740; Cass. 4 aprile 1997 n. 2944) o di cessazione degli effetti civili del matrimonio (Cass. 28 gennaio 1980 n. 661; Cass. 18 agosto 1992 n. 9592; Cass. 19 giugno 1996 n. 5664) oppure dell'interdicendo nel processo di interdizione (Cass. 22 febbraio 1989 n. 1001), ovvero del soggetto ingiunto in materia di sanzione amministrativa (Cass. 21 febbraio 1991 n. 1873; Cass. 29 maggio 1993 n. 6048; Cass. 5 aprile 1996 n. 3196); 6) la morte del magistrato incolpato in sede di procedimento disciplinare (Cass. s.u. 5 marzo 1993 n. 2674) o il suo collocamento a riposo (Cass. s.u. 26 maggio 1995 n. 5805); 7) la transazione stipulata fra le parti dopo l'inizio del processo (Cass. 27 febbraio 1998 n. 2197; Cass. 18 maggio 1998 n. 4963; Cass. 6 giugno 1998 n. 5594).

ITALY

ANDREA GIUSSANI

Professor of Civil Procedure,
University of Urbino, Italy

II.b Briefly describe the highest court (or courts) of your country and indicate its (or their) function within your legal system.

Italy's higest ordinary court in civil matters is the *Corte di Cassazione*: its main function, according to Art. 65 of the Italian judiciary law, is ensuring the exact compliance to national law and its uniform interpretation. The Constitutional Court, by contrast, only deals with the constitutionality of statutory law, mainly of remand from ordinary courts (private parties have no access as of right, albeit they may participate in the proceedings).

III. JUDICIAL DECISION MAKING

(a) Have you observed a similar phenomenon in your judicial system? If so, please identify the area(s) of law in which this has occurred. (Please do not limit yourself to questions involving jurisdiction.

Italy is a civil law jurisdiction. Hence, I interpret the question as follows: A code rule is generally interpreted according to a rationale; does a "reasonableness" standard sometimes limit the scope of the rule interpretation in a way that defeats its rationale?

This is sometimes expressly provided by statutory law; e.g., Art. 156, c. 1, of the code of civil procedure provides that proceedings are void for formal reasons only when the law expressly sanctions with nullity a lack of formality. This too-optimistic rule comes from enlightenment delusions encoded in the Napoleonic code and is obviously aimed at limiting the discretionary power of the judge. Since the nineteenth-century abuse of this rule proved too easy for the parties, both France and Italy introduced a reasonableness standard now encoded in Art. 156 c. 2: the court may also sanction with nullity any lack of formalities deemed functionally "indispensable."

This happens also with rule interpretation: According to Art. 291 of the code, when a null notification is renewed its effects run back from the first null service and not from its subsequent renewal; this rule is aimed at protecting the sender from the risk of mistakes in the delivery process; however, when the results of this interpretation are unreasonably unfair (e.g.. when notice was delivered to a person in a place that has nothing to do with the addressee), courts qualify the notification not as null but as "non-existent" in order to deny retroactivity to the renewal, albeit no code rule contemplates it.

We also have reasonableness standards limiting the scope of rule interpretations; e.g., courts used to say that if a party died or lost capacity, but the lawyer did not formally declare the event, appeal should nevertheless be filed against that party. This formal mechanism helped the appealing party to satisfy the burden of identifying the adversary (a burden especially heavy when there is a succession), according legal relevance only to events formally declared; however, this interpretation was not applied when a parent lost capacity because the minor reached the age of consent. In fact, the adversary could easily predict that event, and the formality rule was therefore unreasonable.

Often, however, these phenomena reveal that the code rule is not sound and encourage legislative reform: Amendment of Art. 153 of the code in 2009 provided courts with a general power to ignore preclusions incurred in by a party whenever enforcing them would put an unreasonably heavy burden on that party.

(b) If you have observed this phenomenon, does it sometimes occur that the judicially developed tests limit the principles that the tests purport to articulate?

I provided *supra* some examples taken from procedural law, guessing that they fit the category you are exploring.

IV. JURISDICTION

(d)(i) Would your country exercise jurisdiction over the foreign manufacturer on a claim against it by the injured party?

Yes.

(ii) On which provisions and/or case law do you base your answer? If your highest court has addressed this or a similar issue, please describe how the court solved it.

Art. 5.3 of EU Reg. n. 44/2001, Art. 3 l. n. 218 of 1995.

(vi) Additional comments. Express any additional comment you may have on the solutions offered by your system and the U.S. system.

Italian law does not provide a "forum non conveniens" rule. However, case law from the EU Court of Justice would govern, and predictability of the forum is deemed relevant (*see, e.g.*, the case eDate Advertising GmbH, C-161-10). I assume that the defendant's conduct in the described case would amount to an assumption of risk of being sued wherever the product could be sold.

V. JUSTICIABILITY

(d)(i) How would the courts of your country resolve the question of whether the mother should be allowed to proceed with her claim?

Under Italian law criminal, prosecution is a mandatory duty of public prosecutors but private parties have no right to control public prosecutors' choices. Moreover, constitutional law cannot be a tool to extend criminal liability: it would contrast with Art. 25. Hence, a mother would have no way to force the father's criminal indictment. She would however obviously have the right to pursue a civil action to obtain support for the child: that claim would be justiciable under current substantive law.

(ii) On which provisions and/or case law do you base your answer? If your highest court has addressed this or a similar issue, please describe how the court solved it.

Public prosecutors' duty to proceed and monopoly of criminal prosecution is provided at a constitutional level (Art. 101 c. 2 and 112). The same holds for parental duties (Art. 30).

(iv) Does your legal system require the same range of considerations to determine whether a party can bring a claim? Are those considerations statutory or constitutional?

Art. 100 of the code of civil procedure provides that only "interested" parties may sue, but interpretation of this requirement is highly disputed. According to some scholars, the rule is pointless. According to others, interest lacks, in a situation such as when the relief sought would not sufficiently protect the violated right. Hence, in theory, a declaratory relief could not be granted by way of a provisional remedy because provisional remedies may always be revoked, while declaratory reliefs protect a right through full *res iudicata* effects. Nevertheless, courts actually used to grant declaratory provisional remedies, notwithstanding their lesser usefulness. Art. 100 is often relied upon to strike moot claims.

(v) Additional comments. Express any additional comment you may have on the solutions offered by your system and the U.S. system.

I am not sure that the examples I have chosen address the issue you aim to develop. I surely agree that in many instances the Italian Supreme Court case law is inspired by docket considerations; however, the most illustrating example is most likely given by case law on formal requirements for appeals.

However, many case law inconsistencies derive also from competing equitable considerations. The main problem in Italy is that equitable considerations in theory should not be relevant to Supreme Court decisions: hence, the Supreme Court relies on them without saying so.

In my opinion, this is why the issue of the preclusive effects of the *decreto ingiuntivo* is still unsettled: courts say that a late challenge is precluded as a rule when they think that the challenge in the specific case is *prima facie* unfounded; they deny the same general conclusion whenever in the specific case the challenge looks sound. The same happens with the alternative between the "certainty" and the "preponderance" standard of proof. Obviously, these phenomena defeat the function of ensuring the uniform interpretation of the law and inflate appeals. On the contrary, inconsistencies inspired by docket considerations tend to discourage them.

Hence, my question is: What exactly are you trying to show?

If you want to show that even in civil law systems courts exploit interstitial interpretative powers to pursue their own ends, often including docket considerations, you have an easy task to fulfill. However this is not so if you want to show that courts own ends amount only to docket considerations.

If you want to show how docket or equitable considerations compete in influencing interpretation of a specific rule in different countries, the task would be most interesting. Perhaps you should select a specific issue.

ITALY

ELENA D'ALESSANDRO

Associate Professor of Civil Procedure,
University of Turin, Italy

II.b. II.b Briefly describe the highest court (or courts) of your country and indicate its (or their) function within your legal system.

In Italy, the highest court in civil and criminal matters is the *Corte di cassazione*, located in Rome. It is divided into six civil sections.

Article 374, Para 1, of the Italian Code of Civil Procedure requires a plenary session when the ground of attack goes to jurisdiction.

In addition, the plenary session may be convened by the president of the court, if the application (*ricorso per cassazione*) involves either a question of particular importance, or a question that has been already decided by single sections in contradiction with one another (Article 374, Para 2 and 3 of the Italian Code of Civil Procedure).

The *Corte di cassazione* reviews appellate judgments or judgments, which may not be brought before the intermediate appellate courts either by law or by agreement of the parties, but rather on points of law only (see Article 360 of the Italian Code of Civil Procedure).

In Italy, there is a constitutional right to review by the *Corte di cassazione*. According to Article 111, para 7, of the Italian Constitution, "Appeal to the *Corte di cassazione* in cases of violations of the law is always allowed against sentences" (judgments on the merit).

The *Corte di cassazione* either affirms the judgments from below, which then become final, or quashes them. In this second case, the *Corte di cassazione* has no power to render a new decision on the merits but must remand the case for a new decision to a different court of appeal, as the court that rendered the judgment that has been quashed (so called *giudizio di rinvio*).

As Supreme Court, the *Corte di cassazione* also ensures the uniform interpretation of Italian law and, consequently, the unity of national law.

Finally, in Italy there is no *stare decisis*; as such, the *Corte di Cassazione* has no power to select cases upon which it has an obligation to rule.

In 2012, the *Corte di cassazione* decided approximately 25,012 cases (http://www.cortedicassazione.it/Documenti/2012_Civ_el_stat.pdf).

Another high court in Italy is the Constitutional Court (Art. 134 *et seq.* of the Italian Constitution). The most important task of the Italian Constitutional Court is to rule on controversies or disputes "regarding the constitutional legitimacy of the laws and acts having the force of law issued by the State and the Regions."

Only the court of a pending proceeding (and not a single party of the proceeding) has the power to refer a question to the Constitutional Court.

III. JUDICIAL DECISION MAKING

(a) Have you observed a similar phenomenon in your judicial system? If so, please identify the area(s) of law in which this has occurred. (Please do not limit yourself to questions involving jurisdiction.)

I have observed a similar phenomenon in the civil procedure area in two cases.

1) Fictitious defendant (*convenuto fittizio*)

First step: According to article 18 of the Italian Code of Civil Procedure, the defendant may be sued before the court of his domicile or residence. However, according to article 33 of the Italian Code of Civil Procedure, causes against more that one defendant that are connected by a common *causa petendi* or *petitum* may be brought in a forum in which any of the defendants reside or are domiciled.

Second step: Interpreting this rule, the *Corte di cassazione* has developed the notion of *causa petendi* and *petitum*.[1]

[1] *See, e.g.*, Cass., ord. 26.02.2009 No 4750 ("quando, in base a titoli contrattuali diversi, sia richiesto nei confronti di più persone il risarcimento del danno per inadempimento, tra le varie domande proposte non sussiste una ipotesi di connessione per il titolo ma ricorre – in relazione al "*petitum*" relativo alla domanda di risarcimento del danno – una ipotesi di connessione per l'oggetto che, ai sensi dell'art. 33 cod. proc. civ., legittima lo spostamento della competenza per territorio"); Cass. ord. 15.07.2005, No 15048 ("L'art. 33 cod. proc. civ., che, in deroga alla competenza territoriale cosiddetta semplice, consente il cumulo delle cause contro più persone presso il giudice del foro generale di uno dei convenuti purchè ricorra una connessione per l'oggetto o per il titolo, trova applicazione anche in presenza di una causa unica ed identica con una pluralità di convenuti, ciascuno dei quali avente una propria legittimazione").

Third step: Additionally, in order to limit the field of application of article 33 of the Civil Code of Civil Procedure, the *Corte di cassazione* has stated that, in any case, article 33 cannot apply if the defendant who has the domicile or the residence in the district of the court hearing the action is a *fictious defendant.*[2]

2) Issue of subject matter jurisdiction (*giurisdizione*)

First step: According to article 37 of the Italian Code of Civil Procedure, the lack of jurisdiction of the ordinary courts over the public administration or of the special courts may be raised for the first time at any stage or level of a proceeding, even before the higher court (*Corte di cassazione*).

Second and third steps: As noted by LAMARQUE, *The Italian Courts and Interpretation in Conformity with the Constitution, EU Law and the* ECHR, Rivista dell'associazione italiana dei costituzionalisti, n. 4/2012, "in 2008 the

[2] *See Cass*, ord. 21.12.2010, No 25891: "*L'art.* 33 *cod. proc. civ.*– relativo alla modificazione della competenza territoriale per effetto del cumulo soggettivo delle domande contro più convenuti – non legittima uno spostamento della detta competenza attraverso la proposizione maliziosa di una domanda verso un convenuto fittizio; tuttavia, affinché il giudice adito possa dichiarare la propria incompetenza, occorre che detta domanda appaia "prima facie" artificiosa e preordinata al fine sopra indicato e – ove non si tratti di competenza territoriale inderogabile – che vi sia stata tempestiva eccezione del convenuto ai sensi dell'art. 38 c.p.c."; Cass. 15.3.2004, No 5243: "In tema di modificazione della competenza per connessione di cause, *l'art.* 33 *c.p.c.* che, in deroga alla competenza territoriale cosiddetta semplice, consente il cumulo delle cause contro più persone presso il giudice del foro generale di uno dei convenuti purché ricorra una connessione per l'oggetto o il titolo – non trova applicazione solo allorché appaia prima facie che la presenza di un convenuto fittizio sia artificiosa in quanto preordinata allo spostamento della competenza. Ne consegue che, in materia di responsabilità civile dei danni da circolazione stradale, non ricorre tale ipotesi nel caso in cui – indipendentemente dall'esito del processo sia convenuto in giudizio il conducente dell'auto su cui al momento del sinistro si trovava il terzo trasportato che ha subito lesioni, giacché l'art. 2054 c.c. esprime un principio di portata generale applicabile a tutti i soggetti che in ogni modo ricevano danni dalla circolazione di un veicolo, in essi compresi i trasportati, quale sia il titolo del trasporto. (L'attrice, trasportata su autoveicolo rovinato in una buca esistente nella strada comunale, aveva proposto azione di danni nei confronti del conducente del veicolo e del Comune: la Corte, nel formulare il principio su richiamato, ha cassato la decisione del giudice di pace, che aveva dichiarato la propria incompetenza territoriale, ritenendo artificiosa – in quanto preordinata alla deroga della competenza – la *vocatio in ius* anche del conducente del veicolo)"; Cass., ord. 25 06.2002, No 9277: "L'art. 33 c.p.c. – relativo alla modificazione della competenza territoriale per effetto del cumulo soggettivo delle domande contro più convenuti – non legittima uno spostamento della detta competenza attraverso la proposizione maliziosa di una domanda verso un convenuto fittizio; tuttavia, affinché il giudice adito possa dichiarare la propria incompetenza, occorre che detta domanda appaia "*prima facie*" artificiosa e preordinata al fine sopra indicato e – ove non si tratti di competenza territoriale inderogabile – che vi sia stata tempestiva eccezione del convenuto, in base alla regola generale stabilita dall'art. 38, comma 2, c.p.c. "

Joint Divisions of the Court of Cassation[3] stated their intention to subject it to an "interpretation with amending effects," in order to contain its substantive scope "within closer limits than those authorised by the letter of the law," in such a manner as to prevent the lack of jurisdiction from being raised once an implicit ruling had been reached on that point, that is whenever the case has been decided on the merits, except in some limited, exceptional cases.

According to the Joint Divisions, in fact, the "core axis" of the new interpretation of the Code's provision must become the constitutional principle of the reasonable length of trials, given that "the traditional interpretation, based solely on the letter of the law, does not strike a correct balance between the constitutional values at stake and leads to an unjustified violation of the principles of the reasonable length of trials and the efficacy of relief (Articles 24 and 111 Const.), since it entails the regression of the trial to its original stage, the overturning of two judgments on the merits and the deferral *sine die* of a valid ruling on the merits." The *Corte di cassazione*, thus, completed this operation in the full light of day without feigning: it struck an autonomous balance of the constitutional values at stake and gave them precedence over the literal meaning of the Code. However, more importantly, between 2008 and the present time, no other court has considered it possible to achieve the same result by following the different path – which moreover is unanimously viewed as the correct one within the literature– of referring the question to the Constitutional Court."

(b) If you have observed this phenomenon, does it sometimes occur that the judicially developed tests limit the principles that the tests purport to articulate?

Yes. See *supra*.

IV. JURISDICTION

(d)(i) Would your country exercise jurisdiction over the foreign manufacturer on a claim against it by the injured party?

Yes, irrespective of whether the foreign manufacturer has a domicile within the EU or a third state.

If the foreign manufacturer is domiciled in an EU Member State, the Italian jurisdiction will be based in article 5, para. 3, of the Brussels I Regulation.

[3] Corte di cassazione, sez. un., 29.10.2008, No 24883; Corte di cassazione, 30.10.2008, No 26019; Cass., sez. un., 27.11.2010, No 26129.

According to article 5, para. 3, of the Brussels I Regulation, a person domiciled in a Member State may be sued in another Member State in matters relating to torts, delict or quasi-delict, in the Courts for the place where the harmful event occurred or may occur.

The ECJ, in the case *Zuid Chemie* (case c-189/08 of 16.07.2009), has clarified that "article 5, para. 3, of the Brussels I Regulation must be interpreted as meaning that, in a dispute concerning the damage caused to an undertaking by the delivery of a defective product, the words 'place where the harmful event occurred' designate the place where the initial damage occurred as a result of the normal use of the product for the purpose for which it was intended."

If the foreign manufacturer is domiciled in a third State, the Italian jurisdiction will be based on article 3 of Law No 215 of 1995 (so-called Italian Rules of Private International and Procedural Law).

In Italy, according to article 3(2) of the Law No 215 of 1995, the special rules of jurisdiction of the Brussels Convention (in this case, article 5 para. 3) apply, even if the defendant is domiciled in a Third State. On this point, the *Corte di cassazione* has clarified that, lacking the Italian legislator's intervention, the reference has to be interpreted as designating the Brussels Convention of 1968 (see *Corte di cassazione*, judgment No 22239 of October 21, 2009). However, from our point of view, in the resolution of our concrete case, there is no significant difference between article 5, para 3, of the Brussels Convention and article 5, para 3, of the Brussels I Regulation.

(ii) On which provisions and/or case law do you base your answer? If your highest court has addressed this or a similar issue, please describe how the court solved it.

See *supra*.

V. JUSTICIABILITY

(d) Your System's Solution[4]

(i) How would the courts of your country resolve the question of whether the mother should be allowed to proceed with her claim?

In Italy, as known, only the court of a pending proceeding has the power to refer a question of constitutionality to the Constitutional Court.

[4] *Ex multis*: Cass. 04.11.2010 No 22502; Cass. 20 04.1991, No 4273 ("il genitore che agisce in giudizio contro l'altro genitore per ottenere il mantenimento del figlio naturale agisce in nome e nell'interesse proprio").

However, a mother may act for the maintenance of the children, against the "natural" father. This is so because, pursuant to article 148 of the Italian Code of Civil Procedure, both parents are jointly obliged to maintain children (*obbligazione solidale*). In other words, if the father fails to maintain the child, the mother has to pay 100 percent of the child maintenance. For this reason, she has a "personal" interest in the action, to recover from the natural father 50 percent of what she paid.

(ii) On which provisions and/or case law do you base your answer? If your highest court has addressed this or a similar issue, please describe how the court solved it.

I base my answer on Article 148 of the Italian Civil Code that states that if

> the parents do not have sufficient means, the other legitimate or natural ascendants are bound to supply the parents with the necessary means so that they may fulfil their duties to their children. This obligation is not limited in time and remains valid even when the children have attained their majority; this duty of maintenance is owed until a child becomes economically independent or until the parents can show that they have given the child the means to work, thanks to the studies he has completed. In a case of need, the right to basic subsistence remains applicable without any limitation in time.
>
> In the event of nonperformance, the president of the court, at the request of any person having an interest, having heard the nonperforming party and having gathered the necessary information, may order that a share of the income of the obligated party should be paid directly to the other spouse or to the person incurring the expenses of the children's maintenance, instruction, and education. The judicial order may be amended or revoked if justified by a change of circumstances.[5]

(iv) Does your legal system require the same range of considerations to determine whether a party can bring a claim? Are those considerations statutory or constitutional?

In Italy, three separate issues must be decided in determining whether a party can pursue a claim (so-called *presupposti processuali attinenti alla parte*).

[5] Please note that Article 148 of the Italian Civil Code has already been emended by the Legislative Decree No 154 of December 23, 2013. Simultaneusly, a new Article (Article 316-*bis*) has been insert to make clear that both parents have parental responsibility over their children. The previous version of Article 148 and the new Article 316-*bis* of the Italian Civil Code cover the same topic and the have, *mutatis mutandis*, the same content.

Currently, I would base my answer on Article 316-bis of the Italian Civil Code.

Firstly, a party must be *legittimata ad agire* (*legitimatio ad causam*). According to article 81 of the Italian Code of Civil procedure, no one is entitled to present a claim to protect the right of another person unless the law requires otherwise.

Secondly, a party shall have the capacity to be "a part" in a civil action (so called *capacità processuale*, according to Article 75 of the Italian Code of Civil Procedure). Usually people acquire the *capacità processuale* by virtue of being 18 years old.

Thirdly, the claimant must have an interest to act (article 100 of the Italian Code of Civil Procedure: *interesse al mezzo processuale; interesse al risultato*).

All those considerations are statutory.

Article 24, para. 1 of the Italian Constitution, only states that "Everyone can take judicial action to protect individual rights and legitimate interests."

REPUBLIC OF LITHUANIA

AURIMAS BRAZDEIKIS

Head of the Legal Research Information Department of the Supreme Administrative Court of the Republic of Lithuania PhD

II. BACKGROUND INFORMATION

a. Please identify yourself, your professional position, and the country on which your answers will be based.

(b) Briefly describe the highest court (or courts) of your country and indicate its (or their) function within your legal system.

A court is an institution administering justice and established by law. In pursuance of the fair and impartial court decisions and in order to prevent any interference in the court activities, the Constitution and the Law on Courts of the Republic of Lithuania establish that in the administration of justice, courts shall be independent from other government institutions, officials, political parties, organizations, and other persons. The law prescribes the liability for the interference in judicial activities.

The system of courts, their competence, their organization, activity and administration, as well as the status of judges, their appointment, career, liability and other issues related to the judicial activities are regulated by the Constitution, the Law on Courts and other legal acts of the Republic of Lithuania.

A court system of the Republic of Lithuania is made up of courts of general jurisdiction and courts of special jurisdiction. There is also the Constitutional Court of the Republic of Lithuania, which is vested with specific tasks.

The Supreme Court of Lithuania (1), the Court of Appeal of Lithuania (1), regional courts (5), and district courts (54) are courts of general jurisdiction dealing with civil and criminal cases. District courts also hear cases of administrative offences coming within their jurisdiction by law. The regional courts, the Court of Appeal, and the Supreme Court of Lithuania have a civil division and a criminal division.

The Supreme Administrative Court of Lithuania (1) and regional administrative courts (5) are courts of special jurisdiction hearing disputes arising from administrative legal relations.

A district court is the court of first instance for criminal and civil cases, and cases dealing with administrative offences (assigned to its jurisdiction by law), as well as cases relating to the enforcement of decisions and sentencing. The district court judge also performs the functions of a pre-trial judge, an enforcement judge, and other functions assigned to a district court by law.

A regional court is the first instance for criminal and civil cases assigned to its jurisdiction by law, and appeal instance for judgments, decisions, rulings, and orders of district courts.

The Court of Appeal reviews cases heard by regional courts as courts of first instance. It also hears requests for the recognition of decisions of foreign or international courts and foreign or international arbitration awards and their enforcement in the Republic of Lithuania as well as performing other functions assigned to the jurisdiction of this curt by law.

The Supreme Court of Lithuania is the only court of cassation instance for reviewing effective judgments, decisions, rulings, and orders of the courts of general jurisdiction. It develops a uniform court practice in the interpretation and application of laws and other legal acts.

According to the Law on Courts of the Republic of Lithuania, for the latter purpose the Supreme Court: 1) shall release a public report about the rulings of the plenary sessions as well as the rulings of the judicial panel of three justices and of the extended judicial panel of seven justices the publication of which has been approved by the majority of justices of the appropriate division. Interpretation in respect of the application of statutes and other legal acts in the rulings published in the Supreme Court Bulletin shall be taken into consideration by courts, states, and other institutions as well as by other persons when applying these statutes and other legislation; 2) shall analyze court practice in the application of statutes and other legal acts and provide their interpretation in the form of recommendations; and 3) may advise judges about the interpretation and application of statutes and other legal acts.

The Law on Courts also provides that the Supreme Court shall analyze and sum up, in accordance with the interpretation by judicial institutions of the European Union, the practice of courts of general jurisdiction in the application of the legislation of the European Union and shall make recommendations on the cooperation between Lithuanian courts of general jurisdiction and judicial institutions of the European Union in ensuring uniform interpretation of legal acts of the European Union and their application in the Republic of Lithuania.

The Supreme Court issues its bulletin "Court Practice," periodically publishing in it major rulings and recommendations, summary reviews of court practice in the application of statutes and other legal acts in cases of separate categories approved by the Senate of the Court, and interpretations in the form of recommendations and other materials for which the necessity of publication has been approved by the Senate.

A regional administrative court is the court of special jurisdiction established for hearing complaints (petitions) in respect of administrative acts and acts of commission or omission (failure to perform duties) by entities of public and internal administration.

The Supreme Administrative Court is the first and final instance for administrative cases assigned to its jurisdiction by law. It is the appeal instance for cases concerning decisions, rulings, and orders of regional administrative courts. The Supreme Administrative Court is the only instance for hearing, in cases specified by law, of petitions on the reopening of completed administrative cases as well as requests to assess legality of normative (regulatory) administrative acts of the central state administration bodies and acts of general nature adopted by public organizations, communities, political parties, political organizations, or associations.

The Supreme Administrative Court develops a uniform practice of administrative courts in the interpretation and application of laws and other legal acts. According to the Law on Courts, for this purpose, the Supreme Administrative Court: 1) shall release a public report about decisions, orders, and rulings rendered by the plenary session of the court, decisions adopted by a judicial panel of three judges or an extended judicial panel of five or seven judges, the publication whereof has been approved by the majority of the Court's judges, as well as all decisions on lawfulness of regulatory administrative acts. Interpretation with regard to the application of statutes and other legal acts found in the decisions, rulings, and orders which are published in the bulletin of the Supreme Administrative Court shall be taken into account by courts, the state and other institutions as well as by other entities when applying these statutes and other legal acts; 2) shall analyze the practice of administrative courts in the application of statutes and other legal acts and provide their interpretation in the form of recommendations; 3) may advise the judges of administrative courts on the issues of interpretation and application of statutes and other legal acts.

The Law on Courts also provides that the Supreme Administrative Court, in accordance with the interpretations of judicial institutions of the European Union, shall analyze and sum up the practice of administrative courts in applying the legislation of the European Union and shall make recommendations on the cooperation between administrative courts of Lithuania and judicial institutions of the European Union in ensuring uniform interpretation and application in the Republic of Lithuania of the legal acts of the European Union.

The Supreme Administrative Court issues its bulletin under the title "Practice of Administrative Courts" and periodically publishes in it major decisions and recommendations, summary reviews of court practice in the application of statutes and other legal acts in cases of separate categories and their interpretation in the form of recommendations, and other materials for which the publication has been approved by the majority of judges of the court.

The Constitutional Court of the Republic of Lithuania ensures the supremacy of the Constitution within the legal system as well as constitutional justice by deciding whether the laws and other legal acts adopted by the Seimas (the Parliament of Lithuania) are in conformity with the Constitution and whether the acts adopted by the President or the Government of the Republic are in compliance with the Constitution and laws.

The Constitutional Court does not perform preliminary judicial review of laws. The Constitutional Court decides the constitutionality issues of enacted laws and other legal acts (*a posteriori* control). The Constitutional Court examines a case only when the entities prescribed by the Constitution address the Constitutional Court with a petition requesting to determine the conformity of a law or a legal act with the Constitution.

The right to file a petition with the Constitutional Court concerning the constitutionality of a legal act is vested in: (1) the government, groups consisting of at least one-fifth of all Members of the Seimas, and the courts for cases concerning a law or other act adopted by the Seimas; (2) groups consisting of at least one-fifth of all Members of the Seimas and the courts for cases concerning an act of the President of the Republic; and (3) groups consisting of at least one-fifth of all Members of the Seimas, the courts, and the President of the Republic for cases concerning governmental acts.

Under the Constitution, laws of the Republic of Lithuania (or a part thereof) or other Seimas acts (or a part thereof), acts of the President of the Republic, or acts of the Government (or a part thereof) shall not be applicable from the day that a Constitutional Court ruling stating that the appropriate act (or a part thereof) conflicts with the Constitution of the Republic of Lithuania is officially published (*ex nunc*). The decisions of the Constitutional Court ascribed to its competence by the Constitution are final and not subject to appeal. Constitutional Court rulings have the power of law and are obligatory for all institutions of authority, courts, all enterprises, establishments and organizations, officials and citizens (*erga omnes*).

III. JUDICIAL DECISION MAKING

(a) Have you observed a similar phenomenon in your judicial system? If so, please identify the area(s) of law in which this has occurred. (Please do not limit yourself to questions involving jurisdiction.)

The Republic of Lithuania is a civil law system. According to the Constitution of the Republic of Lithuania, the judge is obliged to apply the law. Although the Constitution of the Republic of Lithuania establishes a set of general and specific principles of law as well as some concrete rules of law, the legal system of Lithuania is characterized by the feature that there are a great number of statutes passed by the Parliament of the Republic of Lithuania and other legal acts adopted by the Government, ministries and other competent public institutions. These acts regulate particular areas of social and legal relations and lay down concrete rules of law that are aimed to concretize the general principles set by the Constitution. In case the judge does not have doubts that the rules of law established by these legal instruments violate the Constitution, he/she is obliged to apply this rule in a case before him/her.

So, quite often the judge has no need to apply general or special principles of law (such as Due Process Clause), because there is one or more concrete and detailed rule of law in the statutes or other legal acts that regulate particular issue.

For example, there is a set of detailed rules of jurisdiction in the Civil Procedure Code of the Republic of Lithuania. Therefore, the judge usually has simply to check whether these rules allow the claimant to bring a case before a respective court. If the answer is yes, there is almost no way to decline jurisdiction in keeping with the independent reasonableness inquiry (some very limited exceptions are possible in cases with a foreign element). However, reasonableness and other principles of law (justice, fairness) are very important in interpreting the rules of law.

Thus, general principles of law in Lithuania usually and basically serve as guidelines for interpreting norms laid down by the statutes, filling the gaps of law or resolving contradictions between the norms. So the first task that the judge (in the case of the Supreme Court, too) has to perform when he is making a decision in a particular case is to establish which rule or set of rules of law shall be applied in the case.

In order to find the right norm, the judge first of all shall establish the legally relevant facts of the case. One should note that the Supreme Court of Lithuania hears only questions of law. Therefore, the judges of the Supreme Court are bound by the facts established by the appellate court unless the

Supreme Court considers that the establishment of facts at the lower instance court was performed by breaching procedural (e.g., evidence) rules. The situation is different for the Supreme Administrative Court of Lithuania, where the judge reviews the legality of the appealed decision both from the point of law and fact. Thus, the Supreme Administrative Court can decide that the facts were actually different than those indicated by the first instance court and can base its judgment on the newly reassessed facts.

After the legally relevant facts are established, for the purpose of choosing the right rule of law (or set of rules), the Supreme (Administrative) Court quite often shall discuss and interpret the rules of law that *prima facie* is applicable in the case. This can happen because the rule may be unclear (e.g., the facts when the rule shall be applied are vague, obscure, etc.), they may conflict with each other, there can be no specific rule for the particular issue, or the rule may lead to a clearly unfair, unjust, or unreasonable result if it were to be applied forthright. Even if from the first sight it seems that particular rule of law is clearly applicable in the case, the Supreme (Administrative) Court may interpret this rule in such a manner so as to lead to a just and fair result. General and specific principles of law play a major role in interpreting the rules, solving their contradictions, filling the gaps, and putting the arguments for the judgment.

By interpreting the rules, the Supreme (Administrative) Court may control and limit the application of certain rule of law.

For example, at the end of 2012, the Supreme Court explained that the rule that no request for a review of default judgment can be made after three months from the date of its adoption, is only applicable if the default judgment was duly served to the defendant, though no such exception is provided in the Code of Civil Procedure.

Based on this, one may say that trends similar to the described phenomena in the United States can be traced in the decision-making process in Lithuania. Still, the judge in Lithuania will usually begin the decision-making process with a search for a particular rule of law, which has to be applied to the established set of legally relevant facts of the case. In this process, he/she will always be guided, will view, will assess and will interpret the rules in light of the principles that underpin them and thus can limit or widen their application. However, if following a thorough interpretation of the rule, all common and special requirements of the application of this principle are met, the judge usually will consider himself as not having the power to decline the application of rule, even on a basis of reasonableness, fairness, justice, or other similar considerations.

Under the principle of separation of powers, the judge must apply the law, not deny it. Such aspects as reasonableness and fairness are normally assessed and taken into account when giving an interpretation of a particular rule, i.e., not after applicability of the rule is established. If the judge has doubts about the rule of law, which he/she has to apply after interpreting it, he/she in most cases can apply to the Constitutional Court (sometimes to the Supreme Administrative Court) asking to verify its conformity with the Constitution and constitutional precepts of law.

We also must note that it is common practice in Lithuania, especially in difficult cases, to begin the motivation of the judgment from discussing the principles of law, then interpreting particular rule and finally by testing whether it can be applied in a case at hand.

For example, in recent years, the Supreme Administrative Court of Lithuania had significant amount of cases related to a denial of a right to deduction of value added tax (VAT).

In such cases, the Supreme Administrative Court usually begins from the principle that the law on VAT cannot be relied on for abusive or fraudulent ends.

Then it explains that this means that the right to deduct can be refused if a taxable person acted abusively, fraudulently, or knew, or ought to have known, that transaction on which he is relying for the right to deduct was connected with fraud previously committed by the supplier or another trader at an earlier stage in the transaction ("accomplice of a fraud").

Finally, the Court endorses specific tests, when one can conclude that a taxable person knew, or ought to have known, that there was a fraud in a transaction chain.

For example, if a taxable person was aware of the fact that his supplier of goods, who at the moment of concluding and implementing a contract was insolvent, will not pay to the state budget the respective amount of VAT received from a taxable person, but instead will unfairly favor his shareholders or other creditors by transferring a respective amount of money to them, the right to deduction of VAT may be refused. In this situation, it is deemed that the supplier engaged in fraudulent activities and a taxable person knew about it. On the other hand, if a supplier did not pay the respective amount of VAT received from a taxable person to the state budget, but there were no fraudulent transactions or unfair favoring of some creditors, the taxable person's right to deduction of VAT, as a general rule, cannot be refused.

b. If you have observed this phenomenon, does it sometimes occur that the judicially developed tests limit the principles that the tests purport to articulate?

There is no straightforward answer to this question. There can be two or more principles that may point in different directions and to different decisions in a specific case. So when making the judgment, the Supreme (Administrative) Court sometimes simply must decide which principle to favor and to which principle give more weight in a particular case.

However, one (e.g., professors of law) may disagree with a decision of the Supreme (Administrative) Court and may argue that it has not selected the right principle to stand for in a particular case. For example, the Supreme Court has interpreted the rule of law that says that the court of appellate instance shall refuse to admit new evidences, which could be provided to the court of first instance, unless the latter court unlawfully refused to admit those evidences or if the necessity to submit the evidences arose later, in such a way as the submission of new evidences can be refused only in cases, where a person, submitting the evidences, abuses his/her procedural rights, unfairly conceals evidences. This interpretation means that a person who is negligent in conducting his case may in some cases be allowed to submit new evidences to the court of appellate instance and thus likely to protract the proceedings.

So in this situation, the Supreme Court attached greater weight and favored the principle of just decision, not the principle of process economy and concentration. Therefore, one may argue that by the aforementioned interpretation and elaborated test for admission of new evidences at the appellate instance court, the Supreme Court has actually limited the principle of process concentration and economy, which the rule at issue purported to reflect. On the other hand, the Supreme Court in this particular situation decided that new evidences may help to reveal the true facts of the case; therefore, in order to allow a greater chance of arriving at a just decision (by better knowledge of true facts) the Court decided to uphold the principle of justice.

IV. JURISDICTION

(d)(i) Would your country exercise jurisdiction over the foreign manufacturer on a claim against it by the injured party?

Lithuania is a Member State of the European Union. The main international jurisdiction rules of the European Union, which are mandatory in Lithuania too, are laid down by the Council Regulation (EC) No 44/2001 of 22 December 2000 on jurisdiction and the recognition and enforcement of judgments in civil and commercial matters (hereinafter referred to as the "Brussels I Regulation"). The courts of the Republic of Lithuania are bound by the interpretations given by the Court of Justice of the European Union on the Brussels I Regulation, thus the role of Lithuanian courts in interpreting this regulation is rather residual.

The system of common rules of conferment of jurisdiction laid down in Chapter II of the Brussels I Regulation is based on the general rule, set out in the first paragraph of Article 2, that persons domiciled in a Member State are to be sued in the courts of that State, irrespective of the nationality of the parties.

It is only by way of derogation from that fundamental principle attributing jurisdiction to the courts of the defendant's domicile that Section 2 of Chapter II of the Brussels I Regulation makes the provision for certain special jurisdictional rules, such as that laid down in Article 5(3) of the Brussels I Regulation, which provides that a person domiciled in a Member State may, in another Member State, be sued in matters relating to tort, delict or quasi-delict, in the courts for the place where the harmful event occurred or may occur.

It is settled case law of the Court of Justice of the European Union (hereinafter referred to as the "CJEU") that, where the place in which the event that may give rise to liability in tort, delict or quasi-delict, occurs and the place where that event results in damage are not identical, the expression "place where the harmful event occurred" in Article 5(3) of the Brussels I Regulation must be understood as being intended to cover both the place where the damage occurred and the place of the event giving rise to it, so that the defendant may be sued, at the option of the claimant, in the courts for either of those places (Case C-18/02 *DFDSTorline* [2004] ECR I-1417).

It is worth noting that the CJEU has stated that the rule of special jurisdiction laid down in Article 5(3) of the Brussels I Regulation is based on the existence of a particularly close connecting factor between the dispute and the courts of the place where the harmful event occurred, which justifies the attribution of jurisdiction to those courts for reasons relating to the sound administration of justice and the efficacious conduct of proceedings. The courts for the place where the harmful event occurred are usually the most appropriate for deciding the case, in particular on the grounds of proximity and the ease of gathering evidence (Case C-220/88 *Dumez France and Tracoba* [1990] ECR I-49).

The place where the event that damaged the product itself occurred is the place of the event giving rise to the damage. The "place where the damage occurred" is the place where the event that gave rise to the damage produces its harmful effects; that is to say, the place where the damage caused by the defective product actually manifests itself. The CJEU has also stated that Article 5(3) of Brussels I Regulation must be interpreted as meaning that the words "place where the harmful event occurred" designate the place where the initial damage occurred as a result of the normal use of the product for the purpose for which it was intended (Case C-189/08 *Zuid-Chemie* [2009] ECR I-6917).

According to the abovementioned case law of the CJEU, we are of the opinion that the courts of Lithuania can (and must if a claim is brought before them) exercise jurisdiction over the foreign manufacturer, which has a domicile in another Member State, if an initial damage to an injured party occurred in Lithuania and there is no direct contractual link between the manufacturer and the injured party (e.g., an agent sold manufacturer's goods to the injured party on his own name and not on behalf of the manufacturer). We do not think that the fact that the foreign manufacturer has not specifically instructed its agent to market the product in Lithuania can call into question this conclusion. By designating the market where the product could be sold, the manufacturer could actually envisage that the product might be sold in Lithuania and thus could assume the risk of being brought to the jurisdiction of Lithuanian courts.

However, one should note that, to the best of our knowledge, the CJEU has not had an opportunity to deal with the application of Article 5(3) of the Brussels I Regulation when the manufacture did not know to which country his goods will be sold. Therefore, there is a probability that the answer could be different. In addition, we would like to note that there is no place for *forum non conveniens* doctrine in the EU (Case C-281/02 *Owusu* [2005] ECR I-1383). Therefore, if jurisdiction of the court is established on a basis of any of the grounds laid down in the Brussels I Regulation, there is no space for additional considerations of reasonableness, due process, etc., because it is considered that the rules providing grounds of jurisdiction and their interpretation by the CJEU and national courts itself take into account and ensure a sufficient level of due process as well as reasonable and just forum for the case.

The CJEU puts great emphasis on the predictability of the jurisdiction and principle of legal certainty. These principles would be undermined, if after establishing jurisdiction of the court according to the rules of the Brussels I Regulation, this court would be allowed to decline jurisdiction on some other grounds that are not clearly expressed in Brussels I.

If the manufacturer has no domicile in a Member State of the EU and there is no direct contractual link between the manufacturer and the injured party, Lithuanian courts would most likely still have jurisdiction over the foreign manufacturer. In this situation, i.e., when the defendant–manufacturer has no domicile in EU Member State, the jurisdiction of the courts of each Member State shall, subject to Articles 22 and 23 of the Brussels I Regulation, be determined by the law of that Member State (Art. 4(1) of the Brussels I Regulation).

Article 787, paragraph 1, subparagraph 3 of the Code of Civil Procedure of Lithuania provides that Lithuanian courts shall have jurisdiction if an obligation at issue arose in Lithuania or have to be discharged in Lithuania.

In the judgment as of 5 November 2011 in case No 2-2247/2011, the Court of Appeals of Lithuania based jurisdiction of Lithuanian courts on Article 787, paragraph 1, subparagraph 3 of the Code of Civil Procedure in a situation where the parties domiciled in Lithuania brought an action against the United States asking for compensation of personal damages inflicted by alleged defamation of claimants by publishing certain documents. Based on this case, we are of the opinion that the manufacturer, which has no domicile in a Member State of the EU and when there is no direct contractual link between the manufacturer and the injured party, can still be brought before the Lithuanian courts, if the damage actually occurred and thus the obligation to compensate for it arose in Lithuania.

If the manufacturer has a domicile in a Member State of the EU and there is a direct contractual bond between the manufacturer and the injured party (e.g., the agent has made a contract with the injured party not on his own name, but on behalf of the manufacturer) and this contract satisfies criteria set in Article 15(1)[1] of the Brussels I Regulation, then, in accordance with Article 16(1) of the Brussels I Regulation, the injured party–consumer may bring proceedings against the other party to a contract in the courts for the place where the injured party–consumer is domiciled. Thus, in this situation, Lithuanian courts can also have jurisdiction over the foreign manufacturer, if the injured party–consumer is domiciled in Lithuania. This rule of jurisdiction is based on the need to protect weaker contracting party–consumer.

Please also note that, to the best of our understanding, the fact that the manufacturer did not specifically instruct its agent to market the product in the Lithuanian market *per se* does not mean that the contract at issue does not satisfy conditions set out in Article 15(1)(c) of the Brussels I Regulation, which

[1] In matters relating to a contract concluded by a person, the consumer, for a purpose which can be regarded as being outside his trade or profession, jurisdiction shall be determined by this Section, without prejudice to Article 4 and point 5 of Article 5, if: (a) it is a contract for the sale of goods on instalment credit terms; or (b) it is a contract for a loan repayable by instalments, or for any other form of credit, made to finance the sale of goods; or (c) in all other cases, the contract has been concluded with a person who pursues commercial or professional activities in the Member State of the consumer's domicile or, by any means, directs such activities to that Member State or to several States including that Member State, and the contract falls within the scope of such activities.

requires the the activities of a manufacturer be directed to the Lithuanian market in order to apply the jurisdiction rule established in Article 16(1) of the Brussels I Regulation.

The CJEU broadly interprets the requirement of directing activities to a certain Member State as is seen from the Joined Cases C-585/08 and C-144/09 *Pammer and Hotel Alpenhof* [2010] ECR I-12527. So the fact, that the manufacturer did not specifically instruct its agent to market the product in Lithuanian market *per se* does not lead to a conclusion that Article 16(1) of the Brussels I Regulation is inapplicable and that the injured party–consumer cannot rely on this ground of jurisdiction by bringing a claim before the courts of his domicile.

If the manufacturer has no domicile in a Member State of the EU and there is a direct contractual bond between the manufacturer and the injured party (e.g., the agent has made a contract with the injured party not on his own name, but on behalf of the manufacturer), Lithuanian courts can still base their jurisdiction over the foreign manufacturer on Article 787, paragraph 1, subparagraph 3 of the Code of Civil Procedure, arguing that a party, who has domicile in Lithuania, suffered an injury, the damage actually occurred, and the obligation to compensate for it arose in Lithuania, therefore, there is a sufficient link between the case and Lithuanian forum.

(ii) On which provisions and/or case law do you base your answer? If your highest court has addressed this or a similar issue, please describe how the court solved it.

Please see IV(d)(i) for details.

(iii) If you need additional facts to answer this question, please indicate which type of facts you would need and why.

If the manufacturer has no domicile in a Member State of the EU, the country in which the manufacturer has his domicile can be important. If the manufacturer has his domicile in a country with which Lithuania has signed an international agreement regulating jurisdiction of the courts, then this agreement and not the rules of the Code of Civil Procedure indicated in IV(d)(i)) would be applicable. Therefore, in such a situation, jurisdiction of the Lithuanian courts would depend on the rules of jurisdiction set in the international agreement.

If the manufacturer has a domicile in a Member State of the EU and there is a direct contractual link between the manufacturer and the injured party and a contract between the manufacturer and the injured party does not satisfy criteria set in Article 15(1) of the Brussels I Regulation and the injured party brings a claim against the manufacturer based on this contract, then the place of performance of the contract might be significant because Article 5(1) of the Brussels I Regulation says that a person domiciled in a Member State may, in another Member State, be sued in matters relating to a contract in the courts of the place of performance of the obligation in question.

Please note that Article 5(1)(b) of the Brussels I Regulation establishes that for the purpose of this provision and unless otherwise agreed, the place of performance of the obligation in question shall be in the case of the sale of goods, the place in a Member State where, under the contract, the goods were or should have been delivered.

So, Article 5(1) of the Brussels I Regulation in some situations (e.g., where factual control over goods passed to the injured party–buyer in Lithuania) can also provide a basis for a jurisdiction of Lithuanian courts over the foreign manufacturer.

In addition, if according to the direct contract between the manufacturer and the injured party–buyer, the manufacturer had to give over the factual control of the good to the buyer in the territory of Lithuania, there is no reason to conclude that the manufacturer, taking into account Article 5(1) of the Brussels I Regulation, could not expect to be brought before the Lithuanian court, although he did not specifically instructed his agent to sell in Lithuanian market.

We also must note that there might be some other facts that may be important in the assessment of whether Lithuanian courts can exercise jurisdiction over foreign manufacturer in a particular case (e.g., is there an agreement on jurisdiction between the manufacturer and the injured party, etc.); however, but we do not think that it is feasible and necessary to elaborate all of them here.

As it is seen from the above, there is a strong likelihood that Lithuanian courts would exercise jurisdiction over the foreign manufacturer in a given case, if the injured party is domiciled in and/or possesses goods in the territory of Lithuania. This is mainly because the CJEU has clearly indicated that the courts for the place where the harmful event occurred are usually the most appropriate for deciding the case, in particular on the grounds of proximity and ease of collecting evidence. In addition, if the place of the delivery of goods is Lithuania, there is sufficient proximity and an authentic link between the case and Lithuanian courts' jurisdiction, which leads to a conclusion that this forum is fair and proper.

(iv) *Additional comments*

Express any additional comment you may have on the solutions offered by your system and the U.S. system.

N/A.

V. JUSTICIABILITY

(d)(i) How would the courts of your country resolve the question of whether the mother should be allowed to proceed with her claim?

If the Criminal Code of the Republic of Lithuania or the Code on Administrative Offences of the Republic of Lithuania would establish as an offence the refusal to provide support to a legitimate child, we are of the opinion that the mother would be able to contest before the court the decision of the prosecutor or other competent officer refusing to commence an action against the father. The court hearing such an appeal would likely apply to the Constitutional Court of the Republic of Lithuania asking it to examine whether the respective provisions of the Criminal Code of the Republic of Lithuania or the Code on Administrative Offences of the Republic of Lithuania, providing protection only to legitimate child, are in conformity with the Constitution of the Republic of Lithuania, namely the constitutional principal of equality and nondiscrimination. If the Constitutional Court accepts that the criminal laws, providing protection only to legitimate children, violates the Constitution, and declares this rule of law as contradictory to the Constitution, the Parliament would be under an obligation to change the laws respectively and these criminal laws, in so far as they do not match the constitutional principles, would become inapplicable.

Please note that the abovementioned appeal of the mother to the court would not be considered as a civil or administrative claim in Lithuania, but as an appeal against the decision of the prosecuting officer. Rules of appeal against such decisions are established in the Code of Criminal Procedure and Code on Administrative Offences. These codes establish the general rule that if an officer refused to file an action, the person who submitted the request for it might appeal the decision of the officer.

We do not think that it would be possible to succeed with a claim asking to stop the discriminatory application of criminal laws before the courts of civil and administrative jurisdiction because questions of criminal prosecution must, as a general rule, be dealt with by courts having jurisdiction over issues of criminal procedure and not by civil or administrative courts. Please also see V(d)(iv) for more details.

(ii) On which provisions and/or case law do you base your answer? If your highest court has addressed this or a similar issue, please describe how the court solved it.

Article 29 of the Constitution of the Republic of Lithuania prohibits unjust discrimination. Article 6, paragraph 2 of the Constitution provides that everyone may defend his rights by invoking the Constitution.

In addition, there was a case (No N-261-742/2010) before the Supreme Administrative Court in which an applicant sought prosecution of a certain person. However, the Code of Administrative Offences provided immunity for this person with respect to an offence he committed. The court of first instance acquitted this person relying on the rule of immunity. The applicant brought an appeal against this judgment. When hearing the appeal, the Supreme Administrative Court stopped the case and referred to the Constitutional Court the question of conformity of the rule providing immunity to the Constitution. The Constitutional Court declared this provision unconstitutional as it contradicted the principles of equality and nondiscrimination. The Parliament changed the law accordingly. However, the Supreme Administrative Court could not convict this person because of the principle *nulla poena sine lege*. Because at the moment when the aforementioned person committed the deed at issue there was no law clearly establishing liability for him for this offence (there was a rule providing immunity to him with respect to this offence), this person could not be held liable for it. Thus the persons who previously had immunity for some offences can be punished only if they committed deeds after the announcement of the decision of the Constitutional Court.

(iii) If you need additional facts to answer this question, please indicate which type of facts would you need and why.

N/A.

(iv) Does your legal system require the same range of considerations to determine whether a party can bring a claim? Are those considerations statutory or constitutional?

According to Article 5 of the Code of Civil Procedure and Law on Administrative Proceedings of the Republic of Lithuania, every interested entity shall be entitled to apply to the court, in the manner prescribed by law, for the protection of his or her infringed or contested right or interest protected under law. In other words, the law establishes the right to judicial protection for any applicant, *inter alia* public agencies, if their rights or interests protected under law are contested or violated.

Thus in Lithuania, as a general rule, every applicant who brings a claim has to demonstrate a particular interest in bringing it before the court. However, one should note that both the case law and legal theory make the distinction between admissibility conditions and conditions for satisfying a claim.

For an action to be admitted for adjudication in an administrative or civil court, there is no need for a claimant to prove with great certainty that his rights or interests have been infringed. The issue of whether the rights or interests of an applicant have been actually violated is to be dealt with not in the stage of admissibility of the action, but in later stages of particular proceedings, i.e., when examining the case on its substance. Thus, the action may be admitted for the adjudication in an administrative or civil court where the infringement of rights and interests is only likely. However, the action shall be dismissed as unfounded if the administrative or civil court, after thorough examination of the case, finds that the applicant's rights or interests have not been violated or that the defendant cannot be held liable for it. The answer to these questions depends on particular circumstances of the case. However, if the action is not "ripe" or "moot" or if the applicant relies on legally unprotected rights/interests, Lithuanian courts will consider that the applicant did not prove the violation of his/her rights/protected interests. This would lead to a dismissal of an action.

The action shall be also dismissed if an applicant requests that the court defend his or her rights in a manner not provided (allowed) by the law or chooses to ask the court to apply relief, which is inappropriate to defend his or her rights or interests (e.g., it cannot redress the infringed rights or interests).

Based on the aforesaid, it seems to us that all three issues – the party must be the "real party in interest," the party must state a claim upon which relief can be granted, the party must satisfy the "justiciability" doctrine – are common to Lithuania, but under different names, and sometimes with slightly different content. Thus, for example, if the law sets some legal rights but does not provide (allow) any (proper) relief for the violation of them, there is a possibility in any case to bring an action defending the rights at issue, arguing that the statute, which does not allow any (proper) relief, violates constitutional principle *ubi ius, ibi remedium.*

On the other hand, if the applicant relies on legally unprotected rights/interests (e.g., raises some moral questions), the judiciary is not a proper institution to deal with them and a claim can be dismissed on the ground that no violation of the legally protected rights/interests have been committed.

(v) Additional comments. Express any additional comment you may have on the solutions offered by your system and the U.S. system.

N/A.

NORWAY

ANNA NYLUND

Associate Professor at the University of Tromsø, Faculty of Law

II. BACKGROUND INFORMATION

a. Please identify yourself, your professional position, and the country on which your answers will be based.

b. Briefly describe the highest court (or courts) of your country and indicate its (or their) function within your legal system.

The Supreme Court is the highest court in Norway. Norway has just one set of courts, no administrative courts, and very few special courts. Therefore, the Supreme Court is the last instance for almost all cases. The Supreme Court decides cases that have an impact outside the case itself, cases that become precedents. The court therefore clarifies what the law is, and, to some extent, develops the law.

III. JUDICIAL DECISION MAKING

a. Have you observed a similar phenomenon in your judicial system? If so, please identify the area(s) of law in which this has occurred. (Please do not limit yourself to questions involving jurisdiction.)

b. If you have observed this phenomenon, does it sometimes occur that the judicially developed tests limit the principles that the tests purport to articulate?

The Norwegian Supreme Court uses a method that is far less sophisticated than the arguments of many other countries. This is probably both a result of the relative small size of the legal culture (as small legal cultures/nations seldom have developed sophisticated legal theories) and of the very pragmatic character of the Norwegian legal system.

However, it is common that the Supreme Court establishes new rules and subsequently develops them. For instance, the rule on evidence collected in an illegal or undue manner. The rule was first established, then developed, and later specified. Rules are seldom developed in a way that would ultimately make them very elaborate, contradictory to the original idea or far from the wording of the law itself.

IV. JURISDICTION

(d)(i) Would your country exercise jurisdiction over the foreign manufacturer on a claim against it by the injured party?

Normally, the agent would be the party in this case, as the agent has chosen to market the device in Norway. However, if the claimant could prove a real need to include the manufacturer as a party in the case, it could be possible to include the manufacturer. In this case, the courts would also need to assess if the manufacturer has a sufficient relationship to Norway.

(ii) On which provisions and/or case law do you base your answer? If your highest court has addressed this or a similar issue, please describe how the court solved it.

Dispute Act §1–3.

V. JUSTICIABILITY

(d)(i) How would the courts of your country resolve the question of whether the mother should be allowed to proceed with her claim?

It is very unlikely that such a case would be filed in Norway, since going to court is generally not the way to change or challenge legislation. Also, since the case would involve criminal legislation, the reason to do this would probably not be considered worthy of trial. It goes against our values and beliefs.

However, it would probably be rejected by the courts, as the mother lacks an interest in having the law overturned; as he personally, nor the child, will receive no benefit from changing the provision. Also, it is not a direct consequence of changing the law that the father will be punished.

(ii) On which provisions and/or case law do you base your answer? If your highest court has addressed this or a similar issue, please describe how the court solved it.

The provision in the Dispute Act (§1–3) reads:

The claimant must show a genuine need to have the claim determined against the defendant. This shall be determined based on a total assessment of the relevance of the claim and the parties' connection to the claim.

(iii) If you need additional facts to answer this question, please indicate which type of facts would you need and why.

(iv) Does your legal system require the same range of considerations to determine whether a party can bring a claim? Are those considerations statutory or constitutional?

The system is based on statutory considerations. The Norwegian constitution has very few provisions on civil rights. However, the test based on Dispute Act §1–3 and consequent case law is basically the same as the U.S. test.

(v) Additional comments. Express any additional comment you may have on the solutions offered by your system and the U.S. system.

The Norwegian system is based largely on finding a practical solution. It is a highly pragmatic legal system.

RUSSIA

MARIA FILATOVA

PhD, Associate Professor at Russian Academy of Foreign Trade

II.b. The Russian judicial system curently is composed of three independent branches of courts: general courts, commercial courts, and the Constitutional Court. Each of first two branches represents a separate hierarchy headed by a supreme court: the Supreme Court of Russia and the Supreme Commercial Court, respectively. The functions of the Supreme Court and the Supreme Commercial Court are similar: the revision of lower courts' acts and giving directions as to the uniform application of law by lower courts.[1]

III. JUDICIAL DECISION MAKING

(a) Have you observed a similar phenomenon in your judicial system?

As Russia belongs to the civil law family, with its tradition of codification and detailed legal regulation, normally the rules (including procedural ones) are set up by law. When applying them, the highest courts give interpretation when necessary, but as a rule, these interpretations do not go beyond the core of the norm itself.

However, two examples may be given when the interpretation limited the scope of the norm and even was contrary to the meaning of the norm. Both refer to the Supreme Commercial Court's activities since it has been traditionally more inventive and far-going in its interpretation of legal provisions.

The first example addresses the interpretation of norms on arbitrability. According to Russian law, most disputes may be subject to arbitration resolution, with exceptions made for disputes of a public nature (involving

[1] This organization of the judicial system is established by the Constitution; however, it may be subject to drastic changes shortly: the President of Russia proposed to unify the two supreme courts in one, and at the moment of writing this report, there is no clear understanding of how the judicial system will function in the forthcoming period.

State bodies), tax, and family disputes. The scope of arbitrability established by law is really broad.

However, the Supreme Commercial Court, in its Informative Letter N 96 of 22 December 2005, stated that disputes regarding real estate (including actions for recognition of property rights) are of a public nature since they imply the State registration of property rights transfer (§27 of the Informative Letter). Since the State registration is an act of public nature, all transfers of rights requiring such registration are of a public nature, too. Therefore, the disputes about rights that may entail such registration are not subject to resolution in arbitration procedures.

This interpretation, presumably a product of competitive wars between commercial courts and arbitration courts, has been used since then by all commercial courts.

The second example also addresses the Supreme Commercial Court and the limits of its "competence-competence." Until recently, the court, as many of the highest jurisdiction in civil law countries, acted as a court of final review instance (with a model close to this of German Revision). The Supreme Commercial Court quashed final judgments of lower courts when the latter violated the uniformity of law and judicial practice.

Starting from a certain moment, however, the Supreme Commercial Court departed from its role of a guarantor of the uniformity of previously established case law; it began creating such new case law when quashing decisions delivered by lower courts. And thus, decisions delivered in conformity with previously existing case law, could be quashed by the Supreme Commercial Court with a view to modify *ratio decidendi* for similar cases. Quashing of judgments in these cases was not "platonic"; that is, the legal status of parties was amended.

Following these practices, when examining cases similar to one with modified *ratio decidendi*, the Supreme Commercial Court started to send them down to lower courts for a reopening of proceedings, invoking its new *ratio decidendi* as a new circumstance justifying such a reopening.

Obviously, no such grounds for reopening were established by the Code of Commercial Procedure: they were deducted by the way of interpretation given by the Supreme Commercial Court.

After considerable legal debate and opposition, including challenging the constitutionality of this practice before the Constitutional Court, the Supreme Commercial Court's approach has prevailed and is now reflected by the Code of Commercial Procedure. However, the quashing of final judgments as a result of a change in the highest court's position is possible only if such annulment does not affect a private party's rights (the principle of legal certainty). It should be noted that this principle is not always strictly followed by the Supreme Commercial Court.

IV. JURISDICTION

The first question concerns the issue of jurisdiction of the national courts over a foreign manufacturer not represented in the country directly but through an agent and the product of which caused injury to an individual domiciled there.

The issue of the Russian courts' jurisdiction over foreign parties is governed by the procedural codes. The latter establish, in particular, that jurisdiction over a foreign party may be exercised when an action for damages to health caused by a foreign party is brought by a claimant (an individual) having its domicile in Russia (subpara. 4 §3 Article 402 of the Code of Civil Procedure); or when a claim is lodged for damages to property caused by an action or other circumstance taking place on the territory of the Russian Federation, or if the injury occurred on the territory of the Russian Federation (subpara. 5 §3 Article 402 of the Code of Civil Procedure subpara. 10 § 1 Article 247 of the Code of Commercial Procedure). Thus, it appears that such a claim may be lodged before Russian courts.

The case law on the matter is not extensive. For instance, on the open databases, one can find a ruling of the Moscow City Court N 11-14420 of 18 July 2012 by which the court confirmed that a claim for health injury caused by labor trauma against a respondent (an enterprise) residing in another country (Azerbaijan) may be lodged with a Russian court if the claimant has its domicile in Russia.

However, if there is a bilateral treaty establishing other rules of jurisdiction, the latter shall apply, and not the domestic norms.

Nothing in the existing case law shows that additional criteria are applied by courts in determining their competence on the matter, including that referred to in the question (the criterion of due process).

The Code of Commercial Procedure as a separate ground of jurisdiction establishes the criterion of substantive connection between a dispute and the territory of the Russian Federation (subpara.10 §1 Article 247 of the Code of Commercial Procedure). However, this criterion is an autonomous one and is not applied in conjunction with others established by the Code.

V. JUSTICIABILITY

There is no difference in the Russian law in the status of children born from parents forming a married or unmarried couple. The term "illegitimate child" is not used by law. Since all children have equal rights to both their parents' support, a claim for such support (usually alimony) may be brought by either parent taking care of the child.

More generally, the question relates to the issue of standing and justiciability, i.e., the matter of judicial protection. As in many other countries, the right to be justiciable should be established by law, be genuine, and have redress.

The concept of justiciability is not developed in the Russian procedural doctrine nor in the case law. The Russian Constitution enshrines the right to judicial protection in a broadest form: all rights guaranteed by law theoretically may be protected through a court proceeding. Economic and social rights (which usually bring most difficulties from the point of view of justiciability) are enshrined as fundamental rights in the Constitution in a general form (right to a housing, to good environment, to cultural diversity, etc.). However, the law very seldom sets up a particular model of its implementation and concrete measures to be adopted by the State and therefore does not imply any particular form of these rights protection.

In particular, the problem was dealt with by the European Court of Human Rights in the judgment *Balakin v. Russia* (21788/06, 4 July 2013, not final). The applicant in the case is a pensioner, with a handicapped daughter suffering from type 2 diabetes. According to Russian law, the family had a right to improved housing conditions on account of their daughter's illness and were put on the local authorities' "first priority" list. The applicant lodged a complaint with a local court about inaction on the part of the local authorities and their failure to provide him with better social housing. He asked the court to order the local authorities to grant him a three-room apartment and pay the compensation for their inaction.

Having heard the applicant, the Russian Court concluded that it did not have jurisdiction to examine his case and discontinued the proceedings. It held, in particular, that the law does not fix time limits for granting housing to families with disabled children and thus the applicant's claim was not within the competence of this court.

From a procedural point of view, it is interesting that the court discontinued the proceeding referring to the lack of its competence to examine the dispute and did not reject the claim referring to the absence of justiciable right.

The issue of justiciability is thus closely related to that of the limits of judicial protection and of particular remedies to be established by law for the realization of general rights enshrined as fundamental (including constitutional ones).

SLOVAK REPUBLIC

ALEXANDRA HORVÁTHOVÁ

LL.M., SJD Candidate and Researcher at CEU Business School, Budapest, Slovak Republic

II.b The judiciary power is divided into two branches: the general courts and the Constitutional Court. The general courts lie in four tiers: (1) 54 district courts (trial courts), (2) 8 regional courts (courts of appeal), (3) the Supreme Court, and (4) the Specialized Criminal Court. District courts are the courts of the first instance, except for administrative and enumerated civil and criminal cases, whereas the regional courts serve as courts of appeal. The Supreme Court is the highest judicial authority in the country and has the function of an appellate review court. The Specialized Criminal Court was established in 2009 as a substitute for the Specialized Court, which was revoked due to its unconstitutionality.

Under Chapter VII of the Constitution, judicial power in the Slovak Republic is exercised by the Supreme Court of the Slovak Republic and other courts. An independent body to oversee compliance with the Constitution is the Constitutional Court of the Slovak Republic.

Under the law, the Supreme Court is the highest judicial authority of the Slovak Republic. It exercises its jurisdiction through its panels and their presiding judges; through divisions and their presiding judges; and through the President and Vice-President of the Supreme Court of the SR. The distribution of cases at the Supreme Court in a given calendar year is determined by the work schedule formulated by the President of the Supreme Court upon a proposal presented by the presiding judges of the various divisions.

The Supreme Court sits on three-member panels composed of the presiding judge and two judges, and on five-member panels composed of the presiding judge and four judges. The head of the panel is the presiding judge.

Three-member panels rule on regular and exceptional legal remedies that challenge decisions made by regional courts, district courts, the Higher Military Court and military district courts, and other cases as set out in the law; examine the legality of decisions made by central authorities of the state administration, unless the law stipulates otherwise; and decide on the recognition and enforceability of decisions of foreign courts in the territory of the SR in cases prescribed by law or by international treaty.

Five-member panels decide on exceptional legal remedies, which challenge decisions that the Supreme Court panels adopted regarding regular legal remedies. Based on the knowledge derived from their decision-making, the panels suggest which of their final decisions should be published in the Collection of Judicial Decisions and Opinions of the Courts of the Slovak Republic; bring to the attention of the presiding judge of the division those cases in which final court decisions reflect conflicting interpretations of laws and other generally binding regulations; and prepare inputs for the report of the Supreme Court concerning the effects of laws and other generally binding regulations and for the proposals of new legislation.

The courts rule on criminal and civil matters and review the legality of decisions made by administrative bodies. Judges sit on panels unless the law prescribes that the matter is to be decided by a single judge. The law specifies the cases in which the panels include lay judges as well as professional judges. The judgments are announced in the name of the Slovak Republic and are always announced in public.

The other court deciding on constitutional matters exclusively is the Constitutional Court of the Slovak Republic, which was established by the Slovak Constitution as an independent judicial body in order to protect constitutionality. Articles 124–140 of the Constitution of the Slovak Republic, regulates the powers of the Constitutional Court.[1]

Generally, the judiciary is a self-governed branch, with the Judicial Council at its top. Judicial Council is in charge of the administration of judiciary. It is responsible for selecting, disciplining, and removing judges. Judges are appointed for an indefinite term by the President upon proposal by the Judicial Council and can be only removed following disciplinary proceedings conducted by a special judicial ethics panel. The Specialized Criminal Court, hand-in-hand with the specialized prosecution, targets and decides the severe criminal violence and corruption-related crimes.

III. JUDICIAL DECISION MAKING

a. Have you observed a similar phenomenon in your judicial system? If so, please identify the area(s) of law in which this has occurred. (Please do not limit yourself to questions involving jurisdiction.)

[1] For more information, see the Slovak Constitution: http://www.concourt.sk/en/A_ustava/ustava_a.pdf

Generally, we could say that this kind of decision-making process is followed as well in Slovakia. Within the reasoning, courts shall give first the rule, which they decided to apply; and second, the interpretation of the rule: how it should be applied to the case at hand together with the reasons why.

The test to control and limit the scope of the underlying principle and the U.S. "reasonability" is often forgotten. However, according to the decision of the Constitutional Court, Pl. Us 17/2007,[2] the conception of material rule of law includes the requirement for the content quality and value of the norm, which should secure the appropriateness of the used legal tool/statute/principle together with the legitimate aim of the legislator, when the norm was adopted.

Once a norm/statute/law is adopted in Slovakia, the parliament adopts an Explanatory Statement [Dôvodová správa], where it tries to expand on the reasons why the law was adopted and define its aims. Thus, when interpreting the law/provision of law, courts sometimes include a reference also to this Explanatory Statement.

One cannot identify specific areas where this phenomenon has occurred, but rather the court instances, which are generally higher courts, meaning the Supreme Court and the Constitutional Court. But again, it is generally individual, depending on the judge or the senate.

Furthermore, given that the Slovak Republic is a Member State of the European Union, depending on the judge or a senate, some court rulings and decisions refer to the judgments of the European Court of Human Rights, the Court of Justice of the European Union, and sometimes even to decisions of other courts of other EU Member States, most often Czech Republic, Austria, and Germany.

b. If you have observed this phenomenon, does it sometimes occur that the judicially developed tests limit the principles that the tests purport to articulate?

Generally, it is a hard observation to make, but the answer would be "yes." Simply put, the tests and laws evolve and one cannot introduce new tests while not condemning the old ones. However, this happens only to a limited extent.

IV. JURISDICTION

(d)(i) Would your country exercise jurisdiction over the foreign manufacturer on a claim against it by the injured party?

[2] *See* http://portal.concourt.sk/Zbierka/2009/4_09s.pdf [available only in Slovak language].

Yes, it would, according to §1(2) of the law no. 250/2007 Coll. on the protection of consumers.

(ii) On which provisions and/or case law do you base your answer? If your highest court has addressed this or a similar issue, please describe how the court solved it.

As stated in the above answer, there is a specific law, which was adopted in accordance with a number of EU/EC directives on the consumer protection (Directives no. 98/27/EC; 99/44/EC; 2002/65/EC; 2005/29/EC; 87/357/EC; 2001/95 EC; 2004/113/EC; 98/6/EC; 93/13/EC and 2009/22/EC).

(iii) If you need additional facts to answer this question, please indicate which type of facts you would need and why

This law is applicable to the sale of products and the provision of services, where the performance takes place in the territory of the Slovak Republic or is related to business in the Slovak Republic. Simply, if any product was sold here, despite being not aimed at the Slovak market, the law is directly applicable and aims to protect the Slovak consumer, who can then decide where he/she would like to sue the seller or producer.

(iv) Additional comments. Express any additional comment you may have on the solutions offered by your system and the U.S. system.

A new trend in the case law of the Slovak Republic has appeared since 2011. There is one specific court in the republic, the Regional Court in Presov [Krajský súd v Prešove], which very extensively interprets the rights of the consumers – even more extensively than the Court of Justice of the European Union. But given the fact that the Supreme Court has yet to sufficiently address consumer disputes, the decision often depends on the court that renders it.

V. JUSTICIABILITY

(d)(i) How would the courts of your country resolve the question of whether the mother should be allowed to proceed with her claim?

In the Slovak Republic, the procedure would be different.

First, a child represented by the mother would always bring the claim (hypothetically, the mother could bring her own claim).

Second, given the fact that there is no law under which the child could ask for a remedy, as the law awards the right only to legitimate children, the child would have to first contest the law as discriminatory before the Constitutional Court under the Act of the National Council of the Slovak Republic of January

20, 1993 on the Organization of the Constitutional Court of the Slovak Republic, on the Proceedings before the Constitutional Court, and on the status of its judges, claiming the breach of Article 127 of the Constitution.

Several laws have since acknowledged that legitimate and illegitimate children enjoy the same rights.

In the Slovakian civil court, one would have to prove certain determinants before the court would accept the claim. First, the court would assess its own jurisdiction in the case at hand (territorial, subject-matter, and personal). Once it decides that it has the jurisdiction, it will assess the standing of a child, meaning whether it is the appropriate claimant, according to the §19 of the Civil Procedure Code no. 99/1963 Coll. This would be decided affirmatively. Third, from the procedural perspective, the court would assess whether the claim fulfills all the formal requirements established by the Civil Procedure Code.

From here on, the court would decide on the substantive matters and issues (including the statute of limitation). In the claim, the rights, which have been breached, would have to be specified together with the showed causality and specification of the sought remedies. All these aspects would have to be specified in either a specific law – in this case for the rights of children or in general code, the Civil Code. In some cases, a general claim can refer to the Constitution or hypothetically general principles of the EU, but one would have to be specific on the claimed breached rights and remedies.

(ii) On which provisions and/or case law do you base your answer? If your highest court has addressed this or a similar issue, please describe how the court solved it.

See above.

(iii) If you need additional facts to answer this question, please indicate which type of facts would you need and why.

No.

(iv) Does your legal system require the same range of considerations to determine whether a party can bring a claim? Are those considerations statutory or constitutional?

Both, but to a greater extent they are statutory. However, in certain areas, e.g., human rights, there have been claims in which the constitutional principle or right was claimed.

REPUBLIC OF SLOVENIA

PROF. DR. ALEŠ GALIČ

University of Ljubljana, Faculty of Law, Slovenia

1. THE RELATION BETWEEN THE SUPREME COURT AND THE CONSTITUTIONAL COURT IN SLOVENIA

Pursuant to Art. 127 of the Slovenian Constitution, the Supreme court of the Republic of Slovenia (*Vrhovno sodišče Republike Slovenije*) is the highest court in the country. There exists also the Constitutional Court (*Ustavno sodišče*), but it is not a part of the regular court system.

However, a party to civil litigation can, after the exhaustion of all legal remedies within civil procedure, file a constitutional complaint if he or she believes that a judgment rendered in civil litigation violated constitutional rights.

According to Art. 160 of the Constitution, one of the powers of the Constitutional Court is to decide on constitutional complaints in case of alleged violation of human rights and fundamental freedoms by the judgments of (*inter alia*) courts in civil litigation. Despite this competence, the Constitutional Court cannot be regarded as a further court of appeals for civil cases. The so-called "fourth instance doctrine" is (or at least is supposed to be) strictly observed, meaning that the Constitutional court is not just another tier of jurisdiction in a civil litigation, examining the correctness of factual findings and legal views of the lower courts.

A constitutional complaint to the Constitutional Court was adopted following the German model of *Verfassungsbeschwerde* and can roughly be compared to a petition to the European Court of Human Rights (under the European Human Rights Convention[1]). Hence, it is the Supreme court which has the "last word"

[1] There is a major difference between a constitutional complaint and complaint to the ECtHR: the latter can only issue declaratory decisions and award just satisfaction in case it finds violations of human rights. On the contrary, the Constitutional Court may also quash the impugned

when it comes to application of "ordinary law." Only constitutional issues are reserved for a final review of the Constitutional court.

When deciding upon constitutional complaints, the Constitutional Court is not empowered to control the correctness of the application of procedural and substantive law and finding of facts, but only whether an ordinary court has interpreted laws in such a manner that contravenes a certain constitutional right.[2]

The power of the Constitutional Court to decide on constitutional complaints is a consequence of the Constitutional Court's fundamental jurisdiction, which is to review the conformity of statutes with the constitution: the system of constitutional protection is not complete if a law itself is in conformity with a constitution, but is then interpreted in an unconstitutional manner in a particular case.

Courts, including the Supreme Court, are not empowered to decide upon the conformity of the law with the constitution. This is reserved for the Constitutional Court. If, in the course of proceedings, a judge of an "ordinary court" suspects that the law that he/she should apply is unconstitutional, he/she must stay the proceedings and refer the matter to the Constitutional Court (Art. 156 of the Constitution).

For the purpose of the submitted questionnaire, I will consider the Supreme Court of Slovenia as the highest court. Nevertheless, it should be stressed that both mock cases raise constitutional issues (due process of law, right of access to court). Thus it might well be the case that the Constitutional Court would have "the last word" when it comes to the question whether the Supreme court's interpretation of the law was in conformity with these constitutional rights.

1. *Access to the Supreme Court (further appeal on points of law)*

The so-called "revision" (*revizija*) in the Slovenian legal system is a further appeal on points of law, similar to the remedy of the same name in German or Austrian law, for instance, and can also be compared to the *cassation* in French or Italian law.[3] It enables access to the Supreme Court and thereby strives to achieve that this court will be able to effectively fulfil its constitutionally determined role of the supreme judicial authority, responsible for the unifying of case law. In Slovenian law, a revision is considered to be an

decision and order a retrial. But according to statistics, less than 5 percent of constitutional complaints in civil (including labor and family cases) and commercial cases are successful.

[2] *See, e.g.*, Decision of the Const. Court, Up 408/00, 20.11.2001.

[3] *See* L. Ude, *Civilno procesno pravo* [Civil procedure] (Ljubljana, ☒Z UL, 2002), p. 337.

extraordinary legal remedy. It neither prevents the enforceability of the judgment it is directed against, nor its becoming *res iudicata* (Art. 369, CPA).

However, if the revision is well founded, the challenged judgment can be altered or set aside.

The grounds for revision consist of errors in substantive and procedural law; most of the so-called "absolute violations of procedure" may be invoked, but only those "relative violations of procedure" that were committed in the proceedings in the appellate court. Findings of facts cannot be subject to review in the Supreme Court. The differentiation between questions of facts and questions of law is, however, in certain aspects, difficult.

For example, a question whether established facts can be subordinated to a certain legal standard (general clause), such as "due care of a reasonable person," "activity with an elevated degree of risk" (in connection with the issue of strict liability) or "appropriate time-limit" are considered to be questions of law (and therefore can be subject to review in the Supreme Court). Also whether the awarded damages for the established suffering correspond to a standard of a "just satisfaction," is a question of law.[4] With regard to future damages, resulting from the harmful event, the determination of the court that their coming into existence can be expected on the "basis of a regular course of events" (which is a legal precondition for awarding compensation for future damages) is considered to be a question of law.[5] The question of whether one event gave rise to another in the sense of natural science is a question of fact; however, the question of whether a legally relevant causal link is thereby established is a question of law.[6] On the other hand, the determination of the contractual will (in the sence of the goal, which the parties wished to achieve by entering into the contract) is considered to be a question of fact.[7]

The Supreme Court examines the judgment only in respect of those parts that are subject to attack and only within the limits of reasons stated in the revision. Unless the party is himself a lawyer who has passed the state legal exam, both the petition for leave to file a revision as well as the revision must be filed by an attorney-at-law. If this condition is not fulfilled, the application

4 *E.g.*, judgment of the Supreme Court, II Ips 354/98, 11.3.1999.

5 Judgment of the Supreme Court, II Ips 781/94, 6.12.1995.

6 J. Zobec, Ugotavljanje (obsega) škode – pravno ali dejansko vprašanje? [Determination of (the Extent) of Damage – Question of Law or Question of of Fact]v: L. Ude (Ed.), *III. Dnevi civilnega prava* (Ljubljana, Inštitut za primerjalno pravo, 2005), p. *81 et seq*.

7 L. Ude, "Dejstva in pravo – razlikovanje dejanskih in pravnih vprašanj" [Facts and Law – Distinction Between Questions of Law and of Fact]v: L. Ude (Ed.), *III. Dnevi civilnega prava* (Ljubljana, Inštitut za primerjalno pravo, 2005), p. 121.

is rejected as inadmissible without first returning the matter to the applicant for rectification.

With the CPA amendment in 2008, the system of the revision has been considerably reformed.[8] Previously, the decisive admissibility criterion for the revision was solely the amount in dispute (whereby this was set rather low, causing that the access to the Supreme Court was widely available, which resulted in backlogs in the Supreme Court). With the 2008 reform, the legislator has changed the criteria of admissibility of the revision, with the result that the revision now amounts to a remedy, the availability of which depends rather on the discretion of the Supreme Court.

The importance of the role of the Supreme Court in the unifying of case law and the giving of guidance for the application of law is emphasized. Besides, the requirements for the filing and support of a revision have been changed. After the 2008 reform, the revision is admissible only if a leave has been granted by the Supreme Court. The Supreme Court is supposed to give such permission if the case raises a question of law of fundamental significance or if the development of law or the preservation of uniformity of case law requires a decision by the Supreme Court.

The criterion of amount in dispute has been retained only partially. If the amount in dispute does not exceed 2,000 euros or if it concerns a matter where a revision is excluded already by statute (for example, small-claims cases, provisional and protective measures, enforcement of judgments proceedings, certain noncontentious procedures), the revision is inadmissible *per se* and a leave to file a revision cannot be granted. On the other hand, if the amount in dispute exceeds 40,000 euros, the revision is admissible already by statute and it is not necessary for the applicant to obtain a leave from the Supreme Court. However, the limit is set to such a high amount that the majority of revisions dealt with by the Supreme court will be those where it was necessary to first obtain the leave to file the case.

With such reform, the legislative goal of this remedy has obviously shifted – previously the interest of an individual party was the focus and access to the Supreme Court was admissible if the matter was of sufficient significance from the viewpoint of the parties (the amount in dispute).[9] This remedy has

[8] *See, e.g.*, L. Ude, "Reforma revizije in zahteve za varstvo zakonitosti" [A reform of remedies of revision and protection of legality], **33** *Podjetje in delo*, 2007, No. 6-7, p. 1078 *et seq.*, A. Galič, "Za reformo revizije v pravdnem postopku" [In favour of a reform of remedy of revision in civil procedure], **26** *Pravna praksa*, 2007, No. 43 (suppl.).

[9] For Slovenia, *see* The Explanatory memorandum to the draft amendment of the Civil procedure Act, 2008, p. 156

predominantly served a public purpose since the reforms in the countries of the former Yugoslavia.

Whether leave to file a revision should be granted depends on the significance of the case from an objective public point of view, and this significance should, in any case, has significance beyond the particular case at issue.

The above considerations concern the question of preserving or achieving the uniformity of case law or achieving that the highest judicial authority will have an opportunity to resolve an important legal question and thereby contribute to the development of law.[10]

The fact that the appellate court may have decided the case erroneously is not, therefore, sufficient grounds to grant leave.

By introducing such filtering criteria, legislatures in the region have implicitly recognized – and the Slovenian Constitutional Court has even explicitly confirmed – that the role of the Supreme Court is predominantly that of *creating precedents* – thus, in view of the benefit foremost for the justice system as a whole and all future litigants.[11] In summarizing the goal of the reform, the Slovenian Constitutional Court, went on to establish the following:

> When the Supreme Court takes interpretive positions on relevant legal issues, it makes law. It co-shapes the criteria that in similar cases in the future will serve as *ex ante* guidelines for courts and the resolution of legal rules in general. In such a manner it enhances the predictability of legal rules and, by extension, legal certainty.[12]

The party may, within 30 days from the day when a judgment of the court of appeals was served on her, file a petition to grant a leave to revision. The petition must be addressed directly to the Supreme Court and must briefly, but concretely, state the reasons that could justify the granting of the leave to revision. If the appellant invokes that the judgment of the appellate court departs from the case law of the Supreme Court, it must concretely identify the file numbers of the Supreme Court judgments from which the attacked judgment allegedly departs. In a similar manner, the appellant is expected to prove that the decision in his case departs from the case law, which has been uniformly established on the level of appellate courts, concerning questions of law not yet resolved by the Supreme Court.

[10] The Explanatory memorandum to the draft amendment of the Civil procedure Act, 2008, p. 157.

[11] Decision of the Slovenian Constitutional Court, U-I-302/09, 12 May 2011: "This regulation of an appeal on a point of law affirms the role of the Supreme Court as *a precedent court*."

[12] *Ibidem*.

The Supreme Court decides upon the petition in a panel of three judges. If the Supreme Court rejects the granting of the leave to file a revision, it does not need to give reasons for such decision; it is sufficient to briefly state that the case does not fulfil the admissibility criteria as defined by the CPA. The decision of the Supreme Court not to grant the leave to file a revision cannot be appealed against. If, on the other hand, the Supreme Court grants the leave to file a revision (which may be restricted just to certain issues raised by the appellant), the party then has 15 days in which he or she must file a revision with detailed reasons. The revision is filed with the court of first instance, which shall, if the revision is admissible and complete, send both the revision and the previous petition for leave to file it to the opponent, who may submit the replication in 15 days. The file is then sent to the Supreme Court. The Supreme Court decides about the revision in session *in camera*, in a panel of five judges.

III. JUDICIAL DECISION MAKING

Legal writing in Slovenia acknowledges that the basic criterion for determining limits of international jurisdiction is whether there exists a *reasonable and real link* between the state of the forum and the dispute.[13] The Constitutional Court held that if such a reasonable and real link exists, the state is even obliged to offer its courts for a determination of a dispute.[14]

The courts however haven't explicitly answered the opposite question: Does the state violate any constitutional rights (procedural guarantees) if it "too widely opens doors to its courts"? The legal writing warns that such outcomes should be avoided. By allowing their courts to adjudicate in litigation that is in no way connected with the forum state, these states are excessively spreading limits of their international jurisdiction. Thus, they are enabling forum shopping. Also, such an extension of international jurisdiction neglects a need of a proper cooperation and respect between sovereign states. The viewpoint of the defendant's constitutional rights however has not been dealt with.

In any case, the aforementioned principles primarily bind the legislature. There is no room for the court to use discretion to decline jurisdiction if an explicit statutory basis exists. The doctrine of *forum non conveniens* is rejected (both in the context of national law as well as in context of the Brussels I Regulation).

[13] *See, e.g.*, Wedam Luki⊠, Polajnar Pavčnik, Ilešič, MEDNARODNO ZASEBNO PRAVO – ZAKON S KOMENTARJEM, Ljubljana, 1992, p. 87.
[14] Decision of the Constitutional Court, No. Up-13/99-24, dated 8 March. 2001.

Whereas courts must – insofar the wording of the law permits – interpret laws in a manner that does not violate the Constitution, they cannot disregard clear wording of the law. If the court believes that the law is not in conformity with the Constitution, the judge must stay proceedings and submit the matter to the Constitutional Court. But the judge is not empowered to simply disregard the law and determine jurisdiction, e.g., relying on "general principles."[15]

III. JURISDICTION

Slovenia is a EU member state. Therefore, for determining international jurisdiction in civil and commercial matters, it is relevant whether the defendant is domiciled in an EU member state or not. International jurisdiction over disputes concerning defendants domiciled in an EU member state is governed by the Brussels I Regulation (Council *Regulation* (EC) No. 44/2001 of 22 December 2000 on jurisdiction and the recognition and enforcement of judgments in civil and commercial matters). In disputes that concern defendants from third states, Slovenian national law remains applicable – International Private Law and Procedure Act (hereinafter PILPA).[16]

The general criterion for jurisdiction under both regimes (the Brussels I Regulation and the national law) is the same: the defendant's domicile. If the defendant is not domiciled in Slovenia, it must be examined whether the case might fall in the scope of special jurisdiction for matters relating to torts. In this regard, both the Brussels I regulation as well as national law

[15] Such a discussion was some time ago alive in Slovenia with regard to so-called jurisdiction based on the presence of assets. Old Yugoslav legislation, following article 23 of German Civil procedure code (ZPO) based international jurisdiction also solely on a circumstance that a defendant possesses some property within that state, whereby it's not demanded for that property to be in any way connected with the claim (*forum patrimonii*). Neither did these assets need to be sufficient to satisfy the plaintiff's claim. The criticisms of jurisdiction based on a presence of assets as a typical example of exorbitant jurisdiction were not neglected by drafters of the new Slovenian Private International Law and Procedure Act (1999).

A provision on *forum patrimonii* is still included (Art. 58/2 slo PILA), however, with some restrictions. Compared to Art. 54 of the Yugoslav PIL Code, the formulation in the new Slovenian Act is more restrictive in two aspects: only plaintiffs who are residents in Slovenia can invoke this jurisdiction and a certain correlation between the value of the claim and the value of the assets that formed a bases of the jurisdiction must exist (it's not clear whether it is meant that defendant's assets must be of such a value that would cover the whole plaintiff's claim, or that even a [significant] partial payment of the plaintiff's whole claim from these assets would sufficit to invoke this jurisdiction). It however seems that even this more restrictive definition of *forum patrimonii* must be regarded as excessive.

[16] *Zakon o mednarodnem zasebnem pravu in postopku*, Official Gazette, No. 56/99.

provide for a special (elective) basis for jurisdiction in the place where the harmful event occured (Art. 5/3 BU and Art. 53 PILPA). It has already been clarified in the context of the Brussels I Regulation[17] and it is explicitly recognized in the PILPA that this concept covers both – the place where the wrongdoer acted (*forum delicti commissi*) as well as the place of the harmful result (*forum laesionis*). It can be assumed that the answer to the question in the mock case no. 1 would be the same regardless of whether the Brussels I or the national law is relevant for determining jurisdiction.

The ECJ has already confirmed that claims arising out of product liability are based in tort, thus the court where the harmful event occurred has jurisdiction over them.[18] In addition, it has clarified (at least to a certain extent) how to construe both the place where the wrongdoer acted (place of the event giving rise to the damage) but also the place where the damage (injury) occurred (*forum laesionis*). The former relates to the place of the production (manufacture) whereas the latter to the place where the initial damage to the claimant occured "as a result of the normal use of the product for the purpose for which it was intended."[19] ECJ adopted this criteria in the case where a defective product was actually used as a raw-material for production of further products (fertilizers), but the reasoning would – in fact even to a greater extent – relate to cases where there is a direct link between the defect of the product and the damage (e.g., a car accident). It is thus not decisive whether the foreign manufacturer directly marketed its product in the country but instructed its agent to market the product wherever it could be sold.

The ECJ recalled that the special jurisdiction for torts must be construed in a restrictive manner. Nevertheless it held that the jurisdiction in the place where the harmful event occurred – which covers both the place of the act giving rise to the damage and the place of actual damage – is based on the existence of a particularly close connecting factor between the dispute and the courts of the place where the harmful event occurred, which justifies the attribution of jurisdiction to those courts for reasons relating to the sound administration of justice and the efficacious conduct of proceedings.[20] Obviously the aspect of the defendant's reasonable predictability of available forums is not a part of this assessment.

[17] ECJ Judgment in case G.J. Bier B.V. v. Mines de potasse d'Alsace, dated 30 November 1976, C-21/76.
[18] ECJ Judgmennt in case Handte, dated 17 July 1992, C-26/91.
[19] Judgment of the ECJ in the case Zuid Chemie, dated 16 July 2009, C-189/08.
[20] *Ibid.*, at para. 22,24.

Therefore, the answer to case no. 1 is that a Slovenian court would assume jurisdiction in a case based on the given facts. If the Brussels I Regulation were applicable, it would directly rely on the ECJ's judgment in the *Zuid Chemie* case, and if national law were applicable, it would most probably cite this judgment as a persuasive authority. Unfortunately, I cannot report on any judgments of the Supreme Court where the question of limits of jurisdiction in product liability cross-border cases was actually discussed.

IV. JUSTICIABILITY

It is very difficult to answer this case in the context of Slovenian law, which is based on entirely different premises.

There can be no separate private action for declaring a law unconstitutional in Slovenian law. Nor can there be any direct civil claim based on the alleged unconstitutionality of the law; there is no system to make such claims "justiciable." The real party in interest (which here would not be the mother, but the child) may submit the case for review of constitutionality to the Constitutional Court if he or she has "legal interest." However, no "legal interest" exists in cases where the attacked legal norm does not produce immediate effects.[21]

In such case, the party is first expected to pursue its individual claim in (civil, criminal, administrative...) proceedings and argue that the law is unconstitutional there. If the court accepts this view, it shall stay proceedings and refer the matter to the Constitutional Court. If it does not (and in the end, the party's claim is dismissed), the party will be able to submit the matter to the Constitutional Court via the constitutional complaint. Thus, the possibility of a direct access to the Constitutional Court is very limited for *individuals*.

As explained above, the courts are not empowered themselves to exercise judicial review over constitutionality of statutes. They may, if the law at issue is relevant for resolution of a dispute, stay the proceedings and refer the matter to the Constitutional Court.

But the presented case relates to criminal law (definition of criminal offences).

If indictment in criminal case were brought by the public prosecutor (or if he or she refused to start proceedings, then the victim of the crime could still take a role of so-called "private prosecutor"), the court could stay proceedings and refer the case to the Constitutional Court (which would examine the issue

[21] *See, e.g.*, decision of the Constitutional Court No. U-I-80/13-4, dated 4 June 2013.

of discrimination). But this would not be an option in the framework of the pending proceedings since it could not possibly affect its outcome. Even if the law were declared unconstitutional, the offender could not be punished since this would amount to a retroactive application of a law (and would also violate the principle of *lex certa* – a crime must be defined as such in the time when it was committed). Therefore it is practically impossible to argue in a concrete (pending) case that the law is unconstitutional because it does not define certain acts as criminal offences.

The only option to pursue the issue of discrimination in the discussed case would be the following. If the mother (on behalf of child) were unsuccessful in enforcing maintenance against the father, it would theoretically be possible to start a lawsuit against the state for damages. The mother would then need to prove damage (lack of payment of alimonies – maintenance – of the father) and the wrongful act of the state that gave rise to this damage.

The wrongful act of the state would be its omission to provide effective means of enforcement of family support and maintenance rights. So theoretically it would be possible to claim that the wrongful act of the state was a particular omission to act – the omission to adopt legislation necessary for effective enforcement of rights.

However, it would be highly unlikely for the claimant to succeed.

It is practically impossible to establish the causal link in such case. The claimant would need to prove that providing for criminal sanctions against parents who neglect their parental responsibilities is the necessary precondition for effective enforcement of civil rights of their children. This is an unlikely conclusion. It is – in general – not necessary to make violation of civil rights a criminal offence in order to make these rights effective. What is necessary is an effective system of enforcement of civil judgments (in casu: judgments concerning maintenance). And even if it was necessary, it is difficult to prove that liability to criminal prosecution would make enforcement of the maintenance claim in the particular case effective.

In any case, it would not be the mother who could pursue any of the aforementioned claims. It would only be the child (regardless of age) who would have standing to act as a party in proceedings. The mother would only act as a child's statutory representative. This distinction is quite clear in Slovenian law.

As explained, it is difficult to discuss the questions of justiciability, standing, and real party in interest along the lines of the suggested hypothetical case. As explained, the doctrine of justiciability is not developed in Slovenian law. Only if the party with standing (thus: pursuing its civil claims) would file a civil claim pursuing its own interests (e.g., a claim for damages against the state for acts and omissions of the state power), would the question of constitutionality of the law become relevant. But this question would then be – if the judge were of opinion that the law was indeed unconstitutional – submitted to the Constitutional Court.

Otherwise, the doctrine of "standing" in Slovenia is interpreted as meaning that the party may only start civil proceedings for protection of her individual – and real, not just hypothetical – interests. Whereas this is usually obvious in cases where condemnatory relief is sought,[22] the examination of "standing" (also "legal interest") is more relevant in claims for declaratory relief. A careful examination as to the standing in declaratory actions is aimed to prevent the court from being burdened with mock, hypothetical cases and to prevent the court from rendering advisory opinions where no actual dispute as to civil rights and obligations in real relationship exists.[23] The benefit, expected from judicial decision should directly relate to rights and obligations in law, not just economic expectations.[24]

[22] Decision of the Supreme Court No. II Ips 246/2000, dated 8.11.2000.

[23] JUDGMENT OF THE SUPREME COURT NO. II IPS 110/2011, DATED 26.5.2011, DECISION OF THE SUPREME COURT NO. II IPS 734/2009, DATED 20.1.2011.

[24] *E.g.*, decision of the Supreme court No. II Ips 185/2008 dated 17.6.2010.

SOUTH KOREA

PROFESSOR GYOHO LEE

Chung-Ang University School of Law, Seoul, South Korea

*II.b.*Briefly describe the highest court (or courts) of your country and indicate its (or their) function within your legal system.

The Supreme Court (*Daebupwon*) is the highest court in South Korea. Courts in Korea consist of three tiers of courts: the district courts, including the family court and the administrative court; high courts; and the Supreme Court.

The Supreme Court is composed of the Chief Justice and 13 Justices. The Supreme Court hears appeals from judgments or rulings rendered by the High Courts, the Patent Court, the appellate panels of the District Courts, or the Family Court in civil, criminal, administrative, patent, and domestic relations cases. Also, the Supreme Court hears exceptional appeals from the judgments rendered by the courts of the first instance under special circumstances. In addition, the Supreme Court has the power to make a definitive review on the constitutionality or legality of orders, rules, regulations, and actions taken by administrative entities.

The jurisdiction of the Supreme Court is exercised at the Grand Bench or Petty Benches. The Grand Bench consists of more than two-thirds of the Justices with the Chief Justice presiding. A Petty Bench is composed of four Justices. The Petty Benches rule most of the cases appealed to the Supreme Court. However, a case is referred to the Grand Bench in the event that a Petty Bench fails to reach a consensus of the decisions to be rendered or if the case falls under one of the following categories:

(i) Where it is deemed that any order, rule, or regulation is in contravention of the Constitution;
(ii) Where it is deemed that any order, rule, or regulation is in contravention of law;

(iii) Where it is deemed necessary to modify the previous opinion of the Supreme Court on the interpretation and implementation of the Constitution, laws, orders, rules, or regulations; and
(iv) Where it is deemed that adjudication by a Petty Bench is not appropriate.

When the grounds for appeal to the Supreme Court submitted by the appellant do not fall under such categories as are enumerated by the law, the Supreme Court is to dismiss the appeal without further examining the case. In this case, the reasons for dismissal need not be stated.[1]

On the other hand, the Korean Constitutional Court has jurisdiction over constitutional review of statutes, constitutional complaints, competence disputes between governmental entities, impeachments of high-ranking governmental officials, and dissolution of political parties. A decision of the Constitutional Court cannot be appealed and binds all state agencies and local governments.[2]

III. JUDICIAL DECISION MAKING

(a) Have you observed a similar phenomenon in your judicial system? If so, please identify the area(s) of law in which this has occurred. (Please do not limit yourself to questions involving jurisdiction.)

Yes, a similar phenomenon in Korea can be seen in the area of private international law. According to the decisions rendered by the Supreme Court in Korea, the exclusive choice-of-court agreement in international commerce is valid if it meets the requirements,[3] which are as follows:

(i) The case in question should not be subject to exclusive jurisdiction of a court of another country;
(ii) A Korean court must have international jurisdiction on the case in question;
(iii) The case in question must have reasonable relevance to the Korea court;

[1] National Court Administration, The Supreme Court of Korea 13 (2011).

[2] The Constitutional Court of Korea, The Constitutional Court of Korea 22 (2012).

[3] Judgment Rendered by the Korean Supreme Court on April 28, 2011 (Case No. 2009Da19093); Judgment Rendered by the Korean Supreme Court on August 26, 2010 (Case No. 2010Da28185); Judgment Rendered by the Korean Supreme Court on September 9, 1997 (Case No. 96Da20093).

(iv) The exclusive choice-of-court agreement will not be the one that is so strikingly unreasonable and unfair that it can be a legal act against public policy.

b. If you have observed this phenomenon, does it sometimes occur that the judicially developed tests limit the principles that the tests purport to articulate?

The Korean Supreme Court held that

> [In] terms of the said (ii) requirement in international patent dispute, the courts of the country in which the patent at issue was registered or its registration was claimed can, in general, have the exclusive jurisdiction in establishment, validity or revocation of a patent for which registration is required. However, the courts of the country in which registration was made or claimed do not have exclusive jurisdiction in an action for performance of a contract which transfer the patent right because it deals with interpretation and existence of effect, of the assignment contract which has nothing to do with the establishment, validity, or revocation of the patent.[4]

IV. JURISDICTION

(d)(i) Would your country exercise jurisdiction over the foreign manufacturer on a claim against it by the injured party?
Probably.

(ii) On which provisions and/or case law do you base your answer? If your highest court has addressed this or a similar issue, please describe how the court solved it.

In terms of international jurisdiction, Article 2(1) of the Private International Act in Korea prescribes as follows:

1. the court shall entertain international jurisdiction in cases where the parties or disputed subject-matters have a substantial relationship with the Republic of Korea. The court must comply with reasonable principle consistent with allocation of international jurisdiction doctrine in determining whether the parties or the disputed subject-matters are substantially related to the Republic of Korea.
2. The court shall determine whether the parties or the disputed subject-matters are substantially related to the Republic of Korea by taking into account the domestic law's jurisdictional provisions as well as by

[4] Judgment Rendered by the Korean Supreme Court on April 28, 2011 (Case No. 2009Da19093).

> considering sufficiently the special feature of international jurisdiction in light of section 1 mentioned above.

According to the decisions rendered by the Korean Supreme Court,

> [I]nternational jurisdiction is determined by basic ideology that aims at fairness, appropriateness, rapidity, and economy between parties. Specifically, the court will have to take into account personal interests such as fairness, expediency, and foreseeability between the parties to an action, and interests of judicial branch or countries such as appropriateness, rapidity, and efficiency of adjudication and effectiveness of judgments as well. The court must reasonably determine which the interests among them it needs to protect, by basing the subjective standard on substantial connection between the forum state and the parties and between the forum state and the case in dispute.[5]

In this hypo, the place where the injury occurs is the Republic of Korea, and the injured person is located in the Republic of Korea. He or she will file an action for damages so that he or she can sue against the manufacturer at his or her domicile in a domestic case because he or she is allowed to sue against the defendant in the claimant's domicile in the domestic case.

Even though judicial competences in a domestic case are an important factor in determining international jurisdiction, the court will take into account personal interests of the parties, judicial interests, and national interests altogether. Eveb though it is difficult to guess whether the Korean court has international jurisdiction over the hypo case, I can say that there is the substantial connection between the forum state and the parties and between the forum state and the case in dispute.

V. JUSTICIABILITY

(d)(i) How would the courts of your country resolve the question of whether the mother should be allowed to proceed with her claim?

The mother should not be allowed to proceed with her claim as a real party in interest. However, she is permitted to bring an action for affiliation as the legal representative of her illegitimate child after she affiliates her illegitimate child under Article 974, 975, and 863 of the Korean Civil Code.

[5] Judgment Rendered by the Korean Supreme Court on May 24, 2012 (Case No. 2009Da22549); Judgment Rendered by the Korean Supreme Court on January 27, 2005 (Case No. 2002Da59788).

Where the agreement on child support cannot or would not be made between the natural parents after affiliation judgment was rendered by the Family Court, the Family Court shall decide it upon a request of the mother or *ex officio*. The mother can enforce it by virtue of Article 63 bis (Order for Direct Payment of Child Support), Article 64 (Order for Implementation), and Article 67 (Sanctions against Non-performance of Liability) of Family Litigation Act. However, the father will not be criminally liable.

(ii) On which provisions and/or case law do you base your answer? If your highest court has addressed this or a similar issue, please describe how the court solved it.

My answer is based on Articles 974, 975, 837, 837bis, 855, 859, 863, and 864 bis of Civil Code in Korea, and Articles 62, 63, 63 bis, 64, and 67 of Family Litigation Act.

Civil Code
Article 974 (Duty to Furnish Support)
Relatives falling under each of the following subparagraphs shall be under a duty to furnish support to each other:

1. Among lineal blood relatives and their spouses;
2. Deleted; <by Act No. 4199, Jan. 13, 1990>
3. Among any other relatives (limited to cases where they share living accommodations).

Article 975 (Duty to Furnish Support and Ability of Living)
A person under duty to furnish support shall perform his or her duty only in cases where the person entitled to receive support is unable to support himself or herself by his or her own financial resources or labor.
Article 837 (Divorce and Responsibility of Fostering Children)

(1) The parties shall determine by agreement matters concerning fostering their children.
(2) If the agreement as set forth in paragraph (1) shall include matters as follows.
 1. Decision on the custodian;
 2. Child support; and
 3. Visitation right and methods thereof.
(3) Where the agreement as set forth in paragraph (1) harms children's welfare, the Family Court shall order correction or decide *ex officio* matters related to fostering, taking consideration of children's intention and age, each parent's financial status and other circumstances.
(4) Where the agreement on fostering cannot or would not be made, the Family Court shall decide it upon a request of the party or *ex officio*.

In such cases, the Family Court shall take matters as set forth in paragraph (3) into account.

(5) Where deemed necessary for children's welfare, the Family Court may change matters concerning fostering or take other appropriate measures, upon a request of each parent, children or prosecutor or ex officio.

(6) Except for matters related to fostering, the provisions of paragraphs (3) through (5) shall not change the rights and duties of parents.

Article 837 bis (Visitation Rights)

(1) A parent who does not take care of children and his/her children shall have the visitation right.

(2) If it is required for the welfare of children, the Family Court may, upon a request of the party or *ex officio*, restrict or exclude such visitation right.

Article 855 (Affiliation)

(1) A child born out of wedlock may be affiliated by its natural father or mother. When the marriage of the parent becomes null and void, the child born between them shall be deemed to be a child born out of wedlock.

(2) A child born out of wedlock, when its father and mother, shall be deemed to be a child born during the marriage from the time of the marriage.

Article 859 (Effectiveness of Affiliation)

(1) Affiliation shall become effective when it is reported in accordance with the provisions of the Act on the Registration, etc. of Family Relationship

(2) Affiliation may be effected by a will. In this case, the executor of a will shall make such report.

Article 863 (Action Seeking for Affiliation)
A child, any of its lineal descendants or the agent by law of any of them, may bring an action against its father or mother demanding affiliation by its father or mother.
Article 864 bis (Affiliation and Responsibility of Fostering Child, etc.)
The provisions of Articles 837 and 837 bis shall apply *mutatis mutandis* with respect to the responsibility of fostering a child and the visitation right in the case of the affiliation of the child.[6]

II. Family Litigation Act

Article 62 (Prior Disposition)

(1) When deemed specially necessary for the settlement of a case where an action in a family case exists, or a request for an adjudication or a

[6] Judgment Rendered by Seoul High Court on April 13, 1987 (Case No. 87Re20).

conciliation, the family court, conciliation committee, or judge in charge of conciliation may, either *ex officio* or upon request of a party, issue an order to prevent the other party or other interested persons from altering the current status or disposing of the goods, and make dispositions deemed proper, such as disposition for preserving the property related to the case, disposition for custody and fostering of the related person, etc.

(2) In making a disposition under paragraph (1), the sanction under Article 67 (1) shall be notified.

(3) In an urgent case, the presiding judge or chief mediator may independently make a disposition under paragraph (1).

(4) An immediate appeal may be made against a disposition under paragraphs (1) and (3).

(5) No disposition under paragraph (1) shall have any executive force.

Article 63 (Provisional Attachment and Provisional Disposition)

(1) Notwithstanding Article 62, a family court may make a provisional attachment or provisional disposition by making a family litigation case or a family non-litigation case of Category E to be a case on the merits. In such cases, Articles 276 through 312 of the Civil Enforcement Act shall apply mutatis mutandis.

(2) Judgment under paragraph (1) may be rendered without having any security furnished.

(3) In applying mutatis mutandis Article 287 of the Civil Enforcement Act, a request for conciliation under this Act shall be deemed that an action on the merits has been instituted.

Article 63 bis (Order for Direct Payment of Child Support)

(1) Where a person liable to pay child support periodically (hereinafter referred to as "child support obligor") fails to pay the child support not less than twice without any justifiable reasons, the family court may, upon an application by an oblige (hereinafter referred to as "income tax withholding agent"), who bears periodic benefit obligation for a child support oblige, to directly pay the child support to the child support oblige by deducting the child support regularly from the child support obligor's salary.

(2) An order for direct payment under paragraph (1) (hereinafter referred to as "order for direct payment of child support") shall be valid as are a seizure order and an assignment order under the Civil Enforcement Act simultaneously issued and the Civil Enforcement Act concerning a seizure order and an assignment order shall apply mutatis mutandis to payment orders: Provided, That an order for direct payment of child support may be issued for a relevant child support bond whose expiration date has not yet arrived, notwithstanding Article 40(1) of the Civil Enforcement Act.

(3) Where any circumstance is acknowledged to exist that the purpose of order for direct payment of child support may not be achieved, a family court may cancel an order for direct payment of child support upon an application of a child support oblige. In such cases, an order for direct payment of child support shall become invalid for the future.
(4) A family court shall deliver orders under paragraphs (1) and (3) to a child support obligor and an income tax withholding agent.
(5) An immediate appeal may be made for a trial concerning applications under paragraphs (1) and (3).
(6) Where any reason for change occurs in the main source of income, such as job change of a child support obligor, the income tax withholding agent shall notify the relevant family court of the fact of change within one week from the date such reason has occurred.

Article 64 (Order for Implementation)

(1) When a person who is required to implement an obligation falling under any of the following subparagraphs pursuant to the judgment, adjudication, conciliation protocol, decision substituting conciliation or child support order fails to perform the obligation without any justifiable reason, a family court may, upon request of the party concerned, order the person to perform the obligation within a specific period:
   1. Obligation related to property, such as payment of money;
   2. Obligation to hand over an infant;
   3. Obligation to allow visitation to his/her children.
(2) In issuing an order under paragraph (1), a family court shall, unless any special circumstance exists, examine in advance the party concerned, and advise him/her to perform the obligations, and make a notification of the sanction prescribed in Article 67(1) and 68.

Article 67 (Sanctions against Non-performance of Liability)

(1) When the party concerned or interested person violates any order under Article 29, 63bis (1) or (2), or 64 or a disposition under Article 62, without any justifiable reasons, a family court, conciliation committee, or judge in charge of conciliation may, by ruling, punish the party or interested person by a fine for negligence not exceeding ten million Won, either *ex officio*, or upon request of the rightful claimant.
(2) When a person who receives an order for inspection under Article 29 violates again, without any justifiable reason, the order even after being subject to sanctions under paragraph (1), a family court may, by ruling, punish the offender by detention until a performance of liability, within the limit of 30 days.
(3) An immediate appeal may be made against a ruling under paragraph (2).

(iii) If you need additional facts to answer this question, please indicate which type of facts would you need and why.

The natural mother of the illegitimate child needs to affiliate the child in advance before seeking child support against the natural father. If so, she can become the legal representative of the illegitimate child in an action for affiliation against the natural father.

(iv) Does your legal system require the same range of considerations to determine whether a party can bring a claim? Are those considerations statutory or constitutional?

The court makes sure that the complaint meets the procedural prerequisites as to party competence, procedural capacity, and interests in the litigation, including real party in interest, justificiablity, and a claim upon which relief could be granted. These considerations are statutory.

SPAIN

LORENZO-MATEO BUJOSA VADELL

Professor of Procedural Law, University of Salamanca

II.b. Briefly describe the highest court (or courts) of your country and indicate its (or their) function within your legal system.

Tribunal Constitucional. Created by the Spanish Constitution of 1978 and regulated by the *Ley Orgánica* 2/1979, October 3. It is a concentrated court for the constitutional guarantees: It can control the statutory laws (through the *recurso de inconstitucionalidad* and the *cuestión de inconstitucionalidad*), the specific violation of fundamental rights (*recurso de amparo*), and solve conflicts between the Central State and the seventeen Autonomous Communities and two Autonomous Cities (Ceuta and Melilla in the North of Africa) of Spain and, since 2009, conflicts between the Constitutional Organs and the Local (Municipal) Autonomy throughout Spain.

The Spanish Constitution of 1978 declares that the Supreme Court (*Tribunal Supremo*) is the highest court in Spain, except on constitutional guarantees. It has five chambers: civil, criminal, administrative, labor, and military. The main functions of these chambers are the Cassation and the Civil and Criminal Judgment of members of the highest Constitutional Organs.

III. JUDICIAL DECISION MAKING

a. Have you observed a similar phenomenon in your judicial system? If so, please identify the area(s) of law in which this has occurred. (Please do not limit yourself to questions involving jurisdiction.)

As a first step, the legal method in Spain is like the other civil law countries: the law is created by the central Parliament (Bicameral: *Congreso de los Diputados and Senado*) or the seventeen Parliament of the seventeen Autonomous Communities (CCAA), and later it is more or less developed by the Central Government and the seventeen Autonomous Governments in some material areas (not exactly the areas of art. 148 of the Spanish Constitution, which literally exposes the matters attributed to the CCAA, but the matters included in the special statutory laws called *Estatutos de Autonomía*, one for each Autonomous Community. All that has been interpreted later by the Tribunal Constitutional, and this court has the final power to define the constitutional attributions.

We should not forget the application – at times a direct application – of the European Union Law by the Spanish Tribunal. But this is yet more theoretical than it should be according to the European Treatises and European Jurisprudence of the Luxembourg European Court.

At a first glance, the Tribunals only can apply these statutory laws, but can do so flexibly, by the constitutional principles. Thus, they create a jurisprudence that can only integrate or fulfil a complementary function to the statutory law (Art. 1.6 Civil Code). I should immediately add that there is a cause of cassation before the Supreme Court when the minor jurisprudence (the decisions of lower courts) does not respect the higher jurisprudence.

There are two more considerations:

One: The Supreme Court Chambers also create law in another way: there are meetings of the Chamber Magistrates for the unification of criteria on interpreting the statutory law.

Two: The jurisprudence of the Constitutional Court has a formally greater function. The *Ley Orgánica del Poder Judicial* (Law of the Organization of the Judicial Power) in article 5.1 establishes that the Constitution is the highest norm and that binds the decisions of the Judges and Tribunals decisions, who will interpret and apply the statutory laws and government general norms according to the constitutional rules and principles, in accordance with the interpretation made by the Constitutional Court in all kind of constitutional processes.

So it is a clear movement from the classical way of reasoning in Civil Law countries to a way that is more like the Common Law methods. Of course, in that move, the Supreme Court and the Constitutional Court sometimes limit the constitutional and legal provisions by clear political reasons. This has occurred in matters such as within the criminal justice system.

b. If you have observed this phenomenon, does it sometimes occur that the judicially developed tests limit the principles that the tests purport to articulate?

Yes, this has occurred in matters such as the access to the criminal justice *(actio popularis)* or the limitation of the powers of the judge in the criminal process *(exasperation of the accusatory principle)*. But sometimes they have developed the constitutional principles in cases when the law was out-to-date, such as in the privacy regulation and the communications reception.

IV. JURISDICTION

(d)(i) *Would your country exercise jurisdiction over the foreign manufacturer on a claim against it by the injured party?*

(ii) *On which provisions and/or case law do you base your answer? If your highest court has addressed this or a similar issue, please describe how the court solved it.*

(iii) *If you need additional facts to answer this question, please indicate which type of facts you would need and why.*

(iv) *Additional comments. Express any additional comment you may have on the solutions offered by your system and the U.S. system.*

The Spanish Jurisdiction System is a unified one. Spain's sovereignty is divided into seventeen Autonomous Communities and two Autonomous Cities, but none of these has a jurisdictional attribution. The jurisdiction is an attribution of the Spanish Central Power.

So the question is if a Spanish Tribunal, anywhere in Spain, can exercise Jurisdiction over the foreign manufacturer on a claim against it by the injured party.

The answer is not so easy, because there are several regulations on these matters. We must apply the norm that corresponds according to the international treaty or the European Law norm that is applicable to the case. And if there is neither treatise nor European norm applicable, we must apply the norms of extension and limits of Spanish Jurisdiction of the article 22 of the *Ley Orgánica del Poder Judicial*.

According to this subsidiary regulation, there is Spanish Jurisdiction if there is an expressed or tacit agreement between the parties in conflict or when the defendant has his residence in Spain (but I believe that this is not the case in the hypo set forth). When there are neither agreements nor Spanish residence, there are many particular norms. One of those requires that in contracts law, the obligation is generated in Spain or must be carried out in Spain.

In this matter of contract law, the Judges must first apply, when possible, the Regulation Brussels I, which in substance provides also the rule of the place of the fulfillment of the commitments. There is some important jurisprudence from the Luxembourg Court as cases 56/79, 26/85, 288/92, 420/97, ...

When it is a consumer case, there are some special norms, both in Brussels I and in the internal law. Here, a *forum actoris* that is a concretion of the *pro consumatore* principle is applied, with some particular requirements.

VI. JUSTICIABILITY

(d)(i) *How would the courts of your country resolve the question of whether the mother should be allowed to proceed with her claim?*

(ii) *On which provisions and/or case law do you base your answer? If your highest court has addressed this or a similar issue, please describe how the court solved it.*

(iii) *If you need additional facts to answer this question, please indicate which type of facts would you need and why.*

(iv) *Does your legal system require the same range of considerations to determine whether a party can bring a claim? Are those considerations statutory or constitutional?*

(v) *Additional comments. Express any additional comment you may have on the solutions offered by your system and the U.S. system.*

In Spanish Law, there is no difference in the treatment of legitimate or illegitimate children based on the Filiations Law of 1981 (*Ley 11/1981, de 13 de mayo, de modificación del Código Civil en materia de filiación, patria potestad y régimen económico del matrimonio*) that reformed many Civil Code articles. The new article 8.II establishes that matrimonial and nonmatrimonial affiliation produce the same effects, as an application of the equality principle of article 14 of the Spanish Constitution. But that will not impede a case of inequality from being brought before the courts.

If the child is over 18 years old, he or she can directly bring a claim of discrimination. He or she will have the capacity to participate in the lawsuit so long as he or she is the real party in interest, that is, he or she must state a claim against his or her right not to be free of discrimination.

That will be enough for a legal basis of a genuine interest (*interés legítimo*) to file an antidiscrimination claim. The Civil Procedural Law, that is our civil procedural statutory law and is applied also subsidiary to all others processes, included those constitutional ones before the Constitutional Court, requires this in article 10.

But also this Law foresees the moot requirement, but not as a question to be considered directly by the court at the beginning of the trial but to be put forward by the defendant in the demand formal answer, or later, by the defendant or by the court itself, in a specific step that will demand the opportunity of all the parties to discuss on the remaining of the interest of the plaintiff to suit for the alleged discrimination.

When the plaintiff is incapable, because minor, or psychological reasons judicially declared, the mother can represent the son, legitimate or illegitimate, matrimonial or not. The only condition is to have the capacity to exercise the *patria potestas*.

These Law changes of Filiation Law were made by the Parliament. Not by the Courts. These, specially, the Constitutional Court has made a flexible interpretation of the standing requirements based in an open interpretation of a fundamental right established in article 24 of the Spanish Constitution: the fundamental right of the effective judicial protection of rights and genuine interests and the *pro actione* principle lying in it.

SPAIN

J. MIGUEL HERNÁNDEZ GALILEA

Professor of Procedural Law, University of Oviedo, Spain

*II.b.*Briefly describe the highest court (or courts) of your country and indicate its (or their) function within your legal system.

The highest court in the Spanish Judicial System is the Constitutional Court because it has the possibility of annulling the judgments of all other courts. But it is configured as a Court of last instance only in constitutional issues. Because of that, the name of the Supreme Court is reserved in the Spanish Constitution for designating another judicial body that is the highest judicial body in all areas except in constitutional guaranties.

The relationship between these two judicial bodies is not always easy because the border between ordinary law and these constitutional guaranties is often subtle; the Constitutional Court occasionally has penetrated it.

Citizens can present their claim to the Constitutional Court only after appeal to the ordinary jurisdiction, including the Supreme Court. However, each judge or lower court can refer directly to the Constitutional Court for a preliminary ruling on the unconstitutionally of any law through the so-called *cuestión de inconstitucionalidad*.

Under these two courts, each Autonomous Community has its own High Court that is at the same time the court of last instance for the special right of the Community (certain aspects of civil law, mainly), and also the Court of Appeal in social and administrative law and in jury trials.

This description should be completed with a reference to the Court of Justice of the European Union and European Court of Human Rights. The first is really a jurisdictional body managing as a kind of Highest European Court in European Union law's matter; while the second is not exactly jurisdictional; however, its jurisprudence is binding for the Constitutional and highest courts of the European countries (specifically for the members of the European Council).

III. JUDICIAL DECISION MAKING

a. Have you observed a similar phenomenon in your judicial system? If so, please identify the area(s) of law in which this has occurred. (Please do not limit yourself to questions involving jurisdiction).

This phenomenon can also be observed in our country. An example of this is the change of criterion by the Spanish Supreme Court about the increasing competence of the Jury.

In its sentence Nº 728/2009 adopted on June 26, it established that in the presence of any crimes connected between themselves, it was enough that one of them would be under the competence of the Jury for they all were judged by such organ.

With this resolution, the Court was trying to end the phenomenon known *as flight of the Jury*. The Jury Act admitted this interpretation but, as a result of this case law, a lot of complicated trials began to be judged by jurors.

Because of that, in a short period of time, the Supreme Court had no alternative but to change its position again. It established a new criterion that consisted in linking the jurisdiction of the jury with the main crime committed: only when such a crime falls within the competence of the Jury the others connected crimes will be judged by it. If not, all of them will be judged by professional judges. (*See*. Decision of the Court adopted in January 20th, 2010.) As it is evident this criterion is not always easy to apply.

In private matters, the most amazing case refers to the last instance resource, called *recurso de Casación*. This is the specific appeal before the Supreme Court that was modified in 2001 by *Ley de Enjuiciamiento Civil* (the Civil Judgment Act). At the same time, when such Law entered into force, on December 12, 2000, the full Board of the Civil Chamber of the Supreme Court adopted a decision by which a restrictive interpretation of the requirements to accede to the last instance was approved. This restrictive interpretation was motivated by a fear that the Supreme Court would be severely restricted by the new law. But this was not, so to speak, the Parliament`s idea and a few years after it amended this regulation and redacted it again in a different way so that this kind of interpretation was not possible. Nevertheless, the fight has not ended.

Another example is the change of position about the possibility to put into trial a criminal case where the only accuser was the so-called *acción popular*, when neither the public prosecutor nor the victims had filed an accusation. In a first position, the Supreme Court considered that the law does not allow the prosecution of the trial in this case (vid. sentence of the Supreme Court Nº 1045/2007 of December 17th) but three year later, it changed this criterion, adding that when the crime has public relevance and there are no determined victims, it will be possible (vid. sentence of the Supreme Court N° 8/2010 of January 20). We can also found this in medical liability issues, reasoning in a different way about the object of the evidence or the burden of proof, etc.

IV. JURISDICTION

(d)(i) Would your country exercise jurisdiction over the foreign manufacturer on a claim against it by the injured party?

In the hypothesis provided, competence is governed by two regulations. First by the Council Regulation of the European Union (EU) N° 44/2001 of December 2000, 22, *on jurisdiction and the recognition and enforcement of judgments in civil and commercial matters*. This norm is applied to determine the judicial competence in the EU about international private or commercial trials and provides the criteria of connection with the European forum. In general, it is the domicile (*locus domicilii*) of the defendant, but there are exceptions: One of them is precisely the raised hypothesis where the *locus delicti commissi* criterion is used as well as in matters of exclusive competence of the State or implied submission when the competence is not questioned by the defendant. In Article 5.3, the mentioned Regulation provides that "A person domiciled in a Member State may, in another Member State, be sued (...): 3. in matters relating to tort, delict or quasi-delict, in the courts for the place where the harmful event occurred or may occur; also the Spanish Organic Law of Judicial Power established in Article 22 says that in the private order, the Spanish judges and Courts will be competent: (...) in the case of not-contractual obligations, when the fact from which they derive has happened in Spanish territory or the author of the harm and the victim has his habitual residence in Spain.

Funded in these norms, we can say that the Spanish judges could not declare its incompetence in this case.

As it can be seen, both norms give specific criteria about the jurisdiction so that they are not necessarily different categories created by the Courts. This regulation has been applied in all EU countries without any problems at the moment.

(ii) On which provisions and/or case law do you base your answer? If your highest court has addressed this or a similar issue, please describe how the court solved it.

Despite the Regulation mentioned above, we can also cite the Directive of the EU N° 85/374 25 of July 1985 *on the approximation of the laws, regulations and administrative provisions of the Member States concerning liability for defective products* as well as any decisions, such as the following: European Court of Justice in *Declan O'Byrne v. Sanofi Pasteur MSD Ltd.* N° 2006\34, and the Spanish Supreme Court sentence N° 406/2013 June 18.

(iii) Additional comments.

A curious case regarding this issue is the process that follows before the Judge of First Instance in Barcelona and the Provincial Audience of Barcelona in appeal. The families of the victims of an aeronautic accident that took place in Germany brought claims against two U.S. traffic control system manufacturers of the damaged planes. Applying the *forum non conveniens* doctrine, the judge of New Jersey declined its competence in favor of the Spanish Courts only because they had already began a trial, though the only contact with Spain was that it was the destination of the flight. The Judge of First Instance of Barcelona ruled against the U.S. companies, applying the law of Arizona and New Jersey respectively. That way, the sentence was confirmed on appeal by the Provincial Audience of Barcelona sentence N° 230/2012 May 17.

V. JUSTICIABILITY

(d)(i) How would the courts of your country resolve the question of whether the mother should be allowed to proceed with her claim?

In 1995, the Constitutional Court had to deal with this problem in its sentence N° 84/1998 April 20. The mother of an illegitimate child filed a suit against the father, based on article 487*bis* of the Criminal Code, which punished the father's refusal to provide financial support for the child, but only in case of a child born to a married couple. The Judge of first instance and the Court of Appeal dismissed the suit in application of the principle that forbids the punishment when the fact is not provided previously as a crime in the Criminal Code.

The mother went to the Constitutional Court using the so-called *recurso de amparo*. In her complaint, she alleged that the law was unconstitutional because it denied her child's equal protection. When the Court pronounced the sentence we are talking about, the article 487*bis* of the Criminal Code was amended and did not distinguish between matrimonial or nonmatrimonial affiliation. Despite this, the Court did not refuse to get into the gist of the matter and granted legal protection to the mother. The main argument was that though nobody had the right to punish another (because the right to punish is only of the State), it was discrimination to give a different protection to the child because of his nonmatrimonial affiliation.

(ii) Does your legal system require the same range of considerations to determine whether a party can bring a claim? Are those considerations statutory or constitutional?

I think the requirements are similar. One of the reasons is because the constitutional formulation, in Art. 24, though succinct, is forceful anti-formalistic: *All persons have the right to obtain effective protection from the judges and the courts in the exercise of their rights and legitimate interests, and in no case may there be a lack of defense.* And the development of this norm has come into this trend. It is clear for instance, in the Organic Law of Judicial Power, where Article 11 establishes that judges and courts ought to resolve claims and can only refuse to do so for formal reasons. In addition, the Constitutional Court case law has interpreted this matter in a very wide sense as an application of the *pro actione* principle.

Eventually, this trend became a problem because there were so many claims before the Constitutional Court that it wasn't able to resolve them. The same situation happened in the European Court of Human Rights; for that reason, a few years ago, both bodies, almost simultaneously, achieved an amendment of their Rules in order to select among the claims. In the case of the Spanish court, this change was made through the amendment of its law in 2007, which allows the Court to evaluate the *constitutional transcendence of the claim* (vid. Organic Law of the Constitutional Court, article 44). The European Court of Human Rights had also introduced a similar category through protocol 14 of the European Convention on Human Rights.

TAIWAN

PROFESSOR KUAN-LING SHEN

Professor of Law, National Taiwan University, LLM

IIb. Briefly describe the highest court (or courts) of your country and indicate its (or their) function within your legal system.

In contrast to the common law system, there are three kinds of the highest courts in our legal system. Each of them has its own function. The Supreme Court, which is the most relevant in this paper, is the highest court in charge of the last resort for civil and criminal cases. Cases regarding administrative and constitutional issues are under the jurisdiction of the other two highest courts.

The Supreme Court decides issues of law. The Court must base its decision on the facts ascertained in the judgment of the court of second instance. In general, the Supreme Court cannot request new evidence.

When deciding a case, each division of the Court, consisting of four justices presided over by the Division Chief Justice, shall sit in council, and before rendering a judgment, the division shall engage in confidential deliberation, at which a majority concurrence is required.

Only certain cases can be brought to the Court: except for civil cases involving amounts in controversy not exceeding NT $1,000,000 and petty offences enumerated in Article 376 of the Code of Criminal Procedure, any civil or criminal case may be appealed to the Court.

III. *Judicial decision making*

(a) *Have you observed a similar phenomenon in your judicial system? If so, please identify the area(s) of law in which this has occurred. (Please do not limit yourself to questions involving jurisdiction.)*

(b) *If you have observed this phenomenon, does it sometimes occur that the judicially developed tests limit the principles that the tests purport to articulate?*

A similar phenomenon has been occurring in our judicial system, affecting both areas of public law and private law. Usually the courts begin with a rule at issue, which most of the time refers to specific law or provision. Then the courts interpret the identified articles in a way that is consistent with precedents or past decisions by the Supreme Courts. Where there is a lack of authoritative interpretation, the courts might invoke scholars' prevailing doctrines. Finally, the courts apply the rule and interpretation to the facts at issue, deciding whether the parties act against law.

IV. JURISDICTION

(d)(i) Would your country exercise jurisdiction over the foreign manufacturer on a claim against it by the injured party?

Yes. Please see (ii).

(ii) On which provisions and/or case law do you base your answer? If your highest court has addressed this or a similar issue, please describe how the court solved it.

In our legal system, laws concerning international jurisdiction are nowhere to be found. As a result, both scholars and the courts have developed several doctrines determining the international jurisdiction of cases involving foreign elements.

The Supreme Court has dealt with similar issues. According to past court rulings, if a court in Taiwan has local jurisdiction, then it will also have international jurisdiction.

In a hypothetical case, though both the plaintiff and the defendant are foreigners, the plaintiff was hurt when buying the product in our country. According to Article 15 of the Code of Civil Procedure, in matters relating to torts, an action may be initiated in the court of the location where the tortious act occurred. Therefore, if the court determines the tort happened in our country, it is possible that the court will exercise its jurisdiction over this case.

There are other rulings, though they are not the prevailing view, which hold that the courts should apply the Code of Civil Procedure by analogy to deal with this issue.

In addition, scholars have developed ways to determine international jurisdiction. In order to decide whether lawsuits can be brought in our country, the courts should consider not only the characteristics of foreign events, but also all the relevant interests and factors before making its final decision.

Based upon observation of recent Supreme Court decisions concerning international jurisdiction, precedent still prevails among other approaches.

However, "forum non convenience" has been mentioned in some rulings, indicating that the court has taken into account other factors to determine the jurisdiction. Now if the approach applies to the hypothetical case, the court should not only invoke the Code of Civil Procedure for local jurisdiction, but consider all relevant factors: for instance, whether the decision is reasonable for the parties to participate in the proceedings; whether the parties' procedural interests have been protected; whether it is convenient for the court to investigate evidence; or the efficacy of the decisions if being made in our country.

The courts should conduct this delicate examination before determining the jurisdiction.

V. JUSTICIABILITY

(d)(i) How would the courts of your country resolve the question of whether the mother should be allowed to proceed with her claim?

(ii) On which provisions and/or case law do you base your answer? If your highest court has addressed this or a similar issue, please describe how the court solved it.

There is a similar provision in Taiwan Criminal Law Article 294. The article provides that

> If a person who by law, order, or contract has the duty to support or protect a helpless person abandons him or does not give him support or protection necessary to preserve his life, the person shall be punished by imprisonment for not less than six months but not more than five years.

According to the article, only people, who by law, order, or contract have a duty to support or protect someone, may infringe this article. Supreme Court precedent held that, "... Unless otherwise contracted, whether a person is now obliged to maintain the living of the other person should be decided in compliance with Civil Code Article 1115..."

The ruling explicitly indicated that, in general, those who by Civil Code Article 1115 have the duty of care can be claimed in violation of Criminal Law Article 294. This has been widely accepted in judicial practice, so the claim would be invalid based on the hypothetical facts.

To decide whether the party can pursue the claim, we should further look into the Code of Criminal Procedure. Code of Criminal Procedure Article 319 provides that

> The victim of a crime may file a private prosecution, provided that where he is without, or of limited, legal capacity, or is dead, such private prosecution may be filed by his statutory agent, lineal relative, or spouse.

However, Article 321 prohibits private prosecution that is initiated against a lineal ascendant or spouse. If, in a hypothetical case, the illegitimate child is under age 20 and thus does not have complete legal capacity, his or her natural mother can file a private prosecution on behalf of the child. Since the illegitimate child has yet to become the natural father's lineal relative, the prosecution should be allowed.

After filing the prosecution, before entering the trial proceedings, the court or commissioned judge may examine the private prosecutor and the accused and may collect or investigate the evidence; if the court or commissioned judge determines that this is a case for civil action or that the private prosecution procedure is being used to threaten the accused, the private prosecutor may be advised to withdraw the prosecution. If, as a result of the examination and investigation specified above, the court determines that the case contains the circumstances of one of the Articles 252 through 254, the private prosecution may be dismissed by a ruling.

Article 1084 of Civil Code provides that:

> Parents have the rights and the duties to protect, educate and maintain their minor children. Such rights and duties only happen when between the parents and their legitimate children. Assume that, in a hypothetical case, the mother of the illegitimate child claims that the father of the illegitimate child shall maintain the child's living, the mother should firstly claim acknowledgement from the natural father under Civil Code Article 1067. According to this Article, the mother of the illegitimate child and the child both have standing to bring the action.

According to the ruling of the Supreme Court, the claim of acknowledgement is an action for modification of rights. The courts should decide whether the action should be dismissed by examining whether the action complies with Code of Civil Procedure Article 249.

URUGUAY

PROFESSOR SANTIAGO MIGUEL PEREIRA CAMPOS

Head Professor of Procedural Law at the School of Law of the University of Montevideo, Partner of the Law Firm Rueda Abadi Pereira Consultants

.II.b. Briefly describe the highest court (or courts) of your country and indicate its (or their) function within your legal system.

The highest court of our country is the Supreme Court of Uruguay (*Suprema Corte de Justicia del Uruguay*). It has the following functions:

a) Issues the final ruling in cases in which the Judges of the Appellate Court revoke unanimously the ruling of the District Court, and one of the parties files an appeal for cassation against this second judgment. The matter discussed in the legal proceeding must amount to more than 4,000 UR (currently, US$ 125.484), and the appeal can only be based in an error or infraction in the application of the law.
b) Rules in cases regarding:
   (i) Constitution offenders
   (ii) Treaties, pacts, and conventions with other states.
   (iii) Diplomats accredited in Uruguay.
   (iv) Other cases, established by international law.
c) Supervises the Appellate Courts, District Courts and the other offices of the Judicial Power, in administrative matters (not regarding jurisdictional decisions).
d) Drafts the bill regarding the budget of the Judicial Power, and submits it to the Executive Power so that it can be added to the other proposed budgets.
e) With the approval of the Senate, or when it is in recess, of the Permanent Commission, appoints the citizens that will be part of the Appellate Courts.
f) Appoints judges.
g) Appoints the public defenders and judges of the peace.
h) Appoints, promotes, and removes employees of the Judicial Power.

i) Solves the conflict of competence between the authorities of the Judicial Power and those of the Administrative Contentious Courts.
j) Bestows the position of judges.
k) Receives the oath from lawyers, public notaries, and solicitors.
l) Oversees the correct practice of the professions mentioned below.
m) Passes decrees regarding the functioning of the Judicial Power.

III. JUDICIAL DECISION MAKING

(a) Have you observed a similar phenomenon in your judicial system? If so, please identify the area(s) of law in which this has occurred. (Please do not limit yourself to questions involving jurisdiction.)

Yes, this has occurred. An example of this took place in Uruguayan Commercial law, regarding "the two steps test."

Article 1836 of the Civil Code states that no one can commit to render personal services without a due date.

This rule was used by the Courts to establish the right of any of the parties, in a distribution contract (without a term), to put an end to this contract at any time.

Afterward, the Courts understood that, nonwithstanding the principle stated above, if one party put an end to the contract without giving due notice to the other party within a reasonable time in advance, causing damages to the other party, this action could be considered illegal, and therefore, be punished.

After this criterium was established by different rulings, a test was created (by different authors) and accepted by the Courts. This test sought to determine when the ending of a contract without a term was illegal. This test has two parts: first the Judge has to determine if there were good reasons to put an end to the contract. In case the Judge understands there were, then the decision of the party to put an end to the contract is not illegal. But in absence of good reasons, the judge must determine if the party who put an end to the contract acted with good faith. If he did not, then the ending of the contract was illegal, and the party must repair the damage caused.

(b) If you have observed this phenomenon, does it sometimes occur that the judicially developed tests limit the principles that the tests purport to articulate?
Yes, in this case, first the Courts established that a contract without a term implied that any of the parties could put an end to it at any time. And afterward, the Courts limited this right.

Other case in which this phenomenon can be observed, is one regarding Uruguayan labor law. This case refers to overtime.

In case an employee files a claim against the employer, seeking to collect the overtime worked, he has to prove he worked overtime (art. 139 of the General Proceeding Code).

Nevertheless, if the employee alleges that he worked daily 16 more hours than contracted, and the employer does not file the answer to this complaint or contradicts this affirmation, the Court, applying the law (art. 130.2 of the General Proceeding Code), should order the payment of those sixteen hours of overtime per day.

Nonetheless, after this rule was created, the Courts created the principle of "reasonableness," in virtue of which if an employee alleges to have worked twenty-four hours per day, and the employer does not answer the complaint or contradicts it, the Court can establish that its not possible for an employee to work this amount of overtime everyday, and can reduce the overtime subject to claim.

III. JURISDICTION

(d)(i) Would your country exercise jurisdiction over the foreign manufacturer on a claim against it by the injured party?

The solution depends. If our country has a treaty signed with the country of the manufacturer, and this treaty allows our country to exercise jurisdiction over this foreign manufacturer, the solution established in the treaty prevails.

Nevertheless, the general rule in our country (if no treaty was signed) is that the claim must be filed:

a) In the country where the thing—subject matter of the contract—was located, at the time of the execution of the contract, in case the contract refers to a specific identified thing.
b) In the country where the domicile of the debtor was located at the time of the execution of the contract, if the contract refers to things determined by their kind, or to perishable goods.

Therefore, in the hypo explained in letter a) if no treaty establishes differently, if a person is injured by a product manufactured in a foreign country and sold in Uruguay, the court in Uruguay will not exercise jurisdiction over the foreign manufacturer unless the contract referred to an identified thing and this thing was located in Uruguay at the time of the execution of the contract, or if the foreign manufacturer had his domicile in Uruguay at the time of the execution of the contract.

(ii) On which provisions and/or case law do you base your answer? If your highest court has addressed this or a similar issue, please describe how the court solved it.

This solution is established in article 2399 of the Uruguayan Civil Code.

In the ruling 57/09, a Civil Appeal Court established that the defendant PSA Peugeot Citroen (France) was duly summoned in Uruguay with the claim, due to the fact that all the proof filed in the proceeding led to the belief that the defendant had a domicile in Uruguay, although the defendant argued that it did not, and that what it had was a exclusive distributorship agreement with Oversil S.A.

In this case, the Court exercised jurisdiction, because it understood that the domicile of the manufacturer at the time of the execution of the contract was in Uruguay.

(iii) If you need additional facts to answer this question, please indicate which type of facts you would need and why.

As was said, our answer will vary depending if there is a treaty signed between the country of the manufacturer and Uruguay, and if not, depending on the nature of the product sold in Uruguay. If this product was previously identified in the contract, and was located in Uruguay at the time of the execution of the contract, the Uruguayan Court will exercise jurisdiction against the foreign manufacturer. But if the product was not identified (only the kind of the product was mentioned, or it referred to a perishable good), then, being the manufacturer domiciled in a foreign country, Uruguayan Courts will not exercise jurisdiction.

V. JUSTICIABILITY

(d)(i) How would the courts of your country resolve the question of whether the mother should be allowed to proceed with her claim?

In Uruguay, a claim regarding the constitutionality of a law can be filed before any District Court. This Court will suspend the proceeding, and submit the claim to the Supreme Court, for it to rule in this issue.

In the case in hand, the claimant in Uruguay can allege that this law discriminates, because article 8 of our Constitution states that all persons are equal before the law and can only be distinguished attending to their virtues or talents.

Nevertheless, we deem it important to point out that in Uruguay, legitimate and illegitimate children have the same rights.

In this case, the mother´s claim would have to be filed before a Criminal Court, because said law establishes the imprisonment of the parent who willfully refuses to provide for the support and maintenance of his child.

But if the claim of the mother referred to the collection of the alimony, this claim would have to be filed before a Family Court.

Also, it is important to point out that in Uruguay, the Criminal Code states in its article 279 B that the parent who refuses to comply with the duties inherent to the parental guardianship (among them, the support and maintenance of their children) shall be punished with imprisonment, from three months to four years.

As was pointed out above, in Uruguay, if a party files a claim asking for the Court to establish the unconstitutionality of a law that discriminates, the Court will suspend the proceeding and send this claim to the Supreme Court. Then the Supreme Court will rule regarding this claim without analyzing the particular claim of the claimant (in this case, a claim regarding alimony). Therefore, the Supreme Court will not analyze the justiciability of the mother´s claim, but only the law challenged as unconstitutional.

If the Supreme Court deems this law as unconstitutional, it will declare it so, and afterward will send the case back to the District Court, which will rule regarding the specific claim of the mother (not applying the unconstitutional law).

Therefore, in the case at hand, if the Supreme Court decided that this statute was unconstitutional, the Criminal District Court would have to prosecute the defendant, and, proven the parent–child relationship and the fact that the father willfully refused to provide for the support and maintenance of his child, it would proceed to sentence the father to prison.

(ii) On which provisions and/or case law do you base your answer? If your highest court has addressed this or a similar issue, please describe how the court solved it.

I base my answer in articles 508, 510, 514, 520 and 521 of the General Proceeding Code.

Also, I base my answer on article 14 of Act 10.783.

An example of this proceeding can be appreciated in the ruling 135/007 issued by the Supreme Court of Uruguay, in which the Court declared unconstitutional a law in virtue of which the money received in missions of the Armed Forces of Uruguay would not be part of the wages of the employee (and therefore would not be calculated for the alimony).

The claimant was the mother of a child who received alimony, and this sum amounted to a percentage of his father´s wages, without taking into account what he received as a payment for the missions in which he participated.

The mother said that this statute was discriminatory, because the money received by the father of her child benefited the children living with him and not her child.

The Court declared this statute unconstitutional, and therefore, the District Court (Family Court) did not apply this law, and established that the percentage of wages destined for the alimony of the claimants child had to include what was received by the defendant as payment for the missions in which he took part.

(iii) If you need additional facts to answer this question, please indicate which type of facts would you need and why.

(iv) Does your legal system require the same range of considerations to determine whether a party can bring a claim? Are those considerations statutory or constitutional?

Our legal system requires the following considerations to determine whether a party can bring a claim:

- That the claimant has legal capacity to file the claim.
- That the claimant owns the right sought to be enforced, or is authorized to represent this party (only if it is clear that this claimant does not have the said right or representation, the Court can dismiss the claim).
- That the claim filed by the claimant has a possible object.
- Also, the Court will analyze that it is competent to try the case, that there are no pending cases related to this claim that need to be solved in order for the claim to be tried; that the claimant does not lack representation, that the period for filing the claim has not lapsed, that this case has not been tried before (*res judicata*) and that the parties of this proceeding have not already made a deal over what is claimed.

These considerations are stipulated by articles 119 and 133 of the General Proceeding Code (statutory law).

7

Concluding Remarks

The law of procedure provides a civilized method through which to resolve disputes over the substantive rights of contending parties. Ideally, procedure should be no more complicated than necessary to provide a just and speedy resolution of the dispute. But simplicity is not a simple matter in our rapidly evolving global economy. The law of procedure must provide rules and standards that are predictable in consequence but at the same time sufficiently general to permit their application to a range of possibilities, some of which, by the nature of things, are unpredictable. In short, procedure must be simultaneously predictable and, at least as to some of its elements, open to adjustment, innovation or nuance. One way to achieve the balance between predictability and innovation is through a careful "law-making" interaction between legislative and judicial bodies. As we have seen, the modern common law method, which appears to operate independently from the legislature, is not suited to this task.

A common characteristic of modern representative democracies is the separation of powers among specified state institutions, each with an identified authority to act in a particular capacity on behalf of the democracy. The basic model is simple: the legislature makes the laws, the executive administers and executes those laws, and the judiciary interprets and applies them. The nuances and nomenclature may vary from nation to nation, but these fundamental assignments of power and authority are readily discernable across a wide array of designs.

This basic description is accurate to the extent that it reflects the principal allocations of authority among the seemingly distinct governmental units of the state. But beyond those principal allocations, the lines of separation are less clear. Each of these units partakes, to some extent, in the business of the others. A legislature may have the authority to appoint or approve members of the executive or judicial branches; an executive may have the authority to veto legislation or to exercise discretion in enforcing various laws; and the judiciary, or some part of it, may have the authority to fill gaps in the legislatively created program or to declare action by the state unconstitutional.

What we see when we step back from this model of separated and intermingled powers is the organic law-making institution we call the state. I'm interested in the judicial decision-making process as it operates within that organic whole and in the particular context of procedural law.

The challenge is to accommodate the commonly understood function of the judiciary as an interpreter and applier of the law – a principal allocation – with the realistic probability that the judiciary is, as part of the organic law-making whole, also a maker of the law.

Having confronted that probability, I have suggested a method to assess the legitimacy of any particular instance of this judicial law-making authority. The ultimate goal is to provide a descriptive set of guidelines as transnational benchmarks for the practice of judicial decision making. Such guidelines might provide an educational function that would promote across-the-border consistencies through a transnational conformity of judicial practices. They would also provide means through which to anticipate and navigate the potentially less predictable applications or innovations in procedural law, especially those of a constitutional dimension.

There are a variety of methods through which to assess the judicial decision-making process, some are theoretical, some are empirical, and some offer a combination of theory and scientific inquiry. All of these approaches share one thing. They operate across a spectrum of possibilities that fall somewhere between pure formalism and unrestrained realism. The classic formalist inquiry rejects the legitimacy of courts as lawmakers and posits that the sole function of a court is to discover the law either by reference to an authoritative text or to the principles of natural law. From this discovery, the correct answer should reveal itself through the careful application of deductive and analogical reasoning. The realist inquiry, on the other hand, rejects formalism as nonsense and sees courts as active lawmakers, perhaps cloaked in a formalist disguise, but ultimately free to advance social welfare with a keen awareness of the consequences of the choice made.

Formalism operates effectively as an explanatory tool in that vast range of cases where law can, indeed, be discovered and deductively applied, as one may do from a clearly applicable and crisply written statutory text. In theory, a formalist approach to the judicial function would achieve something akin to a perfection of predictability. Yet, realism offers a perceptive insight into the realpolitik of judicial decision making and helps us see what judges do when there is no clear and crisp law to be discovered but where the demands of the case still require a solution.

Both theories falter, however, in their failure to appreciate the value of the other. Formalism overlooks the impossibility of "discovering" the content of the empty gaps in the law or the true meaning to be assigned to those vague texts that offer no more than abstract possibilities. In so doing, formalism fails to account for a vast array of judicial decisions that have stood the test of time. Realism, however, proves too much in underestimating the legitimating role of formal reasoning and in failing to explain how or when a judge's perception of the social welfare should be allowed to override the principal allocation of law-making authority to the legislative arm of the state. Certainly from a transnational litigation perspective, unrestricted realism would provide a strong disincentive for investment in any markets where such judicial practices were extant.

As the preceding paragraph suggests, the ideal (and reality) of judicial decision making operates somewhere between the projects of formalism and realism. It is in that "somewhere" that we must identify the proper role of the judiciary in the law-making process as well as provide an effective method through which to evaluate the judicial function in all of its manifestations. Subpart 23.2 of the UNIDROIT Principles of Transnational Civil Procedure offers this beginning: "The judgment [of a court] should be accompanied by a reasoned explanation of the essential factual, legal, and evidentiary basis of the decision." The commentary on 23.2 does not elaborate on the reasoned-explanation standard, but the welcome announcement of such a standard invites our deeper consideration.

We can begin with the easy cases. Certainly, when the facts are not in dispute (or have been established through proper means) and the standard to be applied to those facts is both identifiable and clear, formalism provides the proper framework from which to assess any judgment applying that law to those facts. It is the court's adherence to the formal rule of law that legitimates the decision. A reasoned evaluation would, therefore, identify the "discovered" legal principle, fairly describe the undisputed or found facts, and offer a deductive map from the principle and the facts to the logical conclusion. But in the not-so-easy cases, when there are potentially conflicting rules or interpretations of a rule, or when the principle to be applied offers a range of possibilities, or when there is no available principle or rule to guide the court, the value of formalist deduction recedes and the need for a more thorough method to appraise the judicial choice steps forward.

When court moves from formalism (law discovery) to realism (law creation), the reasoned evaluation of the judgment should address the following considerations. First, the court should attend to the primacy of legislature in the lawmaking process with respect to matters not of a constitutional dimension. Given that primacy, the default position of a judicial decision should be one of deduction or analogy from established legal principles. Thus, the court must explain why those tools of logic are inadequate to the task at hand – e.g., the applicable procedural code does not address the precise question presented.

Second, the decision should reflect a careful consideration of both the case-specific and broader consequences of the choice made. If, for example, one interpretation of a broadly stated principle is to be favored over a contending interpretation, the court should state a reason for the choice. Here we might expect the court to reason inductively from the particular to the general.

Third, the choice made should be premised on a durable principle capable of application to the fullest possible range of similarly situated cases. This point too calls for a reasoned elaboration of the chosen principle. Hence, the more generally the principle can be stated and defended the better.

Fourth, the choice should comport with the judicial obligation to provide a forum for the vindication of individual claims of right that fall within the court's assigned competence. In other words, the standards created by the court should not create unnecessary obstacles that would hinder access to the judicial process.

Finally, the court should not seek to justify its conclusions through a judicial monologue or argument that does no more than pave the path to a particular result. Rather, the court should identify the range of alternative interpretations to the issue presented and, after careful examination of those alternatives, explain what the law "ought to be."

With this latter approach, which resembles a dialogue with the political community as opposed to a lecture to or imposition on that community, the decisionmaking process is more likely to reach conclusions that are understood and accepted by that community. This may be because, so articulated, such opinions cohere with the broader perspective of the community and are therefore accepted as a moral imperative rather than as an imposition. Moreover, opinions that proceed through a carefully constructed framework of "trial and error" or "conjectures and refutations," appear more "scientific," rather than the product of personal preferences.

Of course, even a careful application of this method will not necessarily lead to a correct result in any particular case. The consistent application of it should, however, lead to a body of results that are more likely to be accepted as legitimate and more likely to create a procedural regime that is perceived as predictable, sufficiently flexible and, in general, compatible with transnational commercial investment activities. It could also induce imitation and the development of sound judicial habits of transnational consequence. Finally, this approach of reasoned evaluation is more likely to create a cooperative effort between the legislative and judicial branches to create a coherent and workable system of procedure.

Index

For EU product safety concerns, contact us at Calle de José Abascal, 56–1°, 28003 Madrid, Spain or eugpsr@cambridge.org.

www.ingramcontent.com/pod-product-compliance
Lightning Source LLC
LaVergne TN
LVHW052220200926
848481LV00001B/165
* 9 7 8 1 3 1 6 6 1 2 8 6 6 *